Race, Ethnicity, and the American Urban Mainstream

Christopher Bates Doob

Southern Connecticut State University

PEARSON

Boston   New York   San Francisco
Mexico City   Montreal   Toronto   London   Madrid   Munich   Paris
Hong Kong   Singapore   Tokyo   Cape Town   Sydney

To the three of them:

Teresa Carballal
Gabriella Monica Doob
Marta Albornoz Carballal

Senior Series Editor: *Jeff Lasser*
Editorial Assistant: *Heather McNally*
Senior Marketing Manager: *Kelly May*
Composition and Prepress Buyer: *Linda Cox*
Manufacturing Buyer: *JoAnne Sweeney*
Cover Administrator: *Kristina Mose-Libon*
Editorial–Production Service: *Matrix Productions Inc.*
Photo Researcher: *Katharine S. Cook*
Electronic Composition: *Omegatype Typography, Inc.*

For related titles and support materials, visit our online catalog at www.ablongman.com.

Between the time Website information is gathered and then published, it is not unusual for some sites to have closed. Also, the transcription of URLs can result in typographical errors. The publisher would appreciate notification where these errors occur so that they may be corrected in subsequent editions.

Library of Congress Cataloging-in-Publication Data

Doob, Christopher Bates.
  Race, ethnicity, and the American urban mainstream / Christopher Bates Doob.
    p. cm.
  Includes bibliographical references and index.
  ISBN 0-205-38624-5
    1. United States—Race relations. 2. United States—Ethnic relations. 3. Minorities—United States—Social conditions. 4. Racism—United States. 5. United States—Social conditions. 6. City and town life—United States. 7. Pluralism (Social sciences)—Canada. 8. Canada—Ethnic relations. I. Title.
  E184.A1D658 2004
  305.8'00973—dc22

                                                                              2004050708

Photo Credits: p. 4: William Lovelace/Getty Images Inc.—Hulton Archive Photos; **p. 12:** Bill Bachmann/PhotoEdit; **p. 19:** John Coletti; **p. 35:** AP Wide World Photos; **p. 52:** Corbis/Bettmann; **p. 63:** Alon Reininger/Contact Press Images Inc.; **p. 78:** Anthony Potter Collection/Getty Images Inc.—Hulton Archive Photos; **p. 94:** Yellow Dog Productions/Getty Images Inc.—Image Bank; **p. 111:** Margot Granitsas/Photo Researchers, Inc.; **p. 126:** Regan/Getty Images, Inc.—Liaison; **p. 139:** Library of Congress; **p. 149:** Bob Daemmrich/Stock Boston; **p. 162:** Jeff Greenberg/PhotoEdit; **p. 175:** Jeff Dunn/Index Stock Imagery, Inc.; **p. 181:** Lewis Hine/Corbis/Bettmann; **p. 201, top:** Stephen Ferry/Getty Images, Inc.—Liaison; **p. 201, bottom:** AP Wide World Photos; **p. 217:** John Coletti/Stock Boston; **p. 228:** Peter Power/Toronto Star/NEWSCOM; **p. 238:** Paul Conklin/PhotoEdit.

Printed in the United States of America
10 9 8 7 6 5 4 3 2   09 08 07 06 05

CONTENTS

PREFACE

> His outwardly smooth sentences were inside of them gnarled and tough with the enigmas of the American experience.
>
> —Carl Sandburg on Lincoln's Gettysburg Address

What role does racial or ethnic membership play in establishing Americans' rootedness in an enigmatic society? Throughout this book I grapple with that question in the setting of the urban mainstream and its varying access to opportunities.

The work builds on C. Wright Mills's powerful principle declaring that a synthesis of history and biography manifests the sociological context shaping contemporary life. History, which stretches across time into the present, analyzes macrosociological forces rooting people into the social world. The historical material helps explain the book's focus on city life, where the most central of the society's developments and changes have originated. Many Americans, including some sociologists, view historical information skeptically, feeling it bears little clear and significant relationship to current realities and serves mainly as a distraction from all-important recent events. In this book I present segments of historical data as essential ingredients for grasping modern racial and ethnic groups' life-shaping experiences.

The biographical aspect of rootedness examines individuals' involvement in social systems, where one's race or ethnicity can be an important, even critical, factor in determining access to such basic resources as housing, schooling, and jobs, and where location outside the mainstream can be highly depriving. In both the biographical and historical areas, I suspect that everyone has a chance to learn about others whose race- or ethnicity-related experiences and opportunities have differed from their own. Throughout the chapters African Americans' consistently oppressive historical and biographical experience receives the most detailed attention.

Sociological ideas guide a reader's perception of material. In a textbook some teachers might expect a heavier dose of sociological thought and analysis. However, while still maintaining effective explanation, I have presented only those select concepts and perspectives that prove helpful in developing an intimate sense of how racial and ethnic membership affect people's lives. This approach has taken me on an exciting, complex journey that has arrived at provocative outcomes.

I seek to engage the reader in a continuous interplay between conception and activity. With that in mind, I develop a narrative flow, featuring Sociological Illustrations as well as a steady stream of brief encounters and quotations, which weave through each chapter to display a detailed sense of participants' behavior. Such information helps promote an interactive classroom setting. I hope this book will contribute to making the course in which it is included a memorable experience.

Each of the following individuals has significantly influenced the nature or content of the text: Eveline Bates Doob, Leonard W. Doob, Dick Gerber, Sherrill Moore, Ian Skoggard, Paul Spector, and Sam Vine.

Jon Bloch supplied two very useful sources, one of which proved particularly helpful early in the process of shaping the project's direction. Tony Doob and Pat Baranek provided several productive observations and sources for the chapter about Canadian racial and ethnic relations, and Tony also made useful comments about crime-related matters.

The dedication is to my wife, daughter, and mother-in-law—the people who give me roots. Teresa Carballal, who remains the essential first reader of my written work, has had a persistent effect on the development of the book.

At Allyn and Bacon, Jeff Lasser was an insightful, supportive editor with whom I've enjoyed working. Donna Simons helped make the book's production a pleasant, efficient process. Aaron Downey's hands-on approach at Matrix Productions proved very useful for resolving a number of thorny issues.

I would also like to thank the reviewers of this book: Ashley W. Doane, Jr., University of Hartford; Paul Lopez, California State University, Chico; Stephanie M. McClure, University of Georgia; Mariela Nunez-Janes, University of North Texas; William L. Smith, Georgia Southern University; and Bruce B. Williams, Mills College.

1

Introduction: The Study of American Race and Ethnicity

Many Americans, particularly in interracial settings, feel uncomfortable talking about race-related matters. Sometimes an individual ends up face-to-face with an awkward moment. Discussion has broached a racial issue, and the person in question feels called upon to express an opinion. Whoops, what to do? Escape might be the coveted option, and the preferred approach is to get there as quickly as possible while making it abundantly clear that one is always very tolerant toward members of other racial and ethnic groups.

So what's happening in people's minds? In two words, I believe, not enough. In spite of the fact that many college-educated adults have had at least one course about race and ethnicity, they emerge from formal education with little grasp of the impact of these issues in our society. Oh, yes, they churn out plenty of facts in their tests and papers but overall display an uneasy lack of coherent thought. To me, there's only one way to initiate the effort to grasp how race and ethnicity fit into modern urban society—provide an effective analytic framework that encompasses relevant discussion, and in the immediate case that means one that carries throughout this book.

The History and Biography Framework

A distinguished social scientist used to tell his students to avoid history courses. "Anything you learn there, you can readily get from reading books," he explained with a dismissing nod. Through the years, however, I've come to appreciate that he greatly undervalued the field—for instance, the study of history is the only way to grasp the full story of how different racial and ethnic groups have ended up with their current opportunities and restrictions. The first section of this chapter begins supplying such information.

In *The Sociological Imagination* (1959), C. Wright Mills appeared to be following a similar line of thought when indicating that two key factors, which he designated "history" and "biography," are necessary for analyzing the social world. In Mills's view, history concerns the major structures and activities that develop across time and space. These broad social conditions concern both the past and present, suggesting that to Mills history was somewhat larger in scope than normally considered. The conventional sociological term for Mills's designation of history is **macrosociological**—involving the large-scale structures and activities that exist within societies and even between one society and another. Mills indicated that history, namely the macrosociological order, affects biography, the lives of people. Once again, conventional sociology employs its own somewhat similar term—**microsociological,** involving the structure and activity of small groups. To help appreciate the related meanings of history and biography, one should consider that during any historical era individuals spend most of their time in such small-group settings as families, friends, and job units.

These dimensions extend throughout the book. In analyzing the historical factor, I consider the impact that different groups' access to work, politics, education, and housing has had on their advancement in American society. In particular, however, I emphasize the great significance of housing, recognizing that sociologists and other social scientists have generally paid limited attention to the impact of housing location in promoting or restricting ethnic and racial groups' successful entry into the American urban mainstream. At the biographical level, I have also had one prominent concern—to provide a variety of descriptions showing how the racialized social system has brought racially discriminatory practice into the immediate social setting where Americans interact with one another. The frequent illustration of this concept permits readers to see the intimate impact of prejudice and discrimination on minority-group members' everyday lives.

In Chapter 2, I examine theories, considering both the historical conditions behind their development and modern conflict theorists' analysis of racialized social systems. The next chapter focuses on the urban history of American racial and ethnic relations, dividing that expanse into five eras and including descriptions of how all the various white groups have eventually been able to escape what for some was initially a racialized social system while African Americans, in contrast, were thwarted in this regard. Chapter 4 looks at housing, surveying five diverse patterns that have developed across time and space and also analyzing how discriminatory practices further promoting housing segregation have been unfolding in the current racialized social system. The next four chapters retain the same perspective, considering how work, politics, community, and family- and education-related activities impact urban racial and ethnic groups. Then Chapter 9 focuses on the contrasting picture presented by urban Canada, and the book finishes with a conclusion that contains both a look toward the future and suggestions about curtailing the racialized social system.

Before moving on to these chapters, I need to provide two preliminary sources of information: first, some introduction to American society's unique racist history and then, second, a set of sociological concepts that serve as useful analytic tools.

The American Racist Tradition

In my college sociology course on race and ethnic relations, the white instructor, with a playful smile toward the class, recounted a conversation following a speech he'd given. A white questioner had asked, "What if your daughter planned to marry a black man?"

"Tell me about him," the sociologist had replied.

"I told you he was black."

"That's a trait that conveys nothing about what he's like as an individual and consequently what he'd be like as a match for my daughter. Tell me about him."

More than forty years later, it still seems a provocative exchange. Clearly, the sociologist was forcefully favoring the idea that race should not be a deterrent in choice of marital partner. The additional reality that he did not address and that intervening experience helps me appreciate is that in spite of an accelerating proportion of whites agreeing with the sociologist, such inclusive views about racial matters have caused considerable struggle for individuals, families, and communities in our society. A look at historical material helps explain why.

In the middle of the fifteenth century, the Portuguese, soon followed by the Spanish, began sailing to Africa, where their superior fire power made it possible to capture and enslave local inhabitants, bringing some of them home in chains where their labor could be exploited. A few leading Catholic priests and theologians debated the morality of enslavement, but the matter was eventually settled in 1550 when the prominent Spanish theologian Juan Gines de Sepulveda concluded that it was legitimate to enslave indigenous populations because of their heathen (unchristian), sinful, uncivilized, and thus inferior natures, which best suited them to serve their biologically and culturally superior Spanish and Portuguese masters. By the early seventeenth century, other Europeans, including the English, had accepted such racist views.

It seems that Protestant powers like England and Germany fostered a particularly potent brand of racism. These countries displayed a religiously inspired zeal for the acquisition of wealth, emphasizing that the attainment of riches in this world was a sure sign of predestination for salvation in the next. The only individuals with a chance to attain wealth were northern Europeans, and all others including racial minorities were regarded as inferior, to be used by the worthy ones in their predestined glory. Although these religious beliefs no longer prevail, the "spirit of capitalism," as Max Weber (1958) called it, has carried over into modern times: Americans praise their occupational commitment, laboring longer hours on the job than anyone else and applauding what's now called "the work ethic."

Meanwhile, whether Protestant or Catholic, the early Christian explorers held fast to the belief that indigenous peoples were inferior and savage. By the 1500s many Christian communities endorsed an old religious myth derived from the Bible claiming that in cursing his son Ham for a transgression, Noah declared that the descendants of Ham's son Canaan would be Africans, whose eternal duty was to serve other people. Through the slavery period and beyond, religious explanations frequently justified whites' domination (Feagin 2000, 71–74; Weber 1958).

It was, however, the actual practice of slavery that stamped in people's minds the link between race and inferiority. In the early 1600s, colonists had little sense of Africans representing a distinctive race. Gradually, however, as they saw blacks only in an enslaved condition, they made a distinct, racially based association. As sociologist Joe R. Feagin wrote:

> In the prevailing European view, the *enslaved status* [his italics] of most black Americans was fundamental: African Americans were inferior because they were enslaved, and they were enslaved because they were inferior. (Feagin 2000, 74–75)

The designations "black" and "white" have been significant. In Old English, "black" meant "sooted," and that meaning resonated with earlier Christian usage that associated black with sin and evil. "White," in contrast, meant to gleam brightly like a candle and always represented purity and cleanliness (Feagin 2000, 75).

The fact that Africans and their African American descendants varied in skin color and other racial features was insignificant to most whites. The so-called one-drop rule, which has prevailed since the days of slavery, stated that a person with any African ancestry was considered black. This standard, which was upheld as recently as 1986 in a case that was appealed to the U.S. Supreme Court, once helped legitimize slavery and afterward promoted a racial caste system. James F. Davis noted, "Most Americans seem unaware that this definition of blacks is extremely unusual in other countries, perhaps even unique to the United States, and that Americans define no other minority in a similar way" (Davis 1996,

This scene in front of a 1940s Dallas bus station displays the daily reality of the segregated South: that the standard represented by the one-drop rule compelled blacks and whites to live ruthlessly separated lives.

42). In other words, our society's historical tradition has supported a uniquely denigrating outlook toward African Americans.

Although historically blacks have been the group most relentlessly victimized by American racism, other groups have also faced discriminatory treatment. In the middle nineteenth century, Irish immigrants were the frequent objects of discrimination, in part because of their religion, but also because of their unusual accents, frequent inability to speak English, and other cultural traits. Eventually, however, most of them were allowed to obtain a firm economic and residential foothold and, with this progress, acceptance into white communities. From the 1880s to the 1920s, various southern and eastern European groups immigrated to the United States and followed a similar pattern. Although initially objects of discrimination, the common result for all these groups was that they were eventually accorded full white status and the mainstream access and rewards associated with it.

While not suffering blacks' lengthy history of oppression, Asians, Hispanics, and other racial minorities have often faced discriminatory treatment. Although many members of Asian American groups have moved into mainstream employment and residential areas, various studies indicate that discriminatory incidents on the job are frequent, particularly for the best educated, who are the most active members of Asian American organizations and other groups seeking to end such treatment. Like Asian Americans, Hispanics report considerable discrimination at work, and once again some indication suggests that those in higher-level jobs are more victimized. Furthermore, each year hundreds of hate crimes against Asian Americans and Latinos occur, and others go unreported (Feagin 2000, 225–26). Often isolated on reservations, Native Americans' disadvantages have been most blatantly underreported: out of sight, out of mind. For instance, it is only in recent years that researchers have started to study Indians' employment data, revealing that although their overall attainment levels stay well below the national average, those remaining on reservations are much more likely to be unemployed (Gitter and Reagan 2002).

Besides the current discriminatory treatment they suffer, poor minority-group members are particularly vulnerable to impact from the fundamental American economic pattern: that big business enjoys lower taxation and fewer limitations imposed on its activities than its counterparts in other postindustrialized societies (Gottdiener and Hutchison 2000, 142–49; Molotch and Vicari 1988; Ullmann-Margalit 1997). Overall the nation might be affluent, but, especially for domestic expenditure, government budgets have been tight. As a result, low-income people, who in American society are disproportionately minority-group members, have fewer financial resources addressed to their basic needs than their counterparts in other modern nations. In upcoming chapters discussions about housing, day care, education, and health care illustrate how this reality plays out in various groups' lives.

The United States, in short, has hardly been an ideal location for African Americans and other racial minorities. Yet even when the immediate circumstances were bleak, courageous individuals and groups refused to accept subjugation. Writing in the 1930s, the renowned sociologist and activist W. E. B. Du Bois described how his exposure to an anthropologist's revealing speech in the midst of an oppressive era inspired him to alter his perception of being black.

> Franz Boas came to Atlanta University where I was teaching history in 1906 and said to a graduating class: You need not be ashamed of your African past; and then he recounted the history of the black kingdoms south of the Sahara for a thousand years. I was too astonished

to speak. All of this I had never heard and I came then and afterwards to realize how the silence and neglect of science can let truth utterly disappear or even be unconsciously distorted. (Du Bois 1975, vii)

To start demonstrating how the science of sociology should prove instructive in this text, I present two sets of concepts.

The Sociological Perspective

These sociological concepts are divided into two broad categories—first, a general set and then a specific set related to race and ethnicity. Even if some of these concepts are familiar, it is well worth taking the time to examine them.

General Sociological Concepts

The most fundamental building block in sociology's long list of concepts is the **group,** which consists of two or more interacting people who share certain expectations and goals. Group experiences differ in many respects, and one significant dimension, which receives extensive attention in this book, involves their extent of cooperation and conflict. "Hmmm," one friend might say to another, "you and your family really rip into each other. It's just the opposite in my home. We're so pleasant and relaxed, it gets boring." In more formal settings, such as on the job, the amount of cooperation or conflict can also vary considerably.

One prominent type of group is a **formal organization,** which is a group characterized by formally stated rules, clearly defined members' roles, and distinct goals. As formal organizations become larger and more complex, they need bureaucracies, which are their administrative sections that have the task of controlling their operations. I single out this concept because in modern urban life, formal organizations are all around us—our schools, the various businesses and other units for which we work, our hospitals, religious structures, political parties, retail stores, restaurants, entertainment centers, and so forth. Since formal organizations are so prominent in modern life, they become the setting for many issues related to race and ethnicity.

Within formal organizations and other groups, people perform roles. A **role** is a set of expected behaviors associated with a certain position in a group or society. As people learn their different roles, they realize that certain rules exist, governing the rights and obligations associated with them. Clearly, everyone does not perform a given role the same way, and yet role performances generally remain within distinct broad limits. My students, for instance, range considerably in test performance, effective participation in class discussions, and attendance, but in class none of them ever starts fights, throws food, or stretches out on the floor to sleep (though admittedly on occasion someone nods off at his or her desk).

The present sociological analysis plays out on an urban stage. A **city** is a large, densely settled concentration of people permanently located within a fairly confined geographical area where nonagricultural occupations are pursued. Most of us spend our lives in cities or the suburbs adjacent to them. Recognizing the interdependence of cities and suburbs, census takers since the 1940s have used the term "Metropolitan Statistical Area" (MSA) to refer to a city of at least 50,000 residents and its surrounding suburbs within a single county. To qualify as an MSA, a sufficient number of local residents must work in the city to produce a functionally integrated relationship between the two entities. In this book we see that at present and also in the past most new arrivals have located themselves in cities, recognizing that their best job prospects lie there.

Cities are an element of the American social system, an important concept in this book. A **social system** is a society's fairly enduring set of interrelated institutions (involving the economy, the family, political order, education, and so forth) that the society's elite seeks to control, both to maximize their own interests and to ensure their citizens' survival and reproduction. Social systems must address various system problems: the establishment of certain goals and the mobilization of units within the system to achieve them; the capacity to obtain necessary goods and services from the environment and to distribute them; the ability to coordinate relationships among the various groups and organizations within a system; and the capacity to mobilize participants to display the appropriate motivation and skills as well as the resources to deal with their tensions and strains. Although all four functions are significant concerns, American society, where achievement and success are such strong frontrunners, has generally featured the first—the achievement of goals through hard work. Sociologist Robin Williams Jr. concluded that "a notable series of observers have overwhelmingly agreed that America is the land of haste and bustle, of strenuous competition, of ceaseless activity and agitation" (Williams 1970, 458).

Such qualities of the American social system diffuse through the major institutions of American society. Furthermore, as discussion in the upcoming section indicates, any additional trait belonging to the American social system, notably its orientation to race, also disperses into various institutional areas.

Race- and Ethnicity-Related Concepts

Several years ago on the opening day of a course on race and ethnicity, I was introducing basic concepts, including "majority group" and "minority group." As soon as I began distinguishing between the two terms, one student said, "I disagree. The key difference involves their size. Majority groups are larger." Although neither of us was inherently right or wrong, the reference in this context should be to sociological usage, where size is not the central element.

A **majority group** is a category of people within a society who possess distinct physical or cultural characteristics and maintain superior power and resources. In contrast, a **minority group** is any category of people with recognizable physical or cultural traits that place it in a position of restricted power and inferior status so that its members suffer limited opportunities and rewards. Minority-group members are aware of their common oppression, and this awareness helps create a sense of belonging to the group. As I already noted, size is not a criterion. Sometimes a minority group is many times larger than the dominant group in the society. Such a situation existed when the European countries established colonies in Africa, Asia, and the Americas. In other cases—African Americans or Asian Americans in the United States, for example—the minority group is smaller in numbers than the majority group.

Individuals' ethnicity and race are two major factors that can determine whether they belong to a majority group or a minority group. **Ethnicity** is a classification of people into a particular category with distinct cultural or national qualities. Ethnic groups differ on such issues as values, language, religion, food habits, sexual behavior, recreational patterns, and outlook on work, and the culture of an ethnic group creates a sense of identity among its members. In American society ethnicity is often synonymous with national-group membership. There are Chinese Americans, Irish Americans, Italian Americans, Mexican Americans, Haitian Americans, Polish Americans, and many other groups. Some ethnic groups are racially homogenous, and others decidedly are not.

Race refers to a classification of people into categories falsely claimed to be derived from a distinct set of biological traits. Western nations, including the United States, tend to use three racial categories generally referred to with Latin-derived designations: Caucasoid, Mongoloid, and Negroid. This scheme—in fact, any scheme of racial classification—is both imprecise and superficial. Many racial groups are omitted. Where, for instance, should East Indians—people with Caucasian features but dark skin—go? Or where does one fit Indonesians, who have thoroughly mixed ancestry? (Marger 1997, 20–21). Another indication of imprecision is that the standard scheme focuses on some shared characteristics and ignores others. Most Americans are unaware, for instance, that if people were grouped according to genetic resistance to malaria or fingerprinting patterns, Norwegians and many African groups would share the same race. However, if digestive capacities became the central criterion for the formation of a racial group, then some Africans, Asians, and southern Europeans would be in one group and western Africans and northern Europeans would constitute another (Schaefer 1997, 10).

Even if one overlooks such inconsistencies and accepts the current scheme, its superficiality should be a dominant concern. Recent genetic findings have indicated that all members of modern humanity are descendants of Africans, only differentiating into racial groups about 50,000 years ago—not a million years ago as previously believed. A pair of experts on human evolution concluded that "Homo sapiens must be a startlingly homogenous species. We simply have not had time to diverge genetically in any meaningful manner" (Stringer and McKie 1997, 15). No evidence suggests that one racial group is more intelligent, more creative, more athletic, more ferocious, in fact "more anything" involving brain power, personality, or capability than any other. Although racist observers will emphasize that often one racial group is more successful than another, evidence to date suggests the key factor is group members' opportunities, not their genetic heritage.

Besides focusing on ethnicity and race, text material often considers the gender dimension. **Gender** consists of the general behavioral standards that distinguish females and males in a given culture. Gender is a status, specifying for both men and women their culturally supported rights and obligations. In the United States, women and men have been expected to dress and to behave quite differently. Across time and space in all racial and ethnic groups, girls and women suffered and continue to suffer **sexism,** a set of beliefs emphasizing that actual or alleged differences between women and men establish the superiority of men. Sexism entails prejudice and discrimination against girls and women.

Invariably, groups with less opportunity have been the victims of prejudice and discrimination. **Prejudice** is a highly negative judgment toward a minority group, focusing on one or more characteristics that are supposedly uniformly shared by all group members. If a person rigidly believes that everyone within a racial or ethnic group is innately lazy, stupid, stubborn, or violent, then that person is prejudiced toward the group in question. Racial, ethnic, gender, and religious prejudice are the most prominently discussed types. In general, prejudice is not easily reversible, distinguishing it from a "misconception," where someone supports an incorrect conclusion about a group but when confronted with facts is willing to change his or her opinion.

When members of one group are prejudiced toward outsiders, they are likely to develop and express stereotypes. A **stereotype** is an exaggerated, oversimplified image, maintained by prejudiced people, of the characteristics of the group members against whom they are prejudiced. In an early study of stereotypes, blacks were considered superstitious, lazy, happy-go-lucky, ignorant, and musical, while Jews were designated shrewd, industrious, grasping, mercenary, intelligent, and ambitious (Katz and Braly 1933). A modern investigation of stereotyping found that "there is a clear, consistent contemporary stereotype of blacks, and that this stereotype is highly negative in nature" (Devine and Elliott 1995, 1146). Corroborating this conclusion, other research found that the use of stereotypes declines with increased education (Plous and Williams 1995).

Whereas prejudice and the use of stereotypes involve negative judgments toward a minority group, discrimination imposes actual limits on the group. **Discrimination** is behavior by which an individual prevents or restricts a minority-group member's access to scarce resources. Prejudice and discrimination are often a one-two punch: The judgment leads to the behavior. However, the two situations do not always appear together. Discrimination sometimes occurs without prejudice. Insecurity can be a distinct contributor, with the individual in question seeking to avoid "rocking the boat." Many white urban homeowners in the North and Midwest claim they are content to have blacks move into their neighborhoods, but they fear what fellow whites will say or do, and so they oppose any significant initiative for integrated housing (Rose 1997, 116). On the other hand, prejudice can fail to evoke discrimination. From 1930 to 1932, Richard LaPierce conducted a classic study on the relationship of the two concepts. LaPierce, a white psychologist, traveled throughout the United States with a Chinese couple. They invariably received courteous treatment at hotels, motels, and restaurants, and yet 90 percent of questionnaire responses sent to the establishments they patronized made it clear that Chinese would be unwelcome (LaPierce 1934). The study contains some problems—for instance, there is no assurance that the person answering the survey was the one who had served the researcher and the Chinese couple—and yet similar findings appear in later research (Kutner, Wilkins, and Yarrow 1952).

Like prejudice, racism has traditionally been defined as an idea—in this instance a belief that actual or alleged differences between racial groups assert the superiority of one racial group. Sociologist Eduardo Bonilla-Silva (2001, 22) has indicated that such a definition has reduced the study of racism to a focus on individual acts: The idea of racism entails a person's prejudice toward minority groups, inducing him or her to engage in discriminatory acts against those groups.

In contrast, Bonilla-Silva has asserted a materialist conception of racism, emphasizing that majority groups receive greater rewards than minority groups. The members of the dominant racial group develop an exploitative structure establishing both practices and a supporting ideology that secure their persistent control. In upcoming chapters both of these elements are discussed at length. The following concept anchors these discussions.

A **racialized social system** is a social system in which people's racial classification partially determines their access to valued economic, political, and social resources. Although other factors such as gender and social class will influence this access, the impact of race on social systems is independently observable (Bonilla-Silva 2001, 37).

Once a majority group establishes a racial hierarchy, making their own group superordinate and another or other racial group(s) subordinate, the system takes on a life of its own, becoming established and legitimate throughout the society's interrelated structures. Sociologist Joe R. Feagin indicated that in a racialist system

> the core racist realities are manifested in each of society's major parts. If you break a three-dimensional hologram into separate parts and shine a laser through any one part, you can project the whole three-dimensional image again from within that part. Like a hologram, each major part of U.S. society—the economy, politics, education, religion, the family—reflects the fundamental reality of [a racialized social system]. (Feagin 2000, 6)

In a society in which racialized hierarchies exist, members of various racial groups will begin to recognize that their interests differ from those of other groups and, in fact, that the respective interests often oppose each other. Both conflict and change revolve around the respective groups' efforts to strengthen their interests. At such times majority-group members are likely to perceive minorities negatively and to engage in racist behavior. In more tranquil times, racism might lie dormant, but when majority groups feel threatened, they will respond punitively.

Racialized social systems can continue to thrive even if some minority-group members move into prominent, influential positions. The key for such systems' survival is the maintenance of a pattern of racial imbalance, in which many members of the majority group are in superordinate roles and, in turn, racial minorities primarily remain in subordinate locations. Figure 1.1 lists major patterns in a racialized social system.

The following Sociological Illustration about a neighborhood in Oakland, California, takes a more detailed look at an interracial setting, demonstrating that even when ethnic and racial relations appear to be smooth and tolerant, the racialized quality of the social system can persist.

FIGURE 1.1   Major Patterns Occurring in the Racialized Social System

I.   A majority group creates a racially based hierarchy that maximizes its economic, political, and social interests. A group's position in that hierarchy significantly affects its members' access to valued economic, political, and social resources.

II. Once the racialized hierarchy develops, racial groups' interests crystallize. Those in control seek to maintain their advantage, and the less privileged maneuver for greater access to valued rewards.

III. Conflict and change occur as various groups in the system seek to promote their often opposing interests.

IV. As long as a racialized social system with its conflicting group interests persists, racism and racial exploitation and stereotyping will thrive.

SOCIOLOGIAL ILLUSTRATION

Oakland's Laurel District and Its Mixed Blessings

If every American residential area had the Laurel District's atmosphere, then this country would undoubtedly have more pleasant and tranquil ethnic and racial relations. This small, diverse neighborhood, where the population is 31 percent Asian, 28 percent white, 23 percent black, 14 percent Latino, and 4 percent biracial, contains individuals and families who feel that it is a very good place for both children and adults who value living in a racially and ethnically diverse environment.

"I like being able to walk down my block and seeing black, white, Chinese people all together. I love it," declared Lydia Jaloma, a middle-aged woman who had felt suffocated in the all-Mexican neighborhood in East Los Angeles where she previously lived (Marech 2002).

Although almost all residents agree that everyone gets along, some observers note that relations between and among various groups are emotionally restrained. Martha Rueca Gustafsson, a Filipina, who is co-owner of World Ground, a popular coffee shop on MacArthur Boulevard, explained, "I don't see the old Chinese men sitting down to have coffee with the old African American guy who sits at another table. I don't see a whole lot of celebration" (Marech 2002).

MacArthur Boulevard, in fact, is what Toni Locke, the white editor of a local newspaper, described as "one of those awful dividing lines that exists in urban areas" (Marech 2002). In fact, it is a street that reveals the relationship between housing value and the racialized quality of the locale. Although the bungalows and houses on both sides of MacArthur are similar in size, quality, and attractiveness, a significant difference in monetary value exists, based on the fact that below MacArthur the proportion of black to white homeowners is nearly double, whereas above the avenue the numbers are almost the same. Certainly residents recognize the difference, with many feeling more comfortable shopping in an area more heavily populated by their own racial group. Dennis Evanosky, a white man who lives close to MacArthur, said he knows many whites who are nervous shopping below the avenue.

"They would rather go to vanilla ice cream Montclair district than the more convenient Laurel shopping district" (Marech 2002). On the other hand, no matter how far above MacArthur some African Americans live, they choose the Laurel shopping area, saying that in contrast to the Montclair locale they feel completely welcome there, with no sense of tension.

Perhaps the most racialized aspect of the Laurel neighborhood involves schooling. Even though whites make up over a quarter of the residents, Laurel Elementary contains barely a handful of white children. Forty-six percent of the students are Asian, primarily Chinese, 39 percent African American, and most of the remainder are Latino. Cheryl Garrett, the principal, indicated that young white couples moving into the area are worried about their child being the only white student in the classroom, and so they either opt for a private school or manage to get their child into the Redwood Heights school, which has a substantial percentage of white students. At Laurel School some race-related disputes occur. Garrett, who experienced racial isolation as the only black student in her San Francisco elementary school, indicated that children tend to make friends across racial and ethnic lines if they are in mixed rather than bilingual classrooms, which in this case generally divides them into two categories—Chinese and non-Chinese. Garrett's opinion, however, displeases many parents. Native speakers say that Chinese teachers' foreign accents impede their children's learning, and Chinese parents claim their children are forced into contact with "bad" classmates. On the last point, Garrett was furious. "I call it racism," she said. "We do our part to make sure kids have an understanding of each other. But they go home to these parents" (Marech 2002).

Although the most obvious race-related clashes occur in schools, other sporadic outbreaks appear. A handful of whites, for instance, complained when to save doing yardwork some Chinese families paved over their yards. "It's cultural," one resident said.

(continued)

Stella Lamb, who is white, indicated she's disturbed when such arguments bubble up in her generally peaceful neighborhood but that "it's a price to pay to raise my daughter in a more diverse place." Lamb paused to think, then added, "Maybe I would move to a place that's diverse but doesn't have some of these problems, if I could" (Marech 2002). When asked to name such a place, she shrugged and conceded that it probably existed only in a utopian world.

At first glance, the Laurel District appears to represent a social system in which race-based interests are muted. However, a closer look reveals various tensions derived from a system in which whites' interests have historically dominated. The residen-

tial settlement pattern often elicits fear; the racialized reality of housing location has prompted many whites to feel uneasy or afraid about shopping in the black-dominated area, and blacks, in turn, react similarly to entering the white section. The topic of schooling produces even greater tension as the various racial groups are all heavily invested in their children's access to effective schooling. In the Laurel District, it is apparent that each of the three groups described—blacks, Chinese Americans, and whites—has had a different agenda. What seems clear is that this underlying source of divisiveness is not likely to disappear in the foreseeable future. That conclusion suggests the abiding impact of the racialized element in the social system.

Although diverse, fairly harmonious urban communities like the Laurel neighborhood exist, it seems that they are fragile. The realities of racialized social systems are visible—in the schools, in at least one residential area on the community's southern border—and such

Although some American families live in communities where extensive racial contact occurs, many never experience close association with the members of other racial groups.

factors as an explosive, race-related incident in the elementary school or a significant economic downturn could further undermine the community's usually tranquil relations. The conclusion of this chapter comments further about the racialized social system.

Conclusion

In *The Pursuit of Loneliness,* sociologist Philip Slater introduced an idea that he designated "the toilet assumption"—the dominant groups' unexamined belief that the best solution for dealing with any distasteful situation, whether it involves human waste products or some racial or ethnic group's issue or problem, is simply to flush the unwanted object from the scene. Out of sight means out of mind, and majority-group members often react petulantly when minority individuals or groups suddenly appear in protests, explosive media stories, or even violent outbreaks. However, such occurrences are exceptional. Most of the time the toilet assumption flows smoothly, often leading to racial segregation and the reinforcement of a racialized social system. Slater wrote:

> The result of our social efforts has been to remove the underlying problems of our society farther and farther from daily experience and daily consciousness, and hence to decrease, in the mass of the population, the knowledge, skill, and resources, and motivation necessary to deal with them. (Slater 1970, 15)

Daily life in American cities testifies to the accuracy of Slater's observations—observations that encapsulate the frequent exclusion of racial minorities in the American social context. In the mainstream world, whether in residential districts, shopping areas, the business world, or the schools, conflicts and problems of race and ethnicity are usually not evident. However, if one visits poor, inner-city residential areas and schools, welfare offices, soup kitchens, the service segments of many businesses, or criminal court, the distinct presence of poor racial minorities' oppressed condition becomes readily apparent.

In the chapters ahead, such realities are examined at length.

DISCUSSION QUESTIONS

1. Evaluate whether or not the United States has had a racist tradition. Indicate why you reach that conclusion.

2. Illustrate the impact that belonging to both a small group and a formal organization has on individuals' outlooks and behavior.

3. Define the concepts of race and ethnicity and provide a specific, preferably real-life example of how each impacts urban residents' everyday life.

4. Define, illustrate, and analyze the concepts of prejudice and discrimination, also considering the relationship of stereotypes to the other two terms.

5. What is a racialized social system? Describe in detail a situation in which the process unfolds.

BIBLIOGRAPHY

Bonilla-Silva, Eduardo. 2001. *White Supremacy & Racism in the Post-Civil Rights Era.* Boulder: Lynne Rienner.

Davis, F. James. 1996. "Who Is Black? One Nation's Definition," pp. 35–42 in Karen E. Rosenblum and Toni-Michelle C. Travis (eds.), *The Meaning of Difference: American Constructions of Race, Sex and Gender, Social Class, and Sexual Orientation.* New York: McGraw-Hill.

Devine, Patricia G., and Andrew J. Elliot. 1995. "Are Racial Stereotypes *Really* Fading? The Princeton Trilogy Revisited." *Personality and Social Psychology Bulletin.* 21 (November): 1139–50.

Du Bois, W. E. B. 1975. *Black Folk: Then and Now.* Milwood, NY: Kraus-Thomson. Originally published in 1939.

Feagin, Joe R. 2000. *Racist America: Roots, Current Realities, and Future Reparations.* New York: Routledge.

Gitter, Robert J., and Patricia B. Reagan. 2002. "Reservation Wages: An Analysis of the Effects of Reservations on Employment of American Indian Men." *The American Economic Review.* 12 (September): 1160–68.

Gottdiener, Mark, and Ray Hutchison. 2000. *The New Urban Sociology,* 2nd ed. New York: McGraw-Hill.

Katz, David, and Kenneth Braly. 1933. "Racial Stereotypes of One Hundred College Students." *Journal of Abnormal and Social Psychology.* 28 (October): 280–90.

Kutner, Bernard, Carol Wilkins, and P. R. Yarrow. 1952. "Verbal Attitudes and Overt Behavior Involving Racial Prejudice." *Journal of Abnormal and Social Psychology.* 47 (July): 649–52.

LaPierce, Richard T. 1934. "Attitudes vs. Actions." *Social Forces.* 13 (October): 230–37.

Marech, Rona. 2002. "Laurel District: Oakland's Mixed Blessings Multicultural Area Hits Snags along Racial Lines." *San Francisco Chronicle.* (May 10).

Marger, Martin N. 1997. *Race and Ethnic Relations: American and Global Perspectives.* Belmont, CA: Wadsworth.

Mills, C. Wright. 1959. *The Sociological Imagination.* New York: Oxford University Press.

Molotch, Harvey, and Serena Vicari. 1988. "Three Ways to Build: The Development Process in the United States, Japan, and Italy. *Urban Affairs Quarterly.* 24 (December): 188–214.

Plous, S., and Tyrone Williams. 1995. "Racial Stereotypes from the Days of American Slavery: A Continuing Legacy." *Journal of Applied Social Psychology.* 25 (May): 795–817.

Rose, Peter I. 1997. *They and We: Racial and Ethnic Relations in the United States,* 5th ed. New York: McGraw-Hill.

Schaefer, Richard T. 1997. *Racial and Ethnic Groups,* 7th ed. New York: Longman.

Slater, Philip E. 1970. *The Pursuit of Loneliness: American Culture at the Breaking Point.* Boston: Beacon Press.

Stringer, Chris, and Robin McKie. 1997. "Neanderthals on the Run." *New York Times.* (July 27): sec. 4, p. 15.

Ullmann-Margalit, Edna. 1997. "The Invisible Hand and the Cunning of Reason." *Social Research.* 64 (Summer): 181–98.

Weber, Max. 1958. *The Protestant Ethic and the Spirit of Capitalism.* Trans. Talcott Parsons in 1930. New York: Scribner.

Williams, Robin M., Jr. 1970. *American Society: A Sociological Interpretation,* 3rd ed. New York: Knopf.

CHAPTER 2

Systematic Equality? Divergent Sociological Thought in Analyzing Urban Racial and Ethnic Groups

The announcer and the athlete are standing in a poor, downtown section of a well-known American city. "So, Lonny, you grew up right here on this block."

"Yes, in that boarded-up building across the street."

"How does it make you feel to be back here?"

"Sad but also fortunate. Sad because of all the family members and friends I left behind, with many dead, on drugs, or in prison, but fortunate because I was able to get out."

"And it was your sport that opened the door for you."

"That's right."

Anyone watching the now-frequent TV biographies of minority-group college and professional athletes is familiar with this type of exchange. Attention is often on the celebrity's escape—how courage and determination were critical requisites for breaking out of the ghetto into a successful, mainstream life. In this chapter we see that one set of theorists have supported a consistent perspective, emphasizing that with the proper work ethic the diverse American citizenry has extensive access to valued opportunities and rewards. On the other hand, another set of theorists focus on the impact of groups' placement in the racialized social system, noting they have appreciably different chances of obtaining systems' economic and political rewards.

These two divergent bodies of theory provide distinctively different perspectives on race and ethnicity and particularly on the significance of the racialized social system. The discussion begins with structural-functional theory at the University of Chicago.

Out of Chicago: Structural-Functional Analysis of Race and Ethnicity in the Urban Context

In 1892 a visitor entering Cobb Hall of the University of Chicago asked a cleaning lady where to find the president. "I dunno," she said. "I jes' scrub." When the visitor repeated the remark to President William Rainey Harper, he quipped that indeed "[w]e are beginning to specialize" (Beadle 1972, 162). Specialization was gaining credibility at this young, flourishing university, where highly recruited, top-level experts were devoting themselves to research in the natural and social sciences, with sociology part of the latter category.

Harper's vision was to establish the University of Chicago as a world-renowned center for research and inquiry, where senior professors were hired both to do their own research and to launch graduate students in their careers. For his cutting-edge programs, this energetic, enthusiastic executive sought first-class academics, whom he offered high salaries along with considerable freedom in their research and classroom activity. Harper was both persistent and pervasive, and though some leading academic figures resisted his offers, he was usually successful, managing to recruit a strong set of senior graduate faculty, including eight former presidents of colleges and universities.

Harper's vision dominated the University of Chicago, but its development would have been impossible without John D. Rockefeller's support. Between 1890 and 1910, Rockefeller gave the university a total of $35 million in endowment and financing for current expenses. This contribution was considerably larger than any other, but the university was established on a firm financial footing only after Harper had tapped a variety of other large corporate sources.

Harper's plans for the new sociology department were vague, little beyond the sense that it could contribute to the solution of social problems. This perspective rang true with the department's founders, who came from liberal Protestant backgrounds and were attuned to the popular midwestern view that sociological investigation could supply information that Christian activists might use to help reform urban life.

The setting for the department's research was the rapidly growing city of Chicago, where an array of social problems gave the department's investigators ample material. When Max Weber, a German sociologist, visited Chicago in 1904, he wrote "it was like looking at a man whose skin had been peeled off and whose intestines are seen at work" (Bulmer 1984, 23). It was a provocative setting for a committed set of urban researchers.

The City as Sociological Laboratory

The central figure in this new sociology department was Robert Park, a former newspaperman, who received a Ph.D. from the University of Heidelberg and between 1914 and 1933 taught sociology at the University of Chicago, where he was the driving force of what became known as the Chicago School of Sociology. From its inception Park urged the department to consider Chicago its laboratory, and its members embraced the proposal.

The initial explorations were descriptions of the city, beginning in Ernest Burgess's course about social pathology with maps showing urban patterns of crime, juvenile delinquency, prostitution, and mental illness (Faris 1967, 52).

Park and Burgess's partnership was intense, inspiring a commitment to urban study that spread throughout the department. Burgess claimed that Park "lived and slept research. I never knew when I would get home for dinner because we would spend whole afternoons discovering both theoretical and practical aspects of sociology and social research" (Burgess 1964, 3). Burgess himself appeared no less committed. While Park developed a methodological overview for projects, Burgess possessed greater skill for conducting empirical study and relating its conclusions to the growing body of urban sociological theory. They also collaborated on the text *Introduction to the Science of Sociology,* which provided the theoretical foundation for the department's expanding body of research.

In the early 1920s, the two men considered themselves pioneers—in the vanguard of the effort to study the social world scientifically. The principal course Park and Burgess fashioned for this purpose was the graduate seminar on field studies, which was structured to help students do empirical research. After several introductory classes, participants were supposed to gather data on a selected topic, engaging in such exercises as conducting interviews, taking detailed notes about meetings, constructing maps of various behavioral patterns, and carefully recording information about a wide variety of urban activities.

Park and Burgess worked closely, frequently sharing information about the student researchers and their work. Graduates of the department recalled that after having a conference with one of them, they would often be drawn into discussion with the other, who invariably was well informed about the particular project (Bulmer 1984, 94–95).

Research in the department focused on two primary areas: the ecological analysis of the city and an array of specific urban topics, including race and ethnicity.

An Overview of the Chicago School's Contributions

The ecological conception of the city emphasizes that much like plants and other animal species, human groups are in competition for space within an urban area. The key component in groups' ability to compete for space is their organization. Those that are highly organized with effective interdependencies among their integral parts—their families; their businesses; and such supportive organizations as schools, health-care facilities, volunteer associations, and religious centers—will be most capable of survival and growth (Hawley 1971, 11–12).

Park, Burgess, and other members of the Chicago School of Sociology were proponents of the **concentric-zone hypothesis**—a proposition asserting that the groups occupying a given space push outward from the city center in a fairly symmetrical pattern along local transportation lines. Burgess, the prime developer of this concept, believed that as with plants, human groups engage in succession, an alternation of stages in which growth is followed by equilibrium, with the cycle then repeating itself over and over. For instance, following a wave of capital investment, business activity expands outward from the center of the city, settles in a particular area, and then later repeats the cycle, perhaps with outward expansion encouraged by recent technological developments. If these businesses were effectively organized, they could meet their expenses and still make a decent profit. With ineffective organization, however, profitable enterprises would not develop, often forcing them to leave this coveted area.

The concentric-zone hypothesis describes five distinct circular areas. At the core is the business district; then a zone of transition, where factories and businesses encroach on housing, causing its deterioration into slums; next a section of workingmen's homes occupied by people who have escaped the slums and now can afford this area, benefiting from proximity to their jobs in the nearby industrial zone; then a residential district of high-income apartment buildings or exclusive single-family dwellings; and finally, the commuter zone within a 30- to 60-minute ride of the central business district.

According to this theory, recently arrived immigrant groups tend to move outward from the city's core, making small moves, not big jumps. As groups push toward the periphery, they tend to assimilate culturally, moving into the political and economic mainstream and also intermarrying as they approach the suburbs.

People living farther from the city's center are usually more affluent, but exceptions develop. In Chicago, for instance, the view of the lakefront with its cooling summer breezes stimulated construction of fashionable apartment buildings in a downtown area that otherwise light industry would probably have dominated (Burgess 1967, 48–52; Faris 1967, 56–58; Hawley 1971, 99–101).

The concentric-zone hypothesis frequently appeared in the department's array of studies on diverse topics. Chicago School sociologists covered a variety of urban issues and problems, including homelessness, juvenile delinquency, family disorganization, and race and ethnicity. Studies of the latter two topics included E. Franklin Frazier's *The Negro Family in Chicago* (1932), which analyzed the linkage between black family experiences and activities, and location in various ecological zones; Louis Wirth's *The Ghetto* (1928), which also used ecological analysis to focus on immigrant Jews whose ghettoized European experiences became more assimilative as their residential locations headed toward the periphery of Chicago and other American cities; and W. I. Thomas and Florian Znaniecki's five-volume work *The Polish Peasant in Europe and America* (1918), which examined the role of such structures as family, friends, the community, the press, schools, and voluntary associations and indicated that frequent social disorganization occurred for newly arrived Polish immigrants because no community organizations effectively mediated the transition from the old to the new society.

No matter whom they studied, Chicago School sociologists tended to downplay inequalities and conflict among groups, suggesting that assimilation was a dominant reality in a given group's future. Herman Schwendinger and Julia R. Schwendinger indicated that the Chicago School's approach to studying cities endorsed a "stable and harmonious capitalist society" (Schwendinger and Schwendinger 1974, 421)—hardly a surprise when one recalls the corporate sponsorship tapped by President Harper. However, the Chicago group claimed ideological neutrality, contending that their supposedly objective research examined universal patterns of social interaction when, in truth, the emphasis on the stability-maintaining process of social consensus and the distinct omission of the disruptive, change-producing process of conflict served to support and endorse the established capitalist order.

That sense of a stable, harmonious social world was on full display in the Chicago School's analysis of race and ethnicity.

Structural-Functional Theory and American Race Relations

In 1933 Ernest Burgess of the Chicago School published a well-known map that identified the spatial location of various ethnic groups, pinpointing Irish, German, Italian, Russian, Swedish, Czech, Polish, and black "ghettos." Later examination, however, revealed that the average number of nationalities per "ghetto" was 22, and that with the exception of Poles and blacks, none of the groups constituted a majority of the population in their designated ghettos. Poles comprised 54 percent of their area, and blacks' percentage was much higher—82 percent (Massey and Denton 1993, 32). Blacks, in short, lived in much more ghettoized districts than the other groups, but Burgess's analysis overlooked that significant reality. As we have noted, the Chicago School tended to deemphasize inequalities, concluding that American society provided substantial opportunity to all groups.

Robert Park's analysis of race relations was consistent with this position. While acknowledging racism, he remained optimistic it would be eliminated, citing what he called "the race relations cycle, which takes the form . . . of contacts, competition, accommodation, and eventual assimilation [and] is apparently progressive and irreversible" (Park 1950, 150).

Contacts, according to Park, occur between different groups when explorers from one group discover new areas that can serve as sites for economic gain. Next, he indicated, competition develops. It is not uncontrolled competition; instead, members of the different racial groups must act within established customs and laws. They adapt to the new situation, accepting work that, while often not personally desirable, contributes to the emerging economy. Eventually a new division of labor forms, incorporating the different racial groups.

With this division of labor in place, accommodation begins. Park asserted that within any established economic system, even one as oppressive as slavery, intimate and personal relations among members of different racial groups develop, undermining the more sinister system elements. According to Park, one indication of accommodation during American slavery was that in spite of legislation and custom strongly supporting the system, the number of slaves given freedom by their masters steadily increased over time (Park 1950, 150).

Assimilation—the elimination of separate racial interests and the development of a common identity involving all racial groups within a society—is the final step. Park suggested that invariably some racial groups assimilate more rapidly than others, and he

A scene like this one, showing harmonious multi-racial involvement in corporate middle management, serves as an illustration of structural-functional theory.

conceded that in the first half of the twentieth century, African Americans had still not fully assimilated—that "though the white man and the Negro have lived and worked together in the United States for three hundred years and more, the two races are still in a certain sense strangers to one another" (Park 1950, 76). Park was vague in analyzing the precise nature of African Americans' incomplete assimilation, indicating that although they were not fully assimilated "in just what sense this is true is difficult to say" (Park 1950, 77).

Milton M. Gordon (1964) sought to be more exact than Park, developing a seven-level framework for analyzing different types of assimilation. To illustrate his scheme, he focused on two hypothetical ethnic groups—the Sylvanians and the Mundovians. Originally they had separate homelands, but at one point Mundovians started moving to Sylvania. By the second generation, the Mundovians were completely assimilated. What were some of Gordon's types of assimilation?

One type was cultural assimilation, with Mundovians adopting all the patterns of the host culture—the language, religion, beliefs, values, norms, and education system—and putting aside their previous cultural standards.

In addition, Mundovians achieved structural assimilation, making friends by joining cliques, clubs, and other Sylvanian organizations and thereby receiving full acceptance in their residential communities.

The Mundovians also experienced civic assimilation, meaning that they made no significant demands on the host culture that would have required its members to make any changes in their established ways of thinking and acting.

All in all, **assimilation** refers to a group's full access to all culturally valued rights, opportunities, and experiences within a society. It represents the achievement of full integration into mainstream life.

Gordon seemed less confident than Park about the occurrence of complete assimilation in the United States. When he examined Americans' friendship patterns and club memberships, it was apparent that many people prefer to associate with their fellow racial and ethnic group members. On the other hand, Gordon noted that by choice some people reach out beyond their own group and seek the friendship and stimulation of those with diverse racial and ethnic backgrounds. Furthermore, contacts among Americans of varied heritages occur because of the racial and ethnic mixing produced in the industrial work world and in higher education systems. Gordon wrote:

> Ethnic communality will not disappear in the foreseeable future and its legitimacy and rationale should be recognized and respected. By the same token, the bonds that bind human beings together across the lines of ethnicity and the pathways on which people of diverse ethnic origin meet and mingle should be cherished and strengthened. (Gordon 1964, 265)

In Gordon's view, ethnic groups function as subsocieties with various friendship networks and voluntary organizations that allow their members to live out their lives within a specific ethnic context. These structures, Gordon suggested, are so compelling for their members that they are likely to stay bound to them even after the ethnic cultural content disappears (Gordon 1964, 158–59). This line of thinking argues that Chinese Americans', Jewish Americans', or Mexican Americans' identity with their respective groups will persist simply because of their involvement in their ethnic-centered families, clubs, or professional organizations even if they no longer continue to make everyday use of their group's traditional values, beliefs, and language.

The latter conclusion shifts away from assimilation, focusing instead on another structural-functional concept—**ethnic pluralism,** which describes ethnic groups' respective contributions to American society, stressing both their current distinctive qualities and their important functions. Unlike assimilation-oriented theories, ethnic pluralism perspectives do not contend that all groups will simply blend into the larger culture. Instead, they argue that various racial and ethnic groups will find it in their interest to retain some of their own cultural traditions and activities.

Nathan Glazer and Daniel Patrick Moynihan (1963), proponents of ethnic pluralism, wrote a well-known book with a decidedly nonassimilationist title. *Beyond the Melting Pot* contended that the early twentieth-century idea that all ethnic and racial groups would simply disappear in the great "American melting pot" has been proved inaccurate. Analyzing the major ethnic and racial groups in New York City, Glazer and Moynihan argued that common history, community ties, organizational linkages, and often religion and language have united members of a given racial or ethnic group, making it likely that affiliation with the group will provide the most efficient means for members to achieve full participatory rights in American political and economic systems.

When, according to Glazer and Moynihan, a racial or ethnic group lacks full participatory rights, members of the group must mobilize to function as an interest group. For example, Glazer and Moynihan contended that in order for blacks to achieve equitable participation in modern society, new, effective African American leaders capable of demanding equal rights for their people had to emerge. Writing in 1963, Glazer and Moynihan suggested that although there had been some promising signs of the emergence of such leadership, black leaders had recently proved ineffective. This failure, the authors argued, was significant, because only African Americans could lead their own people in certain problem areas. They wrote:

> It is probable that no investment of public and private agencies on delinquency and crime-prevention programs will equal the return from an investment by Negro-led and Negro-financed agencies. It is probable that no offensive on the public school system to improve the educational results among Negroes will equal what may be gained from an equivalent investment by Negro-led and Negro-financed groups. (Glazer and Moynihan 1963, 84)

However, solutions to such pervasive problems prove politically formidable and expensive. To expect the emerging leadership of any racial or ethnic minority, particularly one that is underfinanced, to play the major role in their solution without substantial resource support seems both unreasonable and unrealistic.

A decade after their initial statement, Glazer and Moynihan reasserted their thesis, emphasizing two new points: first, that by the middle 1970s, there were more interracial struggles for prestige, respect, political power, and access to economic opportunity than in the past; second, that the use of ethnic groups as interest groups had become a more persistent trend in recent years (Glazer and Moynihan 1975, 5–7).

Once more, in 1990, Glazer and Moynihan reevaluated their version of ethnic pluralism during a panel discussion that occurred following the trial for two white men accused of killing a black man in the Bensonhurst section of Queens, New York. They suggested that the racial unrest and hatred the killing had produced underlined the relevance of their thesis and invalidated an assimilationist perspective—that as a reporter tersely phrased it, "the melting pot metaphor was a crock" (Roberts 1990, B1). Moynihan took the opportunity to criticize Marxist thought, suggesting that the beyond-the-melting-pot position, which emphasizes a prominent advocacy role for race and ethnicity in modern times, has refuted Karl Marx's claim that industrial forces would annihilate the significance of race and ethnicity and create a unified working force whose only interests were those shared by an oppressed, exploited class. Giving his colleague major credit, Moynihan said, "What Karl Marx proposed in the British Museum, Nat Glazer disproved in the New York Public Library" (Roberts 1990, B1).

It is true that Marx was one of several prominent nineteenth-century social scientists who incorrectly discounted the significance of race and ethnicity as major forces in the industrial world. However, his carefully reasoned analysis of the impact of capitalist enterprise on human activity is very useful for analyzing the distribution of wealth, power, and privilege among American racial and ethnic groups. In contrast, Glazer and Moynihan's theory, which gives little attention to such forces operating among groups, suffers from that absence. As an example of that inadequacy, Glazer, who wrote the original chapter on African Americans in *Beyond the Melting Pot,* admitted that his claim that blacks would manage to be as economically and politically mobile as whites proved to be naive (Roberts 1990, B1). Glazer's incorrect prediction about blacks was consistent with the structural-functional perspective's overly optimistic view that minority groups, including blacks, invariably have increasing access to power, wealth, and social position.

Sociologist Stephen Steinberg concluded that ethnic pluralists like Glazer and Moynihan who focused on the ethnic revival of the 1960s were simply witnessing "a dying gasp" on the part of the European ethnic groups who had represented the great waves of nineteenth- and early twentieth-century immigration. According to Steinberg, there are four reasons why European ethnic groups are unlikely to sustain sharply distinct identities in the new land:

■ *Distance from their homelands.* Suddenly cut loose from their traditional moorings, the new arrivals tended to embrace American culture as a means of feeling part of the adopted society. Supporting this trend was the fact that most immigrants arrived poor and disadvantaged and encountered a society with the potent message that mainstream success followed only for those who shed all or most of their traditional ways.

■ *Interdependence of ethnic communities with the general society.* American ethnic communities seldom have basic functions that would have established their distinct separation. In particular, they have generally not possessed a successful economy catering to their members' needs, and as a result most workers needed to look beyond the ethnic locale for employment. In addition, unlike in Canada and other multiethnic countries, public schools have never been under individual ethnic groups' control. Although various religious organizations have developed their own schools, their structures served only a portion of a given group and often, as in the case of parochial schools, were not focused on a single ethnic category.

■ *The decline of ethnic prejudice.* As various groups have assimilated to American culture, the established population has become increasingly tolerant toward their members, eliminating or at least downplaying the need to seek refuge in a separated ethnic community.

■ *Homogenizing trend in modern societies.* In preindustrial times such basic structures as families, religious organizations, and the community played a major role in individuals' upbringing and were often intimately interwoven with specific ethnic identities. Now these structures have lost their dominant functions, with the mainstream mass media and education system, both separated from ethnic values, serving as replacements (Steinberg 2001, 53–59).

These trends, in short, suggest that some basic structural qualities of American society have been more attuned to an assimilationist than an ethnic pluralism perspective. Certainly, historians Stephan Thernstrom and Abigail Thernstrom (1997) agree. In *America in Black and White: One Nation, Indivisible,* they devoted over six hundred pages to developing their decidedly assimilationist subtitle, stressing the economic, political, and social progress that blacks have made in recent decades and downplaying the impact of persistent racism in American institutions. The Thernstroms presented their readers with their conception of the big picture.

> The issue of group differences is actually enormously complicated. American society does not consist of two monolithic racial groups, blacks and whites. It is a complex mosaic of groups with different histories and different cultural traits that have led them to concentrate in different social niches. (Thernstrom and Thernstrom 1997, 541)

The authors followed this general statement with a host of references showing that specific ethnic groups—Cajuns, Armenians, Jews, Puerto Ricans, and others—are skewed either well above or below the national average for income or education. Then the Thernstroms added:

> What explains why some of these groups have done so much better than others is very hard to say. Whatever the answer, the implications for thinking about black-white issues should be clear. Group differences are here to stay, whatever our public policies and however thoroughly we root out discrimination. (Thernstrom and Thernstrom 1997, 543)

At this juncture conflict theorists abruptly part company with the Thernstroms, contending it is invariably clear why some groups have done much better than others— the consistently successful ones have been the beneficiaries of favorable historical and contemporary conditions. Conflict theorists are convinced that, overall, blacks and whites have experienced clear and persistent opportunity differences in American society, diminishing blacks' chances for conventional success and justifying continued efforts to incorporate more of them into the American mainstream. Assimilation proponents like the Thernstroms, they contend, ignore or downplay the major disadvantages many blacks and selected other racial minorities continue to face.

Table 2.1 summarizes the principal differences between the structural-functional and conflict theories of race and ethnicity presented in this chapter and provides highlights for the following discussion.

TABLE 2.1   Summary of Structural-Functional and Conflict Perspectives on Race and Ethnicity

	Structural-Functional Theory	**Conflict Theory**
View of capitalist society	Capitalist leaders support a just, harmonious world.	Capitalist forces structure the world for their own advantage.
Role of minorities in cities	The urban ecological reality permits all groups arriving in cities to enjoy increasing assimilation as they move toward the suburbs.	Modern cities need a large pool of poor minority workers to fill service jobs.
Outlook on racial and ethnic groups' access to economic and political opportunities	All groups eventually have access to mainstream success.	The racialized social system restricts selected minorities.
Dominant ideological setting	Either assimilationist or pluralist opportunities are available to all racial and ethnic groups.	Color-blind racism and other toned-down modern racist forms remain prominent.
Explanation for why a particular group's members do not attain success	Claims of failure are focused on supposed cultural deficiency, such as lack of motivation or discipline.	Embeddedness in the racialized social system makes conventional success remote or impossible.

Conflict Theory's View of Race and Ethnicity in the Urban American Context

Conflict theorists provide quite a different analysis of society than structural-functionalists. Following in a Marxist tradition, they recognize and highlight the oppression caused by the vastly unequal distribution of such prized resources as wealth, power, and social prestige. Some belong to victimized minorities and are committed to altering the inequalities suffered by members of their minority group. Some, like many of us in modern sociology, have been influenced by the 1960s protests, which, as sociologist Todd Gitlin phrased it, "relaunched the long, long trek toward equality" (Gitlin 1989, xi). Conflict theorists are much more attuned than their assimilationist counterparts to the barriers racial minorities can encounter entering mainstream life.

W. E. B. Du Bois, a noted sociologist and social activist, took positions consistent with a conflict perspective. He believed that ignorance lay at the roots of whites' oppression of blacks and that a thorough and objective scientific investigation would reveal the truth and lead to its termination. Du Bois's research, which was sponsored by the University of Pennsylvania and took place in Philadelphia in the 1890s, was well timed. A reform movement was in full swing, and even though Du Bois, a black man with a Ph.D. from Harvard, obtained only the most marginal status—no office at the university, no teaching duties, and the lowly title of "assistant instructor"—he did receive a liveable stipend of $900 for a year's study (Aptheker 1973, 18).

Du Bois plunged into the work, feeling it was a grand opportunity to help his people. He described the project as "an inquiry . . . into the condition of the forty thousand or more people of Negro blood now living in the city of Philadelphia" (Du Bois 1973, 1).

The study concentrated in the seventh ward, which was the historic center of the African American population. Du Bois conducted about 2,500 interviews averaging about 20 minutes each, producing about 835 hours of data (Aptheker 1973, 17–18).

Du Bois was a pioneer, decades ahead of other sociologists in providing hard-hitting evidence of the racialist social system and its destructive impact on African Americans' lives. Although Du Bois was the first sociologist to provide evidence in this area, he was not the first American to analyze his nation's racialized structure.

Early Perceptions of the Racialized Social System

Sixty years before Du Bois started his research, Frederick Douglass, who had escaped slavery in Maryland a few months earlier, began making public appearances. In a fifty-four-year career "as the preeminent spokesman for African Americans," Douglass gave over two thousand speeches, wrote thousands of articles and editorials, and produced three versions of an autobiography, "the first two of which are now commonly acknowledged as masterpieces transcending their genre." In his day, however, Douglass was best known as an orator in an era when the power of oratory was as great as that of television today. Introducing Douglass's selected speeches and writings, Yuval Taylor indicated that "[w]ith his combination of rhetorical power, intellectual acumen, classical eloquence, and physical presence, Douglass may well rank as the greatest American orator of his time" (Taylor 1999, xi). I can add that along with Du Bois's work, Douglass's commentary of the impact of a racialized social system still seems insightful.

In 1865 in a speech at a meeting of the American Anti-Slavery Society, Douglass proved prophetic, anticipating southern whites' tenacious effort to suspend blacks' rights provided during Reconstruction. Southerners, he indicated, are

> loyal while they see 200,000 sable [black] soldiers, with glistening bayonets, walking in their midst. But let the civil power of the States be restored, and the old prejudices and hostility to the Negro will revive. (Foner 1999, 579)

A racialized social system also was entrenched outside the South. Speaking at the Convention of Colored Men in 1883, Douglass indicated that everywhere he sought work, the black man encountered racism.

> If he offers himself to a builder as a mechanic, to a client as a lawyer, to a patient as a physician, to a college as a professor, to a firm as a clerk; to a Government Department as an agent, or an officer, he is sternly met on the color line, and his claim to consideration in some way is disputed on the ground of color. (Foner 1999, 673–74)

Less than two decades later, Du Bois's study, which was entitled *The Philadelphia Negro,* documented the unrelenting presence of the color line in the racialized social system. In Philadelphia African Americans had few opportunities to rise above the most menial jobs. This reality made it almost impossible for young people to feel hopeful about achieving occupational success, instead encouraging idleness, crime, poverty, and a host of problems for the city, whose leaders, according to Du Bois, had no right to complain as long as they failed to address current inequities. The author angrily concluded that job discrimination against blacks was "morally wrong, politically dangerous, industrially wasteful, and socially silly" (Du Bois 1973, 394).

Housing, the research indicated, compounded African Americans' job problems. Blacks often found it cheaper and easier to live close to the most affluent parts of the city, where many had menial jobs in private homes, hotels, and large stores, but because most whites refused to accept black neighbors, their residential locations were greatly restricted. Realtors often took advantage of blacks' limited housing options, charging them more than whites for comparable accommodations.

Du Bois concluded that the core of blacks' problems in Philadelphia revolved around the negative interplay of job and housing restrictions:

> that here is a people receiving a little lower wages than usual for less desirable work, and compelled, in order to do that work, to live in a little less pleasant quarters than most people, and pay for them somewhat higher rents (Du Bois 1973, 296).

The book ended on a plaintive note, suggesting that "without any danger to the supremacy of the Anglo-Saxon," whites could risk the "little decencies of daily intercourse" such as exchanging greetings on the street. Positive actions would help members of both races "realize what the great founder of the city meant, when he named it the City of Brotherly Love" (Du Bois 1973, 397).

Du Bois's frank analysis was almost unprecedented in his day when few blacks dared to speak or write freely. Although Du Bois suffered no immediate punishment for his strong stance, his white colleagues generally ignored his meticulous research, and in the next decade his single-handed effort to conduct a systematic study of American blacks collapsed from lack of funds. Joe R. Feagin, a theorist in urban sociology, indicated that Du Bois's pioneering work merits considering him *a* if not *the* founder of urban social science in the United States, but he has received limited recognition because, until recently, social scientists have downplayed black scholars' work highlighting the role of racial oppression in the growth of American society (Feagin 1998, 1–2).

Feagin, along with Mark Gottdiener, developed a conflict theory called the **new urban paradigm,** which focuses on the factors determining why cities develop their respective forms and functions (Feagin 1998; Gottdiener, Collins, and Dickens 1999; Gottdiener and Feagin 1988; Gottdiener and Hutchison 2000). Like all conflict theories, this one emphasizes that human existence involves a struggle for scarce resources—most notably wealth, power, and social recognition. The new urban paradigm, in line with Karl Marx's contribution to conflict theory, acknowledges the preeminent role economic forces play in determining people's life chances. The theory examines five factors: the global context of economic activity; land development; local government's role in growth coalitions; cultural forces; and the racialized social system, particularly involving employment. At various points throughout this book, it becomes apparent that one or more of these factors have an influence on racial and ethnic groups in the urban/suburban setting. Briefly consider each of them:

1. *The global context:* Since the middle 1970s, a dispersion of international economic activity has occurred, with major American cities becoming centers for servicing and financing of international trade and investment and headquarters for corporate operations. Regional cities have developed similar functions within more localized territories (Sassen 1996).

2. *Land development:* Inevitably, wealth and power are linked, and perhaps nowhere is that physically more obvious than in cities. Major businesses establish the character of cities throughout the nation, with owners' and chief executives' decisions about locating their production and distribution operations affecting the lives of most urbanites. Such corporate decisions as building a skyscraper in a downtown district, moving headquarters to a nearby suburb, or simply leaving one American city for another or for a foreign location can have a significant impact on major urban activities, including employment, especially if the business in question is a large one with functional links to many other companies (Feagin 1988).

3. *Local government's role in growth coalitions:* Since this nation's formation, government subsidy for business expansion has occurred. Alexander Hamilton, the first secretary of the treasury, stated that this assistance "is a species of encouragement more positive and direct than any other, and for that reason, has a more immediate tendency to stimulate and uphold new enterprises" (Judd and Swanstrom 2002, 373). Currently, public and private leaders still maintain this outlook, contending that a city must provide incentives for businesses to establish themselves in its locale, thereby increasing jobs and creating a healthy tax base, conditions that establish a vibrant urban economy and a good business climate, encouraging renewed business investment and a continuing positive economic cycle (Judd and Swanstrom 2000, 373).

4. *Culture and the city:* **Culture** consists of all human-made products associated with a society. Nonmaterial products such as values, beliefs, and norms are the foundation for a culture. Established values like achievement and success, freedom, progress, and equality convey a basic sense of our cultural emphases, and in various ways we see evidence of these values in American cities. Whether it is corporations headquartered in massive skyscrapers or families' spacious homes, the large size has symbolized achievement and success. Such culturally influenced choices in the use of space have significantly influenced how much space in cities remains for various other uses.

5. *A racialized social system:* The new urban paradigm emphasizes the necessity of obtaining a steady supply of largely minority service workers so that the urban corporate world can function smoothly. Chapter 3 indicates that this relationship between business and cheap labor is hardly new. Each successive wave of immigrants has been welcomed to cities for their economic contribution, but the groups' foreign ways created fear and hostility. How did established citizens deal with their ambivalence? In brief, they permitted minorities in cities but kept them under supervisory control. No more potent example exists than African Americans' relentless oppression in urban housing during the first forty years of the twentieth century—an experience that imposed limitations still operating today.

The remaining portion of this chapter examines the development of the racialist social system.

The Racialized Social System
in Modern American Society

As the time allotted for class discussion came toward an end, a member of one group drew me over, saying there was a story I should hear. A middle-aged man explained that he'd grown up in a racially mixed neighborhood in Bridgeport, Connecticut, where the children played freely together and no racism was apparent. Then one day a local girl had her thirteenth birthday party, and he was the only African American present. "We were about to sit down to cake and ice cream when her father told me my mother had phoned to say I should come home right away." So without a thought, the boy ran home and asked his mother what she wanted. The woman looked puzzled and said she'd never called. Thinking there must have been a mistake, the boy headed back to the party.

When he knocked at the front door, the father appeared and said, "Oh, Joe, you've returned. . . . You might as well go home. The party's almost over." In class the man shook his head and pursed his lips. "That was over thirty years ago, but it's still painfully fresh in my mind."

Modern conflict theorists contend that whether the focus is neighborhood relations, school attendance, jobs, politics, or some other activity, whites have systematically imposed territorial limits on racial minorities, especially African Americans. How do whites justify such discrimination?

Andrew Hacker, a well-known observer of American race relations, speculated that among most whites "there remains an unarticulated suspicion: might there be something about the black race that suited them for slavery?" Hacker added, "This is not the least reason why other Americans—again, without saying so—find it not improper that blacks still serve as maids and janitors, occupations seen as involving physical skills rather than mental aptitudes" (Hacker 1992, 14).

Historically, American whites have been ambivalent about southern blacks migrating to northern and midwestern cities seeking jobs. Although blacks' cheap labor was welcome in the burgeoning industrial age, their migratory numbers to cities, which rose from 174,000 in the 1890s to 777,000 between 1900 and 1920, aroused whites' alarm and hostility. Sociologists Douglas Massey and Nancy Denton described how two classes of whites responded to blacks' growing presence during the so-called Great Migration.

> Middle-class whites were repelled by what they saw as the uncouth manners, unclean habits, slothful appearance, and illicit behavior of poorly educated, poverty-stricken migrants who had only recently been sharecroppers. . . . Working-class whites, for their part, feared economic competition from the newcomers; and being first- or second-generation immigrants who were themselves scorned by native whites, they reaffirmed their own "whiteness" by oppressing a people that was even lower in the racial hierarchy. (Massey and Denton 1993, 29)

Early in the twentieth century, many blacks were convinced that the first English word European immigrants learned was "nigger."

Soon the white urban leadership mobilized to restrict African Americans' opportunities. As blacks' numbers grew in northern and midwestern cities, newspapers increasingly used such pejorative terms as "darkey" and "nigger," also providing unflattering stories about crime and vice. Then between 1900 and 1920, a series of race riots against African Americans occurred, with those living outside recognized "black" neighborhoods having their homes bombed, ransacked, or burned and those caught in "white" neighborhoods beaten, shot, or lynched. The tide of violence also inspired a hardening color line in jobs, schooling, and housing. Blacks living outside recognized Negro areas were relentlessly driven into what became known as "black belts," "darkytowns," "Niggertowns," or "Bronzevilles."

In the next two decades, the migration of southern African Americans continued, totaling about 1,277,000. Although housing segregation persisted, the dominant group altered its strategy, using effective legal procedures outlined in upcoming chapters.

By 1940 in northern and midwestern cities, this systemic, white-controlled process had established the boundaries of modern black ghettos, where many residents have been trapped in poverty for successive generations extending up to the present. White immigrant groups such as Jews, Poles, Italians, and Czechs arriving in the same cities in the late nineteenth and early twentieth centuries also encountered hostility and discrimination about residential location but never were as relentlessly forced into isolated living areas as were blacks and then, once established occupationally, were permitted to move elsewhere (Massey and Denton 1993, 27–42). Blacks, however, remained trapped in ghettos, experiencing the racialized social system at its most malignant.

Once such a system develops, it takes on a life of its own, with most whites unquestioningly accepting the ongoing discriminatory treatment within it and giving little attention to either the treatment inflicted on the minority group or the historical advantages the European groups received. For instance, in the middle nineteenth century, nativist groups declared Irish immigrants racial inferiors, imposing on them a racialized social system that channeled them into physical labor and stereotyped them as drunken, bellicose ruffians unsuited for more refined work. Upward mobility in the next century, however, permitted Irish American men to attain success in a wide variety of fields, and, in consequence, the earlier stereotypes largely disappeared.

For African Americans, in contrast, a racialized social system has continued to persist, splaying out into various institutions and structures. Consider five prominent areas where the impact of the system remains strong:

1. In urban areas the majority of blacks still find barriers to obtaining housing outside ghettoized areas, putting them at a disadvantage in seeking jobs, obtaining quality schooling, and procuring other services and opportunities. Housing studies done in various American cities conclude that in the nation's cities and suburbs African Americans are highly segregated, living in areas that on average are 78 percent black.

2. Because of their inferior housing location, urban African Americans compared to white suburban dwellers receive much less effective schooling, often suffering deteriorated buildings, overcrowded classes, deficient books and equipment, and underpaid and disillusioned teachers.

3. In politics such mechanisms as the annexation of largely white areas, multimember legislative districts, election runoffs, and at-large district elections have the appearance of being race-neutral and promoting democracy, but they have served to dilute the impact of black voting. Thus, in spite of African Americans' voter registration increasing since 1965, black elected officials currently make up no more than 1 to 2 percent of elected officials—a proportion that is at least six times smaller than their portion of the population.

4. Widespread evidence indicates that the criminal-justice system operates in a distinctly discriminatory manner. When blacks and whites who have committed the same crimes are compared, blacks receive substantially greater penalties for weapons possession, sale of drugs, rape, and murder. For over twenty years, the incarcerated proportion of blacks has consistently been about six times greater than that of whites.

5. Employers often rely on informal social networks to locate employees, and blacks tend to be out of these loops. In addition, blacks and some other minorities face racist treatment in the employment process. Over the past twenty years, studies comparing sets of research subjects belonging to different racial groups and matched on various job-related traits have consistently demonstrated more discrimination against blacks and Latinos seeking jobs (Bonilla-Silva 2001; Center for Regional Policy Studies 2001; Doob 1999; Feagin 2000; Massey and Denton 1993).

Besides African Americans, other groups have also experienced racialized settings. Certain jobs such as domestic housework and gardening lock individuals into racialized roles. Sociologist Pierrette Hondagneu-Sotelo concluded that relationships between domestic workers and their employers

> have always been imbued with racial meanings: white "masters and mistresses" have been cast as pure and superior, and "maids and servants," drawn from specific racial-ethnic groups (varying by region), have been cast as dirty and socially inferior. (Hondagneu-Sotelo 2001, 13)

By the late nineteenth century, the racialization of domestic work was established, with what Anglo-Saxon employers saw as "inferior" white groups cast in the role. At that time single young Irish, German, and Scandinavian women who had migrated from the country to cities worked as live-in "domestic help," often leaving those jobs when they married. By the onset of World War I, the decline of European immigration encouraged a black exodus to the North. For many whites, black women as house servants was the preferred choice, and by 1920 they constituted the largest group of domestics in both the South and the Northeast. In mid-nineteenth-century northern California, the rapid influx of Anglo settlers and miners and scarcity of women meant that the first option was Chinese men, who served as "houseboys," laundrymen, and cooks and were followed by other Asian groups—Japanese men and then Japanese women, who remained in domestic activity until World War II.

In many western states, however, Spanish American women have numerically dominated domestic work. From the 1880s until World War II, it provided the largest source of nonagricultural employment for Mexican women, and in the United States today, immigrants from Mexico, Central America, and the Caribbean represent the major source of domestic workers. Unlike the earlier European groups, they reach the United States at a time when the economy is less expansive, and as a result the opportunity to advance occupationally, particularly for those without papers legalizing employment, is distinctly limited (Hondagneu-Sotelo 2001, 13–15).

FIGURE 2.1   Concepts Analyzing the Workings of the Racialized Social System

Four Types of Capital
- Social capital
- Cultural capital
- Human capital
- Financial capital

Ideology of Color-Blind Racism
Various social functions such as justifications of the established system and scripting of race relations

Camouflaged Racism
Sparked by the race-related threats majority-group members can experience

Social Class
Underlying, often ignored impact on ethnic and racial relations

As Figure 2.1 indicates, sociologists have found certain concepts useful for examining racialized social systems.

Concepts for Analyzing the Racialized Social System

Once racialized social systems develop, they take on a life of their own. Whether members of minority groups or majority groups, individuals find themselves caught in their processes—affected by such conceptual realities as capital, color-blind racism, and social class, which are now examined.

In the social world, individuals accumulate what sociologist Alford A. Young Jr. (1999) has described as **capital**—the material or nonmaterial means that provide resources or access to resources promoting mainstream success. According to Young, people living in a racialized setting, such as the low-income men living in Chicago he studied, accumulate certain items of capital—perceptions, knowledge, and skills—but seldom the varieties for obtaining success in the mainstream society.

Young designated four types of capital—social, cultural, human, and financial—that can be used for analyzing the racialized social system:

- Social capital is the ability to secure advantage through the organizations and social networks to which individuals belong. Poor urban blacks' friends and families, for instance, are not likely to help them gain access to jobs outside the inner city.

- Cultural capital involves the development of a sense of how the social world works, particularly a competence at engaging in the practices necessary to move toward mainstream success. Although urban minorities attain extensive cultural capital to survive in difficult, physically threatening neighborhoods, they might not have the experience needed to obtain the social skills necessary to deal with employers, colleagues, and customers in entry-level jobs.

■ Human capital is the acquisition of the skills or abilities that secure the likelihood of access to occupational and income success. In racialized settings inferior education is often a major disadvantage in obtaining any jobs outside of unskilled labor.

■ Financial capital concerns the material sources used to obtain other capital. Throughout this book it is apparent that majority groups' advantageous locations for housing and jobs provide further advantage toward accumulating other capital. Minorities, sometimes described as "disadvantaged" groups, tend to have limited financial capital and its associated assets.

Whites tend to maintain comfortable lives isolated from those blacks and other minority-group members who suffer diminished opportunity, restricting them to essential but unrewarding service jobs. To keep American citizens, at least majority-group citizens, satisfied with the current arrangement, an ideology comes into play. An **ideology** is a practical set of ideas and concepts that provides a working theory of everyday life (Bonilla-Silva 2001, 137). In this instance the ideology justifies the perpetuation of a racialist social system.

Modern racist ideology is more polite and toned down than "old-fashioned" racism, which is a clear belief in whites' racial superiority (Sears and Jessor 1996). According to various social scientists, contemporary racist ideology now centers on the claim that minorities' cultural deficiency leads to behavior unacceptable to upstanding citizens and warrants, even requires, exclusion from mainstream opportunities and rewards (Bobo and Smith 1996; Gaertner and Dovidio 1986; Jackman 1996; Tuch and Hughes 1996). For example, those subscribing to "polite" racism will assert that blacks are "undisciplined," "unmotivated," or "prone to violence." Although proponents of this form of racism are focusing on alleged cultural deficiencies, their assessments of racial minorities project a fatalistic sense of inferiority reminiscent of old-fashioned racists. Sociologist Stephen Steinberg, in fact, has described such racism as "the new Darwinism," in which a sense of deep-seated cultural difference between or among racial groups replaces the once immutable biological basis for invidious interracial comparisons (Steinberg 2001, 77–81).

Sociologist Eduardo Bonilla-Silva (2001) developed a useful concept for analyzing modern racial and ethnic relations. **Color-blind racism** is an ideological position asserting whites' frequently proclaimed desire to live in a society in which race no longer matters. Supported by this ideology, many white Americans argue that ours is an open, largely discrimination-free society in which racism is minimal and declining in significance. Color-blind racism displays certain distinct elements:

■ An abstract liberalism stressing equal opportunity, opposing affirmative action, and ignoring the impact of past and present discrimination on minorities' lives. (Example: "I am for equal opportunity, and that's why I oppose affirmative action.")

■ A "biologization of culture" in which the majority group evaluates selected minorities' inferior status as the result of deficient culture. (Example: "Blacks are poor because they have weak values.")

■ A minimization of racism and discrimination, acknowledging its existence but describing it as rare. (Example: "There are racists out there but very few of them.")

In a 1998 Detroit study on white racist ideology, Bonilla-Silva found that 84 percent of his respondents cited each of these three elements (Bonilla-Silva 2001, 141–42).

Like any ideology color-blind racism provides social functions in support of established structures—in this case, the persistence of a racialized social system. In particular, this ideology supplies the above set of toned-down, seemingly nonracial assertions that justify keeping the current system and its exploitation of minorities intact. An additional function an ideology provides is the scripting of race relations, informing individuals about how they as members of a given racial group should perceive themselves in relation to other racial groups. For white Americans the scripting is that in a practical sense their racial character is invisible or nonexistent: They do not need to be burdened by it, and in modern times they no longer receive rewards for being white (Bonilla-Silva 2001, 71–75).

What I have called camouflaged racism is a different reaction to the modern racialized reality—not a toned-down effort to justify the system as occurs with color-blind racism, but a sudden reaction to the fear and frustration many whites continue to maintain in the modern setting. **Camouflaged racism** involves distinctly racist behavior that bursts into public view from individuals whose racist outlooks and behavior generally remain hidden behind public statements and actions favoring racial equality. Both survey data and personal observations suggest to me that most majority-group members consider themselves untainted by racism and want to function in a racism-free environment, where, as the idea of color-blind racism suggests, race becomes a nonissue. Majority-group members' racism breaks out of its camouflaged cover only when a race-related threat materializes, revealing, in essence, whites' "true colors." This sense of threat might appear:

■ When whites feel an uncomfortable number of blacks have moved into their neighborhood, arousing concern about crime, violence, and disorder.
■ When extensive minority competition for jobs develops.
■ When an unwanted push to promote school integration occurs.
■ When a seemingly unjustified insult or disturbing physical action comes from a minority-group member (Doob 1999, 16).

The core image supporting whites' sense of threat is one involving imminent invasion by a large number of poor, uneducated, even dangerous minority-group members considered unsuitable as neighbors, fellow employees or students, or individuals sharing some fairly intimate setting. In contrast, if whites sense stability in a situation, they are often quite comfortable with quite large numbers of minority-group members in their neighborhood, workplace, or whatever (Yinger 1995, 120–22).

One critical idea related to this concept is that given the deep-seated fear that ghettos create and the reality of those fears nurturing racism, it appears highly unlikely that race-related fears will disappear or even significantly decline until ghettos are no longer perceived as a major threat in our society. Racist fears motivated the creation of ghettos, which now help keep racism alive. Although not referring to race, Franklin

Roosevelt seemed attuned to a similar dynamic when he declared, "The only thing to fear is fear itself."

The concept of camouflaged racism suggests that whites' primary fears about minorities are directed against individuals who both belong to racial minorities and come from lower-class origin—in particular, poor, black males, who are, it turns out, in such ways as inadequate schooling, rates of unemployment and underemployment, incarceration, and early death, the most victimized racial or ethnic category in the United States. On the other hand, whites are likely to accept, even embrace middle-class minority-group members, particularly those who in their eyes have proved themselves worthy. Mike Tyson, the boxer, and Colin Powell, the general and Secretary of State, are two contemporary celebrities representing the contrasting majority-group reactions related to camouflaged racism. Tyson's host of violence-laden or debauched actions or expletive-laden interviews have drawn massive media attention, which caters to an audience who appears simultaneously repulsed and titillated. Powell, in contrast, seems a secure representative of the social world many Americans embrace—one where issues of race and ethnicity scarcely touch their lives and where selected minority-group members' mainstream assets make them seamlessly acceptable.

As successive generations of white immigrants have found upward mobility into the economic and social mainstream available to them, ethnic affiliation has tended to lose its power and significance. With the passage of time, speaking the group's native language, maintaining its religious practice, marrying within the group, and honoring its traditional customs have often faded in significance.

Attuned to this process of assimilation, Americans are inclined to speculate why certain groups, particularly blacks, are less successful than recently arrived ethnic groups. Usually, the upshot of the discussion is some truncated cultural explanation—that members of the less successful group are undisciplined, lack a tradition of committing to educational and occupational success, or something similar. An accurate explanation, however, requires a comparative analysis of the two sets of historical circumstances. In the frequent comparison of blacks and Asians, for instance, the observer needs to begin by acknowledging the discriminatory legacy imposed on African Americans. Then he or she should recognize that Asians comprise at least twenty-five ethnicities, which have a wide range of traditions and experiences. Some groups, notably recent arrivals from southeast Asia, have tended to be poor and uneducated and have often had a difficult time establishing themselves in the United States. On the other hand, newly arrived groups who have been most strongly touted as disciplined and hardworking, such as Indians and Koreans, have heavy concentrations of professionals whose middle-class backgrounds give them substantial advantage for obtaining high-status jobs, not only compared to blacks but compared to the general citizenry (Steinberg 2001).

The last point suggests one more concept to use in the analysis of racialized social systems. Differences in social class exist within any racial or ethnic group—the lower class or poor, working class, middle class, and upper class. A **social class** is a large category of people who are similar in income level, educational attainment, and occupational prestige ranking. Individuals' racial or ethnic classification can serve as either an advantage or a disadvantage, but the impact of social class also needs to be appreciated.

In *The Ethnic Myth: Race, Ethnicity, and Class in America,* sociologist Stephen Steinberg has argued against widespread support for "the iron law of ethnicity," which claims that

In a racialized social system, members of racial minorities represent a disproportionate number of victims. Clearly that is the case for this woman, her seven-week-old son, and the estimated one hundred homeless African Americans living under the I-395 overpass in Miami and waiting in line for food.

"traditional hatreds" between proximate ethnic groups invariably lead to conflict. Rather, Steinberg contended, such conflicts break out along ethnic lines "when ethnic groups are found in a hierarchy of wealth, power, and status"—in short, when at least one ethnic or racial group is distinctly disadvantaged in social-class location. Then conflict, including violent conflict, is likely or inevitable. In contrast, where there is "social, economic, and political parity among the constituent groups"—in essence, the social-class distribution of respective members is fairly similar—then conflict will be muted and rarely spill over into violence. Steinberg compared the situations in Northern Ireland and Switzerland. In the Irish case, most public attention has focused on "traditional hatreds" between Protestants and Catholics, but it seems highly unlikely that frequent violence would have continued had not the Protestants sustained their decisive political, economic, and status advantages. In Switzerland, in contrast, the German, French, and Italian ethnic groups demonstrate fairly similar social-class distributions, and as a result, most conflicts between members of different ethnic groups are quite easily settled through informal discussion or the judicial process (Steinberg 2001, 169–70).

So how does American society, which fits neither of these national patterns, relate to this analysis? The two largest racial minorities, namely African Americans and Hispanic

Contrasting Perceptions of Men and Jobs

The white driver steers his pickup truck down the street of the poor, black downtown section of Washington, D.C. He stops near a man sitting on a cast-iron porch and asks if he wants a day's work. The man shakes his head, and the truck moves on, stopping each time a man comes within calling distance, but all turn him down. He reaches the New Deal Carry-out shop, where five men briefly discuss the possibility but decline the offer. The truck passes the corner, then repeats the same process on the next block. Move ahead and pause, move ahead and pause. In the far distance, the observer sees one man, then another hop into the back of truck, and it moves on.

Elliot Liebow, the anthropologist who conducted a year-long study focused on the Carry-out corner, speculated what the truck driver concluded based on his drive through the area. He wrote:

> He had been able to recruit only two or three men from each twenty or fifty he contacts. To him, it is clear that the others simply do not choose to work. Singly or in groups, belly-empty or belly-full, sullen or gregarious, drunk or sober, they confirm what he has read, heard, and knows from his own experience: these men wouldn't take a job if it were handed to them on a platter. (Liebow 1967, 30)

Liebow asked readers to accompany him back to the Carry-out corner and evaluate the truck driver's probable perception against concrete realities in the lives of the approximately twenty men inclined to spend time there. To begin, the truck driver's critical analysis can't apply to all the men, because a few actually accept the offer. What about the others?

The most basic reality the truck driver misses is that a high percentage of these men are employed and are out on the street this weekday morning because the room or apartment where they live is depressing, either because it is a small, drab space offering nothing to do or because they feel oppressed by a wife, girlfriend, or someone else living there. Some like Boley, who belongs to a trash-collection crew, work Saturdays and are off this particular day while others like Sweets work nights cleaning and tidying up such largely middle-class facilities as office buildings, hotels, restaurants, and other public locations dirtied during the day.

Still others at the corner work for such retail businesses as liquor or hardware stores that don't open until ten o'clock. Some laborers, like Tally, have already returned, unable to work this day because the ground is too wet for pick and shovel or the temperature too low for pouring concrete. A few have personal reasons for missing work today—Clarence is attending a funeral, and Sea Cat has to answer a subpoena in a criminal case.

Others unwittingly contribute to the driver's stereotype, appearing able-bodied but, in truth, incapable of physical work. The man on the cast-iron porch rubs one gnarled arthritic hand with the other and murmurs that he doesn't know if he'll live long enough to collect Social Security. The quiet man sitting in front of a nearby brownstone building has a steel hook strapped onto his left elbow. Raymond, who looks like he could tear the nearby fire hydrant out of the ground, coughs up blood if he bends over or moves suddenly.

A few men have been working but are recently laid off and are collecting unemployment compensation, giving them nothing to gain from accepting work like this that pays little more and often less than what they are currently receiving.

Some like Bumdoodle, the numbers man, are hustling to make money in illegal ways—buying and selling sex, liquor, drugs, stolen goods, or something else with monetary value.

The few remaining include Tonk, who fears that if he leaves the corner his wife will be unfaithful to him, and several like Leroy and Sea Cat who at the moment are unwilling to work. The truck driver feels that the latter category represents the vast majority of men in the area, but that is a misperception. Most presently unwilling to work are taking a temporary leave from unrewarding jobs that seldom can support a couple and one or more children. Soon, however, economic pressure will force them to return.

The truck driver, however, is oblivious to these details. He has passed by men whose complicated lives derive from conditions in the racialized social system, a system from which this man is isolated and does not comprehend. All in all, because he already has a set of negative expectations and generally receives a uniform rejection to what he considers a grand opportunity, his stereotyped evaluation of poor, black men has been effectively reinforced.

Americans, are much less advantaged overall in such social-class components as income, political power, and social position than European Americans. However, there is a distinct social-class distribution within both groups, with about a third of African Americans and nearly as many Hispanics located economically, occupationally, and socially in the middle class. Such mainstream success militates against open strife with the majority group.

On the other hand, blacks, in particular, have a large poverty-stricken group, most of whose members have little prospect of obtaining mainstream success. In the 1960s some African Americans in the poor, inner-city areas of American cities became involved in violent outbreaks, and sporadic incidents have occurred since then. Could the United States become another Northern Ireland?

It seems unlikely. As the discussion of urban politics in Chapter 6 suggests, the American political leadership has developed a national strategy for addressing minority-related urban problems, undercutting any major inner-city rebellion if not curtailing the underlying sources of disadvantage. In addition, as the chapter opener emphasized, the American mass media have engaged in a relentlessly optimistic effort to portray both the success that racial minorities have obtained and a sense that such opportunities widely persist.

Regardless of their social-class membership, however, minority-group members, most notably blacks, are widely at risk for encountering various types of racist treatment. Journalist Ellis Cose (1999) listed "a dozen demons" middle-class blacks can encounter in the job world, but perhaps the most publicized recent example has involved racial profiling: DWB ("driving while black") is now recognized as a tongue-in-cheek "offense," which occurs when police without probable cause of guilt for any crime but relying on racist stereotypes have stopped and searched cars driven by blacks and Latinos. The fact that widespread press coverage has revealed that many victims have been successful professionals has brought considerable public sympathy and encouraged states like New Jersey, North Carolina, and Connecticut to start curtailing the process. However, the courts, including the U.S. Supreme Court, have generally not sought to control racial profiling (Cole 2001), and so minority-group members appear likely to remain vulnerable to such victimization.

Destructive as such racist incidents can be, the most oppressed minority victims are poor individuals. Television, newspapers, and other media sources usually do not convey any more than superficial information about the disadvantaged locations in which they find themselves, and as the previous Sociological Illustration demonstrates, majority-group members often have little knowledge about the challenges such individuals face.

As the previous discussion indicated, Americans have distinctly different perceptions on how the social world functions. Throughout this chapter that theme has been readily apparent.

Conclusion

In the examination of sociological theory, we have analyzed two bodies of thought—one asserting that the United States is an open, equality-oriented society permitting all ethnic and racial groups eventual access to mainstream economic, political, and social rewards. Starting with the Chicago School members, structural-functionalists have found capitalist society a comfortable fit, producing studies that assured theirs has been a just, harmonious world where social consensus prevails over conflict.

In contrast, conflict theories have developed in a Marxist tradition, emphasizing the role of wealth and power in structuring groups' opportunities for mainstream success. The new urban paradigm, which is a conflict perspective on the development of cities, emphasizes the important but restricted role many minority-group members fill in cities' service sectors. Although assimilation into the mainstream has been available to the majority of individuals from most ethnic and racial groups, particularly the European ones, African Americans and some other people of color often find themselves victims of a racialized social system. Color-blind and camouflaged racism supply ideological support for the modern version of that system.

Because the two bodies of theory discussed here have distinctly different outlooks, readers will obtain varied insights and understanding from them. Many individuals might well have a preference for one, but the potential exists, I suspect, for many to learn something substantial from each.

DISCUSSION QUESTIONS

1. Analyze the Chicago School of Sociology, considering both its contributions to and limitations for the study of race and ethnicity.

2. Do you have bits of information that support and/or dispute the concentric-zone hypothesis?

3. Having gained some sense of what Frederick Douglass and W. E. B. Du Bois said about American racism, what single idea expressed in that discussion seems the most compelling or powerful? Why?

4. Examine the concepts of color-blind racism and camouflaged racism, considering how they relate to the maintenance of a racialized social system.

5. Discuss the contributions the different forms of capital provide.

6. Indicate how individuals' racial, ethnic, and social-class membership have an impact on their access to two types of capital.

7. Elliot Liebow discussed the impact of the racialized social system on men living near the Carry-out corner. Are you aware of a setting where an astute observer might detect similar effects?

BIBLIOGRAPHY

Aptheker, Herbert. 1973. "Introduction," pp. 5–31 in W. E. B. DuBois, *The Philadelphia Negro*. Milwood, NY: Kraus-Thomson.

Beadle, Muriel. 1972. *Where Has All the Ivy Gone: A Memoir of University Life*. Garden City, NY: Doubleday.

Bobo, Lawrence, and Ryan A. Smith. 1996. "From Jim Crow Racism to Laissez-Faire Racism," pp. 151–63 in Wendy Katkin and Andrea Tyree (eds.), *Beyond Pluralism: Essays on the Conceptions of Groups and Identities in America*. Urbana: University of Illinois Press.

Bonilla-Silva, Eduardo. 2001. *White Supremacy & Racism in the Post-Civil Rights Era*. Boulder: Lynne Rienner.

Bulmer, Martin. 1984. *The Chicago School of Sociology: Institutionalization, Diversity, and the Rise of Sociological Research*. Chicago: University of Chicago Press.

Burgess, Ernest W. 1964. "Research in Urban Society: A Long View," pp. 2–14 in Ernest W. Burgess and Donald J. Bogue (eds.), *Contributions to Urban Sociology.* Chicago: University of Chicago Press.

Burgess, Ernest W. 1967. "The Growth of the City: An Introduction to a Research Project," pp. 47–62 in Robert E. Park, Ernest W. Burgess, and Roderick D. McKenzie. *The City.* Chicago: University of Chicago Press.

Center for Regional Policy Studies. 2001. "Census 2000 Factsheet: Residential Segregation in United States Metropolitan Areas." www.sppsr.ucla.edu.lewis.

Cole, David. 2001. "The Color of Justice," pp. 122–23 in John A. Kromkowski (ed.), *Race and Ethnic Relations 01/02.* Guilford, CT: McGraw-Hill/Dushkin.

Cose, Ellis. 1999. "A Dozen Demons," pp. 18–24 in Christopher G. Ellison and W. Allen Martin (eds.), *Race and Ethnic Relations in the United States: Readings for the 21st Century.* Los Angeles: Roxbury.

Doob, Christopher Bates. 1999. *Racism: An American Cauldron,* 3rd ed. Reading, MA: Addison Wesley.

Du Bois, W. E. B. 1973. *The Philadelphia Negro.* Milwood, NY: Kraus-Thomson. Originally published in 1899.

Faris, Robert E. L. 1967. *Chicago School 1920–1932.* San Francisco: Chandler.

Feagin, Joe R. 1988. *Free Enterprise City: Houston in Political-Economic Perspective.* New Brunswick, NJ: Rutgers University Press.

Feagin, Joe R. 1998. *The New Urban Paradigm.* Lanham, MD: Rowman and Littlefield.

Feagin, Joe R. 2000. *Racist America: Roots, Current Realities, and Future Reparations.* New York and London: Routledge.

Foner, Philip S. (ed.). 1999. *Frederick Douglass: Selected Speeches and Writings.* Chicago: Lawrence Hill Books.

Frazier, E. Franklin. 1932. *The Negro Family in Chicago.* Chicago: University of Chicago Press.

Gaertner, Samuel L., and John F. Dovidio. 1986. "The Aversive Form of Racism," pp. 61–89 in John F. Dovidio and Samuel L. Gaertner (eds.), *Prejudice, Discrimination, and Racism.* Orlando: Academic Press.

Gitlin, Todd. 1989. *The Sixties: Years of Hope, Days of Rage.* New York: Bantam Books.

Glazer, Nathan, and Daniel Patrick Moynihan. 1963. *Beyond the Melting Pot.* Cambridge: MIT Press and Harvard University Press.

Glazer, Nathan, and Daniel Patrick Moynihan. 1975. "Introduction," pp. 1–26 in Nathan Glazer and Daniel Patrick Moynihan (eds.), *Ethnicity: Theory and Experience.* Cambridge: Harvard University Press.

Gordon, Milton M. 1964. *Assimilation in American Life: The Role of Race, Religion, and National Origins.* New York: Oxford University Press.

Gottdiener, Mark, Claudia C. Collins, and David R. Dickens. 1999. *Las Vegas: The Social Production of an All-American City.* Oxford: Blackwell.

Gottdiener, Mark, and Joe R. Feagin. 1988. "The Paradigm Shift in Urban Sociology." *Urban Affairs Quarterly.* 24 (December): 163–87.

Gottdiener, Mark, and Ray Hutchison. 2000. *The New Urban Sociology,* 2nd ed. New York: McGraw-Hill.

Hacker, Andrew. 1992. *Two Nations: Black and White, Separate, Hostile, Unequal.* New York: Scribner.

Hawley, Amos H. 1971. *Urban Society: An Ecological Approach.* New York: Ronald Press.

Hondagneu-Sotelo, Pierrette. 2001. *Doméstica: Immigrant Workers Cleaning and Caring in the Shadows of Affluence.* Berkeley and Los Angeles: University of California Press.

Jackman, Mary R. 1996. "Individualism, Self-Interest, and White Racism." *Social Science Quarterly.* 77 (December): 760–67.

Judd, Dennis R., and Todd Swanstrom. 2002. *City Politics: Private Power and Public Policy,* 3rd ed. New York: Longman.

Liebow, Elliot. 1967. *Tally's Corner.* Boston: Little, Brown.

Massey, Douglas S., and Nancy A. Denton. 1993. *American Apartheid: Segregation and the Making of the Underclass.* Cambridge, MA: Harvard University Press.

Park, Robert E. 1950. *Race and Culture.* Glencoe, IL: Free Press.

Roberts, Sam. 1990. "Moving Beyond the Melting Pot 25 Years Later." *New York Times.* (May 17): B1.

Sassen, Saskia. 1996. "A New Geography of Centers and Margins: Summary and Implications," pp. 69–74 in Richard T. LeGates and Frederic Stout (eds.), *The City Reader.* London: Routledge.

Schwendinger, Herman, and Julia R. Schwendinger. 1974. *The Sociologists of the Chair: A Radical Analysis of the Formative Years of North American Sociology (1883–1922).* New York: Basic Books.

Sears, David O., and Tom Jessor. 1996. "Whites' Racial Policy Attitudes: The Role of White Racism." *Social Science Quarterly.* 77 (December): 751–59.

Steinberg, Stephen. 2001. *The Ethnic Myth: Race, Ethnicity, and Class in America,* 3rd ed. Boston: Beacon Press.

Taylor, Yuval. 1999. "Introduction," pp. xi–xvi in Philip S. Foner (ed.), *Frederick Douglass: Selected*

Speeches and Writings. Chicago: Lawrence Hill Books.

Thernstrom, Stephan, and Abigail Thernstrom. 1997. *America in Black and White: One Nation, Indivisible.* New York: Simon and Schuster.

Thomas, W. I., and Florian Znaniecki. 1918. *The Polish Peasant in Europe and America.* Chicago: University of Chicago Press.

Tuch, Steven A., and Michael Hughes. 1996. "Whites' Racial Policy Attitudes." *Social Science Quarterly.* 77 (December): 723–45.

Wirth, Louis. 1928. *The Ghetto.* Chicago: University of Chicago Press.

Yinger, John. 1995. *Closed Doors, Opportunities Lost: The Continuing Costs of Housing Discrimination.* New York: Russell Sage Foundation.

Young, Alford A., Jr. 1999. "The (Non)Accumulation of Capital: Explicating the Relationship of Structure and Agency in the Lives of Poor Black Men." *Sociological Theory.* 17 (July): 201–27.

3 An Ambivalent Balance: Welcomed Workers versus Stigmatized Settlers

In William Kennedy's *Quinn's Book,* Daniel Quinn described the Irish arriving in Albany in large numbers following the outbreak of the 1840s potato famine. They, the "famine Irish," were considered "villains in this city." It hadn't been that way when Quinn was a child, but now they not only were likely to carry the cholera plague but were viewed

> as a plague themselves, such is their number: several thousand setting up life here in only a few years, living in hovels, in shanties, ten families to a small house, some unable to speak anything but the Irish tongue, their wretchedness so fierce and relentless that not only does the city shun them but the constabulary and the posses meet them at the docks and on the turnpikes to herd them together in encampments on the city's great western plain. (Kennedy 1988, 111)

The "Albany wharf rats and river scum," some of whom were Irish themselves, eagerly endorsed the general plan, stoning the canal boats trying to unload newcomers in downtown areas. The immigrants soon realized they were "finding in this new land a hatred as great as that which drove them out of Ireland" (Kennedy 1988, 112).

In the opening two decades of the twentieth century, southern blacks also encountered intense hosility and violence as they too entered northern cities seeking jobs. Those living outside recognized "black" neighborhoods had their houses vandalized or burned, and if unlucky enough to be caught in "white" neighborhoods, could be beaten, shot, or lynched. With the rising tide of violence, "blacks were increasingly divided from whites by a hardening color line in employment, education, and especially housing" (Massey and Denton 1993, 30).

Numbers were the lynchpin. When both the Irish and blacks first arrived in northern cities, their modest totals failed to arouse the local people. Only later, as increased numbers seemed to signal an invasion, did established groups turn hostile.

Both these situations illustrate the opposing majority-group reactions that materialize when new ethnic or racial groups have entered American cities. On the one hand, they have represented a cheap, abundant source of labor for physically taxing or unpleasant work that established citizens have often been unwilling to do. On the other hand, the dominant citizenry encounters what they consider alien, even frightening ways, and sometimes the new arrivals have become competitors for jobs. So the majority group has normally settled for an ambivalent balance, allowing the new arrivals to remain but keeping a vigilant control on their residential location and activities.

The majority group has imposed demanding standards on the recent arrivals. Yes, they have been accepted in the new land if they contribute to established people's own economic success, but like everyone else, they have been expected to sink or swim with little outside help. Over time as immigrant groups establish themselves, they become ready converts to these standards, often applying them harshly to later immigrant groups or to people of color, particularly blacks.

Analyzing American cities over time, observers can see that newly arriving groups have often been subjected to discriminatory treatment, placing them at a disadvantage in access to employment, education, housing, and other basic resources. Throughout the historical discussion, components of the new urban paradigm, which was introduced in Chapter 2, will appear, particularly the role of business leadership, local government, and a racialized social system.

In this chapter we consider five historical eras—the colonial, preindustrial/commercial, early industrial, advanced industrial, and postindustrial. These historical glimpses convey a general sense of the racial and ethnic settlement of American cities.

The Colonial Period: Up to 1790

In the spring of 1638, John Davenport and Theophilus Eaton, the leaders of the New Haven Colony, purchased a large tract of land from the Quinnipiack tribe. Shortly afterward, under the direction of surveyor John Brockett, the settlers laid out the town plot in the form of nine squares. With the central square serving as a marketplace, land in the other eight squares provided home-building sites for the chief shareholders in the Davenport-Eaton company. The thirty-odd additional settlers, who were too poor to buy a share, were forced to settle "in the suburbs" (Osterweis 1953, 12). From the earliest times, more affluent individuals and families have had advantageous residential locations, and this pattern has persisted.

The early American urban settlements were instruments of control, not laboratories for democracy or experiments in individual freedom. Wealth and social rank received explicit recognition, with, according to law, social-class membership determining where people lived, the materials used in producing and decorating clothing, and even the assignment of seats in church (Glaab and Brown 1983, 5).

By modern standards the colonial seaport cities were very small. Boston was the largest of the seventeenth-century towns, barely surpassing 7,000 inhabitants in 1700. Its population reached about 15,000 in 1750 while Philadelphia surged ahead, attaining 40,000 on the eve of the American Revolution. At that time New York City had 25,000 inhabitants, and besides those three the other two major seaports were Baltimore and Charlestown, the only southern representative. At the end of the eighteenth century, about 200,000 people representing 5 percent of Americans lived in twenty-four urban locations of 2,500 or more.

Commerce was the focus of urban enterprise. Colonial businessmen created prosperous trade connections featuring such extractive products as fish, furs, wheat, rice, tobacco, indigo, lumber, and minerals. Then as more sophisticated trade routes formed with Europe, Africa, and the West Indies, it became profitable to establish industries producing a variety of goods—flour milling, for instance, became a major enterprise in New York City, Philadelphia, and Baltimore; and New England ports dominated shipbuilding, with Boston alone providing over two hundred ships annually.

Inevitably, urban growth required addressing such issues as fire and police protection, water supply, assistance for the poor, and the construction and repair of streets and harbors. Leading merchants headed the municipal corporations that ran the cities, and they recognized that to maintain prosperity, citizen-subsidized services needed to address pressing urban issues.

Normally, a city starting a new service copied procedures successfully established elsewhere. Boston, for instance, led the way in fire protection after a huge fire in 1711 left a hundred families homeless and motivated the formation of a fire department. By 1720 the city possessed six engines and twenty firemen in ten fire wards. Sixteen years later in Philadelphia, Benjamin Franklin used the Boston model to organize the famous Union Fire Company, which was so efficient that he could eventually brag that since the company's inception fire had never destroyed more than one or two houses at a time and that often flames were extinguished before the building in question was half consumed.

After the 1793 yellow fever plague caused great loss of life and temporarily immobilized the city, Philadelphia's civic leadership, which suspected a relationship existed between polluted water and various diseases, hired the famous architect Benjamin Latrobe to design a public water system. It was completed in 1801 and became a much admired and visited municipal asset (Glaab 1963, 24; Mohl and Betten 1970, 30–31).

One quality separating these youthful cities from their European counterparts was the absence of walls and moats protecting them from outside invasion, which ceased as a danger once the two wars with Great Britain had ended. As a result, when cities started to expand during the early nineteenth century, they were quite unrestricted in their growth, eventually becoming susceptible to urban sprawl (Monkkonen 1988, 54–55).

In both Great Britain and the colonies, growth was a frequent topic of discussion. The arguments were well articulated in English parliamentary debate. During one speech Sir John Holland referred to balancing such advantages as more commerce, increased trade, and rising property values against the discontent and agitation produced by foreigners' presence. English legislators' greatest concern was that intermarriage would "blot out and extinguish the English race" (Muller 1993, 16)—a fear so intense that for decades it ended debate about a liberalized immigration policy in that country.

The colonies, in contrast, were much more accessible to continental Europeans, whose numbers were well represented in the nation's first census in 1790. While nearly half of those inhabitants, about 1.55 million, were English, about 600,000 were African, 222,000 German, 210,000 Scottish, 155,000 Scotch-Irish, 95,000 Irish, and 85,000 Dutch (Parrillo 2000, 130).

The colonial elite recognized that skilled and commerce-oriented aliens had contributed to British economic expansion at home and would undoubtedly prove to be assets in the New World. So their policies became more encouraging to such non-English-speaking immigrants as Germans, Dutch, and French Huguenots. These groups often possessed education and job training that made them more versatile workers than either the largely unskilled Scotch-Irish, who generally arrived as indentured servants, or the paupers and crimminals whom the English government decided to ship oversees.

During the colonial era, episodes of anti-immigrant sentiment did occur. In the 1680s Governor William Penn of Pennsylvania recognized that a need to populate the vast territory overrode foreigners' alleged negative qualities, and so he encouraged German immigration, promising both religious freedom and large plots of land. In 1729, however, Pennsylvania legislators became fearful that as Germans' numbers grew, the colony would lose its dominant English character. They passed a hefty entrance tax to be levied on all resident foreigners, and though it was quickly repealed, this short-lived law was the first in a long line of anti-immigration legislative efforts (Muller 1993, 17–18).

Leading citizens stressed their concern. In 1750 Benjamin Franklin, Philadelphia's most prominent inhabitant, was outraged about the German "invasion." Angrily he asked:

> Why [should] the Pennsylvanians . . . allow . . . Germans to swarm into our settlements, and by herding together to establish their Language and Manners to the exclusion of ours? Why should Pennsylvania, founded by the English, become a colony of Aliens, who will shortly be so numerous as to Germanize us instead of our Anglifying them? (Parrillo 2000, 147–48)

Because of the historic struggle between Great Britain and the Roman Catholic Church, the most virulent anti-immigrant feelings during colonial times were directed against Catholics, who by 1700 received full civil and religious rights in Rhode Island. Anti-Catholic bigotry reached its zenith following the English Parliment's passage of the 1774 Quebec Act, which showed religious tolerance toward Catholics in Canada and therefore appeared to many American colonists to represent an English effort to mobilize a subversive movement against them. Only Catholic France's aid during the American Revolution and passage of the First Amendment kept intense anti-Catholic feeling in check for a generation.

While bigotry was alive and well in early American cities, New York, at least for wealthy men, represented an exception. A historian noted, "[T]rue to its Dutch origins, [the city] put money first and honored the men who made it no matter where they came from, who they were, or what, if anything, they believed in" (Epstein 2002, 28). When at the end of the seventeenth century the British took over New York, they retained the Dutch system of loosely regulated commerce, opening its port to doing business with pirates and even allowing the notorious Captain Kidd to occupy a pair of townhouses on what is now Pearl Street. In the nineteenth century, the city retained its tolerance toward diversity in commerce, enticing individuals like John Jacob Astor, a semiliterate fur trader with a thick German accent, to leave Oregon, set up business in New York, and by the time of his death in midcentury become established as the richest man in the country.

Actually, the Founding Fathers themselves were fairly tolerant toward European immigrants. One contributing factor was their classical education. Upper-middle-class or even upper-class men well schooled in the Old Testament, Greek philosophy, and the Renaissance were hardly inclined to consider northern Europeans intellectually superior to the continent's southern residents. Thomas Jefferson was particularly eager to attract immigrants from the Mediterranean basin, primarily from Italy, believing their artists, artisans, and other skilled workers could help enact his plan of creating a capital city modeled after classical Rome.

The new nation's hospitality, however, did not include blacks. The Naturalization Act of 1790 restricted citizenship to "free white persons" who had resided in the United States for at least a year. This limitation was meant to appease the slaveholding states, assuring their nervous whites that free blacks from the Caribbean would not become citizens (Muller 1993, 18–20).

In the North, in fact, there seems to have been limited support for black citizenship, and legislators tended to restrict free blacks' rights without much discussion (Jacobson 1998, 29). In the next era, newly arrived white groups also faced discriminatory treatment.

The Preindustrial/Commercial Period: 1790–1860

Between the American Revolution and the outbreak of the Civil War, an urban explosion occurred. Although the economy was still agriculturally centered, business was leading to the formation of many new cities and the rapid growth of those already established. During that time period, New York's population rose from about 33,000 to over 800,000, and Philadelphia's went from 42,000 to about 565,000. Baltimore, Boston, and other seaport cities also grew rapidly. In addition, new river cities such as Pittsburgh, Cincinnati, Louisville, St. Louis, and New Orleans spearheaded the westward expansion, becoming regional markets and manufacturing centers and stimulating the settlement of adjacent farmlands.

Canals and then railroads developed as transportation sources for carrying a variety of foodstuffs and other products from such processing and distribution centers as Buffalo, Cleveland, Detroit, Milwaukee, and Chicago to the seaport cities. As the inland urban centers expanded commercially, their coastal counterparts began moving into manufacturing. By 1860 New York and Philadelphia were the largest manufacturing sites in the country, producing woolen goods, finished clothing, boots and shoes, leather goods, and cotton textiles. In inland cities, urban entrepreneurs developed local industrial specialites such as flour milling, meatpacking, and lumber preparation. The establishment of factories also stimulated the formation of a host of smaller eastern and midwestern cities, and by the 1850s the growth of specialization and a complex division of labor along with the decline of household manufacture and local handicraft industries signaled the end of the preindustrial era.

In both eastern and midwestern cities, business leadership was prospering, becoming rich and powerful. Meanwhile, cities were sprawling and unplanned, containing working poor crowded into tenements, cellars, and shacks without adequate facilities for sewage and garbage disposal (Mohl and Betten 1970, 91–93). In 1839 George Templeton Strong wrote that New York was "one huge pigsty" but that any sensible farmer would keep his pigs out to avoid catching the plague. A local ordinance requiring responsible disposal of waste products was never enforced, and so people threw garbage, feces, and urine out their doors and windows. By 1857 only 138 miles of sewers had been constructed in nearly 500 miles of streets, leaving almost three-fourths of the city unsewered, including the densely populated, filthy sections where new immigrants resided. Each day some 24 million gallons of sewage matter flowed into yards, alleys, gutters, and streets (Ernst 1970, 117). Strong concluded that "our streets have been horrible enough in times past no one denies, but they are now . . . more abominably filthy than ever" (Glaab and Brown 1983, 77).

Most of the urban poor were immigrants, whose numbers in American cities increased from a trickle at the turn of the nineteenth century to a flood tide of over 4 million between 1840 and 1860. The majority came from Germany and Ireland. Like the Irish, whom we discuss momentarily, the Germans left impoverished conditions. Departing from rural and agricultural areas in the southern and western regions of the country, they escaped crop failures, high rent, inflation, and the disruptive changeover to an industrial economy. The earliest arrivals wrote glowing letters to relatives and friends back home, stimulating a steady flow of new arrivals and making Germans the largest immigrant group during the era (Dinnerstein and Reimers 1999, 21–22). Most of those new settlers remained in cities and provided a cheap pool of labor. By 1860, 50 percent or more of the populations of New York, Chicago, St. Louis, Milwaukee, and San Francisco were immigrants.

During this period blacks also lived in cities, but in small numbers. In the South, where blacks were concentrated, the slave population of cities declined significantly in the four decades beginning in 1820 (Wade 1970). This oppressive practice ran smoothly when unskilled agricultural workers were under overseers' tight, physically abusive supervision, but cities represented a very different setting. Having experienced both situations, Frederick Douglass wrote:

> Slavery dislikes a dense population, in which there is a majority of non-slaveholders. The general sense of decency that must pervade such a population does much to check and prevent those outbreaks of atrocious cruelty, and those dark crimes without a name, almost openly perpetrated on the plantation. He is a desperate slaveholder who will shock the humanity of his non-slaveholding neighbors by the cries of the lacerated slaves; and very few in the city are willing to incur the odium of being cruel masters. (Douglass 1994, 218–19)

Although prejudice toward blacks was intense, they were generally not considered a threat because outside of slavery their numbers were small. Instead, nativists, who sought to protect native-born Americans' rights, focused their discriminatory efforts on European immigrants, whose sharply rising numbers frightened them. Many nativists were working-class artisans and craftsmen who were appalled by foreigners' mass employment in factories, where the output endangered or even eliminated their own jobs. Indisputably, as the following Sociological Illustration suggests, the fiercest nativist attacks were against the Irish.

SOCIOLOGIAL ILLUSTRATION

The Famine Irish's Reception in American Cities

In the late 1840s, the failure of the Irish potato crop precipitated a massive famine that between 1847 and 1854 spurred a migration of about 1.2 million Irish Catholics to the United States.

The immigrants generally settled in cities and towns. By about 1870 fully 75 percent of American-born Irish lived in urban-industrial areas compared to about 25 percent of the overall American citizenry, making Irish Americans the most urbanized ethnic group. The famine Irish tended to move to northeastern, midAtlantic, or midwestern cities, with at least 60 percent residing in New York, Massachusetts, Pennsylvania, and Illinois. In 1860 a full quarter of both New York City's and Boston's populations were Irish-born.

Like earlier Irish immigrants, these recent arrivals found that without marketable skills the available jobs entailed hard physical labor and domestic work. As common laborers Irish men's tasks included serving as longshoremen on the docks, coal heavers, lumberyard workers, quarrymen, pipe layers, street pavers, boatmen, brick layers, plasterers, and cartmen and teamsters transporting goods throughout the city. Besides being domestic servants, where the position featured cleaning, cooking, washing, sewing, and mending, Irish women engaged in such jobs as bringing washing or textile work into their homes, providing lodging to boarders, or working outside the residence as needleworkers, bookbinders, peddlers, and makers of umbrellas and paper boxes. Those women unable to obtain employment in any of these jobs were often financially compelled to turn to prostitution, with one-third of two thousand prostitutes interviewed by an investigator in New York City in 1855 born in Ireland.

These immigrants were willing to work long hours for low pay at a variety of tasks that proved highly beneficial for their employers or, when engaged in public works, the citizenry at large. However, in spite of such contributions, the nativist populace's perception of the famine Irish was decidedly negative. Working-class citizens saw them threatening their job security, and middle-class individuals feared that they would become a permanently depressed, lower-class group crowding into cities, overburdening urban services, and raising tax rates (Kenny 2000, 109–11). The common contempt for Irish workers was apparent in the following ad, which appeared in the New York *Daily Sun* on May 11, 1853, and read: "Women wanted to do general housework . . . English, Scoth [*sic*], Welsh, German, of any other country or color except Irish" (Kenny 2000, 116).*

Let us consider the context in which these viewpoints developed. In the 1840s and 1850s, the famine Irish arrived, fortunate to have survived the trip. Thousands died of disease or starvation either before departure or on the nightmarish passage in the cramped, foul steerage quarters of "coffin ships." At New York City, the principal port of entry, they left the boat and soon found themselves on Manhattan streets with little or no clear sense of where to go. Those without relatives or friends often fell prey to dishonest business representatives of waterfront boardinghouses, promising to provide comfortable living quarters that often turned out to be rat- and roach-infested windowless rooms, each containing several families.

Living in such squalid, crowded conditions, the worst any mid-nineteenth-century immigrant group encountered, the famine Irish fell victim to such infectious diseases as tuberculosis, pleurisy, pneumonia, yellow fever, and cholera, and thousands of children died of malnutrition, suffocation, and neglect (Kenny 2000, 104–08; Shannon 1989, 39).

Still, life was not entirely bleak. For new immigrants the pull was to locate near relatives and friends who were already settled. Frequently, the established residents held Saturday-night "kitchen rackets" welcoming the newly arrived "greenhorns." Adults would help both men and women find jobs, and for a half-century these poor communities, with

*In opposition to the position developed in this chapter and in most source material, historian Richard Jensen (2002) asserted that historical records display limited evidence of anti-Irish job discrimination.

(continued)

SOCIOLOGIAL ILLUSTRATION   Continued

life centered on loyalty to the family, neighborhood, and the Catholic Church, formed the center of an Irish American world that persisted well into the twentieth century. A mayor of New York City once asked the well-known Irish American politician Al Smith what he thought of vice conditions in midtown Manhattan. "I don't know, Mr. Mayor," replied this eventual Democratic candidate for the presidency. "I don't get above Fourteenth Street once in a year" (Shannon 1989, 34).

Although the children received support from their families and communities, they confronted an often alien outside world. In school the textbooks described individuals with Anglo-Saxon names like Jones and Robinson and featured scenes that were idyllically rural, where middle-class families resided in immaculate white cottages surrounded by trees, grass, and farm animals—settings entirely fanciful for children who knew only cold-water, crowded, usually filthy tenements. Meanwhile, the schools hammered away at the importance of individual striving, where success achieved in the competitive commercial world then denied to recently arrived Irish was the cherished goal.

How could Irish American boys surrounded by poverty and remote from access to jobs leading toward commercial success engage in personally satisfying pursuits? Many joined gangs, where behavior supported two significant cultural emphases in members' lives—first, the respect accorded loyalty, cooperation, and obedience nurtured in the family and community and, second, the importance of individual success achieved through acts of courage and daring that resonated with the personal achievement standard prominent in the society at large.

The gangs, possessing such picturesque names as the Dead Rabbits, the Forty Thieves, the Road Guards, and the Plug Uglies, thrived because of their members' alienation and poverty and their physically confrontational style, which followed a tradition started in the homeland's rural settings. Gang activity encouraged criminal involvement, and by the 1850s the number of Irish American men imprisoned in American cities was disproportionately high. In 1859 in New York City, for example, five times as many Irish as native-born men were convicted of crimes, with drunkenness and disor-

derly behavior especially common (Kenny 2000, 108; Knobel 1996, 48; Shannon 1989, 35–36).

At that time Irish males also engaged in many collective violent acts. A famous case was the Astor Place Riot, which occurred in May 1849 in New York City when aroused Irish gang members stormed the theater where an English actor had the lead in a performance of *Macbeth* competing with another rendition featuring the gang's preferred choice. As police tried to subdue the rioters, one Irishman ripped open his shirt, bared his chest, and demanded, "Fire into this! Take the life of a free-born American for a bloody English actor! Do it! You darsen't!" (Shannon 1989, 40).

During these years the stereotypic view of Irishmen was changing. A study of literature written from the 1820s to the mid-1840s described Catholic Irish as *wicked, ignorant,* and *stupid;* following the surge of immigration in the famine years, characterizations became more inclined to project a violent image with such designations as *dangerous, quarrelsome,* and *reckless* (Knobel 1986, 24–27).

Nativist groups were aroused. As the Irish population increased, the Catholic Church grew, and starting in the 1830s, nativist groups mobilized against it, claiming that it represented foreign power and engaged in corrupted, depraved practices. In 1834, as hundreds of people watched, a mob of forty to fifty men burned a Boston convent, forcing a dozen nuns and sixty students to flee by the rear entrance. Although eight men were indicted for arson, the trial took place in a highly charged, anti-Catholic atmosphere that assured their quick release (Shannon 1989, 42–43).

Two years later Maria Monk's *Awful Disclosures* appeared. It was the most prominent of a body of anti-Catholic works that one scholar described as "a form of nineteenth-century pornography" (Kenny 2000, 80). Ghosted by a professional writer hired by nativists, *Awful Disclosures* told the fictional tale of a young woman named Maria Monk who supposedly was educated in a Catholic convent in Montreal, converted to Catholicism, decided to become a nun, and then along with other young nuns was forced to engage in sexual intercourse with priests. Children born of these affairs were supposedly baptized, strangled, and buried in mass graves, and Maria's only hope to save her own unborn child was to flee to New York.

The one accurate part of the story was that Maria did have a child out of wedlock, but it was undoubtedly not fathered by a priest but by a boyfriend, who helped her escape a Catholic asylum for delinquent girls. Although Maria's mother revealed she had never been a resident of the convent described in the book, *Awful Disclosures* retained its sense of authenticity, producing twenty printings and selling over 300,000 copies.

By the 1840s anti-Catholic, anti-Irish sentiments were strong and violent incidents common. The most serious outburst occurred in Philadelphia after Bishop Francis Kenrick convinced the leaders in the local school system to allow Catholic children to read the Douai instead of the King James version of the Bible in public schools and also to be excused from the standard religious instruction in the school curriculum. Nativists attacked the decision, calling it interference by a "foreign prelate," holding protest meetings in a largely Irish residential area, and eventually rioting. Through the spring and summer of 1844, sporadic outbursts led to thousands of Catholics fleeing the city as nativist gangs roamed around the city searching for Irishmen.

Although most middle- and upper-class nativists were initially enthusiastic about the outbreaks, many became horrified with scenes that seemed like reenactments of the French Revolution. On May 8 George Templeton Strong, a wealthy New Yorker, wrote enthusiastically in his diary about the outbreak of rioting. "Great row in Philadelphia," he stated. "This'll be a great thing for the Natives, strengthen their hands amazingly if judiciously used." But when two months later the nativist mobs attacked the local militia, his view changed. They were "pelting the military, not with paving stones but with grapeshot and scrap-iron out of ten-pounders; the state of things is that the city is growing worse and worse every day." Strong considered the violence so disruptive that he "wouldn't be caught voting for a 'Native' ticket again in a hurry" (Shannon 1989, 45).

A decade later, however, with the emergence of the American or Know-Nothing Party, the nativist movement made its strongest political surge. The name developed because the original members, who belonged to a secret nativist organization called the Order of the Star-Spangled Banner, always displayed their ignorance, replying "I know nothing" when asked about their suspected clandestine activities. In the elections of 1854–55, the party moved squarely into the public eye, campaigning against the pope and his American followers and winning seventy-five congressional seats.

At that time anti-Catholic, anti-immigrant issues resonated with a signficant proportion of the population. For the Know-Nothings and other nativist groups, a motivating factor was their staunch support for what they called "free labor"— an outlook that celebrated unskilled physical work as both dignified and independent, supposedly representing for most citizens a way station on the road toward eventual entrepreneurial success. Historian Kevin Kenny concluded that many of the stereotypic traits "the nativists chose—drunkenness, ignorance, laziness, moral laxity, idolatry, and political indoctrination—were clearly seen as obstacles to a self-sufficient work force as well as a virtuous citizenry" (Kenny 2000, 117).

As long as Know-Nothing Party members were able to nurture anti-Irish sentiments that appeared to underlie their commitment to free labor and simultaneously avoid the slavery issue, they thrived. The problem was that taking a position about the slavery issue, which represented the antithesis of the party's strong support for free labor, became impossible to avoid. By 1856 a North/South split began to develop, with northern nativists joining the new Republican Party opposing slavery and their southern proslavery counterparts becoming Democrats. The political heyday of nativism had passed (Kenny 2000, 116–17).

Although they were victims of nativist attacks, the famine Irish could also be oppressors. In 1843 John Finch, an English traveler, wrote that

> [i]t is a curious fact that . . . the poor class of Irish immigrants in America are greater enemies to the negro population, and greater advocates for the continuance of negro slavery than any portion of the population in the free states. (Ignatiev 1995, 97)

For Irish immigrants, labor competition was a major concern because emancipated blacks often competed with them for unskilled jobs. Another

(continued)

important factor, namely racism, came into play. The Irish, after all, were white and quite willing to reach alliances with various white groups, notably Germans with whom they had experienced fierce, even violent competition. In relating to blacks, however, they embraced the prevailing American standard— that they were inferior beings to exploit mercilessly and never accept as equals.

In sharp contrast to African Americans, the famine Irish and their descendants were permitted to steadily improve their economic prospects. By 1870 many of them had begun to achieve an economic foothold in the commercial world, moving up the class structure and leaving about 40 percent of their members among the working poor still doing unskilled labor jobs (Kenny 2000, 129). Irish Americans' growing prosperity continued into the twentieth century. Contributing factors were their steady gains in education and tendency to monopolize certain job areas—for instance, by 1900 95 percent of longshoremen in New York City were Irish (Jensen 2002), and their members often dominated police and fire departments in many eastern and midwestern cities.

During the middle nineteenth century, Irish immigrants were locked into a racialized social system where conflict and violence frequently erupted. The generation arriving shortly after the famine faced various difficult conditions, including the following:

- Intense restriction in jobs, housing, and education with little short-term opportunity to advance into mainstream life.
- Hostility from nativist groups fearing competition for jobs and the pervasive impact of Catholicism.
- Stereotyping and a racist ideology from nativists and other established residents rationalizing harsh, restrictive treatment.
- Limited capital development—for instance, in the realm of human capital, little chance to obtain reading or writing skills for seeking office positions; or in the area of social capital, a deficiency in well-placed friends or acquaintances for gaining access to any but the most difficult, low-paying jobs.

Following the Civil War, the racialized pattern began to break down, allowing Irish Americans to improve their jobs, housing locations, and access to schooling.

The most dramatic winners in the emerging industrial age were white Anglo-Saxon business leaders and their families, but all white groups and even racial minorities were at least modest beneficiaries.

The Early Industrial Period: 1860–1924

During this time span, advances in communication, transportation, and various other innovations promoted industrial growth. Although New York City, Philadelphia, Boston, and Baltimore continued to increase in population, the midwestern cities grew much more rapidly. Chicago, for instance, had barely 100,000 residents in 1860, but by 1890 it possessed over a million and just two decades later over 2 million. The most explosive growth, however, occurred in smaller cities like Omaha, Wichita, Duluth, and Spokane, which during the 1880s increased in population anywhere from three- to thirty-five-fold. In fact, over the half-century from 1860 to 1910, the national percentage of the population living in cities of 2,500 or more increased from 20 to nearly 46 percent.

As in the past, however, urban growth came at a price. In both the 1870s and 1890s, industrial depressions brought poverty, disorder, and sometimes violence. In addition, as urban populations grew, cities were faced with the challenge of providing such services as drinking water, sewage disposal, policing, firefighting, and health-care regulation (Mohl and Betten 1970, 177–78).

Instead of taking a passive role in providing services, business and political leaders began to realize that if their cities were going to be pleasant, comfortable places to live and work, they needed to take an active stance in their development. These services were often controversial, however, both because of their expense and because of the unsettling nature of some new practices. For instance, in the 1850s when Philadelphia reorganized and modernized its police force, government officials demanded that officers wear uniforms. The response was vigorous resistance, with many quitting and all protesting about the insult of wearing "servants' livery" (Monkkonen 1988, 95–100).

Urban leaders often found themselves unprepared to respond to the growing challenge of running rapidly growing cities. Political machines frequently replaced them, featuring a membership undaunted by the expanding demands of political leadership. In New York City, the renowned William Marcy Tweed, better known as Boss Tweed, made certain that streets were extended, franchises granted for horsedrawn railways, and planning for Central Park advanced. In the process Tweed gained enormous illicit wealth and power.

Toward the end of his life, Boss Tweed candidly summarized his view of the urban scene in which he participated:

> The fact is New York politics were always dishonest—long before my time. There never was a time when you couldn't buy the Board of Alderman. A politician in coming forward takes these things as they are. This population is too hopelessly split up into races and factions to govern it under universal suffrage, except by the bribery of patronage or corruption. (Glaab and Brown 1983, 205)

In modern times Tweed's assertion could still provoke an interesting debate. Like many political machines, the so-called Tweed Ring depended on German and Irish immigrants, who provided votes in exchange for the location of housing and jobs and the provision of financial aid.

As Chapter 6 indicates, the political machines went into decline when the ethnic composition of immigrants began to change. Between 1890 and 1915, 18 million new arrivals crowded off ships into the United States. Eighty percent came from southern and eastern Europe, with the new century's opening decade bringing in 5.8 million people from Austria-Hungary, Spain, Italy, and Russia.

It was a very different ethnic mix from preceding decades. For instance, in 1882, the peak nineteenth-century year for immigration when more than three-quarters of a million Europeans reached eastern U.S. ports, a third were from Germany but only 32,000 came from Italy and just 17,000 from Russia. In contrast, 1907, the peak year in the twenty-five-year span ending in 1915, the trend reversed, with Germany sending only 37,000 while Italy provided 285,000 of its citizens and Russia another 250,000. For the forty-year period starting in 1881, Italy led the list, sending 3 million immigrants followed by 2 million Jews, mostly from Russia, and 1 million Poles.

Four of five new arrivals settled in eastern and midwestern industrial cities, where friends and family members had informed them that jobs were available. Members of a certain ethnic group often headed for a given city if they were skilled in trades in which jobs

In the late nineteenth and early twentieth centuries as immigrants from southern and eastern Europe poured into American cities, they often ended up in busy neighborhoods like the Lower East Side of New York City, where the streets were crowded with a variety of commercial wares, vehicles, and people as well as laundry hung from windows and fire escapes.

were plentiful—for example, Russian Jews who had been tailors migrated to the garment districts of New York City and Chicago. If unskilled, they simply went to cities where economic opportunities were expanding—for instance, Italians looking for construction jobs and Poles moving into steel manufacturing headed for such rapidly growing cities as Buffalo, Cleveland, Detroit, and Milwaukee as well as some of the older eastern cities (Yancey, Eriksen, and Juliani 1976, 393).

Native-born Americans now faced what many considered a startling reality—that 75 percent of the populations of such cities as New York City, Boston, Chicago, and Cleveland were either immigrants or the children of immigrants. Like new arrivals before them, most started at the bottom of the occupational ladders, doing low-paying, taxing jobs like construction, mining, smelting, factory work, and domestic service (Bailyn et al. 1977, 948–50).

One account from an anonymous Italian source addressed the gap between what immigrants had heard about the new land and what they discovered:

> Well, I came to America because I heard the streets were paved with gold. When I got here, I found out three things: first, the streets weren't paved with gold; second, they weren't paved at all; and third, I was expected to pave them. (Chermayeff, Wasserman, and Shapiro 1991, 56)

Whether paving streets or engaging in another task, recently arrived immigrants faced a demanding existence. Often exploited by their bosses, who could be natives or immigrants themselves, they lived in slums and eked out a decidedly meager living. Around 1910 the standard rate for Jewish women working in New York's garment district was 8 cents an hour; Slovak steel workers in Pittsburgh made about $12.50 for a 60-hour week (Bailyn et al. 1977, 950).

The largely urban states like Connecticut, Illinois, Massachusetts, New Jersey, and New York tended to thrive economically. For instance, between 1880 and 1920, New York, which received more immigrants than any other state, increased its per capita income 3.7 times and moved its rank in state income from ninth to first. As these urbanized states continued to prosper, they kept drawing immigrants, and with reason. Living standards for recent arrivals started to rise. Some ethnic groups benefited from an **ethnic agglomeration effect,** referring to the causal impact produced when increasing numbers of a given ethnic group settle in a city and create more jobs for the group's members. In New York City, for example, Jewish- and Italian-owned shops and small factories created job opportunities usually reserved for members of their respective groups (Muller 1993, 75–76).

The new arrivals often came from cultures where national origin had less impact than region, locale, or village. While outsiders simply saw Italians, Poles, Hungarians, or Russian Jews, residents often shared highly localized homeland identities, in which common patron saints or other religious figures, feast days, and even civic associations prevailed.

Over time, however, these new immigrant communities grew in strength, and the preeminence of neighborhoods gave way to increasing ethnic identification as churches, foreign language newspapers, and service organizations like the Sons of Italy and the Pan-Hellenic Union helped weld those sharing an ethnicity into vibrant subcultures. Edward Corsi, who grew up in New York City and later became President Hoover's commissioner of immigration and naturalization, recalled the lively commercial life that developed in East Harlem's multiethnic world, where cafés, ratskellers, cabarets, and dance halls seemed to recreate Old World urban scenes. Corsi said, "We have Yiddish theaters and Italian marionette shows, not to mention movie and vaudeville houses. Our secondhand books shops are as good as those of Paris. So are our music stores" (Bailyn et al. 1977, 951).

Meanwhile at both the national level and in individual cities, the primarily northern European political and economic leadership was concerned about what appeared to them as teeming hordes of new arrivals. Many, like President Theodore Roosevelt, feared that the "tangle of squabbling nationalities" represented "the one certain way of bringing the nation to ruin" (Bailyn et al. 1977, 952).

Such a statement resonates with the doctrine of **social Darwinism,** an ideology loosely borrowing from Darwinian thought and emphasizing that the most capable groups will rise to the top of economic, political, and social hierarchies and establish the most productive arrangement for the distribution of wealth and power for society at large.

Social Darwinists considered white, Protestant males the most elevated category of people, and all non–Anglo-Saxons as representing varying degrees of inferior beings, who were primarily valued as sources of cheap, unskilled labor. Chapter 7 describes how until at least the 1920s nativists of northern European origin considered various other Europeans to be members of inferior races (Hofstadter 1955).

Leading intellectuals often supported social Darwinism. For instance, in the first quarter of the twentieth century, several well-known psychologists administered early versions of intelligence tests in English to both northern and southern Europeans, usually interpreting lower scores for Italians, Jews, or Poles as decisive proof of biological inferiority. The blatant fact that many of the southern Europeans were foreign-born with limited or no English literacy was conveniently ignored (Kamin 1974, 15–19). These test results became a clear support for legislating a sharp restriction in southern Europeans' immigration.

Before moving on to that era, however, I want to look more closely at some of the new urban arrivals at the turn of the twentieth century. To begin, several conditions combined to encourage blacks to migrate north in record numbers. Starting in 1906 the Mexican boll weevil began devastating the cotton crop, and that factor along with a number of disasterous floods in the following decade prompted many southern planters to switch to growing food crops and raising livestock, which are less labor intensive than raising cotton. At the same time, the outbreak of World War I temporarily blocked the flow of European immigrants, and so recruiters for northern factory workers stopped going to Europe and simply headed south seeking black workers. During the 1890s about 174,000 blacks migrated north, and in the next decade the number increased to 197,000. Then between 1910 and 1920, the impact of recruiting southern blacks produced dramatic results, with 525,000 African Americans arriving in the North (Massey and Denton 1993, 28–29). In Chapter 2 we saw that as the so-called Great Migration occurred, whites responded with intimidation and violence, including riots in the century's first two decades, forcing African Americans into restricted locations that by 1940 marked the perimeters of the current, inner-city black ghettos. Housing segregation has been the foundation for implementing the racialist social system imposed on African Americans.

Southern blacks often found the North an unsettling place to live. Richard Wright, later a well-known writer, who migrated northward in the 1920s, represented a case in point. Wright hated the southern existence, in which whites paraded their sense of racial superiority, but soon after arriving in Chicago, he began to realize that he had entered a territory where the standards of race relations on the job were no longer clear. At least in the South, he had known where he stood, but now "I had embraced the daily horror of anxiety, of tension, of eternal disquiet" (Wright 1991, 253).

How did African Americans of this era respond to the discrimination they encountered? W. E. B. Du Bois described two principal ways. One was Booker T. Washington's approach, which emphasized blacks' complete cooperation with whites, thus accepting the racialist social system. Under "the benevolent leadership of white capital," a corp of black skilled labor would develop. Using portions of their wages to educate and elevate the children, this pioneer group would produce a black middle class, whose members would hire African American laborers and continue to cooperate with white capitalists. Critical of Washington's approach, Du Bois declared, "He did not know the difficulty, indeed the practical impossibility, of this program, when capital was willing to exploit race prejudice and the rivalry of race groups in industry" (Du Bois 1975, 214).

Du Bois's own approach was decidedly more militant, taking advantage of the accumulating power of the growing black communities in the North. In 1905 Du Bois and other African American leaders convened the Niagara Movement, which produced a bill of rights. Five years later that same leadership group allied with a number of white liberals to form the National Association for the Advancement of Colored People (NAACP). In its early years, this organization was very active, winning many cases before the Supreme Court, including ones addressing residential segregation, voter discrimination, and lynching (Du Bois 1975, 215).

At that time blacks remained a fairly modest numerical presence in most cities. Italians, with 4 million arriving between 1880 and 1920, were the most populous urban newcomers. As in the Irish case, Italians' Catholicism branded them a religious anathema to the Protestant majority group, who tended to stereotype them as uncouth, dark-skinned peasants. This type of perception helped rationalize such job discriminations as an ad for laborers to build a reservoir in New York City offering daily wages of $1.30 to $1.50 for "whites" and $1.15 to $1.25 for "Italians" (Gambino 1975, 77). The dominant white group, in short, set early Italian immigrants apart from other white groups, just as a half-century earlier it did with the famine Irish. Still, Italians entered the United States in large numbers, and many found a much better existence than in the homeland.

In 1982 I had a ninety-two-year-old Italian American landlord, who had arrived in this country at the dawn of the new century. Although Sal had made several trips back to his southern Italian village to visit family members, he never considered permanently returning. He simply loved and valued this country too much, often telling me how wonderful its opportunities were for immigrants like him. If one were willing to work hard as Sal had done at a variety of jobs, success was inevitable. A case in point, he proudly indicated, was his own family, notably his grandchildren, who had attended excellent schools and were now establishing themselves as successful professionals.

Like other groups, Italian immigrants tended to settle in urban communities containing residents from their town or region, most likely finding familiar names, faces, dialects, and customs a comforting reminder of the old country (Nelli 1970, 259–61). Rosario Ingargiola, who emigrated to New York City in 1911, described this pattern:

> While the Italians stayed together, there was a tendency to gravitate toward people from the same area of Italy. There were so many of us from my home town of Marsala, some three to four hundred, that we tended to stay together in this circle. The Italians from different sections got along with one another, although it was different with other nationalities like the Irish. (La Gumina 1981, 182)

Not only was living close to others from the homeland pleasant and comforting, but it also provided important social capital. Neighbors and friends in the new communities served as a **social network,** a set of contacts involving friends, acquaintances, or business associates that individuals use to obtain information about or advantage in seeking jobs or other valued opportunities. Most residential or job settings, however, contained people from outside narrow homeland locales, and as they extended their social horizons, Italian immigrants began to think of themselves more broadly—as Italians.

One means of solidifying that sense was various mutual benefits organizations like the Sons of Italy, which helped immigrants address the complexities of urban life. For dues-paying members, these organizations offered recreation, companionship, a sense of identity and strength in numbers, and such practical aids as medical care and sickness and death benefits.

Another important development was Italians' gradual occupational advancement. By 1900 they had begun going from unskilled labor into such job areas as printing, bricklaying, carpentry, banking, law, and medicine (Nelli 1970, 264–69). Once they started to prosper, Italians, like other white groups, began moving toward cities' peripheries, seeking higher-priced, more desirable housing and integrating into the general white, middle-class community.

At this time groups from outside Europe began arriving in fairly substantial numbers. Among Asians, Chinese men were the earliest immigrants, and although the first were railroad laborers, some soon settled in cities. Regardless of where they lived, they rapidly gained a reputation as hardworking and effective. Considering the modest numbers—about 225,000 between 1850 and 1882—they faced marked hostility, including the 1871 massacre of twenty-one Chinese in Los Angeles (Parrillo 2000, 278–80). Clearly, many whites feared competing with them on the job. Two years before the killings in a speech that might have helped nurture that violence, a California senator candidly addressed this perceived threat:

> It is the duty of every class of men to unite to prevent the introduction of the Chinese. If they come into contact with only the common laborers to-day, tomorrow they will be in competition with the mason, the bricklayer, the carpenter and the machinist, for they are the *most frugal, industrious and ingenious people on the face of the earth.* (Brown and Pannell 2000, 292)

According to this senator, the Chinese had various laudable qualities, but as non-members of the white, Anglo-Saxon set, they qualified for social Darwinist–style treatment. The Chinese Exclusion Act of 1882, which barred Chinese immigrants for ten years and later was extended indefinitely, provided a tidy legislative solution. Following its passage, daily existence for the Chinese already in the United States became more difficult. Restricted to living in so-called Chinatowns in such cities as San Francisco, New York, Los Angeles, and Denver, they were susceptible to various harassments, including immigration agents' efforts to deport them if they had arrived after 1882.

Following the enactment of the Chinese Exclusion Act, labor recruiters sought Japanese workers, particularly as farm laborers. As a result, Japanese immigration increased, reaching almost 130,000 in the twentieth century's first decade. Nearly half of these new arrivals settled in California, gradually moving from common labor positions to becoming owners of their own farming and fishing businesses. When the California Alien Laws of

TABLE 3.1   **Five Historical Eras in the Development of American Cities**

	Dominant Population Patterns	**Major Ethnic and Racial Trends**
Colonial Period: Up to 1790	Location on eastern coast. Small in population and slow in growth	Predominantly English with several northern European groups and Africans represented
Preindustrial/ Commercial Period: 1790–1860	Rapid growth of seaport cities and formation of inland cities on rivers	Influx of immigrants from northern Europe, especially Germany and Ireland
Early Industrial Period: 1860–1924	Expansion of eastern cities and explosive growth in the country's western half	Between 1890 and 1924, new arrivals primarily from southern and eastern Europe reversing the earlier northern European domination; additional residents from Asia and Mexico
Advanced Industrial Period: 1924–1970	Spread of established cities into suburbs	Great Migration of southern blacks
Postindustrial Period: 1970 to the present	Shift into postindustrial economy leading to population decline, especially in many eastern and midwestern cities	New immigrants from a wide variety of countries, with Asians and Latin Americans most heavily represented

1913 deprived Japanese immigrants of the right to land ownership, many moved to cities, where they established a variety of successful small enterprises, including produce markets, flower shops, and nurseries (Miyares, Paine, and Nishi 2000, 268–70).

During these years Mexicans seeking jobs as farm laborers arrived in fairly substantial numbers, but it was not until the advanced industrial era that more than a few began living and working in cities. Table 3.1 provides information about the five eras examined in this chapter.

The Advanced Industrial Period: 1924–1970

Throughout most of this era, an accelerated movement toward the suburbs occurred. This pattern, which started in the late nineteenth and early twentieth centuries, began because of white Protestants' hostility toward Catholic and Jewish immigrants as well as the desire to escape noise, pollution, and the fast-paced, impersonal urban life. The escapees' idea was to live in the suburbs but to keep working in nearby cities and also to continue using them for obtaining various goods and services. At the turn of the century, trolleys and intercity railroads promoted the process, but by the 1920s automobiles played an increasing role, augmented by the foundation in the late 1940s of a federally subsidized highway system facilitating and speeding movement between cities and their suburbs.

It was not unmitigated progress. The business and political leadership in American cities never committed to comprehensive urban planning, where a carefully conceived and executed design would seek to smoothly coordinate cities' expanding physical structure and activities. As a result, new housing developments and business ventures produced urban/suburban sprawl, which has featured traffic problems and pollution along with cheaply constructed, ugly homes and businesses.

Outside cities suburban proliferation occurred, leading to growing government complexity. A large city eventually had a network of surrounding suburbs, each of which duplicated such services as fire protection, water distribution, and sanitation, thereby increasing costs and wastefully raising municipal taxes. By the 1960s Chicago and its suburbs had over 1,100 overlapping but independent local governments and New York City's suburban network encompassed portions of three states (Feagin 1988; Mohl and Betten 1970, 271–72).

Although such structural complexity was just starting to develop in the 1920s, another major problem was already consuming many American cities. The legacy of prejudice and fear felt toward southern and eastern European immigrant groups supported the introduction of restrictive legislation. Three citizens' actions contributed. First, although the progressive movement, which was a middle-class reform effort that emphasized the destructive impacts of rapid urban growth and corporate greed, had peaked in popularity before World War I, its emphasis on assimilating aliens already in the country before admitting more continued to receive widespread support during this decade. Second, in the 1920s the Ku Klux Klan was alive and well, drawing support not only from Southerners but also from disgruntled lower-middle-class and working-class groups in northern cities and directing its verbal and physical attacks against Catholics, Jews, and, above all, blacks.

Finally, the most important development was the **eugenics movement,** which was an initiative founded by late nineteenth-century intellectuals who claimed science could improve the quality of the human race, primarily by promoting the "purification of the Anglo-Saxon race." The movement, whose members included the previously mentioned developers of intelligence tests, rapidly gained support from prominent physical and biological scientists, sociologists, and psychologists as well as an array of wealthy and powerful urban leaders. The proponents gradually broadened their range of inferior groups, at first focusing on blacks and Asians but then including Mediterranean groups, who they claimed were tainted by African blood and thus were "colored."

Leading intellectuals' public statements had a decisive influence on immigration policy. E. G. Conklin, a Princeton biologist, declared, "How insignificant are the considerations of cheap labor and rapid development of natural resources when compared with these [race-mixing] biological consequences of immigration." William Ripley, a Harvard economist, claimed that the new wave of immigrants was "a menace to our Anglo-Saxon civilization," with cities now reduced to producing "a swarthy and black-eyed primitive-type" population (Muller 1993, 39–40).

Besides these citizens' actions, economic conditions supported restrictive legislation. By the 1920s industrial growth had slowed down, and the combination of new labor-saving technology and a substantial urban population swelled by nearly a century of mass immigration meant that a continuing supply of European workers became less pressing (Steinberg 2001, 39–40).

Some fairly prominent groups had interests that opposed restrictive legislation. Many business owners felt that continuing immigration helped keep workers' wages low, undercut organized labor's effort by providing a steady supply of replacements, and also offered a steadily expanding market for their goods and services. Furthermore, such ethnically attuned organizations as the National Catholic Welfare Conference, the American Jewish Congress, the Polish-American Alliance, and the American-Italian League voiced disapproval. Opposition, however, was insufficient to carry the day.

The House of Representatives passed the National Origins Act of 1924, requiring that a quota system based on national origin be established, and with just minor variations that standard remained until 1965. The new restriction established that the size of any nationality's annual quota of immigrants could only be 2 percent of that group's American population based on 1890 census figures. The use of the 1890 population profile was the eugenics movement's master stroke. At that time the flood of immigrants from southern and eastern Europe had barely started, and so with the passage of the 1924 law, the number of new arrivals representing those nationalities shrunk drastically. For Italy and Russia together, average annual immigration in the first two decades of the twentieth century was 270,000, but with restrictive legislation the figure slipped to barely 6,000. Greeks faced an even more drastic reduction, going from 17,000 annually to a quota of 100 (Muller 1993, 43–47).

The result was decisive. Immigration from southern and eastern Europe went from a flood to a trickle, but now the counterweight in "the ambivalent balance" provoked a major question: In an industrially expansive era, where could employers find a supply of cheap, unskilled workers?

The labor recruiters, who had initially headed south with World War I's curtailment of European immigration, now returned. During the 1920s black migration northward reached the unprecedented figure of 877,000, and many whites sensed an invasion.

By this time, however, the antiblack violence of the earlier two decades was rapidly declining. Although such activity had successfully intimidated blacks, the white leadership realized that it both unnecessarilly destroyed property and also could bring legal charges and unfavorable publicity. Influential white groups now used a more restrained but equally effective approach: Establish neighborhood "improvement associations" such as Chicago's Hyde Park Improvement and Protective Club or the Woodlawn Society and New York City's Property Owners' Improvement Corporation or the Gates Avenue Association. To the members of these organizations, "improvement" simply meant keeping blacks out of their neighborhoods (Massey and Denton 1993, 35).

Leaders made bold, unambiguous statements that displayed a sense of both the power and the righteousness of their eugenics-inspired cause. Soon after rapidly building the Hyde Park Improvement and Protection Club to 350 members, Francis Harper, a prominent lawyer, issued a manifesto confining blacks to specific areas. Threatening to blacklist any real-estate firm that opposed the manifesto, Harper declared, "The districts which are now white must remain white. There will be no compromise" (Spear 1970, 330).

As affluent and well-connected members of their communities, participants in these improvement associations had an array of available options to ensure the desired results:

lobbying city councils for zoning restrictions to eliminate hotels and rooming houses that attracted blacks; threatening to boycott real-estate firms or other enterprises that might bring African Americans into their areas; seeking public investment in the locale to raise property values and make it economically prohibitive for African Americans to buy homes there; and raising money either to purchase black-owned houses or to give cash bonuses to black renters to leave the district.

While these tactics all proved useful, the centerpiece of neighborhood improvement associations' strategy was the **racially restrictive covenant**—a contract among property owners in an area prohibiting selected minorities from buying, leasing, or occupying property in that locale. No other measure to restrict African Americans' location matched this one's efficiency. The typical covenant required the support of 75 percent of property owners, lasted twenty years, and was renewable.

Statistics demonstrate the collective effectiveness of these actions. Between 1900 and 1930, the typical black residents of most cities lived in areas with a steadily rising **index of isolation,** which is the citywide average of a particular racial or ethnic group's membership within the selected neighborhoods where that group resides. The higher the percentage goes, the greater a group's isolation. For African Americans Chicago, going from 10 to 70 percent, had the greatest acceleration. Cleveland went from 8 to 51 percent, New York City from 5 to 42 percent, and St. Louis from 13 to 47 percent. A similar pattern developed in southern cities, but it was more gradual than in the North both because of slower industrial growth and because whites' greater sense of social control over blacks made them less fearful of having African American neighbors.

European ethnic groups never experienced such high indices of isolation, and by 1930 descendants of southern and eastern European immigrants encountered increasingly less housing restriction; steadily became more assimilated educationally, occupationally, and socially; and progressed up the social-class ladder. Consider intermarriage rates over time for four initially restricted southern and eastern European groups. If one compares the cohort born between 1916 and 1925, usually immigrants' children, with those born between 1946 and 1955, usually immigrants' grandchildren, the intermarriage rate rose from 43 to 73 percent among Italians, 53 to 80 percent for Poles, 74 to 91 percent among Czechs, and 76 to 92 percent for Hungarians (Jencks 2001, 59).

Meanwhile, during the first four decades of the twentieth century, blacks in northern and midwestern cities were increasingly isolated through a systematic process examined in the next chapter. The Sociological Illustration later in this chapter indicates why the resulting ghettos have been a troubling element in many modern American cities. The focus shifts to that era.

The Postindustrial Period: 1970 to the Present

In the 1950s manufacturing in cities ruled the roost. The typical city was a prosperous industrial center, where factory employees, often immigrants or recent descendants of immigrants, lived in modestly thriving, working-class neighborhoods. Then, gradually, a massive economic change initiated by major manufacturers began to unfold, not only in the United States but also in other highly industrialized nations. Because they could pay workers considerably less and function with little or no governmental supervision, factory owners began moving either out of the country or to the southern United States.

During the 1970s the United States and western Europe lost 8 million manufacturing jobs. The loss was particularly pronounced in eastern and midwestern cities. It involved not only a decline in manufacturing jobs but also a population decrease as affluent urban residents left deteriorating cities for the suburbs. Between 1970 and 1980, for instance, Detroit's population dropped by 20.5 percent, New York City's by 10.4 percent, and Chicago's by 10.1 percent. On the other hand, in the 1970s and 1980s, vibrant Sunbelt cities like Los Angeles, Houston, and Jacksonville expanded their populations.

When manufacturing left cities, service industries catering to corporations and banks became the dominant economic activity. Early analysts of the postindustrial transformation predicted that these services, which include financial and business consulting, insurance, real estate, legal expertise, and communication and transportation support, would fully replace industry, maintaining cities' industrial prosperity. That result did not materialize. The postindustrial city has increasingly shifted toward a two-tiered employment reality. At the top resides a select core of primarily white, well-educated, highly paid professionals, and below them lies a large segment of largely minority, poorly educated, low-paid service workers (Gottdiener and Hutchison 2000, 78–84). A substantial number of these service workers are recent immigrants, reflecting the increase of new arrivals since the beginning of the postindustrial era.

During the preceding four decades when the National Origins Act of 1924 was in effect, immigration fell to about 4.5 million, with Europeans representing about 80 percent of the total and Latin Americans, primarily from Mexico and Puerto Rico, about 15 percent. Then the immigration picture abruptly changed.

The Immigration Act of 1965 passed Congress when unemployment was at a record low and the citizenry was in a benign mood about minority groups' rights. The new law discarded the 1890 census standard for determining a country's yearly quota and replaced it with an annual maximum of 20,000 immigrants per country. Applications receiving preference came from family members, professionals, and skilled workers. Within a few years, most congressional members were surprised, even shocked to discover that the priority given family members greatly expanded Asian immigration, which grew from about 150,000 in the 1950s to more than 2.7 million three decades later.

Although over the next thirty-five years some modifications in the 1965 law occurred, its central thrust continues: After priority for family members and preferred occupations, immigrants enter on a first-come, first-served basis, with the annual maximum per country now raised to about 28,000 individuals.

These revised laws have promoted increased immigration, allowing 23 million foreigners to enter the country between 1966 and 1997—over five times as many as arrived in the previous forty years. Now about 16 percent of recent immigrants are European, 37 percent Asian, and 40 percent Latin American or Caribbean. The countries supplying the largest number include Mexico, providing about 12.5 percent of the annual total, Russia,

Vietnam, El Salvador, China, the Dominican Republic, India, Korea, Jamaica, Poland, and Haiti (Fernandez 2000, 18–21).

Presently, in a society where racist and anti-ethnic positions are muted compared to the past, Americans' outlook on immigration continues to vary with their economic location. Christopher Jencks wrote:

> Under America's current immigration policy, the winners are employers who get cheaper labor, skilled workers who pay less for their burgers and nannies, and immigrants themselves. The losers are unskilled American-born workers. (Jencks 2001, 63)

Jencks was implying that one might visualize immigration policy in social-class terms, with higher categories benefiting and the working poor facing stiff competition for low-paying jobs.

A substantial percentage of impoverished immigrants are illegal. Congress required the Immigration and Naturalization Service to focus its restrictive effort on the Mexican border, tripling between 1982 and 1997 the number of border patrol agents. No evidence exists that this effort has curtailed the influx. Whether they can enter legally or not, the residents of many countries are convinced that modest though the initial opportunities are by most Americans' appraisal, this postindustrial economy offers far better jobs and standards of living than exist in the homeland (Fernandez 2000, 22–23; Muller 1993, 47–49).

American cities, particularly the large ones with diversified economic activity, can be lodestones for poor immigrant groups, who have often arrived illegally seeking a better life. In Los Angeles a wide array of professionals in the business and finance, hi-tech, and entertainment sectors rely heavily on Latino immigrant workers from Mexico, El Salvador, and Guatemala to perform bottom-rung, low-wage service jobs. In this setting where hundreds of thousands work as domestics and gardeners, sociologist Pierette Hondagneu-Sotelo concluded:

> For the masses of affluent professionals and corporate managers in Los Angeles, relying on Latin immigrant workers has become almost a social obligation. After relocating from the Midwest to Southern California, a new neighbor, the homemaker wife of an engineer, expressed her embarrassment at not hiring a gardener. It's easy to see why she felt abashed. (Hondagneu-Sotelo 2001, 7)

Immigrant Hispanics, who have usually come from poor, politically turbulent homelands, tend to be optimistic about what they often find is a more positive life in the United States. A *New York Times/CBS News* poll indicated that 83 percent of foreign-born Hispanics expected life for the next generation to be better than life today. That figure contrasted with 64 percent for Hispanics born in the United States. The overall Latino number of 75 percent turned out to be much higher than the figure for non-Hispanics—39 percent. A specialist on Hispanic trends indicated that in cities like Los Angeles with many Latinos, there exists "a sense of ascendancy" that is most apparent among new arrivals. However, it remains unclear whether this outlook will continue to develop (Romero and Elder 2003).

Unlike Latinos, Native Americans entering cities cross no national boundaries, but the move is likely to have a strong effect on their lives. About half of the nation's nearly

Like other recently arrived immigrants, these Cuban Americans in Miami have started small businesses that are often located in their own residential areas.

two-and-a-half million American Indians have become urban residents, after finding that on reservations the Bureau of Indian Affairs has provided few jobs, poor schooling, and deficient health and family services. Although those migrating are more likely to be working than those remaining behind, it generally takes fully five years to show economic gain. About three-quarters of urban Native Americans live in poor neighborhoods and, lacking the necessary educational credentials and job skills, experience a level of poverty similar to what they left behind but without the significant presence of the tribal support system.

Nonetheless, Indians in or near cities run a variety of businesses, featuring facilities catering to tourists and other visitors, including casinos, museums, gift shops, gas stations, hotels, and restaurants (Gottdiener and Hutchison 2000, 179–80; Thornton 2001, 146–47).

Difficult as Indians' urban experience has been, they have not been forced like millions of African Americans to live in ghettos. The following Sociological Illustration describes the human impact of that practice.

Not surprisingly, the deterioration of the country's black ghettos have an impact on cities at large, contributing both to taxpayers' financial overload and to the psychic burden accompanying fear of drugs, crime, and violence. Figure 3.1 compares African Americans' and Irish Americans' historical experience. Approaching the end of the chapter, we might consider whether the modern American urban scene could have been more equitable and universally beneficial.

S O C I O L O G I A L   I L L U S T R A T I O N
Chicago's Black Ghettos at the Onset of the Postindustrial Period

In introducing his book about the disappearance of work for Chicago's largely black urban poor, sociologist William Julius Wilson noted that although the city's black ghettos were low-income and crowded, many once functioned as viable communities with a solid business core. In Chicago's Woodlawn neighborhood, for instance, this primarily black area had over eight hundred commercial and industrial enterprises in the 1950s, but by the 1990s the number had fallen to about a hundred, often functioning as marginal businesses with only one or two employees. A researcher studying the area's decline indicated that according to residents what had been a lively, crowded business section now

> has the appearance of an empty, bombed-out war zone. The commercial strip has been reduced to a long tunnel of charred stores, vacant lots littered with broken glass and garbage, and dilapidated buildings left to rot in the shadow of the elevated train line. At the corner of Sixty-third Street and Cottage Grove Avenue, the handful of remaining establishments that struggle to survive are huddled behind wrought-iron bars. The only enterprises that seem to be thriving are liquor stores and currency exchanges, these "banks of the poor" where one can cash checks, pay bills and buy money orders for a fee. (Wilson 1996, 5)

Not only the Woodlawn neighborhood, but black ghettos in many American cities became victims of industrial decline. Low-skilled African American workers, whose residence in ghettos restricted their access to mainstream success, were hit harder than most other groups by manufacturers' departures from northern and midwestern cities. During the 1970s this factor accounted for about half their increase in unemployment. Instead of finding jobs in manufacturing, construction, or some other blue-collar position like their fathers, sons and daughters could only seek much lower-paying service jobs as waiters, custodians, or fast-food attendants.

What happened? Wilson indicated that ghetto dwellers face disadvantages that make them unusu-ally vulnerable to changing economic conditions. Two factors account for much of this vulnerability. First, because of their poverty, ghetto neighborhoods contain schools where crowded classrooms, underpaid and overworked teachers, poor facilities, and deficient supplies leave their students less effectively prepared for the job world than those in other urban areas. Second, unlike more affluent areas, black ghettos provide few job opportunities. As a result, job-seeking residents need to go elsewhere, where they must pay the added expense of transportation and where they lack effective social networks—individuals who can help them locate jobs or perhaps put in a good word with a prospective boss. Middle-class people often take for granted the distinct advantage such social networks offer.

A twenty-nine-year-old black male from one of Chicago's poorest neighborhoods commented on how limited employment in the locale impacted his life. In the past, he said, jobs had been plentiful:

> You could walk out of the house and get a job. Maybe not what you want but you could get a job. Now, you can't find anything. A lot of people in the neighborhood, they want to work but they can't get work. A few, but a very few, they just don't want to work. The majority they want to work but they can't find work. (Wilson 1996, 36)

As joblessness in Chicago's ghetto neighborhoods has increased, it has obviously nurtured poverty, which has impacted communities in a variety of ways. For instance, residents are less able to maintain their homes and less capable of supporting local businesses, which often are forced to close. More affluent families of all races and ethnicities leave the deteriorating area, and new arrivals are invariably individuals who are too poor to afford living elsewhere.

Although youthful inhabitants have very limited connection to people promoting quality education and interesting, well-paid jobs, they have abundant access to a different type of social network. A seventeen-year-old black male who worked part-time, attended college, and lived in an impoverished ghetto on Chicago's West Side commented on this reality:

> Well, basically I feel if you are raised in a neighborhood and all you see is negative things, then you are going to be negative because you don't see anything positive. Guys . . . see drug dealers on the corner and they see fancy cars and flashy money and they figure, "Hey, if I get into drugs I can be like him." (Wilson 1996, 55)

In this young man's neighborhood, the most available social network provides access to drugs and crime. In the 1980s the advent of crack, which accelerated drug use, created a highly competitive atmosphere, where dealers became more inclined to use guns to obtain and hold prime drug-selling locations. Even after crack declined in popularity, widespread use of guns continued.

Family life can hardly thrive in such an impoverished, violent, drug-ridden context. Wilson entitled the relevant chapter "The Fading Inner-City Family," providing a variety of trends and respondent statements that support that reality. In the 1990s young men who impregnated women were much less likely to stay with them and, in particular, to marry them than two or three decades earlier. In modern times a key factor undermining family stability has been ghettoized black males' earning power, with most either jobless or less regularly employed at jobs paying a livable wage than those in the previous generation.

A sociologist who had three decades of inner-city research experience in Chicago suggested to Wilson that because of declining income and other debilitating conditions of ghetto life, it appeared that family norms were loosening. He stated:

> I think that families now exert less pressure on men to remain involved than they once did. I found no instance, for example, of families urging their children to marry or even to live together as was common when I was studying the parents of my informants in the mid-1960s. (Wilson 1996, 102)

This material has suggested that ghettos like those just described represent the racialized social system in a setting where the structural elements interplay negatively. Because of entrenched poverty, local schools were poorly funded, meaning students received inadequate financial capital preparing them for the occupational world. That might have been less of a problem if as in the past industrial jobs were still available, but local factories have shut down. The lack of ghetto employment has helped make many young residents vulnerable to the drug culture and its seemingly easy wealth and ostentatious lifestyle. Furthermore, consuming poverty has helped make many young men less willing to maintain a stable family life.

Conclusion

Endowed with the power to make a single historical change that would have helped level the playing field for American citizens, what might we do? With the current book's topics in mind, I would opt for something simple and fairly modest: during Reconstruction to have seized former slaveowners' land and provided each newly freed black family the 40 acres that Congressman Thaddeus Stevens proposed. Then, instead of being poverty-stricken, rootless, and isolated from the various structures that provide access to mainstream success, black families would have had a firm economic base from which to start a new life. Assuming they had been permitted to retain those properties and the subsequent wealth that they obtained from them, there is every reason to believe that before the end of the nineteenth century African Americans would have established an economic, political, residential, educational, and social foothold in the nation and been spared the unique levels of indignity and horror the racialized social system has imposed on them.

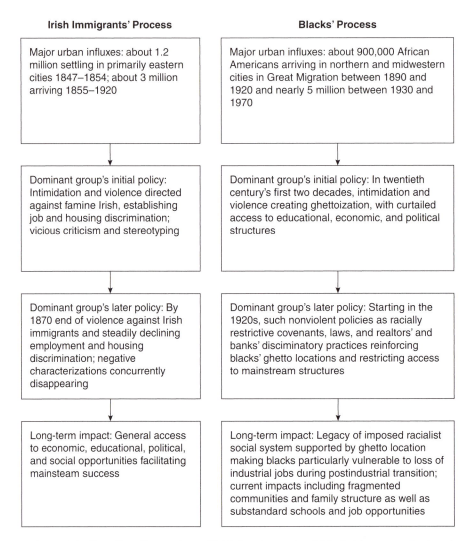

FIGURE 3.1 Four-Step Comparison of Irish Immigrants' and Blacks' Access to the American Urban Mainstream

From its introduction, however, Stevens's proposal never had a chance. "No man in America," declared the *Nation,* whose readership at that time was primarily educated Republicans, "has any right to anything which he has not honestly earned, or which the lawful owner has not thought proper to give him." Such critics felt Stevens's plan had socialist overtones, making it unpalatable in a capitalist society. "An attempt to justify the confiscation of southern land under the pretense of doing justice to the freedmen," stated an editorial in the *New York Times,* "strikes at the root of all property rights in both sections. It concerns Massachusetts quite as much as Mississippi" (Bailyn 1977, 743). Southern plantation owners might have been defeated enemies, but they were Northerners' *equals*—fellow property owners and fellow whites, who would once again share a common economic system. Such a monumental reward to blacks at their expense appeared to threaten society's very fabric. So blacks received no such boost toward equality. Quite the contrary.

Throughout American urban history, newcomers have encountered an ambivalent reception. The faster they have been accorded equitable access to mainstream resources, the more quickly and comfortably they have assimilated. The most dire exception to the historical urban pattern has been African Americans, whose long history of systemic discrimination continues to unfold in modern times.

DISCUSSION QUESTIONS

1. Discuss how the political and economic leaders of American cities viewed the newly arrived immigrant groups during the preindustrial/commercial period (1790–1860).

2. If you were a member of one of those newly arrived ethnic groups, what would be your greatest challenges? Discuss.

3. List and examine the various conditions promoting restrictive legislation on immigration in the 1920s. Then describe the central elements of the current legislation.

4. Analyze how the experiences you faced would have changed if you belonged to an African American family moving from the South to a northeastern or midwestern city in each of the following three years: 1895, 1915, and 1935.

5. Evaluate the following statement, assessing what it implies about both leaving one's country of origin and prospects for success in the United States: "It seems surprising that so many Hispanics and Asians currently leave their homelands to come to American cities."

BIBLIOGRAPHY

Bailyn, Bernard, et al. 1977. *The Great Republic: A History of the American People.* Lexington, MA: Heath.

Brown, Catherine L., and Clifton W. Pannell. 2000. "The Chinese in America," pp. 283–309 in Jesse O. McKee (ed.), *Ethnicity in Contemporary America.* Lanham, MD: Rowman and Littlefield.

Chermayeff, Ivan, Fred Wasserman, and Mary J. Shapiro (eds.). 1991. *Ellis Island: An Illustrated History of the Immigrant Experience.* New York: Macmillan.

Dinnerstein, Leonard, and David M. Reimers. 1999. *Ethnic Americans: A History of Immigration,* 4th ed. New York: Columbia University Press.

Douglass, Frederick. *Autobiographies: My Bondage and My Freedom.* 1994. New York: Library of America. Originally published in 1855.

Du Bois, W. E. B. 1975. *Black Folk: Then and Now.* Milwood, NY: Kraus-Thomson. Originally published in 1939.

Epstein, Jason. 2002. "Up with Downtown." *New York Review of Books.* 49 (December 19): 28+.

Ernst, Joseph Albert. 1970. *The Forming of a Nation, 1607–1971.* New York: Random House.

Feagin, Joe R. 1988. *Free Enterprise City: Houston in Political-Economic Perspective.* New Brunswick, NJ: Rutgers University Press.

Fernandez, Ronald. 2000. *America's Banquet of Cultures: Harnessing Ethnicity, Race, and Immigration in the Twenty-First Century.* Westport, CT: Praeger.

Gambino, Richard. 1975. *Blood of My Blood.* Garden City, NY: Anchor Books.

Glaab, Charles N. 1963. *The American City: A Documentary History.* Homewood, IL: Dorsey Press.

Glaab, Charles N., and A. Theodore Brown. 1983. *A History of Urban America,* 3rd ed. New York: Macmillan.

Gottdiener, Mark, and Ray Hutchinson. 2000. *The New Urban Sociology,* 2nd ed. New York: McGraw-Hill.

Feagin, Joe R. 1988. *Free Enterprise City: Houston in Political-Economic Perspective.* New Brunswick, NJ: Rutgers University Press.

Hofstadter, Richard. 1955. *Social Darwinism in American Thought,* rev. ed. Boston: Beacon Press.

Hondagneu-Sotelo, Pierrette. 2001. *Doméstica: Immigrant Workers Cleaning and Caring in the Shadows of Affluence.* Berkeley and Los Angeles: University of California Press.

Ignatiev, Noel. 1995. *How the Irish Became White.* New York: Routledge.

Jacobson, Matthew Frye. 1998. *Whiteness of a Different Color: European Immigrants and the Alchemy of Race.* Cambridge and London: Harvard University Press.

Jencks, Christopher. 2001. "Who Should Get In?" *New York Review of Books.* 48 (November 29): 57+.

Jensen, Richard. 2002. " 'No Irish Need Apply': A Myth of Victimization." *Journal of Social History.* 36 (Winter): 405–29.

Kamin, Leon J. 1974. *The Science and Politics of I.Q.* New York: Wiley.

Kennedy, William. 1988. *Quinn's Book.* New York: Viking.

Kenny, Kevin. 2000. *The American Irish: A History.* New York: Longman.

Knobel, Dale T. 1986. *Paddy and the Republic.* Middletown, CT: Wesleyan University Press.

Knobel, Dale T. 1996. *"America for the Americans": The Nativist Movement in the United States.* New York: Twayne.

La Gumina, Salvatore J. 1981. *The Immigrants Speak: Italian Americans Tell Their Story.* New York: Center for Migration Studies.

Massey, Douglas S., and Nancy A. Denton. 1993. *American Apartheid: Segregation and the Making of the Underclass.* Cambridge and London: Harvard University Press.

Miyares, Ines, Jennifer A. Paine, and Midori Nishi. 2000. "The Japanese in America," pp. 263–82 in Jesse O. McKee (ed.), *Ethnicity in Contemporary America,* 2nd ed. Lanham, MD: Rowman and Littlefield.

Mohl, Raymond A., and Neil Betten (eds.). 1970. *Urban America in Historical Perspective.* New York: Weybright and Talley.

Monkkonen, Eric H. 1988. *America Becomes Urban: The Development of U.S. Cities and Towns, 1780–1980.* Berkeley: University of California Press.

Muller, Thomas. 1993. *Immigrants and the American City.* New York: New York University Press.

Nelli, Humbert S. 1970. "Italians in Urban America: A Study in Ethnic Admustment," pp. 258–70 in Raymond A. Mohl and Neil Betten (eds.), *Urban America in Historical Perspective.* New York: Weybright and Talley.

Osterweis, Rollin G. 1953. *Three Centuries of New Haven, 1638–1938.* New Haven: Yale University Press.

Parrillo, Vincent N. 2000. *Strangers to These Shores,* 6th ed. Boston: Allyn and Bacon.

Romero, Simon, and Janet Elder. 2003. "Hispanics in U.S. Report Optimism." *New York Times.* (August 6): A1+.

Shannon, William V. 1989. *The American Irish: A Political and Social Portrait,* 2nd ed. Amherst: University of Massachusetts Press.

Spear, Allan H. 1970. "Black Chicago: The Making of a Negro Ghetto," pp. 324–34 in Raymond A. Mohl and Neil Batten (eds.), *Urban America in Historical Perspective.* New York: Weybright and Talley.

Steinberg, Stephen. 2001. *The Ethnic Myth: Race, Ethnicity, and Class in America,* 3rd ed. Boston: Beacon Press.

Thornton, Russell. 2001. "Trends Among American Indians in the United States, pp. 135–69 in Neil J. Smelser, William Julius Wilson, and Faith Mitchell (eds.), *America Becoming: Racial Trends and Their Consequences.* Vol 1. Washington, DC: National Academy Press.

Wade, Richard C. 1970. "Slavery in the Cities," pp. 140–60 in Raymond A. Mohl and Neil Batten (eds.), *Urban America in Historical Perspective.* New York: Weybright and Talley.

Wilson, William Julius. 1996. *When Work Disappears: The World of the New Urban Poor.* New York: Vintage Books.

Wright, Richard. 1991. *Black Boy.* New York: Library of America. Originally published in 1944.

Yancey, William L., Eugene P. Eriksen, and Richard N. Juliani. 1976. "Emergent Ethnicity: A Review and Reformulation." *American Sociological Review.* 41 (June): 391–403.

4

Starting from Home: Residential Location

Urbanized Housing Patterns
Ghettoized Living Strategy
Forced Relocation
Incarceration
Ethnic Urban Villages
Suburban Residence

Current Major Trends in Housing
Locating a Home: Perils of the Process
Initiating the Search
Completing the Search
Conclusion

The traditional American dream includes owning one's own home—a pleasant, comfortable dwelling in what's regarded as a good location. It's something many Americans take for granted. Benefiting from decent locations, they give little thought to the connection between living in a comfortable, safe, financially secure area and good opportunities for education, employment, valued contacts, and high-quality goods and services—issues to be explored in later chapters. What they are likely to heed is the steady stream of media stories about violence, crime, drug use, and other brutalities linked to "inner city" districts.

One evening in class a young white woman spoke to me following a discussion about urban neighborhoods. "I've got this friend," she said in a tense, earnest way. "I told him I was afraid to walk alone through the Briarwood area, and he said that was a racist reaction. " Fighting back tears she asked, "Is it racist to be afraid to enter a neighborhood everyone knows is dangerous?"

The topic of residential location has great significance in this book. Many sociologists, however, give it little attention. Textbooks on race and ethnicity have ignored or almost ignored the subject. The prevailing sense seems to be that if American citizens are free to pursue their occupational goals, then they will readily obtain decent housing. Case closed.

It is perplexing and disturbing that the historical pattern of systematic housing discrimination against blacks has been a largely overlooked topic. After all, as detailed commentary in upcoming chapters demonstrates, people's residential location is a fundamental starting point in their lives, affecting their chances for stable families, effective schooling, useful networking contacts, productive job training, and access to various jobs.

The opening three chapters have already suggested the important role of housing in American racial and ethnic history. We have seen that while white immigrant groups might initially encounter housing discrimination and difficult living conditions, they invariably found the restrictions waning as they gained an economic foothold. African Americans, we noted, were forced to live "history in reverse," starting to develop a firm residential and occupational foundation in many cities but within a few decades facing a relentless, widely supported campaign to set a color line that greatly restricted both their housing and job options.

In this section I look deeper into the macrosociological conditions affecting residential location, describing five prominent patterns of housing that have developed in American society. In each case, it is clear that the majority group has not only approved the option but also played the most decisive role in its implementation. The other principal section is microsociological, focusing on the unfolding of housing discrimination in interpersonal settings.

Urbanized Housing Patterns

It is safe to say that in most countries, including the United States, no major policies and approaches develop and unfold without wealthy and powerful groups' approval and support. That reality is apparent with the first pattern examined.

Ghettoized Living Strategy

A **ghetto** is an area of a city, often within its inner portion, where one ethnic or racial group predominates, usually because of restrictions the majority group imposes. The first application of the term was to the Jewish section of Venice, and by the sixteenth century European Jews, who originally clustered in voluntary ghettos for mutual convenience, faced growing legal restrictions compelling them to reside in what became compulsory ghettos.

In the United States, newly arrived European immigrants often gathered in neighborhoods surrounded by family members and friends, but these neighborhoods were seldom true ghettos, where a single ethnic group was numerically dominant (Borchert 1998).

The exception was blacks. As we noted in Chapter 2, the white majority group in eastern and midwestern cities greeted large numbers of migrating southern African Americans with unrelenting repression, at first using violence and intimidation and then a variety of legal means to force them into ghetto living. Recent statistics testify to the legacy these policies have produced: In 2000 the 30.5 million blacks living in U.S. cities and suburbs on average resided in an area that was 78 percent black—clearly representing numerical dominance (Center for Regional Policy Studies 2001).

The centerpiece in the creation of ghettos was the **racially restrictive covenant,** which was a contract among property owners prohibiting selected minorities from buying, leasing, or occupying property in that locale. In analyzing these covenants, we can see an interplay among various power groups bonded by their common segregationist purpose.

The first victims of restrictive covenants were Chinese immigrants. In 1892 in a California case, a panel of judges made the following ruling:

> It is understood and agreed by and between the parties hereto, their heirs and assigns, that the party of the first part shall never, without the consent of the party of the second part, his heirs or assigns, rent any of the buildings or ground owned by said party of the first, and fronting on said East Main Street, to a Chinaman or Chinamen. (Jones-Correa 2001, 548, 550)

It was not until thirty years later, however, that racially restrictive covenants became widespread. Between 1917 and 1921 when the Great Migration of southern blacks was at its height, riots directed against blacks occurred in fourteen different cities, sparking frequent lynchings, fire bombings, and assaults throughout the era. Although local economic and political leaders initially supported the riots, they eventually found them troublesome, leading to significant property loss and a host of civil suits. Racially restrictive covenants proved to be a more practical option.

By the late 1920s, private organizations throughout the North and Midwest had established many racially restrictive covenants, which one enthusiastic judge, who belonged to the Chicago Real Estate Board, lyrically declared were "like a marvelous delicately woven chain armor . . . [excluding] any members of a race not Caucasian" (Jones-Correa 2001, 559). Clearly, influential whites were deeply committed to segregated housing.

Real-estate boards, along with neighborhood and homeowners' associations, initially sponsored racially restrictive covenants in various cities. In fact, the Chicago Real Estate Board was particularly active, not only making certain that every all-white area in the city received covenants' protection but also promoting the foundation of the National Association of Real Estate Boards (NAREB), which headquartered in Chicago. In 1927 NAREB officials produced a standard racially restrictive covenant, which they shared with local real-estate boards around the country.

In the 1930s the federal government became increasingly involved in local issues including housing, and by 1938 Federal Housing Authority (FHA) officials had accepted NAREB standards, declaring that "if a neighborhood is to retain stability, it is necessary that properties shall continue to be occupied by the same social and racial classes" (Jones-Correa 2001, 565). The emphasis on "neighborhood stability" became a code phrase for restricting government housing assistance to whites. The new FHA standards made it much more likely that families living in all-white areas would receive low-interest federal loans than those residing in racially mixed or all-black areas.

In the 1940s and 1950s, the FHA continued to support segregated housing, making loans only to suburban developers who committed to keeping their housing all-white. Even though in 1948 the Supreme Court declared racially restrictive covenants unenforceable, the FHA fixation on preserving neighborhood stability by maintaining racial separation continued much longer. If for the years 1934 to 1960, for example, one assesses the volume of FHA mortgages given to a respective city's suburbs compared to its inner-city area, the proportion of per capita mortgage spending of suburb to city was five times greater for St. Louis's suburbs than for the city itself. Washington, D.C., and New York City displayed even more inequity, with the dispersal of mortgages to suburban Nassau County eleven times greater than to urban Brooklyn and sixty times greater than to the urban Bronx (Massey and Denton 1993, 53–54).

The overall chronology is clear. In cities influential whites initiated the use of racially restrictive covenants, which became the cornerstone of the ghettoized living strategy. The formation of NAREB led to nationally standardized racially restrictive covenants, and later FHA officials supported the exclusionary approach, establishing federal policies to produce racial segregation throughout the nation's urban and suburban communities.

It was a smooth coordination of government and private business—a partnership bolstered by the fact that FHA officials at both federal and local levels were former real-estate professionals well schooled to carry their segregationist standards from the private to the public sphere (Jones-Correa 2001, 565–66). Perhaps most important, the longtime use of racially restrictive covenants solidified an urban-based cultural tradition of housing discrimination, which, as the second major section of this chapter indicates, still resonates with many modern Americans.

The impact of these practices is unquestionable. Between 1930 and 1970, blacks' isolation in cities sharply increased. During that time span, nearly 5 million African Americans entered northern cities searching for industrial jobs, and they had no choice but to live in ghettos. The numerical changes were dramatic.

During those four decades, the average index of black isolation for neighborhoods of eighteen northern cities went from 31.7 to 73.5 percent. That means that in 1930 the average neighborhood for all African Americans living in those cities was 31.7 percent black; forty years later the black percentage in that average neighborhood had more than doubled—to 73.5 percent. In twelve southern cities, for which the 1930 indices of black isolation are not available, the 1970 average was slightly higher—76.4 percent (Massey and Denton 1993, 48).

In 1970 the indices of black isolation would have been lower if blacks who could have afforded housing outside ghetto areas had been able to obtain it. However, even though the Supreme Court in 1948 declared racially restrictive covenants unenforceable, a survey of real-estate practices revealed that in most American cities the mind-set that had supported them persisted. The study found, for example, that in the 1950s in Chicago 80 percent of realtors refused to sell blacks homes in white neighborhoods and 68 percent would not rent them property (Helper 1969). Banks and savings associations cooperated as realtors generally denied blacks loans.

In the 1950s and 1960s, suburbs prospered and expanded while cities, particularly their black sections, became increasingly impoverished. As poor southern blacks entered in large numbers and officials raised taxes to pay for increased services, whites continued to retreat to the suburbs to escape blacks, the growing tax burden, and the deteriorating urban setting.

Because northern and midwestern cities were in disarray, the influential groups whose activities or investment in capital and infrastructure required them to remain—various large businesses as well as universities, hospitals, libraries, and foundations—lobbied the federal government for help. Relief came with two national housing acts that provided local political leaders federal funds to purchase slum properties, clear "blighted" areas of residents and buildings, and then "redevelop" districts for business, high-priced apartments, extensions of hospitals and universities, or other facilities the elite would value. Part of the arrangement was that local governments had to supply replacement housing for uprooted residents.

One of the difficulties with these "urban renewal" programs was that guiding legislation was vague enough so that the local political and economic elite were able to annihilate any neighborhoods, most of which were black or primarily black, that they felt encroached on valued downtown territory (Massey and Denton 1993, 54–55).

William Ryan, a psychologist who was an astute observer of American cities in the 1960s, commented on the program's intent. He declared:

> In almost every urban renewal project, the objective was to get rid of a slum neighborhood (and the "undesirables" who lived there) to make room for "higher uses." The rehousing of the poor was never a matter that had the slightest priority. (Ryan 1976, 185)

The negative impact on inner-city areas, including many viable communities where people lived modestly but well, proceeded quickly. A major problem was that replacement housing was usually scarce, and relocated families often found themselves shuttled from one condemned neighborhood to another, perhaps just a few months ahead of the wrecker's ball. The toll on family stability had to be tremendous.

While doing a study of an agency battling poverty problems in Albany, New York, I attended a community meeting at which a topic of discussion was the circumstances leading to a local black teenager's indictment for murder. Toward the end of the discussion, the agency's widely respected director concluded, "For me the crowning event in this man's young life was the fact that over the past two years urban renewal initiatives forced his family to move nine times. Nine times! I defy anyone to maintain a stable family life in such circumstances" (Doob 1969, 66).

Most people displaced by such programs ended up in public housing, which ideally could have provided a positive living experience. However, the overriding commitments in public-housing construction involved, first, restricting its location to the scarce pockets of land lying next to or within recognized ghettos and as a result seldom if ever replacing as many units as were destroyed and, second, keeping costs minimal. Local political leaders usually authorized drab, poorly constructed, multi-unit, often high-rise projects, where most tenants felt little if any pride in their apartments and the surroundings and little incentive to maintain them in good condition. Through the 1950s and 1960s, as thousands of African Americans continued to pour into what had become increasingly restricted black, inner-city districts, they became more and more crowded.

William Ryan concluded that urban renewal did great damage to the poor, primarily black people living in the areas where it took place:

> Urban renewal is to the slum housing problem approximately as a crash reducing diet is to the problem of malnutrition. In the face of a problem that can only be solved by the massive construction of new low-income housing, urban renewal keeps destroying low-income housing. (Ryan 1976, 188)

At the time, however, most observers failed to appreciate this dire process. Public-relations messages touted urban renewal as a progressive policy for the entire local citizenry. In New Haven, for instance, commercial and residential revitalization in the downtown area had projected Mayor Richard Lee and his program into national prominence. Then in 1968, surprisingly and inexplicably, riots broke out in this "model city." Gradually, the truth dawned. Not all the local citizenry benefited from what indeed was a crash diet in the context of malnutrition. Quite the opposite.

A glimpse at recent housing conditions in inner-city areas suggests that the shortage has persisted. Low-cost rental housing, such as the Section 8 Program providing rent subsi-

TABLE 4.1   Historical Development of Blacks' Housing Segregation in Northern and Midwestern Cities

Dates	Blacks' Population Movement	Dominant-Group Behavior
1890–1900	Influx of about 174,000 blacks scattered through largely white residential areas	Little or no hostile response
1900–1920	Arrival of about 772,000 blacks	A series of race riots and violent actions supported by white leadership and restricting blacks' housing location
1920–1940	About 1,277,000 African Americans arriving from the South	White "improvement associations" using various legal means, including racially restrictive covenants, to restrict blacks' housing location; by 1940 boundaries of modern ghettoes established
1940–1990s	Crowded, deteriorating living conditions in inner-city areas, with blacks' average indices of isolation[1] more than doubling from 31.7 to 73.5 in eighteen northern cities between 1930 and 1970	Systematic exclusion of blacks from white-dominated residential sites and provision of limited, often poorly constructed public housing for crowded ghetto areas
2000	Urban and suburban blacks living in areas that average 78 percent black	Slight decline in discrimination against black renters and buyers

[1]An index of isolation is the citywide average percentage of a particular racial or ethnic group's membership within the selected neighborhoods where that group resides.

dies to low-income tenants in private housing, is badly underfunded, producing lengthy waiting lists. In 2002 in New Orleans, for instance, the waiting list for Section 8 vouchers had 19,000 names (Housing Authority of New Orleans 2002). Another bit of evidence about the housing shortage for poor blacks appears with statistics on homelessness. On any given day, there are between about 365,000 and 567,000 African Americans who are homeless—a much higher proportion than any other group demonstrates (Burt 2001; Burt, Aron, and Lee 2001). Table 4.1 summarizes the history of events producing blacks' housing segregation.

In the twenty-first century, most Americans no longer openly support a total residential separation of races. Yet a few do. Perhaps 20,000 Americans belong to between 250 and 300 white separatist groups declaring that both blacks' and whites' best interests are served if the two races remain apart. Matt Hale, leader of the National Socialist White Americans Party, phrased the position this way:

> We are separatists. We are—we don't consider ourselves supremacists in a sense because we are not out to rule anyone. We do believe the white race is a superior race, but we're not looking for the old, white supremacy where the white man's on top, the black man's on bottom, and the black man is working for the white man, etc. We'd like to have a total geographical separation where no race is oppressing the other. (Dobratz and Shanks-Meile 2000, 106)

Although white separatist groups' membership is fairly small, it appears that perhaps an additional 150,000 to 175,000 active sympathizers buy literature, make contributions, or attend occasional meetings (Dobratz and Shanks-Meile 2000, 25).

White supremacists would probably support a second approach to housing, which produces complete racial separation. Both forced relocation and incarceration, the subsequent housing pattern, often exist outside of cities. However, they often appear to be urbanized in character—both because they are the products of problems that have developed in cities and because their inhabitants tend to be urban in origin.

Forced Relocation

Whereas the ghettoized living strategy requires a racial minority to reside in a restricted part of a city, forced relocation compels the entire group to move to another, often distant place, destroying whatever pattern of living they have established. Native Americans' forced relocation onto reservations is a distinct American illustration. Sometimes the distances were great and the circumstances harsh. In 1838 federal government officials compelled 13,000 Cherokees to march over 1,000 miles from Georgia, Tennessee, and North Carolina to Oklahoma, with over 4,000 dying along the way from disease, starvation, and malnutrition (Parrillo 2000, 235–36).

The most publicized illustration of forced relocation occurred about a century after the so-called Trail of Tears. In 1942 the compulsory evacuation of Japanese American citizens living on the West Coast to "relocation centers" in the interior is the topic of the following Sociological Illustration.

SOCIOLOGICAL ILLUSTRATION
Japanese Americans' Forced Relocation

Shortly after the United States entered World War II, President Franklin Roosevelt signed Executive Order 9066, which excluded all people of Japanese descent living in Washington, Oregon, California, and Arizona from access to airports, dams, power plants, railroads, shipyards, and military institutions, where authorities believed they might commit serious acts of sabotage. In order to ensure that such destruction would not occur, the 110,000 Japanese Americans living in those four states received orders to secure or sell all personal possessions except those they could carry and to report to specific control stations, where government officials registered and labeled them with tags. Next they were sent in buses and trains to "assembly centers," which were off-season racetracks, unused fairgrounds, and abandoned stockyards that housed them for about three months while more permanent internment camps were built. Then "the internees," as they were officially designated, were moved to these ten concentration camps that were surrounded by barbed wire and under armed guards' surveillance. In remote sections of Utah, Arizona, Colorado, Wyoming, California, Idaho, and Utah, they remained for over three years until the war ended (Wakida 2000, xi–xii).

A variety of powerful interests supported the Japanese relocation. Political leaders like California Attorney General Earl Warren, later Chief Justice of the Supreme Court, described Japanese American citizens as a threat, singling out as most dangerous those children sent to Japan for schooling, where

> they are indoctrinated with the idea of Japanese imperialism. They receive their religious instruction which ties up their religion with their Emperor, and they come back imbued with the ideas and the policies of Imperial Japan. While I do not cast a reflection on every Japanese who is born in this country—of course we will have loyal ones—I do say that the consensus of opinion is that taking the groups by and large there is more potential danger to this State from the group that is born here than from the group born in Japan. (O'Brien and Fugita 1991, 47)

Warren went on to say that the difference between people of Japanese heritage and those of German and Italian ancestry, whose countries of origin were also opposing the United States in that war, was that the Japanese Americans came from a culture and way of life that was far more difficult for white Americans to understand and evaluate. Warren conveniently ignored the seemingly pertinent fact that the other two groups were white and Japanese Americans belonged to a racial minority.

Although some political officials like Earl Warren and Secretary of the Navy Frank Knox fanned the flames of public fear, other prominent individuals like liberal columnist Walter Lippmann, Mayor Fiorello La Guardia of New York City, and President Franklin Roosevelt, all of whom often championed minorities' rights, remained uncharacteristically silent, thereby tacitly supporting the relocation.

One reason some individuals and groups supported the Japanese relocation was the potential economic benefit. During about a half-century of residency in the United States, many Japanese Americans had become increasingly successful, starting as farmers but then moving into a variety of medium-sized urban businesses, particularly after restrictive legislation about owning and leasing land made it difficult to keep farming (Schaefer 1994, 376–77). When asked whether agribusiness officials had a self-serving profit motive fueling their support for Japanese relocation, the secretary of California's Grower-Shipper Association tersely replied, "We do" (Taylor 1942, 66).

With widespread, powerful support and little opposition, the relocation operation appeared to the public to run smoothly. For the inmates, however, that was hardly the case. Jeanne Wakatsuki Houston was a child when she and her family were sent to the Manzanar internment camp in the remote Owens Valley of California. She wrote, "The simple truth is the camp was no more ready for us when we got there than we were ready for it" (Houston 2000, 104). The family living quarters had bare floor, blankets as partitions separating rooms, and open ceilings allowing mischievous boys to scoot over-head and intrude into families' lives.

Many people who had lived in southern California were unaware they were going to be shipped to a much colder climate. The government issued clothing—military surplus from World War I, which usually proved several sizes too large for the often diminutive Japanese. The clothes, Houston noted, "flopped, they dangled, they hung." She added, "It seems comical, looking back; we were a band of Charlie Chaplins marooned in the California desert. But at the time, it was pure chaos" (Houston 2000, 105).

An uninterrupted chain of daily indignities became the standard way of life, but many families also faced life-threatening situations made much more difficult by restricted camp life. For instance, one woman gave birth in the camp, and because of the fact that there was no anesthesiologist present they couldn't operate, instead using huge forceps to remove the child and in the process cutting off her access to oxygen long enough to produce permanent brain damage. Gradually, painfully, the mother saw her daughter's distinct disadvantage revealed:

> There was another lady who had a baby about the same time and her baby started sitting up at six months or so. Well, my baby couldn't, and so I could see that her development was behind. Other children started walking, at around a year, and Madeline couldn't walk. She couldn't walk until she was twenty-two months, so I knew she was way behind in her development. (Ota 2000, 173)

Meanwhile, the woman's father, who earlier had been diagnosed as diabetic, was in another camp where the poor diet and the medical staff's refusal to accept that previously confirmed diagnosis contributed to his rapid decline and death (Ota 2000, 175–77).

Although some people were more effective than others in adapting to camp life, all internees were victims, forced to compete with each other for various scarce resources. Yoshiko Uchica, who was a resident of a camp in Topaz, Utah, explained:

> Most internees got into the habit of rushing for everything. They ran to the mess halls to be first in line, they dashed inside for the best tables and then rushed through their meals to get to the washtubs before the suds ran out. (Uchida 2000, 76)

All in all, most inmates learned to survive in this new, difficult, and crowded world. Survive, yes, but as one internee explained,

> the entire situation there, especially in the beginning—the packed sleeping quarters, the communal mess halls, the open toilets—all this was an open insult to that other, private self, a slap in the face you were powerless to change. (Houston 2000, 107).

In later years when former internees met for the first time, conversation often began with the question, "What camp were you in?" and proceeded with exchanges of personal camp experiences that were so intimate and detailed that listeners who were not in the camps felt excluded (Ima 1982, 266).

Over forty years after the war ended, the U.S. attorney general officially apologized to Japanese Americans for inflicting this destructive and demeaning experience on them. Congress allotted $20,000 to each surviving internee—an amount that, according to Congressman Ronald Dellums, who testified in favor of the allotment, was "meager . . . compensation for the pain and the agony" camp inmates experienced (Dellums 2000, 34).

Is forced relocation likely to occur again on American soil? A *Newsweek* poll conducted immediately after the September 11 terrorist attacks revealed that 32 percent of respondents favored forced relocation for Arab Americans and 62 percent opposed such an action (Levitas 2002, 23). Eight months after the attacks, a review of surveys indicated that the public was scarcely more supportive of restricting the freedom of Arab Americans than of limiting other ethnic groups. Some groups, notably African Americans, showed much greater concern than whites about individuals' potential loss of civil liberties (Clymer 2002).

Actions authorized by U.S. Attorney General John Ashcroft, however, were less restrained. A report issued by his department indicated that following the attacks of September 11, 2001, 762 people, mostly Arab and Muslim men, were detained, often with flimsy or inconsistent evidence and under harsh conditions. Although the numbers were much smaller than either the 110,000 Japanese American citizens placed in internment camps or the thousands of immigrants imprisoned for radical views

(continued)

during the Palmer raids of the 1920s, the approach was distinctly similar.

Eric L. Muller, a law professor specializing in immigrant groups' relations with the government, concluded that admittedly such cases are complicated. Following the September 11 attacks, it was reasonable to take ethnicity into account when evaluating suspects but not to place large numbers of Arabs in detention. Muller indicated that government politics were "not good yet in confining our uses of race and ethnicity to very moderated, limited intrusions. We just don't do it very well" (Liptak 2003, 14). It appears, in short, that federal officials like Ashcroft have learned little from the tragic experience of the Japanese relocation.

The case of Japanese relocation has revealed the precarious location minorities experience in a racialized social system, where majority-group interests dominate. Before World War II, many Japanese Americans were effectively establishing themselves

This young Japanese American girl was tagged for shipment to the relocation center in Owens Valley, an inland area in California, where, as her clothes suggest, it was likely to be much colder than in her coastal home.

in small businesses and in their communities, but the various forms of capital they had accumulated were lost when the political leadership opted to uproot them. The racialized nature of the political setting in which relocation developed was apparent when leaders normally sympathetic to racial minorities failed to be supportive.

Once placed in internment camps, Japanese Americans faced a brutalized structure that reflected the low priority the racialized system accorded them—deficient housing, clothing, sanitation facilities, food, medical treatment, and so forth. In the context of World War II, the political leadership appeared quite comfortable with the arrangement: in line with the toilet assumption (described in Chapter 1), out of sight, out of mind, with little or no attention to the indignities Japanese Americans suffered in their daily lives.

Incarceration, which is another housing option, actually constitutes a form of forced relocation.

Incarceration

The statistics are staggering. With 5 percent of the world's population, the United States criminal-justice system incarcerates 25 percent of the world's prisoners. In 2000 the total was 2 million individuals, a figure that had tripled since 1978. Because of its mammoth size, what critics call "the prison-industrial complex" is costly. For instance, over the past twenty years, California, which possesses the largest prison population of any state, has increased its annual prison budget sixfold to $31 billion. It now costs the state nearly twice as much per year ($20,925) to incarcerate an individual as it would to place the same individual on full scholarship in the University of California system of higher education ($10,592).

For all major racial and ethnic categories, the totals have been well above those for most other countries. All major western European nations have incarceration rates that are about or below 100 per 100,000 members of the population. In rising order, here are the figures for six categories of Americans per 100,000 population members:

- White women, 63
- Hispanic women, 117
- African American women, 380
- White men, 683
- Hispanic men, 1,715
- Black men, 4,777

For the year 2000, half the 2 million American prisoners were black (Braz, Brown, and DiBenedetto 2000; Duncan 2000; *Factbook: Race and Prison* 2002).

Why are such a disproportionate number of African Americans in prison? A number of analysts refer to the sense of threat that blacks create for whites. In a tradition dating back to slavery, both public officials and the white public have historically felt that blacks are inherently violent and rebellious and that the only way to deal with them is control and punishment. During slavery, corporeal punishment, often for nonexistent or minute infractions, was a constant. After the Civil War, lynching, beatings, killings, and race riots were means of imposing punitive control. In modern times the chief form of punishment is incarceration. The sense of threat whites feel from blacks' alleged violent tendencies is apparent in the pattern showing that the racial disparity in sentencing is greatest when the crime involves violence. For weapons and drug charges, for instance, blacks' sentences are about one-and-a-half times longer than whites', and over time the disparity has been increasing. Furthermore, in murder cases involving blacks and whites, prosecutors are much more likely to demand the death penalty if the victim is white and the alleged killer black than in the three other relationships (Bonilla-Silva 2001, 104–05; Cureton 2000; Cureton 2001; Eitle, D'Alessio, and Stolzenberg 2003; Doob 1999, 88–90; *Factbook: Race and Prison* 2002).

The mass media has been an important contributor to this sense of threat. Even though crime, including violent crime, has been dropping, media coverage of violence has sharply increased. Overwhelmingly, the central representations have involved black men. A former producer of the long-running TV reality show *Cops* admitted that most of the episodes displayed black men engaged in criminal acts and that although personally he regretted such a focus, the emphasis on hate and violence guaranteed the show's sustained success (Moore 2002).

Besides the threat issue, other conditions in blacks' lives increase their vulnerability to imprisonment. Consider the major issue of drug offenses, which has become the crime for which the largest number of individuals are imprisoned. Although evidence indicates that blacks are no more likely than whites to be involved in illicit drug offenses, two conditions make them more susceptible to arrest. First, African Americans, who disproportionately reside in poor areas with small, crowded apartments, often must do the transactions outdoors in streets, alleys, or abandoned buildings or in such public indoor places as bars or restaurants, whereas working-class or middle-class purchases are more likely to occur in more spacious, secluded private dwellings and other protected indoor locales. Second, dealers in unstable, poor areas have little choice but to sell to strangers, readily exposing them to undercover busts, in contrast to sellers in more stable settings, who are more likely to know their clientele and thus avoid comparable risk. In addition, since the mid-1980s, penalties for drug crimes have become steadily harsher, further accentuating the racial gap in incarceration. A particularly potent development is that federal law equates one gram of crack cocaine, primarily used by urban blacks and Hispanics, with 100 grams of powder cocaine, which is pharmacologically indistinguishable but used primarily by middle-class whites.

Over time the impact of this set of factors has greatly widened racial disparities in drug arrests. In 1965 the arrest rates for both nonwhites (primarily blacks) and whites were below 100 per 100,000 members of the population. Two decades later the nonwhite rate had shot up to nearly 1,500 while the white rate rose much more modestly—to about 200 (Tonry 1999). Although political leaders are often aware of why disparities in arrest rates occur, most continue to support current policies, finding that a "get tough" policy remains popular with many voters.

Such realities hit home for African Americans as they experience the incongruities the criminal-justice system imposes. In his youth Nathan McCall faced charges for two felonies, with very different results. In *Makes Me Wanna Holler,* this man, who eventually became a well-known journalist, explained:

> I shot and nearly killed Plaz, a black man, and got a thirty-day sentence; I robbed a white business and didn't lay a finger on anybody, and got twelve years. I got the message. I'd gotton it all my life: Don't fuck with white folks. (McCall 1994, 144)

Try to visualize a typical court scene for a poor black male. The defendant, if unable to afford bail, is likely to enter the courtroom handcuffed, immediately conveying an aura of guilt. His lawyer is likely to be fairly young and inexperienced, usually supplied at public expense, and even if committed to the defendant, probably carries a large case load, making it difficult to invest much time and energy in the case, which is likely to be a hard one to win. Many defendants will have a difficult history of family disorganization, juvenile and perhaps adult offense, and failed rehabilitative attempts. When the prosecutor recites the list of infractions, it is likely to sound convincing to many juries or judges that both as a means of forcefully instructing a wrongdoer that he cannot be allowed to keep breaking the law and also as a way of protecting society from a dangerous individual, prison is the most sensible option. Statements by lawyers, family members, or others, even if they are eloquent recitations of a defendant's disadvantaged circumstances and positive accomplishments, often fail to win over those making judgment in the contemporary world where what is perceived as the threatening presence of such defendants readily arouses camouflaged racism.

As blacks' numbers in prison have increased, a strong sense of resentment has built. Several decades ago writer Eldridge Cleaver, a longtime prisoner himself, stated:

> One thing that the judges, policemen, and administrators of prison seem never to have understood, and for which they certainly do not make any allowances, is that Negro convicts, basically, rather than see themselves as criminals and perpetrators of misdeeds, look upon themselves as prisoners of war, the victims of a vicious, dog-eat-dog social system that is so heinous as to cancel out their own malefactions: in the jungle there is no right or wrong. (Cleaver 1970, 64)

Besides black inmates, other members of black communities have adopted some version of this stance. For instance, **jury nullification** is the acquittal of a defendant, basing the decision on the alleged injustice the criminal-justice system has historically delivered to the defendant's racial or ethnic group and not on the evidence in the case at hand. This approach has been most prevalent in such urban environments as the New York City borough of the Bronx, where black and Latino juries have acquitted African American defendants in felony cases 48 percent of the time—nearly triple the 17 percent national acquittal rate for all defendants (Holden, Cohen, and de Lisser 1996).

This strategy receives cautious support from some legal experts. Paul Butler, an associate professor at the George Washington University Law School, posed the rhetorical question of whether black juries should exercise the practice in all cases or employ a more restrained standard. Butler's conclusion was that these jury members should be constantly aware of the political nature of their decisions, using their power in the black community's best interests. He added:

> In every case, the juror should be guided by her view of what is "just." (Have more faith, I should add, in the average black juror's idea of justice than I do in the idea that is embodied in the [abstract] "rule of law)." (Butler 1996, 337)

Whereas incarceration, forced relocation, and ghetto living have often been negative settings for their inhabitants, ethnic urban villages represent a more diversified context for living.

Ethnic Urban Villages

"I couldn't believe it," a flabbergasted associate told me recently. "There I was, lost in the middle of Los Angeles, with nobody around who could give me directions in English. I might as well have been in Mexico or Peru." Although exaggerated, this statement does introduce a current reality: California now contains over 11 million Hispanics, with at least a third living in Los Angeles County (U.S. Census Bureau 2000).

Many recently arrived members of racial minorities find that both comfort and practicality suggest that they locate in neighborhoods where their own ethnic group is the numerically dominant presence. Historically, they had neither the majority group's consent nor the economic resources to live elsewhere. Before World War II, restrictive covenants in housing often singled out Catholics and Jews along with blacks, thus greatly limiting where these groups could live (Brodkin 1999, 46–48).

In the late 1950s, sociologist Herbert J. Gans (1962, 4) used the term **urban village** to describe a city-based community where the members of one or more ethnic groups seek to adapt their own cultural standards and activities to the new, sometimes disorienting setting.

Studying the largely Italian American West End of Boston, Gans learned that while a range of options on sociability existed, most residents chose to be friendly and fairly outgoing and, as long as they weren't negatively affected, tolerant toward such offbeat types as alcoholics, mentally ill individuals, or "bohemians"—middle-class people with a looser, more raucous lifestyle than generally practiced during that fairly sedate era. Members of this urban village also maintained a set of shared attitudes toward their community—an appreciation of the low rents, modest cost of living, and easy access to downtown stores and jobs as well as a sense of common fate in dealing with such trials as irresponsible absentee landlords or overdue bills. For many families issues like job layoffs, illness, mental illness, alcoholism, desertion, or death were never far away, and when an emergency occurred, neighbors readily helped each other (Gans 1962, 14–15).

Urban villages are hardly new. In Chapter 3 we saw that Irish immigrants arrived during the famine era and Italians several decades later almost invariably moved into them, taking a generation or more to improve their economic status and then with rising social-class position venturing out from the city's core toward the suburbs. Other European immigrant groups followed a similar pattern, with most newly arrived groups facing distinct housing and job discrimination.

Eastern European Jews, most of whom settled on the Lower East Side of New York City between 1880 and 1920, were a notable case. Living in a dense, segregated urban village, many who had been students, professionals, or intellectuals in Europe found these job options unavailable. They accepted their working-class status, considering themselves exploited workers who in a Marxist tradition needed to struggle to overcome the injustices inflicted on them. Political radicals were central players in creating the basic elements in this urban community, where mutual aid societies like the Workmen's Circle, secular schools, literary and theatre societies, and summer camps all featured criticism of capitalist society and the need to redistribute wealth by establishing a socialist economy.

The International Ladies Garments Workers Union and the Amalgamated Clothing Workers Union were prominent supporters of socialist values. These unions initiated a massive wave of strikes, beginning with female shirtwaist makers in New York City in 1909 and continuing both there and in Chicago until 1914. In the first two decades of the twentieth century, Jewish women on the Lower East Side were not only active participants in union activity but also were the major actors in meat boycotts, food protests, and rent strikes (Brodkin 1999, 108–20).

After World War II, Jews were beneficiaries of an expanding, more pluralistic economy. Jewish intellectuals, writers, actors, and comedians gained mainstream recognition, further promoting Jews' widespread acceptance and motivating them to tone down earlier radical views and actions. As their economic foothold deepened, Jews moved out of urban villages into suburbs, where, unlike blacks, they almost always obtained full acceptance (Brodkin 1999, 138–55).

Newly arrived immigrant groups, however, still live in urban villages. The 2000 census indicated that on average the 30.7 million Latinos in American cities and suburbs inhabited areas that were 64.6 percent Latino (Center for Regional Policy Studies 2001), suggesting that many if not most resided in urban villages.

New York City's East Harlem, where in 1966 I lived and conducted my dissertation research, represented such a setting. It was a vibrant Puerto Rican community. On pleasant evenings people sat on their stoops or in nearby chairs chatting or playing cards; middle-aged men gathered for chess or checkers in front of the men's club in one brownstone's basement; and children were everywhere, some occupied with swings or the jungle gym in the concrete-floored park across the street while several girls played jacks or jumped rope on the sidewalks, and many boys engaged in stickball or football in the street. I joined many of the boys' games and soon learned that there was an added element to the inner-city version missing from my previous experience: the frequent presence of cars. Not a major problem since block traffic ran one-way and the first observer's loud "CAR!" quickly alerted us to stop all action—unless a play was under way. Then someone would shout for the car to halt, and it would wait until the action ceased. I never saw a close call nor even heard a horn beep in impatience. Drivers in the area appeared to realize that travel east or west through the blocks' village-like interior would not be as speedy as the rapid north/south passage on the avenues bordering the blocks.

The street was the center of so much activity: the place to catch up on the latest news about either Maria's planned visit to the island or José's likely promotion; to get the recipe from Alicia for the tasty cake she made for the church bake sale; to buy a watch, radio, or custom jewelry from the thin man who at dusk regularly slipped through the block selling what was known to be "hot" merchandise; or just a few steps off the street to enter a ground-level apartment and place a few dollars on the numbers.

Although everyone was poor, they helped each other with advice, emotional support, child care, rides, running errands, and money. Even an outsider was a beneficiary. Nearly every evening at about ten o'clock, I showed up at my friend Tony's apartment, where his fiancée's father promptly appeared with a loaf of steaming hot, thickly buttered Spanish bread and a bag of frosty cokes.

Like Puerto Ricans in New York City, Mexicans in Los Angeles have often developed urban villages. In the 1920s, driven by poverty and political turmoil, substantial numbers of Mexicans came to the Los Angeles area. By modern standards, however, the totals were modest, not exceeding more than 40,000 before 1950. The new arrivals took a variety of low-paying positions—in construction, the garment industry, restaurants, service stations, and laundries, with women concentrated in the garment industry. They tended to secure jobs by underpricing those already there, and besides chronically low pay, found themselves facing such issues as underemployment, seasonality, and poor working conditions. Still it was a start—in a country whose welcome was often inhospitable but whose opportunities were considerably greater than those available in Mexico.

Most believed they would return to the homeland. This outlook hardly set them apart from other immigrant groups; the difference was that proximity to Mexico made migration to the United States a less arduous process than other groups experienced.

The earliest arrivals often had homes that were mere shacks built of old oil cans, tin slabs, scrap lumber, or boxes. Within a few years, however, some modestly successful workers were buying pleasant bungalows located on hilltops, shaded by large pepper trees, and surrounded by flower and vegetable gardens. All of these urban villagers were living in *México de afuera*—Mexico outside the homeland. It was a new Mexico, where, surrounded by family, friends, and other compatriots and with fewer troubles than in the old country, the sense of a better life often prevailed (Monroy 1999, 37–39).

Living in *México de afuera,* especially for the children of immigrants, often meant living between two cultures and not belonging fully to either one. Although family and community provided a grounding and protection in the new urban setting, young people often felt the drawing power of *americano* popular culture—its movies set new romantic standards, its shops and magazines modeled the latest clothing styles, and its lifestyle represented a more liberated way of life, especially for women. Battles with parents could be titanic. In 1932 eighteen-year-old Henrietta complained:

> I never had any fun since I was 16 years old. As soon as I was 16, my father began to watch me and would not let me go anywhere or have any friends come home. He was born in old Mexico but he has been here long enough to know how people do things. The way it is with the Mexicans, the bigger a girl is, the farther they pull her into the house. (Monroy 1999, 168)

Although Mexican immigrants and the children of immigrants found themselves caught between two cultures, they controlled local Mexican American clubs and social networks, permitting them to dominate new arrivals. Nowadays, for instance, in the city of Santa Paula located sixty miles northeast of Los Angeles, recent immigrants seeking full social inclusion in the local urban village must conform to long-term residents' cultural standards—speaking English effectively, adopting modern clothing styles, and finding an urban-based job, decidedly not work in the citrus industry (Menchaca 1995, 213–14). In an upcoming Sociological Illustration, the discussion focuses on Mexican American life in Santa Paula.

Suburban living, the last of the five housing patterns, produces a distinctly different lifestyle from residence in an urban village.

Suburban Residence

A **suburb** is a politically independent municipality that develops next to or in the vicinity of a central city. In the nineteenth century, modern-sounding appraisals of suburban living began appearing. In 1851 Nathaniel Willis, a prosperous resident of suburban Westchester county, some twenty miles removed from the filth, overcrowding, and hustle-and-bustle of New York City, lamented the area's tedious homogeneity. "Miles upon miles of unmitigated prosperity weary the eye," he complained.

> Lawns and park-gates, groves and verandahs, ornamental woods and neat walls, trim edges and well-placed shrubberies, fine homes and large stables, neat gravel walks and nobody on them—are notes upon one chord, and they certainly seemed to me to make a dull tune of Westchester. (Stilgoe 1988, 68)

Nowadays, critics of suburbs around the country offer similar complaints. They are sites of placid homogeneity, where most residents are escaping urban problems to lead a disengaged, almost anonymous existence.

Sociologist M. P. Baumgartner (1988) concluded that the dominant suburban theme is what he called "moral minimalism," where people are willing to interact with each other only when circumstances are easy. They shun confrontation and conflict, often going to extensive lengths to avoid pursuing grievances and initiating police intervention only if they can remain anonymous in the process. Moral minimalism also applies to mutual aid. Research has shown that as contact among residents becomes less intimate, they are increasingly disinclined to provide material aid or emotional support when a neighbor could use assistance. Both conditions, especially the second, stand in distinct contrast with urban villages' way of life.

This lack of community distinctly affects suburban residents' existence, perhaps most notably for youths, who are developing their basic sense of how to relate to others. Baumgartner described the case of Bob Zimmer, a teenager from a middle-class family. One Sunday morning Zimmer returned home to find his new stereo tapedeck missing from his car. Because the car had been parked behind his house, he concluded that it was unlikely that someone had just happened upon it and stolen the tapedeck. After some thought he concluded that a particular friend was the culprit. Zimmer's basis for the conclusion was that the friend had a history of committing thefts and had frequently been in trouble with the police; besides, the young man knew about the tapedeck and was aware that the family would be at church that morning. Zimmer's parents and siblings agreed with his conclusion, and the parents, who had distinct misgivings about the friendship, urged that he terminate the relationship. Zimmer did just that; he never confronted the former friend with the evidence, nor did he contact the police. Baumgartner concluded, "In a classic case of avoidance, he simply altered the terms of the relationship drastically and without notice" (Baumgartner 1988, 78).

Not surprisingly, in such a detached atmosphere it is not easy to interest suburban dwellers in addressing nearby urban problems. For several years I belonged to a group composed of both urban and suburban residents promoting regionalism—a recognition of the interdependent relationship of a city to its suburbs and the necessity for those distinctly wealthier suburbs, which receive various important benefits from the city, to assist in addressing its problems. In our case the dominant position was that the poverty and decline of New Haven, the region's central city, invariably affects its suburbs, whose residents often depend on the city for their jobs as well as a wide variety of services, including hospitals, specialty stores, restaurants, and theaters: in short, help New Haven improve its employment opportunities and schooling and overcome its scarcity of housing or suffer the impact of its continuing decline. Suburban meetings, usually in churches supporting the initiative, might draw anywhere from 100 to 200 people for a community's first gathering, but few of those individuals signed up for subsequent involvement. The regionalism group maintained about a dozen members for over three years, and then when it became apparent that the suburban political leaders and citizens wanted little involvement in the cooperative venture, it disbanded.

One potent reality confronting supporters of regionalism is that usually they find themselves attempting to organize primarily white, middle-class suburbanites, who often moved out of the city to escape racial minorities and urban problems. It appears that people who are used to living in racial separation are not likely to embrace integration. One of housing researchers' findings is that most whites are willing to remain in a given area if the black population is under 8 percent, but once it passes that "tipping point," they move out, often in droves (Hacker 1992, 36). So an occasional black family in a white suburb is not a difficulty, but increasing numbers can cause growing concern and eventually contribute to changing the area's racial character. In contrast, recent research shows that among whites a comparable concern does not exist toward Latino or Asian families, who are generally accepted in substantial numbers in the suburbs (Emerson, Chai, and Yancey 2001).*

Some whites, however, are dissatisfied with suburbs' frequent racial homogeneity. In David K. Shipler's *A Country of Strangers,* he described a recent college graduate who lamented that both her residential and work sites in Washington, D.C., were almost completely segregated. "Where I get on the Metro [subway] is sort of a splitting point," she explained.

> My train I get on, it goes to Virginia, and it's primarily white people who take that train. And the other train, it must go to Southeast or Northwest {Washington, D.C.], it's the Green Line, and there's not a single white person. It's like they put all the black people on the train and take them away, and they put all the white people on the train going the other direction and take them away. (Shipler 1997, 32)

On those limited occasions when suburban schools cooperate to integrate urban, primarily black students, the results are mixed. To begin, the numbers of students brought in are likely to be small, perhaps 2 or 3 percent of the total student body since large numbers of blacks make whites uncomfortable. Lexington's coordinator of the Metro program, which brought blacks from Boston to this large white suburban high school, explained that

---

*In the next section, we examine this issue in greater detail, finding that whites' attitudes toward blacks' presence in their neighborhoods is a more complex issue than described here.

most observers saw the children as living in two very different worlds. She indicated that urban and suburban settings were highly divergent ways of living—"that it has to do with street savvy or street naîveté. It has to do with whether or not you know how to ride the T!" (Shipler 1997, 65). She laughed at her own reference to riding the subway system, which was a normal experience for city kids but alien to most suburban teens.

A handful of Metro students indicated that a number of teachers discriminated against them, and David Wilson, the principal, agreed, illustrating with the case of a biology teacher, whom he had to confront because over several years there were six or seven convincing cases where black students alleged discriminatory treatment. Wilson was one of a number of white staff members at the school who felt that among students, whites' much greater affluence drove a wedge between the two groups. To compensate for this disadvantage, each black child had a host family in Lexington, which served as a home base for after-school visits and overnight stays. Some youngsters formed lasting attachments to these families, who would sometimes show up at games or plays in the role of substitute parents. In spite of the power of these attachments, however, the black students were left with an often stark contrast between this suburban family life and the struggles they and their families faced back in Boston.

All the differences, however, did not favor the suburban students. Peggy Dyro, who taught English and history, loved having blacks from Boston in her classes, detecting a sense of community missing in the suburban children's lives. In contrast, Dyro asserted, the Lexington parents were much more focused on "earning and getting," leaving them little time to relate to their own children. She added:

> But there isn't the richness of culture that I see in a lot of black kids coming from in the city. They [whites] don't have such touch with their families—you know, grandparents, that sort of stuff. There isn't that much conversance with what struggle really is: reaching down and finding—when you've got nothing left—new resources. There isn't a whole lot of that. By the same token, because there is this created thing called poverty, and this created culture called inner-city life, it lives on the underbelly of capitalism. It wants really fancy sneakers and real fancy leather goods and real shiny gold. (Shipler 1997, 68)

If nothing else, these two sets of students in the Lexington schools had the chance to interact with each other, obtaining some sense of each other's world. Normally, both suburban and inner-city students are isolated from such exposure.

Whereas these blacks students were isolated from the suburbs, others reside in them. A study of the 102 most populous metropolitan U.S. areas indicated that between 1990 and 2000 the segment of suburban dwellers belonging to racial and ethnic minorities increased from 19 to 27 percent. From least to most, the percentages of suburban dwellers for the four largest racial/ethnic categories were the following:

- Blacks, 39 percent
- Hispanics (of any race), 50 percent
- Asians, 55 percent
- Whites, 73 percent

Thirty-five of the urban areas in this study were designated "melting pot metros," serving as immigration magnets because of their employment potential. The suburbs of such melting pot metros as New York, Los Angeles, San Francisco, Miami, and Chicago have shown particularly high proportions of racial minorities, especially Hispanic and Asian Americans.

Although whites represent nearly three out of four suburban residents, they left the suburbs in substantial numbers during the 1990s. The largest white suburban losses were in melting pot metros—areas where minority numbers had sharply increased. There continue to be thirteen largely white metropolitan areas in the South and West, notably in the vicinity of cities like Seattle, Tampa, and Colorado Springs (Frey 2001).

Will these changing racial/ethnic compositions influence suburban dwellers' outlooks and activities, perhaps promoting activism on such issues as regionalism? Although such a potential exists, no current evidence has supported such a trend.

Besides these five broad patterns, which are summarized in Table 4.2, certain distinct trends in housing are presently apparent in our society.

Current Major Trends in Housing

The standard measure of housing segregation is the **index of dissimilarity,** which indicates the percentage of a particular racial group that would need to change residential location in order to achieve racial evenness—a condition in which that racial group's representation throughout a city's census districts would be dispersed proportionate to its overall representation in relation to non-Hispanic whites in the city. Consider, for instance, a city where a certain group is 20 percent of the overall population, but that group represents 60 percent of the population in the districts where its members reside. In this case the group has an index of dissimilarity of 40, meaning that 40 percent of its members would need to move into other census tracts in the city to obtain racial evenness. High indices of dissimilarity represent high levels of segregation.

Over time one dominant pattern has been apparent. Nancy Denton and Douglas Massey, a pair of sociologists specializing in housing discrimination, wrote, "Blacks represent a major exception to the pattern of declining segregation with rising socioeconomic status" (Denton and Massey 1988, 798). As we noted in earlier chapters, most ethnic and racial groups move into the residential mainstream over time. Even as they advance occupationally, African Americans often face discrimination in this regard.

Recent urban/suburban housing patterns involving other racial minorities are also noteworthy. The decades of the 1980s and 1990s brought a sharply rising influx of both Hispanic and Asian immigrants, most of whom were low-income and took modestly paying jobs that financially restricted their residential location. As a result of these rising immigrant populations, both groups have recently become slightly more residentially segregated from whites. During these same years, African Americans have actually decreased their indices of dissimilarity (Darden 1998; Emerson, Chai, and Yancey 2001, 932).

Census data comparing 1990 to 2000 dissimilarity indices for the three largest minority groups living in American cities and suburbs provide the following figures:

- Asian/Pacific Islanders, 41.2 percent to 41.4 percent
- Hispanics, 49.7 percent to 51 percent
- African Americans, 67.8 percent to 64.3 percent (Center for Regional Policy Studies 2001)

TABLE 4.2 **Characteristics of Urbanized Housing Patterns**

	Most Prominent Participants	**Major Impetus Producing It**	**Negative Qualities**
Ghettoized living strategy	Racial minorities, particularly blacks	Majority group's containment and control of enlarging minority group employed for low-income jobs	Highly discriminatory restriction curtailing mainstream options and producing serious social problems
Forced relocation	Various racial minorities, notably Native Americans and Japanese Americans	Control of an entire minority group seen as an immediate threat	Loss of physical freedom creating isolation from general society in a debilitating setting
Incarceration	Disproportionate representation of racial minorities, especially African American men	Majority group's control of selected minority-group members considered an immediate threat	Loss of physical freedom creating isolation from general society in a debilitating setting
Ethnic urban village	Various groups, particularly newly arrived ethnic groups	Group members seeking cheap, hospitable living quarters	The variety of problems facing low-income, urban communities, including stereotyping and discriminatory treatment
Suburban living	Disproportionately white membership especially in wealthier areas	Affluent people looking for spacious, quiet, clean residential location	Sanitized setting, encouraging moral minimalism and often isolation from minority groups

Although African Americans' index of dissimilarity has shown a slight decline, recent data indicate that across four income groups blacks remain highly segregated from non-Hispanic whites, with blacks' indices of dissimilarity actually increasing as income rises. Furthermore, middle-class blacks who have white neighbors tend to be distinctly more affluent than those whites. Meanwhile, Hispanics and Asians have not only been less segregated than African Americans, but their indices of dissimilarity have declined sharply with rising income (Alba, Logan, and Stults 2000; Massey and Fischer 1999).

One contributing factor has been whites' perception of blacks. A recent national study of almost 1,700 randomly chosen white Americans found that the respondents reported that the percentage of Hispanics or Asians in a neighborhood did not matter but that with African Americans once the figure rose above 15 percent, they were unlikely to buy in that area. This refusal was particularly pronounced with individuals having children under eighteen (Emerson, Chai, and Yancey 2001).

Sociologist Joe T. Darden suggested that in evaluating Asians, white Hispanics, and blacks, the white majority group uses different criteria—the "criteria of ethnicity" for

Asians and white Hispanics, meaning that with occupational progress both those groups are encouraged to follow European groups' progress into the residential mainstream. For blacks, Darden indicated, whites employ "a racial criterion," promoting a uniquely exclusionary housing pattern for occupationally mobile blacks (Darden 1998).

Whites' attitudes toward blacks promote their residential segregation, but it is hardly the only contributing factor. Recall the general statement about racism and the racialized social system in Chapter 2: Once established as racialized, the system takes on a life of its own and produces a more significant impact than the racist ideology itself.

Writing about housing segregation, sociologist John Yinger reached a similar conclusion. According to Yinger, whites are less concerned about the number of blacks in their neighborhood than about the avoidance of the embodiment of the racialized social system, namely a ghetto and its inhabitants—a commitment to stay as far as possible from what is perceived as the destructive impact of a "black area." A study comprising a large sample of metropolitan areas found that the more segregated the area in which blacks live, the greater the discrimination they face from realtors in seeking new housing. On the other hand, if whites do not feel the ghetto's encroachment, they become fairly relaxed about the number of minorities in their neighborhood. As discussed earlier, it is apparent that the prospect of contact with ghetto residents draws out the fears associated with camouflaged racism.

A study of Chicago's metropolitan areas demonstrated that about a tenth of the city's population lived in neighborhoods that displayed a well-integrated combination of whites, blacks, and Hispanics that had remained stable for well over a decade. Most of these areas were adjoining the suburbs, distinctly separated from the expanding ghetto districts in Chicago's western and southern portions (Yinger 1995, 120–22). All in all, the potency of the racialized social system triggers whites' race-related fears, making them concerned about the negative impact of black ghettos on the value of their properties and schools as well as both safety and comfort. This line of thought suggests that in a racialized social system, many whites' opposition to desegregation centers on attributes of the ghetto, perhaps more than a racist ideology directed simply toward all blacks.

In fact, whites have not been the only group displaying this reaction. Research indicated that when middle-class African Americans in all-black Chicago neighborhoods described their locales as changing racially, they meant that poor blacks were coming in, lowering property values and causing them to be pessimistic about the area's future (Shipler 1997, 438).

Often trapped by the racialized social system, African Americans have had different housing experiences from those Europeans encountered. The impact of the racialized social system should remain in mind as the focus shifts from the larger, macrosociological picture of housing patterns established over time and space to microsociological immediacies of buying and renting houses and apartments.

Locating a Home: Perils of the Process

In 1991 my wife and I sold a condominium to a black couple. Three times in the course of the sale the buyer's agent, who was white, behaved badly, twice showing up very late for appointments with the buyers and once failing to transmit information about a necessary repair. Was racism involved, or was the agent simply an equal-opportunity incompetent? We'll never know.

What we do know is the result of a form of experimental research referred to as "paired testing," where two individuals, one white and one a minority-group member and closely matched on such factors as income, job type, financial assets, and credit rating, answer the same housing advertisement and then record their experience, determining on a number of dimensions whether or not discrimination occurred. In 1977, 1989, and 2000, the U.S. Department of Housing and Urban Development (HUD) conducted the Housing Discrimination Study (HDS). In 2000, 4,600 paired tests took place in twenty-three metropolitan areas nationwide. Based on the findings, observers concluded that between 2 and 3 million cases of housing discrimination occur annually (HUD User 2003; Minerbrook 1996; National Fair Housing Alliance 2003).

Our current discussion involves two stages—initiating the search and completing the search.

Initiating the Search

In the 2000 HDS, when compared to whites, prospective renters belonging to three major minority groups experienced some form of discrimination in the following proportion of cases:

- Asian and Pacific Islanders, 21 percent (tested in eleven metropolitan areas)
- African Americans, 22 percent
- Hispanics, 26 percent
- Native Americans, 29 percent (tested in three states)

Among potential buyers the figures were as follows:

- African Americans, 17 percent
- Native Americans, 17 percent (only tested in New Mexico)
- Hispanics, 20 percent
- Asian and Pacific Islanders, 20 percent (tested in eleven metropolitan areas)

For Hispanics and African Americans, the only two groups compared to whites in the earlier studies, the discrimination totals fell somewhat lower in the 2000 HDS. The major discriminations these two groups suffered entailed learning of fewer units and seeing fewer than white counterparts (HUD User 2003; HUD News Release 2003; NAHREP 2003).

The 2000 HDS also addressed another important issue. A truism in the real-estate industry is that the three most important issues in clients' search are location, location, and location. A common tactic that appears when clients are trying to locate a home is **steering,** which is a real-estate agent's effort to direct customers toward residential areas where their racial or ethnic group is concentrated. Historically, the practice has been most common with black clients, whom agents have sometimes tried to steer away from all-white or nearly all-white neighborhoods, knowing that current and prospective white residents often resist more than a small percentage of black neighbors.

The 2000 HDS provided data on different kinds of agents' behavior related to steering. In the areas of recommending and showing homes to prospective renters and buyers, the research found a slight tendency, which was weakly significant statistically, to show biased treatment toward both blacks and Hispanics.

As far as agents' commentary was concerned, however, the difference was more substantial. Blacks were 15 percent less likely than whites to hear positive comments about homes in census districts with high concentrations of whites and also heard 12 percent fewer positive comments about more affluent areas. The respective numbers for Hispanics were much lower—6 percent and no difference respectively (Reade 2000). These data suggest that especially for African Americans steering persists but more subtly than in the past.

Historically, as the following episode suggests, real-estate agents could simply build steering into their regular practice. Shortly before the upcoming exchange between Puerto Rican writer Piri Thomas and his real-estate agent occurred, Thomas himself had located a buyer for his house. At first the agent was enthusiastic. However, when Thomas handed him a piece of paper on which the buyer's name and address were written, the enthusiasm quickly faded. "What was the matter?" Thomas wanted to know.

> "Was the family black?" Mr. Hendricks asked.
>
> "That's right. Why" I asked knowing the why all the time.
>
> "Really, Mr. Thomas, I don't know quite how to say this, but you certainly must know that Silver View is a, er . . . white community and they wouldn't be happy there . . . and you bought your house from Mr. Baldwin, who's lived here many years and his parents before him, and, well, you being, er . . . Spanish is not like. . . ."
>
> My blood was tearing itself into my eyeball.
>
> "Why don't you just come out with it, fella?" My eyes just stared into his.
>
> "Well, it's not that I mind, but the people, I mean their homes, they've worked hard and do mind, ah . . . mixing, and well, dammit, I have lived here all my life.
>
> "Real estate is my livelihood, and if I sold to a colored family property in Silver View, well. . . . Can you understand? I mean put yourself in my place." (Thomas 1973, 210)

No, he wouldn't do that, Thomas replied. He dismissed the agent and prepared to sell the house directly to the black family, but threatened by members of the all-white Better Civic Improvement Committee, the prospective purchaser withdrew.

Although steering is fairly common, encounters with it can catch clients by surprise. Several years ago, one of my students described a situation in which she and her husband wanted to see homes in a particular area. The real-estate agent, a polite, seemingly accommodating individual, appeared to have misunderstood their preference and instead offered to take them to another area. Thinking the agent was confused, the wife repeated the request, and the agent again gave the same reply. Then the husband repeated the question with an identical result. "Finally," the woman told the class, "it was clear he understood us perfectly, and that no matter how many times we asked, he was going to use that evasive technique to keep a black couple from seeing a house in that neighborhood."

Although steering remains a common practice, blockbusting was effectively banned following the passage of the Fair Housing Act of 1968. **Blockbusting** is a realtor's attempt to convince individuals to vacate an area where they own or rent property, telling them that an influx of a nearby racial or ethnic group is imminent. Typically, blockbusting involved all-white neighborhoods where real-estate agents used letters, telephone calls, or home visits to induce panic selling by "warning" white residents that blacks from an adjacent ghetto were about to "invade" their community. In one situation involving mail solicitation, owners were urged to sell "before it was too late" or "before the value drops further" (Feagin and Feagin 1986, 94).

The earliest practice of blockbusting occurred in the opening two decades of the twentieth century—after whites had begun forcing blacks into ghettos. The blockbusting agents, sometimes called "white blackmailers," usually operated outside the bounds of the mainstream real-estate and finance industries, which at least officially shunned the practice.

During the 1950s and 1960s, however, blockbusting remained a popular enterprise, involving many neighborhoods in such cities as Chicago, New York, Cleveland, Washington, Baltimore, Philadelphia, and Boston (Orser 1998). Realtors not only received their normal commissions but often engaged in financial speculation, clearing very large sums when one distraught white family after another sold a house for a modest amount and then within one or two weeks a black family paid double the price. Frequently, a neighborhood turned over quickly. A white resident of Mattapan, a neighborhood bordering Boston's black ghetto of Roxbury, indicated that blockbusting "became a nightmare. Out of 141 white families on my street, only seven were left within two years" (Yinger 1995, 123).

For what portion of black ghettos' girth is blockbusting responsible? To my knowledge no expert hazards a guess, but since the practice was a sixty-year stimulus to ghettos' expansion, the actual figure must be impressive.

Although blockbusting and other realtors' practices have been central to housing discrimination, homeowners and landlords can also contribute. A telephone audit study in Philadelphia found clear evidence of discriminatory responses, with not only race but social class having an impact. The auditors represented six categories of race-class-gender: white middle-class females, white middle-class males, black middle-class females, black middle-class males, black lower-class females, and black lower-class males. Apparently, over the telephone the landlords could effectively identify the different types, and there was a distinctly discriminatory pattern involving such issues as informing the caller of available units, returning phone messages, and charging an application fee. While whites received a more positive response than African Americans, there were further distinctions made among blacks: Lower-class blacks obtained less access to rental housing than middle-class blacks, and black females encountered more discrimination than black males. Lower-class black females were distinctly the most disadvantaged group (Massey and Lundy 2001).

In another study the researchers quoted from a respondent whose experience demonstrated the significance of the social-class factor. The woman was interested in an apartment advertised in the newspaper:

> She called, and they told her that the apartment was rented. And she called [a friend] on the phone and said, "I'd like for you to call them because you sound like a white person." And [the friend] called and the apartment was still unrented. (Feagin and Sikes 1994, 229)

Once customers have examined available units, they are interested in closing a deal, and the second stage begins.

Completing the Search

The HDS studies described a variety of ways real-estate agents and others discriminated in completing a transaction. Sometimes agents were biased in encouraging the minority testers to conclude the transaction, making fewer follow-up calls or arranging fewer future meetings, and also providing less assistance with financing (HUD User 2003; NAHREP 2003). More factors than agents, however, affected the completion of a housing search.

To complete a sale, prospective buyers usually need a loan from a bank or lending agency. Historically, African Americans have had more difficulty than whites in getting

Over time, housing discrimination against blacks has been declining.

loans, including mortgages. A major contributor has been that in the past before credit evaluations, white officials at banks and lending agencies were much less likely to trust blacks than whites. Whites, they tended to believe, were good credit risks but not blacks, making it much more likely that members of the latter group were forced to turn to loan sharks and other disreputable sources. As a result of using such sources, blacks developed a general reputation, both among whites and even among blacks, as being bad credit risks. Actually, no national evidence indicates that when both blacks and whites are examined for loans, blacks are more likely to be rejected because they check out as bad credit risks. Historically, however, the reputation for bad credit has preceded them (Ards and Myers 2001).

A well-known lending bias blacks have traditionally endured is **redlining,** which is the discriminatory practice of refusing to provide mortgage loans or property insurance or only providing them at accelerated rates for reasons not clearly associated with any conventional assessment of risk. The term developed because lenders and insurers literally circled in red local urban areas they declared off-limits for their services. The most frequent culprits have been large mortgage-lending banks. Redlining has tended to target low-income, largely black districts.

Besides redlining, there are additional practices that subtly discriminate. Underwriting rules might set eligibility limits on older or lower-valued homes that disproportionately bar minorities from loans or restrict loan giving to white-dominated suburban rather than minority-populated urban areas.

Because of the discriminatory loan practices just described, it is hardly surprising that data released through the Home Mortgage Disclosure Act demonstrated that when blacks and whites are matched for similar economic characteristics, blacks' denial rate was 10.6 percent higher (Reibel 2000; Squires 1998; Squires and O'Connor 2001).

Blacks not only suffer from the impact of discriminatory lending practices, but their frequent location in areas with fewer bank branch offices and less targeted advertising represent additional disadvantages (Yinger 1995, 68–69).

Not surprisingly, a large national study of representative American families conducted since 1968 has found that black householders have been significantly less likely to translate their housing desires into a residential move they found satisfactory. With rising incomes whites' ability to accomplish this goal has improved, but not blacks'. The author of the study concluded that this outcome

> point[ed] to the persistence of racial barriers in the nation's housing market and indicat[ed] that, in comparison to that of whites, the mobility of black householders is more subject to external forces and affected less by personal expectation. (Crowder 2001, 1392)

Table 4.3, which summarizes central elements in the process of locating a house, features lists of discriminatory elements.

A number of initiatives have helped minority clients overcome discriminatory disadvantages. The opening volleys against discriminatory lending practices were pieces of federal legislation—the Fair Housing Act of 1968, the Home Mortgage Disclosure Act of 1975, and the Community Reinvestment Act of 1977. Following in the wake of this legislation, the federal Office of Fair Housing and Equal Opportunity created the Housing Opportunities

TABLE 4.3   Two Stages in Locating a Home

Initiating the Search	Completing the Search

Possible discriminatory elements include:
 	
    Realtors' showing clients fewer units
 	
    Steering
 	
    Blockbusting (in the past)
	Possible discriminatory elements include:
	
	    Such home-sale issues as fewer follow-up calls, arranging fewer meetings, or offering less financial advice
	
	    Redlining and other biased lending practices
	
	    Such rental issues as fewer requests to call back or fewer offers of special rental incentives

Project for Excellence (HOPE), which provides assistance to individuals who want to learn about fair-housing enforcement or want to take legal steps to combat housing discrimination they experienced (HOPE 2002).

This federal legislation has also encouraged the development of community groups, which have negotiated over $60 billion in investments from banks and lending organizations (Squires 1998). The most prominent of these organizations has been the Association of Community Organizations for Reform Now (ACORN), which since 1986 has developed home ownership and counseling programs in twenty-nine cities, helping over 45,000 families become first-time homeowners. The organization's offices are located in low- and very low-income neighborhoods where over 90 percent of the residents are African American, Mexican American, or recent immigrants from Central America or the West Indies. The ACORN website indicates that its staff members "roll up their sleeves and dirty their hands on the front lines of direct service delivery" (ACORN 2002). ACORN counselors supply their clients detailed information and assistance in achieving home ownership, including a credit review, a personalized financial plan, and consultation throughout the home-purchasing process.

Although organizations like ACORN help large numbers of low-income minorities obtain housing, affluent minority-group members, particularly blacks, can also need housing assistance. Attorney Reed N. Colfax, director of the Washington Lawyers' Committee Fair Housing Project, claimed that his firm has a 95 percent success rate handling cases in which clients have encountered the range of discriminatory treatments described in the Housing Discrimination Study. Colfax noted, "Real estate companies and agents often use the tactics of discouragement, steering, and delay to keep African Americans out of certain neighborhoods. Those tactics," he added, "may be more subtle than the blatant and explicit refusals to sell, seen frequently in the past, but they still prevent Africans Americans from purchasing their desired homes and that violates the law" (Jackson 2002, 170).

Although African Americans have been the most relentless victims of housing discrimination, the following Sociological Illustration indicates that other minorities have also suffered its effects.

SOCIOLOGICAL ILLUSTRATION

Santa Paula: A Sense of Social Apartness

In *The Mexican Outsiders,* anthropologist Martha Menchaca (1995) indicated that her study of Santa Paula, a city of about 26,000 located 60 miles northeast of Los Angeles, provided clear evidence about housing segregation imposed on Mexican Americans. In this city, where nearly two-thirds of the citizens are working-class, Menchaca interviewed sixty-four Mexican Americans and twelve Anglo Americans.

Property-tax records in Santa Paula indicated that by 1902 residential segregation was established, with citizens of Mexican heritage restricted to the East Side along Santa Paula Creek and prohibited from buying property in the new sections of town where Anglo-Americans lived. Natalia, a respondent who was also a local historian, indicated that town real-estate regulations ensured that no neighborhood in Santa Paula would be racially integrated. She explained:

> On this side of town land wasn't sold to Mexicans. We only sold them cheap worthless rocky land on the East Side. Real estate practices restricted selling land to Mexicans within the city limits. (Menchaca 1995, 27)

Because Mexicans were dependent on the local citrus growers for jobs, they felt powerless to challenge the standards of residential segregation, which their bosses had helped establish. Not surprisingly, the first individual to break the pattern was financially independent of the growers—Martin Morales, a successful businessman who in 1953 wanted to move from the East Side to Virginia Terrace, an affluent Anglo-American neighborhood. At first Morales encountered sharp resistance, with residents circulating a petition against Mexicans moving into the area. Eventually, the petition was brought to the Chamber of Commerce, where its membership composed of leading businessmen supported Morales's right to live in Virginia Terrace. It turned out that he was a prominent member of the Chamber, who often donated money to city projects and charities.

Morales moved into Virginia Terrace, and by the late 1950s some other affluent Mexican Americans began buying homes along the border between the Anglo and Mexican neighborhoods. However, most Mexican Americans, about 68 percent, remained on the East Side. In the 1960s the city council decided to support the construction of a new freeway through that area, creating extensive noise and air pollution, the loss of several neighborhoods' secluded, nearly rural way of life, and also the devaluation of residential property (Menchaca 1995, 118–20).

By the 1990s the majority of Mexican American residents of Santa Paula lived on the East Side in what was an ethnically homogenous urban village. Studying the community, Martha Menchaca concluded that a dominant reality involved what she called "social apartness," in which little shared sense of solidarity existed between Mexican and Anglo inhabitants and the Anglos exploited the separation.

Clearly, Menchaca found, there was a distinct relationship between residential segregation and public-school segregation: Because school districts have been based on residential location, the distinct majority of Mexican American students attended largely segregated schools. In the late 1970s, the school board evaluated the situation, contending that the segregated outcome had developed simply because Mexican Americans were poorer, not because of discriminatory housing practice. Without firm evidence of actual discrimination, that body concluded, little justification existed for such aggressive steps as redistricting or busing.

Upon review of the relevant information, analysts found abundant evidence of discrimination. Although, overall, Anglos had higher income, both groups were primarily working-class. The key difference involved the impact of housing policy: Historically, Mexicans have been restricted to the East Side, a devalued residential area from which few could afford to relocate. Anglos of comparable income were always free to live wherever they chose. Located in segregated residential areas, the Mexican children attended segregated, less well-funded schools, whereas Anglo children coming from families of comparable income went to all-white or nearly

(continued)

all-white schools, which because they drew students who were more economically diversified ended up being better funded (Menchaca 1995, 173–76).*

The relationship between residential segregation and school segregation, however, was not widely understood, particularly since the school board's official stance helped cover it up. In fact, Menchaca found that living apart from Mexicans, her Anglo respondents readily embraced what in essence was color-blind racism, using such rationales as "No one is holding these people back" or "Those people prefer to be among their own kind" (Menchaca 1995, 172).

Meanwhile, in the urban village on the East Side, the legacy of racism negatively impacted the residents. Menchaca concluded that the Anglo-American racist outlook on Mexican Americans and their culture has apparently generated a cultural ranking system among many East Side residents, who have elevated Anglo-American culture and sought to replicate it while stigmatizing Mexican traditions. To be seen as truly American, respondents indicated that an individual needed to speak English outside the home, celebrate American holidays, not play Mexican music in public, and to associate only with native-born people. Mexican immigrants were widely considered backward peasants, whose primary jobs were in unskilled farm labor.

Miriam, a respondent in the study, indicated how she encountered discrimination from native-born students in high school:

> The native-born think that all the immigrants are wetbacks, and the immigrants think that all the native born are *pochos* [not real Mexicans or Anglo Americans]. For example, when I was in high school I was popular with a lot of the native-born, but then some of them found out I was an immigrant. They stopped talking to me. (Menchaca 1995, 211)

In spite of rifts among different categories of residents, they were sometimes willing to suspend their differences and act as a cohesive group, especially when facing a common threat from the Anglo American contingent. In 1986, for instance, two groups of Mexican American teenagers became engaged in a dispute, and they spraypainted graffiti in each other's neighborhoods—an act referred to as "bombing." One of the gangs resided on the West Side, a primarily Anglo area, and once its neighborhoods were bombed, the city government called an emergency meeting and Anglo businessmen offered rewards for information leading to the bombers' arrest.

At this point the Mexican American community mobilized. An activist group called *Lucha* (struggle) attempted to diffuse the situation, asking parents to attend the city-council meeting and to stop the authorities from harassing the Mexican American youth. At the meeting Daniel, a member of *Lucha,* spoke for the entire group, arguing that the bombing was the mischievous work of a few youngsters and not the manifestation of an uncontrollable delinquency problem on the East Side as some politicians alleged. Daniel also moved to the offensive, asking why the city council acted so quickly when bombing occurred on the West Side after taking no action for months regarding graffiti on East Side walls. Apparently, the combination of Daniel's speech and the parents' presence was effective, encouraging the city council to drop the charges against the teens and to order the walls cleaned in both the East Side and West Side neighborhoods (Mancheca 1995, 119–20).

Such events suggest that in spite of the legacy of discrimination the Mexican American urban village in Santa Paula has experienced, the community can function quickly and powerfully in support of its members' interest.

All in all, this study of Santa Paula revealed the racialized nature of the local social system. Although Mexican Americans in that city had not been as systemically ghettoized as blacks, they did face housing discrimination that limited their educational and job opportunities. Furthermore, whites' racist system of ranking has been replicated among Mexican Americans, with new arrivals stigmatized. In addition, recent events indicated that whites' hostile attitudes and acts have continued to fuel a sense of exclusion.

---

*As discussion in Chapter 8 indicates, a significant amount of funding for public education comes from local property tax, which provides greater revenue in more affluent areas.

After reviewing the chapter's coverage, I return to the idea of replacing racism with justice.

Conclusion

Throughout the chapter the focus has been on the development of various housing patterns in which urban/suburban Americans live—first at the macrosociological and then at the microsociological level. In the Sociological Illustrations—first on Japanese relocation and then on the legacy of racism in Santa Paula—attention turned to the impact of housing on daily living.

In upcoming chapters many discussions examine the impact of individuals' and groups' residential location on jobs, education, health, safety, and various other issues.

Now, however, I want to end the chapter with a prediction: In the next several decades, audit studies will continue to show distinct housing segregation practices. Black ghettos are at the core of the racialized social system, and it seems that their continued presence will often encourage citizens, realtors, and bankers to support housing segregation. Opposing this outcome is a complex task, requiring effective government-financed programs targeting the various conditions keeping segregation intact. For instance, if someone could do a magic-wand wave and remove all whites' prejudice about African Americans living in their neighborhoods, that would hardly be enough: Substantial numbers of blacks are currently too poor and too badly prepared for the job world to enter the home-buying market. So powerful, unprecedentedly effective programs would need to address this significant deficiency (Massey and Denton 1993, 220).

Still, a number of housing experts seem to agree that if the political will existed to implement the current fair-housing standards, considerable progress in curtailing housing segregation would occur. That political will requires HUD's deep commitment to fair-housing enforcement, emphasizing such steps as these five:

■ HUD needs to establish a permanent testing program featuring the regular administration of large-scale housing audits, with any instances of realtors' discrimination turned over to the Attorney General's office for prosecution.

■ Another productive move would involve increased HUD funding to local fair-housing organizations to investigate and prosecute minority-group members' complaints of housing discrimination. Presently, long waiting lists testify to the limited number of personnel available for this task.

■ An additional policy initiative would entail the creation of a staff under the Assistant Secretary for Fair Housing and Equal Opportunity to investigate lending practices, once again referring discriminatory cases for prosecution.

■ HUD's Hope VI is an encouraging idea that seems worthy of expansion—to dismantle large public-housing projects and replace them with smaller developments mixing families of varied incomes and also promoting private apartment and house ownership. Impressive challenges face the program, such as preparing previously unemployed public-housing tenants to enter high-school equivalency or training programs so that they can obtain jobs and sufficient income to pay rent; finding landlords willing to house those leaving the razed projects; and ultimately building replacement housing of sufficient quality so that the new tenants will feel strongly motivated to do what is necessary to remain there. All in all, it is a promising venture.

■ Finally, HUD might subsidize minority families' settlement outside of ghettos. Because of intense resistance to public-housing projects beyond inner-city areas, research suggests that one of the most promising ventures for producing success in schooling and jobs seems to be federally subsidized rental vouchers allowing poor blacks to leave segregated areas and move into more affluent, integrated districts (Belluck 2001; Fiss 2003, 28–43; Massey and Denton 1993, 230–31; Meares 2003).

Such measures will hardly eliminate housing segregation, but they represent vigorous, innovative moves in the right direction.

DISCUSSION QUESTIONS

1. Analyze in detail the impact of racially restrictive covenants on the formation and maintenance of black ghettos.

2. Give your personal view of urban villages, describing their advantages and disadvantages.

3. List and evaluate at least two positions about the prevailing national policy toward incarceration, tying the discussion to the topics of race and ethnicity.

4. Evaluate whether or not living in the suburbs affects people's willingness and ability to function effectively in a racially or ethnically diverse setting.

5. Are you aware of any incidents of housing discrimination involving real-estate agents, bank staff members, or other loan officials? In class it might be interesting and useful to enact a hypothetical conversation between a real-estate agent and a minority-group client in which steering or some other discriminatory practice unfolds.

6. Discuss whether or not discrimination against minorities in housing is likely to decline in the next two or three decades.

BIBLIOGRAPHY

ACORN. 2002. "Acorn Housing Corporation." (June 3). www.acornhousing.org/TEXT/wwa.html.

Alba, Richard D., John R. Logan, and Brian J. Stults. 2000. "How Segregated Are Middle-Class African Americans?" *Social Problems.* 47 (November): 543–58.

Ards, Sheila D., and Samuel L. Myers Jr. 2001. "The Color of Money: Bad Credit, Wealth, and Race." *American Behavioral Scientist.* 45 (October): 223–39.

Baumgartner, M. P. 1988. *The Moral Order of a Suburb.* New York: Oxford University Press.

Belluck, Pam. 2001. "Razing the Slums to Rescue the Residents," pp. 152–57 in Fred Siegel and Jan Rosenberg (eds.), *Urban Society,* 10th ed. Guilford, CT: McGraw-Hill/Dushkin.

Bonilla-Silva, Eduardo. 2001. *White Supremacy & Racism in the Post-Civil Rights Era.* Boulder: Lynne Rienner.

Borchert, James. 1998. "Ghetto," pp. 322–24 in Neil Larry Shumsky (ed.), *Encyclopedia of Urban America,* vol. 1. Santa Barbara: ABL-CLIO.

Braz, Rose, Bo Brown, and Leslie DiBenedetto. 2000. "Overview: Critical Resistance to the Prison-Industrial Complex." *Social Justice.* 27 (Fall): 1–5.

Brodkin, Karen. 1999. *How Jews Became White Folks & What That Says About Race in America.* New Brunswick, NJ: Rutgers University Press.

Burt, Martha R. 2001. "What Will It Take to End Homelessness?" Urban Institute. www.urban.org/housing/homeless/end homelessness.html.

Burt, Martha R., Laudan Y. Aron, and Edgar Lee. 2001. *Helping America's Homeless: Emergency Shelter or Affordable Housing?* Washington, DC: Urban Institute Press.

Butler, Paul. 1996. Racially Based Jury Nullification: Black Power in the Criminal Justice System," pp. 334–38 in Richard C. Monk (ed.), *Taking Sides: Clashing Views on Controversial Issues in Race and Ethnicity,* 2nd ed. Guilford, CT: Dushkin.

Center for Regional Policy Studies. 2001. "Census 2000 Fact Sheet: Residential Segregation in United States Metropolitan Areas." www.sppsr.ucla.edu/lewis.

Clark, William A. V. 1996. "Residential Patterns: Avoidance, Assimilation, and Succession," pp. 109–38 in Roger Waldinger and Mehdi Bozorgmehr (eds.), *Ethnic Los Angeles.* New York: Russell Sage Foundation.

Clymer, Adam. 2002. "U.S. Attitudes Altered Little by Sept. 11, Pollsters Say." *New York Times.* (May 20). www.nytimes.com/2002/05/20/politics/20CIVI.html.

Cleaver, Eldridge. 1970. *Soul on Ice.* New York: Dell.

Crowder, Kyle D. 2001. "Racial Stratification in the Actuation of Mobility Expectations: Microlevel Impacts of Racially Restrictive Housing Markets." *Social Forces.* 79 (June): 1377–96.

Cureton, Steven R. 2000. "Justifiable Arrests or Discretionary Justice: Predictors of Racial Arrest Differentials." *Journal of Black Studies.* 30 (May): 703–19.

Cureton, Steven R. 2001. "An Empirical Test of the Social Threat Phenomenon Using 1190 Census and Uniform Crime Reports." *Journal of Criminal Justice.* 29 (March/April): 157–66.

Darden, Joe T. 1998. "Housing Segregation," pp. 362–63 in Neil Larry Shumsky (ed.), *Encyclopedia of Urban America,* vol. 2. Santa Barbara: ABL-CLIO.

Dellums, Ron. 2000. "The Total Community," pp. 33–34 in Lawson Fusao Inada (ed.), *Only What We Could Carry: The Japanese American Internment Experience.* Berkeley: Heyday Books.

Denton, Nancy A., and Douglas S. Massey. 1988. "Residential Segregation of Blacks, Hispanics, and Asians by Socioeconomic Status and Generation." *Social Science Quarterly.* 69 (December): 797–817.

Dobratz, Betty A., and Stephanie L. Shanks-Meile. 2000. *The White Separatist Movement in the United States: "White Power, White Pride!"* Baltimore: Johns Hopkins University Press.

Doob, Christopher Bates. 1969. *How the War Was Lost: A Description and Analysis of Anti-Poverty Organizations in Two Areas.* Unpublished manuscript.

Doob, Christopher Bates. 1999. *Racism: An American Cauldron,* 3rd ed. Reading, MA: Addison Wesley Longman.

Duncan, Garrett Albert. 2000. "Urban Pedagogies and the Celling of Adolescents of Color." *Social Justice.* 27 (Fall): 29–42.

Eitle, David, Stewart J. D'Alessio, and Lisa Stolzenberg. 2002. "Racial Threat and Social Control: A Test of The Political, Economic, and Threat of Black Crime Hypotheses." *Social Forces.* 81 (December); 557–76.

Emerson, Michael O., Karen J. Chai, and George Yancey. 2001. "Does Race Matter in Residential Segregation? Exploring the Preferences of White Americans. *American Sociological Review.* 66 (December): 922–35.

Factbook: Race and Prison. 2002. "Drug War Facts." www.drugwarfacts.org/racepris.htm.

Feagin, Joe R., and Clairece Booher Feagin. 1986. *Discrimination American Style: Institutional Racism and Sexism,* 2nd ed. Malabar, FL: Robert E. Krieger.

Feagin, Joe R., and Melvin Sikes. 1994. *Living with Racism: The Black Middle-Class Experience.* Boston: Beacon Press.

Fiss, Owen. 2003. "What Should Be Done for Those Left Behind?" pp. 3–43 in Joshua Cohen, Jefferson Decker, and Joel Rogers (eds.), *A Way Out: America's Ghettos and the Legacy of Racism.* Princeton: Princeton University Press.

Frey, William H. 2001. "Melting Pot Suburbs: A Census 2000 Study of Suburban Diversity." www.brookings.edu/urban.

Gans, Herbert J. 1962. *The Urban Villagers: Group and Class in the Life of Italian-Americans.* New York: Free Press.

Hacker, Andrew. 1992. *Two Nations: Black and White, Separate, Hostile, Unequal.* New York: Scribner.

Helper, Rose. 1969. *Racial Policies and Practices of Real Estate Brokers.* Minneapolis: University of Minnesota Press.

Holden, Benjamin A., Laurie P. Cohen, and Eleena de Lisser. 1996. "Color Blinded? Race Seems to Play an Increasing Role in Many Jury Verdicts," pp. 244–46 in John A. Kromkowski (ed.), *Race and Ethnic Relations 96/97,* 6th ed. Guilford, CT: Dushkin.

HOPE. 2002. "Mission Statement." www.thechamber.com/hope/legalrig.htm.

Housing Authority of New Orleans. 2002. "Housing New Orleans." www.hano.org/S8WL percent20Update.htm.

HUD News Release. 2003. "HUD Study Shows More Than One in Four Native American Renters Face Discrimination." www.hud.gov/news.

HUD User. 2003. "Discrimination in Metropolitan Housing Markets: National Results from Phase 1, Phase 2, and Phase 3 of the Housing Discrimination Study (HDS)." www.huduser.org/publications/hsgfin/hds.html.

Houston, Jeanne Wakatsuki. 2000. "Farewell to Manzanar," pp. 104–07 in Lawson Fusao Inada (ed.), *Only What We Could Carry: The Japanese American Internment Experience.* Berkeley: Heyday Books.

Ima, Kenji. 1982. "Japanese Americans: The Making of 'Good' People," pp. 262–302 in Anthony Gary Dworkin and Rosalind J. Dworkin (eds.), *The Minority Report,* 2nd ed. New York: Holt, Rinehart and Winston.

Jackson, Lee Anna. 2002. "The Prosecution Won't Rest." *Black Enterprise.* 32 (February): 170.

Jones-Correa, Michael. 2001. "The Origins and Diffusion of Racial Restrictive Covenants." *Political Science Quarterly.* 115 (Winter): 541–68.

Levitas, Daniel. 2002. "The Radical Right After 9/11." *Nation.* 275 (July 22/29): 19–20+.

Liptak, Adam. 2003. "The Pursuit of Immigrants in America After September 11." *New York Times.* (June 8): sec. 4, p. 14.

Massey, Douglas S., and Nancy A. Denton. 1993. *American Apartheid: Segregation and the Making of the Underclass.* Cambridge, MA: Harvard University Press.

Massey, Douglas S., and Mary J. Fischer. 1999. "Does Rising Income Bring Integration? New Results for Blacks, Hispanics, and Asians in 1990." *Social Science Research.* 28: 316–26.

Massey, Douglas S., and Garvey Lundy. 2001. "Use of Black English and Racial Discrimination in Urban Housing Markets: New Methods and Findings." *Urban Affairs Review.* 36 (March): 452–69.

McCall, Nathan. 1994. *Makes Me Wanna Holler: A Young Black Man in America.* New York: Random House.

Meares, Tracey L. 2003. "Communities, Capital, and Conflicts," pp. 51–57 in Joshua Cohen, Jefferson Decker, and Joel Rogers (eds.), *A Way Out: America's Ghettos and the Legacy of Racism.* Princeton: Princeton University Press.

Menchaca, Martha. 1995. *The Mexican Outsiders: A Community History of Marginalization and Discrimination in California.* Austin: University of Texas Press.

Minerbrook, Scott. 1996. "Home Ownership Anchors the Middle Class," pp. 171–75 in John A. Kromkowski (ed.), *Race and Ethnic Relations 96/97,* 6th ed. Guilford, CT: Dushkin.

Moore, Michael. 2002. *Bowling for Columbine.* A Film by United Artists and Alliance Atlantis.

Monroy, Douglas. 1999. *Rebirth: Mexican Los Angeles from the Great Migration to the Great Depression.* Berkeley: University of California Press.

NAHREP. 2003. "Hispanics Face More Discrimination When Looking for a Home." www.nahrep.org/Real Voices/Hispanics face more housingdi/hispanics face more housing di.html.

NFHA: National Fair Housing Alliance. 2003. "National Fair Housing Alliance 2003 Fair Housing Trends Report." www.nationalfairhousing.org.

O'Brien, David J., and Stephen S. Fugita. 1991. *The Japanese American Experience.* Bloomington: Indiana University Press.

Orser, W. Edward. 1998. "Blockbusting," p. 84 in Neil Larry Shumsky (ed.), *Encyclopedia of Urban America,* vol. 1. Santa Barbara: ABL-CLIO.

Ota, Mabel. 2000. "Insufficient Care," pp. 173–77 in Lawson Fusao Inada (ed.), *Only What We Could Bear: The Japanese American Internment Experience.* Berkeley: Heyday Books.

Parrillo, Vincent N. 2000. *Strangers to These Shores: Race and Ethnic Relations in the United States,* 6th ed. Boston: Allyn and Bacon.

Reade, Julia. 2000. "Testing for Housing Discrimination: Findings from a HUD Study of Real Estate Agents." www.bos.frb.org/commdev/c&b/2003/spring/testing.pdf.

Reibel, Michael. 2000. "Geographic Variation in Mortgage Discrimination: Evidence from Los Angeles." *Urban Geography.* 21 (January 1–February 14): 45–60.

Ryan, William. 1976. *Blaming the Victim,* rev. ed. New York: Vintage Books.

Schaefer, Richard T. 1994. *Racial & Ethnic Groups,* 5th ed. New York; HarperCollins.

Shipler, David K. 1997. *A Country of Strangers: Blacks and Whites in America.* New York: Knopf.

Squires, Gregory D. 1998. "Redlining," p. 630 in Neil Larry Shumsky (ed.), *Encyclopedia of Urban America,* vol. 2. Santa Barbara: ABL-CLIO.

Squires, Gregory D., and Sally O'Connor. 2001. *Color and Money: Politics and Prospects for Community Reinvestment in Urban America.* Albany: State University of New York Press.

Stilgoe, John R. 1988. *Borderland; Origins of the American Suburb, 1820–1939.* New Haven: Yale University Press.

Taylor, Frank J. 1942. "The People Nobody Wants." *Saturday Evening Post.* (May 9): 24–25+.

Thomas, Piri. 1973. *Savior, Savior, Hold My Hand.* New York: Bantam Books.

Tonry, Michael. 1999. "Racial Politics, Racial Disparities, and the War on Crime," pp. 374–81 in Christopher G. Ellison and W. Allen Martin (eds.), *Race and Ethnic Relations in the United States: Readings for the 21st Century.* Los Angeles: Roxbury.

Uchida, Yoshiko. 2000. "Desert Exile," pp. 69–80 in Lawson Fusao Inada (ed.), *Only What We Could Carry:*

The Japanese American Internment Experience. Berkeley, CA: Heyday Books.

U.S. Census Bureau. 2000. "Profile of General Demographics: 2000 (California)." http//factfinder.census.gov/servletQTTTable?name=DEC 2000 SF1 U&geo id=0400US06&qr name=DEC 2000 SF1 U DP1.

Wakida, Patricia. 2000. "Preface," pp. xi–xiv in Lawson Fusao Inada (ed.), *Only What We Could Carry: The Japanese American Internment Experience.* Berkeley, CA: Heyday Books.

Yinger, John. 1995. *Closed Doors, Opportunities Lost: The Continuing Costs of Housing Discrimination.* New York: Russell Sage Foundation.

5 Employment Legacies: The Urban Job World

A century ago Horatio Alger's novels about pious, disciplined poor boys who in later life achieved great wealth and prominence sold millions. The rags-to-riches story is the embodiment of the American dream, lionizing such coveted American values as competitiveness, individuality, and self-reliance. Both a century ago and now, however, such an impressive outcome, which celebrates the potential opportunities represented by laissez-faire capitalism, has distinctly been the exception, not the rule.

Although a popular claim is that ours is a society in which the opportunity for wealth and high position is available to all citizens, the historical reality has been that distinct conditions have sharply favored economic and occupational success for members of select groups. As an ironically tinged observation phrased it, "They chose their parents well."

The opening section examines the macrosociological factors affecting job access, indicating how certain broad conditions affect groups' advantage or disadvantage. Then the focus shifts to microsociological realities—the three stages of the employment process as well as the challenge of welfare to work, where the majority of family heads are women of color.

The discussion opens with a look across the historical expanse, revealing selected factors affecting various groups' access to mainstream employment.

Ethnic Succession and the Context of Job Access

If a ticket for a concert or a game is scarce and highly prized, some people are willing to wait in line for hours, even camping out overnight. Everyone understands the necessity of queuing for valuable items. The fact is that for access to many of society's most valued material and nonmaterial rewards, the process of lining up is largely or perhaps entirely out of people's hands. Ethnic succession is a prime case in point. In essence, the critical queuing involved some Americans' ancestors hundreds of years ago and for others is just now occurring.

Ethnic succession is the process by which the presence of established ethnic groups affects the economic opportunities of the groups arriving afterward. Members of a given group move out of a job market or residential area only when it serves their purpose to do so. Often they leave because better opportunities exist elsewhere, and the new arrivals face a setting in decline. In the 1970s Latinos, primarily Mexican Americans and Puerto Ricans, began moving into neighborhoods on the northwest, southwest, and southeast sides of Chicago that Polish immigrants had dominated fifty years earlier. By the time Latinos became numerous in that area, the well-paid, unskilled jobs in local heavy industry were becoming scarcer and what remained were minimum-wage service positions. Meanwhile, thanks to the benefits produced by industrial jobs, the Polish families were able to afford to move toward the city periphery. In those areas the children were the beneficiaries of improved schools that often effectively prepared them for jobs in the urban middle-class mainstream (Kantowicz 1994).

An analysis of ethnic succession might start at the top. A number of studies have found that since the nineteenth century the country's top business leaders have been white males, at least half of whom have had English or Welsh ancestry and the remainder have been primarily of Scottish or Irish origin. They have tended to be Protestants and prominent Republicans, who have shared various common experiences and privileges (Burris 2000; Domhoff 1998; Ingham 1978, 14–16; Miller 1949, 202; Wahl 2003).

The Corporate Community

The economically privileged group, which political scientist G. William Domhoff designated "the corporate community," began to develop soon after the nation's independence. By 1845 about eighty men, known as the "Boston Associates," controlled thirty-one textile companies that handled 20 percent of the nation's textile business, but their members were board members for other corporate activities—notably, seventeen filling that role at Boston's banks, twenty at insurance companies, and eleven for railroads.

Currently, members of the corporate community are very active on the boards of directors of the largest companies. Most are business executives, commercial bankers, investment bankers, and corporate lawyers, but they also include university administrators, foundation presidents, and previously elected officials. The members of the corporate community are 90 to 95 percent male, 95 percent white, 3 to 4 percent African American, and 1 to 2 percent Latino and Asian American. In the past three decades, they have included a few more women and minorities but have carefully restricted their membership to individuals sharing the same outlooks and values as the white male core. Black and Latino participants tend to have lighter skin color than most leaders of their respective groups (Domhoff 1998, 40–42; Wellner and Fetto 2003).

Members of the economic elite have often been born to privilege and have had access to special social networks that assure their sustained economic prominence. Education is one such avenue. Upper-class individuals often attend select boarding schools, where they not only receive high-quality formal education but also learn the style of dress, aesthetic tastes, manners, and values considered appropriate for their station in life. In addition, these schools provide important social contacts. One interviewee in a study of upper-class women explained: "Where I went to boarding school, there were girls from all over the country, so I know people from all over: It's helpful when you move to a new city and want to get invited into the local social club" (Ostrander 1984, 85). From these schools the youthful members of the economic elite proceed to select universities, particularly Ivy League schools and prestigious state institutions.

Just as private schools serve as an important influence in upper-class children's lives, adults of the corporate community find social clubs a pervasive influence. Many belong to upper-class country clubs or clubs specializing in such sporting activities as yachting and sailing, tennis, and squash. Although initiation fees, dues, and other expenses can reach tens of thousands of dollars a year, money is hardly the only requirement for acceptance. Each club has a rigorous screening process, in which negative votes from two or three members of a ten- to twenty-member committee means exclusion. Upper-class individuals often join clubs in several cities, creating a national pattern of overlapping memberships.

The select individuals who belong to both prominent clubs and major corporate boards have wide access to useful information and also exert considerable influence among their peers. Large corporations' leaders are committed to participating in the most prestigious clubs. For instance, a majority of the twenty-five wealthiest corporations in the country have one or more directors in eleven very prestigious clubs.

The most widely known of these organizations is the Bohemian Club, which every year holds a two-week retreat on its 2,700-acre forest 75 miles north of San Francisco. The all-male gathering includes not only the upper-class corporate members but also celebrities, government officials, and several hundred associate members who pay lower dues in exchange for producing plays, skits, and other forms of entertainment. On the weekends the Bohemians and their guests total from 1,500 to 2,500 individuals, but during the week as few as 400 men are in residence. The opening ceremony, which involves more than 250 Bohemians, features the so-called "Cremation of Care," the burning of an effigy called Dull Care, who represents these prominent men's burdens and responsibilities put on hold for two weeks.

Although formal business is not conducted, the retreat, which maintains a festive atmosphere, gives members and their friends ample opportunity to listen to top leaders' speeches and to meet and discuss what they consider the important issues at hand (Domhoff 1998, 86–91).

Sociologist Thomas Powell, who studied such upper-class clubs, summarized their function:

> The clubs are places in which the beliefs, problems, and values of the industrial organization are discussed and related to the other elements in the larger community. Clubs, therefore, are

not only effective vehicles of informal communication, but also valuable centers where views are presented, ideas are modified, and new ideas emerge. Those in the interview sample were appreciative of this asset; in addition, they considered the club as a valuable place to combine social and business contacts. (Powell 1969, 92)

The clubs, in short, lie at the heart of the corporate community, whose members recognize that a critical step in advancing their common interests involves sustained social interaction with elite peers in a pleasant, relaxed setting. The clubs and corporate boards are part of an elite economic and social network remote to most Americans. Many of these upper-class individuals are direct descendants of those largely British Americans who led the ethnic succession.

At this juncture we move back in time to the middle nineteenth century when many ancestors of current corporate community members were already established in the urban business world. Who followed these prominent people in the ethnic succession?

Paths for the Next in Line

Several important avenues for advancement existed. For some groups urban politics helped promote job opportunities. Political organizations, including political machines, could play a central role in individuals' advancement, with Irish and German immigrants often becoming prominently involved in them.

Supporters voted machine politicians into office, not only providing their own vote but for a fee registering and voting as "all sorts of people who were not qualified, including the dead, the departed, and the unborn" (Kenny 2000, 161). In exchange for such support, political machines helped needy immigrants locate food, housing, and, above all, jobs. Leaders of political machines used the city budget and municipal jobs as a so-called "spoils system" to reward supporters and allies. Faithful Irish backers of political machines often received positions in the police and fire departments as well as other city agencies, giving these job-holders the first step toward an economic foothold in the new land (Healey 2003, 487–88).

In many cities such practices continued long after the celebrated political machines had been destroyed. In New York City, for instance, the Tweed Ring, the most famous of all political machines, was defeated in the 1870s, but in the 1940s the local Democratic Party was still providing Irish Americans jobs for votes. In his autobiography Irish American writer Pete Hamill explained how at Christmastime in 1945, his impoverished family received a delivery of coal and a turkey in exchange, his father emphatically explained, for doing "the most important thing in life"—voting the straight Democratic ticket. Then the next year the unemployed father's loyalty to the Democratic Party really paid off. Hamill wrote:

> In the spring of 1946, . . . I realized what a [party] Big Shot could do when my father finally went back to work. One of the Big Shots had arranged for a job, right across the street in the Factory. On Thirteenth Street, we had lived in its cold shadow; now the Factory would give my father a living. (Hamill 1994, 69)

The Irish have hardly been the only group in New York City trading votes for Democratic Party support in finding work. For three decades blacks were able to get jobs in the urban government, particularly in such rapidly expanding areas as social services. By the late 1990s, however, such government agencies were under pressure to downsize, particularly in those once expanded areas. H. Carl McCall, the New York State comptroller and a thirty-year observer of African Americans in city government, concluded: "Public sector jobs helped establish a stable middle class for the minority community, but the next generation will not have that opportunity" (Johnson 1997, 36).

Besides blacks, other twentieth-century groups in New York City established niches in selected government areas, then dispersed jobs to their respective members. Niches included construction for the Irish, sanitation for Italians, and school teaching for Jews (Waldinger 1996, 302). In many other city governments, similar patterns developed.

Historically, unions have been another means for advancing groups. Starting in the late nineteenth and early twentieth centuries, various white ethnic groups played a role in the development of unions, with the Irish representing about one-third of union leadership in the early twentieth century. In 1935 the passage of the National Labor Relations Act required the federal government and corporate management to recognize the legitimacy of independent unions. This law not only helped the membership of many industrial unions obtain improved wages and benefits, thereby giving those families a firm economic foothold in American society, but union leadership became increasingly powerful and prominent.

In most unions the workforce tended to be multiethnic and multilingual, and so the leaders not only had to represent unions' general interests but also had to communicate with and satisfy the various participating ethnic groups. As a result, union organizers often became significant intermediaries among the different groups (Bailyn et al. 1977, 1086–87).

In modern times similar situations sometimes develop. The 275,000 participants of the Hotel Employees and Restaurant Employees union (HERE) are ethnically and racially diverse. For instance, in Las Vegas, where the local chapter won significant pay gains and increased its number from 18,000 in 1989 to nearly 50,000 in 2001, its membership was 40 percent Latino and 10 percent Asian, along with particularly energetic participation from new immigrant workers. John Wilhelm, the union's chief organizer in Las Vegas, encouraged widespread membership involvement. In the past the bartenders and banquet waiters had dominated union activities, but Wilhelm insisted on promoting minorities, women, and lower-paid unskilled workers to leadership positions. In the course of the fight to win decent wages and benefits for the membership, Wilhelm, who became HERE's national president, argued that

> the forms of democracy without the organization and involvement of the membership isn't worth much. I believe strongly in the involvement of members at every level. . . . The forms of democracy are not nearly as important as the practice of democracy. (Moberg 2001, 28)

Besides labor unions and political organizations, other prominent avenues for ethnic succession have included the church, crime, and sports. In the case of the Catholic Church, the Irish were the first large group of immigrant Catholics arriving in the United States, and so they were best positioned to dominate the church hierarchy, first as priests and then as bishops and even cardinals. Later, as Catholic Italians and Poles arrived in substantial numbers, they demanded their own parishes, where they could speak their native languages and celebrate their own customs and festivals. Although the church hierarchy remained disproportionately Irish, Italians and Poles along with members of other European as well as Hispanic Catholic groups have progressed up the church hierarchy.

In such areas of ethnic succession as crime and sports, modern observers' views are often frozen in time, stereotyping a particular ethnic or racial group as the sole or dominant representative. Many citizens, especially those who grew up with *The Godfather* and other gangster films showing Italian Americans running organized crime, are unaware that before the 1920s Germans and Irish controlled its activities and that nowadays blacks, Latinos, Asians, and Russians are prominently represented. Or, in the sport of boxing, many Americans do not know that the current reign of black and Latino boxers follows an ethnic succession of Irish, Italian, and Jewish domination (Healey 2003, 487–94).

While ethnic succession involves advancement in established structures, groups have also benefited from structural change. **Structural mobility,** which involves changes in the economy and the labor market affecting workers' advancement, can have a major impact on economic success, especially when coupled with education. In the late nineteenth and early twentieth centuries, large numbers of southern and eastern Europeans and the first Chinese and Japanese arrived in the United States. These groups were able to establish themselves sufficiently well in industrial jobs and businesses that their children were effectively well placed to obtain such educational credentials as college or postgraduate degrees, making them eligible for the steady increase in white-collar positions developing since the 1940s.

In contrast, other racial minorities were historically less well situated to initiate the advancement process. At the turn of the twentieth century, blacks and Mexican Americans were located primarily in unskilled agricultural jobs, and Native Americans were isolated on reservations (Alba 1985, 62–64; Healey 2003, 452–53; Rader 1983, 90–106).

In current times newly arrived immigrants face structural conditions that sharply diverge from those of earlier eras. Nowadays in American cities, globalization and economic restructuring have produced a labor market that features a majority of low-paying service jobs requiring limited schooling and skill as well as an expanding segment of good-paying positions needing extensive formal education and high-level English competency.

Recent male immigrants tend to have rates of labor-force participation at the 90 percent level or higher. A variety of factors can determine employability. For instance, Southeast Asian men, who in 1990 were more than twice as likely as other groups to be economically inactive, suffered from limitations in education, English proficiency, job skills, and access to employment networks. A notable contrast occurred with Mexican workers, who were the most disadvantaged group in job skills and English proficiency but ended up being the highest employed because they had extensive access to employment networks.

Among women, patterns of labor-force participation vary considerably with different groups. Recent research revealed that when compared to immigrant men, the women were much less likely to be employed and when working tended to be disproportionately underemployed. Nonworking women were similarly disadvantaged to men in education, job skills, and access to employment networks. Some also withdrew from the labor market because of marriage and childbearing.

Partial employment and, in particular, unemployment are obvious disadvantages for the advancement up the socioeconomic ladder. The sharpest dividing line between those who do and do not advance occupationally involves the possession of strong human capital: Individuals with a good education, marketable skills, and English proficiency have a decisive advantage (Massey 1996; Portes and Zhou 1999; Zhou 2001).

Invariably, structural opportunities have been more accessible to some minority groups than to others.

Examples of Groups' Contrasting Access to Economic Success

Several ethnic groups have made abundant use of **ethnic enclaves,** which are interconnected sets of small businesses belonging to a single ethnic group, located in its own neighborhood, and usually serving both the immediate ethnic community and the society at large. They might include restaurants, retail stores, and a variety of services such as gas stations, laundries, and repair shops. While not the typical American practice, ethnic enclaves have appeared in Chinese, Cuban, Dominican, Greek, Japanese, Jewish, Korean, and Lebanese urban communities. When researchers have analyzed these structures across time and space, they have discovered two common characteristics:

■ "Bonded solidarity," which is an ethnic group's shared sense of fate created by the dual recognition of being foreign and treated by outsiders as different. As consumers, members of an immigrant group usually prefer items associated with their culture of origin, both because the items represent their ethnic identity and because their familiarity means a greater personal value placed on them. As jobholders they often feel more comfortable and secure working with individuals who share their language and customs. Finally, as investors they tend to have greater confidence in firms centered in the ethnic community than toward outside organizations.

■ "Enforceable trust," which means a shared belief among business colleagues that established customs and rules will prevail. Beyond cultural loyalty, the basis for this conclusion rests on the recognition that violators of standard practices will commit occupational suicide, cutting themselves off from ethnicity-based credit unions and other key opportunities critical for business survival and growth (Portes and Manning 1986; Portes and Zhou 1992).

Among Chinese immigrants to American cities the core element in the economy has been the *hui,* the single most important capital-raising practice imported from the homeland. A businessman in need of money arranges with a number of friends and relatives to pay a fixed sum of money into a common pool. The organizer obtains first use of the sum of money, and then in successive months the *hui* reconvenes, with each participant in turn becoming the monthly beneficiary (Lyman 1974, 120–21). Bonded solidarity is the basis for forming and maintaining the group; the process permits each member to receive the temporary benefits of a large sum of money that otherwise might be unavailable, and the monthly meetings usually involve a pleasant combination of business and social contacts. Furthermore, enforceable trust prevails because each member realizes that once involved, a

This Korean American man arranges the salad bar in a New York City store owned by his family. In this city, the Korean ethnic enclave dominates this line of business, owning and operating 900 of 1,100 fruit and vegetable stores.

failure to support the *hui* by not returning loans in full represents a betrayal of friends and allies and inevitably does irreparable harm to one's reputation.

Although the majority of immigrant groups that have developed ethnic enclaves arrived in this country as poor people, their cooperative activities have helped them gain a distinct economic foothold, which in turn helped advance their children's educational and economic opportunities into mainstream society. Many Americans who superficially observe such immigrant groups as the Chinese, Cubans, Koreans, Jews, and Dominicans are oblivious to the major contribution ethnic enclaves have made in their lives. What they see is ethnic groups in which many members have risen quite quickly from poverty to middle-class status while other groups, such as blacks, who have often been in the country longer, have had less success.

What is a popular explanation? Since biologically based analyses of success or failure are now designated racist, a more readily acceptable substitute analysis focuses just as broadly and vaguely on cultural factors: The groups that do well economically have dynamic, success-oriented cultures while those that fail lack them. In contrast to these vague, unsubstantiated claims, I offer one that can be validated: Through such structures as ethnic enclaves or other forms of support, advancing groups are able to obtain the critical resources to achieve economic success that deprived groups, such as African Americans, are less likely to obtain.

Comparing Chinese, Japanese, and African American self-employment between 1880 and 1940, sociologist Ivan Light emphasized that unlike the two Asian groups, blacks lacked necessary social capital, particularly established financing practices like the *hui* (Light 1972; Light and Gold 2000, 9–11).

Historically, African Americans have suffered a distinct structural disadvantage in business access. During the years 1910 to 1930 when rapid industrialization occurred, the white-dominated power structure in American cities imposed increasing segregation. Elite black businessmen and professionals, who once lived in primarily white neighborhoods, were forced to move and to break contact with the social and economic networks that were establishing them firmly in the middle-class economic mainstream. While ethnic concentrations of Italians, Poles, and other recently arrived European groups were increasingly free to live where they chose, African Americans were driven into isolation. It is important to realize that this forced isolation occurred at a time of unparalleled opportunity. During the industrial era, white-collar positions in both management and a variety of professions increased, but invariably these positions required formal schooling—at a minimum, college graduation and often advanced degrees. Blacks' systematic isolation in ghettos, however, meant little or no access to higher education, and so for the majority of African Americans the opportunity to move ahead in the industrial age was abruptly stunted. Because of this uniquely oppressive set of circumstances, it seems accurate to conclude that blacks have "lived history in reverse" (Logan and Molotch 1987, 127–28).

American Indians' difficulties in the labor market have received much less attention than blacks', but they too have been historically victimized. Once they were militarily defeated and isolated on reservations, their situation received little attention. It is well known that the economic problems of Indians living on reservations have been particularly acute, but until 2002 research had not examined the impact of reservation life on employment rates. Using data from the National Longitudinal Survey of Youth, Robert J. Gitter and Patricia B. Reagan (2002) found that compared to a representative American sample, Indian males born between 1957 and 1964 were 10 percent less likely to be employed. Furthermore, if residing in a county with a reservation, they were 11 to 14 percent less likely to be working than Indian men living elsewhere.

Some situational factors associated with reservation life can affect employability. For instance, among North Cheyenne families a study demonstrated how what the author designated "native capital"—a type of cultural capital obtained from family and community members—affected young people's job prospects. If the older individuals were well educated and effectively positioned in the mainstream economy, then the youths in question were more likely to seek educational credentials and higher-level jobs. Other young people, whose native capital was less attuned to the general society, tended to restrict themselves to the less prosperous reservation economy, often ending up in low-paying agricultural or service positions or unemployed (Ward 1998).

Although no other racial or ethnic group can duplicate Native Americans' and blacks' history, the developmental path for poor Latino and Asian groups currently arriving in substantial numbers and currently concentrated in low-paying service jobs remains unclear. In this postindustrial economy, where higher-level positions are scarce, it is hard to visualize the widespread upward mobility most earlier immigrant groups experienced.

S O C I O L O G I C A L   I L L U S T R A T I O N

The Koreatown That Never Was

In 1968 Hi Duk Lee arrived in Los Angeles from Korea with a degree in chemical engineering and a dream. In 1975 he opened one of the first Korean restaurants in L.A., called Young Bin Kwan (the VIP Palace), along with a shopping center next door known as the VIP Plaza. Lee imported blue Korean roof tiles and painted the buildings in ornate Korean style. As he explained a quarter of a century later, "I planned to make Koreatown. Chinese people have Chinatowns everywhere: New York, San Francisco, Los Angeles, Montebello. But there's no Koreatown" (Quinones 2001).

The Los Angeles Korean business sector was certainly a promising place in which to develop new business ventures. In Los Angeles and other cities, Korean immigrants had arrived well educated and experienced about urban life. They were often the beneficiaries of ethnic enclaves or the physically more dispersed ethnic middleman businesses, both of which use rotating credit and other means to promote each other's business growth. In Los Angeles the high-profile enterprises included restaurants, groceries, gas stations, liquor stores, and real-estate agencies. When the VIP Palace opened, the Korean population of the city had expanded to 65,000, a six-fold increase in a decade. There were about 4,000 Korean-owned businesses in the county (Portes and Manning 1986, 55–58; Yoon 1999, 123). It was Lee's plan to draw many of the dispersed middleman businesses into a large ethnic enclave, where economic solidarity would be the foundation for a more general social and political community.

From this business base, Lee planned to produce his vision of Koreatown. The opening of the VIP Palace was an optimistic start. The restaurant was very popular, hosting wedding banquets, business meetings, political dinners, and family gatherings. Within two or three years, about forty businesses were operating in an adjacent five-block area, which Lee owned. To promote his dream, Lee sought to lobby city officials, acting in his capacity as director of the Koreatown Chamber of Commerce, the Koreatown Development Association, and the Korean-American Friendship Association.

Lee envisioned the borders of Koreatown extending from 8th and 11th Streets to the north and south and Western and Vermont Avenues to the west and east, with the entire area bisected by Olympic Boulevard. He wanted to have two large Korean-style gates erected on Olympic at Western and Vermont. Although Mayor Tom Bradley, with Lee and other L.A. Korean leaders at his side, set up a sign for Koreatown on the Santa Monica Freeway, the gates were never installed. Lee gave a party for Korean property owners, who showed up to drink his liquor and eat his food, but at the end of the evening, they gave no donations for the gates.

Pushing ahead on his own, Lee planned a 230-room, five-story VIP hotel on Olympic Boulevard. He had already invested a half-million dollars in the project when interests rates rose sharply. That development along with the fact that many of Lee's VIP Plaza tenants were behind in their rent forced him to file for bankruptcy, and by 1982 he had sold all his real-estate holdings.

Why did the Koreatown dream fail to catch on? In the first place, Korean merchants, who as we noted are well educated and sophisticated about urban life, are also quite independent-minded (Yoon 1999, 123). So while they will often cooperate in specific economic ventures, they are unlikely to buy into someone's grand scheme unless it effectively addresses their own interests. Lee's vision seems to have struck many Korean entrepreneurs as old-fashioned. David Hyun, a major Korean developer in L.A., said, "Koreans are so keen on becoming Americanized and forgetting their Korean roots, especially the young folks" (Quinones 2001). Hyun added that part of the Americanization process was focusing on current commercial ventures and putting traditional culture aside. It appears that Lee did not appreciate that the forces promoting assimilation in American society make it very difficult for ethnically based community-wide structures to develop and persist.

(continued)

To be sure, some traditional cultural elements still seem to function in Koreatown. At the Wilshire B.B.Q. House on Wilshire Boulevard, Korean businessmen finalize deals deep into the night, conversing in time-honored tradition over *soju* (Korean vodka) and spicy dried octopus or seafood pancakes.

Throughout the area, in fact, restaurants thrive, with the number leaping from 160 in 1992 to 400 nine years later. Reporter Linda Burum indicated that

> the streets are ablaze with restaurant "grand opening" banners. Dinner-time traffic can be a madhouse, with mini-mall parking lot attendants heroically juggling twice as many cars as the lots can hold. (Burum 2001)

Although the area is known as Koreatown, some parts are more distinctly Korean than others. Korean business ventures have shifted north and west from Olympic and Normandie to Wilshire and Western, deserting the old center of Koreatown, which has started to deteriorate.

In that locale Oaxacans, primarily Zapotec Indians from the Mexican state of Oaxaca, have moved in, representing at least a partial ethnic succession. Oaxacan businessman Fernando Lopez converted the VIP Palace into La Guelaguetza, an Oaxacan restaurant. "It's no longer Koreatown," Lopez said. "It's Oaxacatown" (Quinones 2001).

That is an exaggeration. A large concentration of Korean businesses is still in the area, but perhaps as many as 200,000 Oaxacans have moved into Los Angeles and represent a significant buying power in the Koreatown area. According to Lopez, Oaxacans retain a passion for their traditional culture. He explained, "We might have left 20 or 30 years ago but we've still got its taste in our mouth, the colors in our heart. When we're away and we go for a while without tasting a chile verde, a mole, we almost die. That's not a lie." Oaxacans "miss their place," he added. "It's like believing in God. It's a necessity to believe in God. It's a necessity that we have our culture near us" (Quinones 2001). That appears to be a desire members of many groups share, but the efforts to satisfy this goal are not likely to lead to the fruition of Hi Duk Lee's dream.

In Chapter 2 we noted that throughout American history a distinct set of factors has opposed ethnic groups establishing a lasting control over their business communities. In Los Angeles both Koreans and Oaxacans have been encountering that reality.

The adjacent Sociological Illustration describes an ambitious plan, which reveals the complexity of creating a community built around ethnic business.

Moving on to job realities for small groups and individuals, we can perceive the impact of the broad historical factors just examined.

Down the Racialized Pipeline

Pete Rivera was a gentle, quiet, introspective man whom I met while doing my dissertation in the East Harlem section of New York City. Pete was one of several workers in an employment center that was run by and for Puerto Ricans.

For Pete it was a frustrating job. No more than a trickle of workers came to the center, and although it was fairly easy to obtain entry-level positions for qualified applicants, the jobs left Pete uninspired. He explained:

> So maybe some guy gets so he can sweep a floor neater than anyone else, or he learns to turn a broom neat, so he can save two or three seconds. He can't go out and brag to the world about that. Nobody's interested, and they'd just laugh at him. (Doob 1967, 144)

It seems reasonable to visualize the employment process as a pipeline, where individuals in a given line of work are in a specific channel that steers them into certain activities and groups and away from others. As we move through the three stages of the employment pipeline—the job-candidate, the job-screening, and the job-promotion stages—we see that some people's tunnels are spacious, pleasant, and easily traveled while others, like those Pete described, are cramped, forbidding, and distinctly racialized.

The Job-Candidate Stage

This opening phase focuses on access to an employment pool. Two basic realities concern the availability of useful social networks and the presence of selective recruitment. Recall that a **social network** is the set of contacts involving friends, acquaintances, or business associates that individuals use to obtain both information about or advantage in seeking jobs or other valued opportunities. It is a form of social capital that in the employment process often distinctly favors selected groups.

The process usually unfolds informally, with employers giving little thought to favoring members of their own group. In Boston an Irish American contractor explained standard hiring practice. "A good number of building contractors drinks in the pub, and the lads come in and they give them work" (Light and Gold 2000, 21). Since such contractors favored Irish-owned pubs, the potential workers were generally Irish.

In his autobiography *Makes Me Wanna Holler,* Nathan McCall described his experience as a black teen seeking a job in a setting where most effective social networks were highly racialized. As he started to look, McCall saw that the young whites his age had summer jobs "in air conditioned offices where they could learn things." So when McCall saw white teens working in such places, he would fill out an application. The people running the office looked at him as if he were crazy, and the white teens displayed an air of superiority. McCall explained:

> Their attitude got on my nerves, but everything I saw around me suggested to me that they might be right. They had a serious inside track on the best summer gigs in town. When looking for work, many of them had to look no further than their own neighborhoods, where people owned their own businesses or held influential government or civilian positions and could set aside jobs for young white kids before openings were even posted. (McCall 1994, 84)

McCall noted that black parents' only job contacts involved manual-labor positions and that even there they were not influential enough to assure their children got the inside track.

In two regards McCall's experience was typical for young urban blacks. First, since he lived in a small city, he undoubtedly sought employment at small firms, which often lack a personnel office and thus more readily use social networks than their larger counterparts. Second, the use of social networks is more prevalent with lower-level jobs such as those high-school students seek.

With lower-level jobs, the development of effective social networks is sometimes quite intricate. In her study of Latina domestic workers in Los Angeles, Pierrette Hondagneu-Sotelo described Lupe Vélez, a housecleaner, who had the almost unheard-of success of having a surplus of houses to clean. Because of her thorough, expert work and the decision to never turn down a job, she faced a situation in which the only way to expand further was to take on an assistant or pass along referrals. Vélez refused to do either, however, fearing damage to her reputation with employers. On the topic of referrals, she explained:

> I . . . don't like to recommend other people . . . because you don't know what's going to happen, and you are the one responsible. So they may have the need, but I'm not going to recommend them, because then I'm going to look bad. (Hondagneu-Sotelo 2001, 73)

Social networks can also be used for higher-level jobs. In a study of 4,078 employers, the openings of those who said they relied on social networks as a chief means of recruitment for college-degree jobs were more likely to be filled by whites than were those of employers who indicated limited reliance on these networks.

Besides affecting whether individuals will be hired, access to social networks influences employees' income. In the same investigation, black high-school graduates who used segregated networks averaged $5.69 per hour, those who did not use networks averaged $5.74 per hour, and, in contrast, those who had access to integrated networks averaged $6.45 an hour (Braddock and McPartland 1987).

For employers in large organizations, the use of social networks can become part of a larger strategy. **Selective recruitment** is a policy of pursuing racially restrictive population segments in an effort to produce a workforce with certain targeted characteristics. In Chicago and surrounding Cook County, a study of 185 employers hiring for entry-level positions found that employers generally claimed that their basic intention was simply to obtain "better quality" workers, not to exclude minorities. However, their procedures often sharply reduced or eliminated blacks and some other minorities (Neckerman and Kirschenman 1999).

Selective recruitment allows employers to avoid hiring from certain largely black "bad areas," particularly public-housing projects, where they believe job candidates are less effectively prepared to work and less motivated. These individuals sometimes engaged in what appeared as camouflaged racism, seeing the ghetto inhabitant as someone pressured by peers to facilitate a robbery by revealing information about the security system or the arrival of a valuable shipment. As one research subject said, "[H]e lives in an area where he may be physically . . . in danger for his life if he doesn't provide the information to the people that live around him" (Wilson 1997, 114).

Over 40 percent of the employers in the Chicago study said they did not use newspaper ads for entry-level positions but instead relied heavily on employee social networks. Many who opted for ads did so only as a last resort after employee social networks had proved inadequate. In addition, about two-thirds of city employers who used newspaper ads did not place them in metropolitan newspapers, where urban blacks generally look for job listings, but chose neighborhood, suburban, or ethnic papers, which targeted white or Hispanic groups.

Employers were also selective about choosing organizations from which to recruit workers. Among schools, recruiters were particularly inclined to visit Catholic schools and those from the city's white northwestern neighborhoods. On the other hand, many employers scrupulously avoided state employment service and welfare programs, which disproportionately referred inner-city blacks. Job recruiters were often highly critical of such programs. One said participants were "the dregs of the year." Another was less blatantly racist, raising the issue of whether young people brought up in inner-city areas and schools are adequately prepared for employment.

> Any time I've taken any recommendations from state agencies, city agencies, or welfare agencies I get people who are really not prepared to come to work on time, not prepared to see that a new job is carried through, that it's completed. I mean there just doesn't seem to be a work ethic involved in these people. (Neckerman and Kirschenman 1999, 281)

Reading this statement, one cannot determine whether the speaker's comments are directed solely at blacks, or at a combination of whites, blacks, and perhaps additional groups. Job recruiters like this person must be concerned about what is called "job readiness"—the social and task skills job candidates bring to the application process—and those with clear deficiencies are likely to encounter significant difficulties successfully completing work-related tasks.

Nearly three-quarters of the 170 respondents in the Chicago study expressed negative views about inner-city blacks when evaluating a list of employee traits. The chairman of a car transport company, for instance, offered the following stereotype-laden response when asked whether he thought various groups had different work ethics.

> Definitely! I don't think, I know; I've seen it over a period of 30 years. I have it right in here. Basically, the Oriental is much more aggressive and intelligent and studious than the Hispanic. The Hispanics, except Cubans, of course, they have the work ethnic [*sic*]. The Hispanics are mañana, mañana, mañana— tomorrow, tomorrow, tomorrow.
> *Interviewer:*   You mentioned the case of native-born blacks.
> *Respondent:*   They're the laziest of the bunch.
> *Interviewer:*   That would relate to your earlier remarks about dependability. What is the reason for that?
> *Respondent:*   The parents are that way so, what the hell, they didn't have a role model to copy; that's part of it. (Wilson 1997, 112)

The material just completed suggests certain conclusions about the job-candidate stage. First, the relevance of residential location as a foundation for the racialized social system is apparent. Blacks living in isolated inner-city areas are not only less likely than whites to have social networks promoting good jobs, but using selective recruitment employers are often inclined to avoid going to those neighborhoods. Second, the line between a fairly objective assessment of a candidate's job readiness and a racist reaction to him or her is not always readily apparent to the observer. Finally, some employers like the last individual quoted seem convinced that no members of certain specified minorities can attain acceptable standards.

Moving along the employment pipeline into job screening, we continue to perceive evidence of a racialized social system.

The Job-Screening Stage

At this point candidates come face-to-face with the recruitment process, or do they? In the past employers could screen out some job candidates with newspaper ads. During the nativist movement of the 1850s, white Protestant employers in the coastal cities published advertisements declaring "No Irish need apply" (Shannon 1989 41).

A century later a selection of newspaper advertisements published in four newspapers for January 2 and 3, 1960, revealed that employers were still just as blatant in expressing their preferences, using newspapers to screen out racial categories. For instance, an ad in the *Los Angeles Times* for January 2, 1960, read:

> HOUSEKEEPER—European or Oriental—2 adults, private quarters, under 45. References. [555]-4891

And a job listing in the *Chicago Tribune* for January 3, 1960, stated:

> WHITE married men who can furnish and operate air conditioned Cadillac limo. Good opportunity. [555]-4864

Some ads, such as the following one in the *New York Times* for January 3, 1960, targeted minority-group members for low-status jobs, where the prospective employer felt their presence was particularly appropriate.

> COOK, housekeeper, Negro preferred, experience essential, prominent family, permanent position, high salary, [555]-5369 (Darity and Mason 1998, 66)

Although job recruiters can no longer use newspapers to screen out job candidates, they can still do it from a distance—with the telephone. Discrimination occurred in an experimental study in which white and Hispanic pairs working for the research team responded to randomly sampled job vacancies listed in newspapers and at employment agencies in Washington, D.C., and its surrounding suburbs. Although the qualifications for the white and Hispanic applicants provided were similar, the latter group, whose members displayed a slight Spanish accent and Spanish surnames, received a less favorable response in 22.4 percent of the calls; in particular, the Hispanic applicants were less likely to be asked to appear for a job interview (Bendick, Jackson, Reinoso, and Hodges 1993; Stolzenberg and Tienda 1997).

A screening interview is also common, with one early study finding that many companies frequently eliminated 30 to 40 percent of applications using that method. In such situations employers did not need to refer directly to race, even among themselves. Instead they could use code words, discussing impressions of candidates' "intelligence," "appearance," "vigor," and "self-confidence," with such references intentionally or perhaps unintentionally playing into interviewers' racial stereotypes (Lopez 1976).

Intelligence, for instance, can be a powerful code word. When researchers asked members of the college class of 1957 from three Ivy League colleges, which have traditionally supplied about two-fifths of America's business elite, whether they agreed with the conclusion that blacks are as intelligent as whites, just 36 percent of the Princeton class, 47 percent at Yale, and 55 percent at Harvard agreed (Jones 1986, 88).

Job interviewers' stereotypes can simultaneously screen ethnic categories out of higher positions and into lower ones. A widespread perception exists that Asian and Asian American women are docile, diligent, and loyal, helping to explain their overrepresentation as cashiers, file clerks, office machine operators, and typists. They are much less likely to obtain higher-status jobs as secretaries and receptionists, where good social skills are necessary, or as supervisors, where leadership abilities are required (Lai 1998; Woo 1998).

Many poor minority-group members can find the context of a job interview unsettling. The situation requires that they be friendly and able to communicate well with people who tend to be white, middle-class, and suburban. Job-readiness skills include the ability to discuss such abstract issues as their philosophy of work and their strategy for self-advancement. In reviewing their past work history, they must be forthright and honest about what potentially is a difficult topic for people whose ghetto location has often severely limited their job prospects.

These can be troublesome demands as comments from respondents in the Chicago study show. A manufacturer indicated that residents of public-housing projects were not well equipped to "come in and really sell themselves." An employer of clerical workers noted, "You don't need to look at the address to know where they're from; it's how people come across; they don't know how to behave in an office." A number of respondents commented on the background differences between poor, black job applicants and the largely middle-class whites screening them in interviews. A manufacturer observed that "we don't realize that their rules are very different than ours" (Neckerman and Kirschenman 1999, 284). Once again, the observer is left wondering whether recruiters were engaging in racism, whether they were grappling with the complexities of job readiness, or perhaps doing some of both.

Besides interviews, job recruiters also use testing as a screening device. In the Chicago study, 40 percent used skill tests to screen their sample; clerical employers were especially inclined to test, measuring such skills as spelling, composition, math techniques, typing, and filing speed. While firms with a higher proportion of black applicants were more likely to test, the research could not determine whether that was because they were less confident of black applicants or because their hiring needs differed from those who did not test (Neckerman and Kirschenman 1999, 285).

While studies involving interviews with job recruiters reveal extensive information about the screening process, another source of information is less detailed but still compelling: data about minorities' almost complete absence from certain job categories.

For blacks many of the underrepresented categories have been professions requiring formal education they were often denied, but in other instances that was not the case. Political scientist Andrew Hacker speculated about why so few blacks entered these job areas.

> The suspicion arises that proprietors of restaurants and lounges may feel that their white clienteles do not want their food and drinks handled by black employees. Or it could stem from the belief that if a place has "too many" blacks on its staff, it will drop to a lower status. . . . Perhaps most revealing of all is the small number of black dental hygienists. While

white patients seem willing to be cared for by black nurses, they apparently draw the line at having black fingers in their mouths. (Hacker 1992, 110)

While African Americans are more likely than other groups to be screened out in the employment process, black males are particularly vulnerable. An experimental study featured black and white male research assistants who sought entry-level jobs with 350 employers in Milwaukee, Wisconsin, and randomly described themselves as having or not having a criminal record. For each position a pair of black and white research assistants applied, offering matched qualifications for education level, work experience, and other relevant factors.

The results were dramatic. For the white applicants without a criminal record, 34 percent were called back and were offered either a job or a formal interview. In contrast, 17 percent of white applicants with a criminal record received a similar call. For blacks 14 percent of those without a criminal record were recalled, and a mere 5 percent with a criminal record obtained the positive call. In short, this last category of applicants—black men with a criminal record—had their chances of passing the screening process reduced by 85 percent compared to the white applicants without a criminal record.

These results strongly suggest that the impact of a criminal record for black applicants has a lasting impact on wages. The far-ranging implication of this finding becomes clear when one appreciates that about 27 percent of black males under forty have been in prison (Pager 2003; Western 2002).

Another group that is broadly screened out occupationally is Hispanics. While representing about a tenth of the U.S. population, they account for only about 3.5 percent of the journalistic workforce. For instance, according to one national survey, only 1.2 percent of the employees in magazine editorial departments are Latinos. Angelo Figueroa, editor of *People en Español,* indicated that possessing a national readership, magazine executives do not face local newspaper editors' necessity of responding to regional demographics. "They just don't feel they have to tailor to Hispanics because they assume that Latinos are not reading their magazines," Figueroa said (Torres 1999, 26).

When a particular racial or ethnic group is widely screened out of certain occupations, its members are inclined not to apply for such positions. Asian Americans, who are underrepresented in such occupations as law, social science, journalism, and administrative management, tend to avoid seeking such openings, believing that white employers consider they lack both the necessary language and interpersonal skills and only succeed in positions featuring technical skills (Chun 1993).

At the end of the employment pipeline lies the job-promotion stage, where racialized issues can also appear.

The Job-Promotion Stage

In November 1996 Texaco Inc. agreed to pay more than $140 million to resolve a federal lawsuit brought by minority employees. Although Texaco's public statements about minority hiring and promotion strongly emphasized equal opportunity, only six—or .7 percent—of the jobholders making over $106,000 were black. A Labor Department invesitgation found that minority employees did indeed need to wait far longer for promotions. During court testimony employees indicated that their white managers subjected them to racial insults, which they did not report for fear of losing their jobs. One black employee noted:

> Throughout my employment, three supervisors in my department only discussed their view that African Americans are ignorant and incompetent, and, specifically, that Thurgood Marshall was the most incompetent person they had ever seen (Eichenwald 1996, 1).

Although the details of this well-publicized case shocked many Americans, Texaco's promotion policies were not drastically out of line with those at other businesses. A national survey of senior executives found that during the 1980s African Americans increased their miniscule percentage of top corporate positions from 0.2 to 0.6 percent, and Hispanics (three-quarters of whom were either Mexican American or Puerto Rican) modestly expanded theirs from 0.1 to 0.4 percent (Sklar 1995). Furthermore, evidence about the membership of the corporate community suggests that during the 1990s little if any change occurred (Domhoff 1998, 43). Consider the process at the job-promotion stage.

Minorities often face a stern set of challenges that psychologist Thomas Pettigrew referred to as "a triple jeopardy"—racial stereotyping, the token role (being considered inferior by whites if they obtained their positions through affirmative action), and the solo role (being the only member of a racial minority at the work site). The impact of these three factors is likely to affect racial minorities negatively if they apply for promotion (Pettigrew and Martin 1987).

When supervisors or colleagues use stereotypes toward minorities, that stereotypic image becomes the dominant tool for analyzing specific behavioral acts, encouraging the use of double standards. If an African American employee does something that a supervisor can interpret negatively, such as speaking somewhat harshly to a colleague, then that behavior is more likely to be attributed to a basic deficiency in the person's character than if a white person acted similarly. In the latter instance, the white colleague would probably attribute the harsh statement to a situational factor, saying, "Oh, she's just having a bad day."

On the other hand, when minority workers perform effectively, stereotypes can rationalize the situation. White colleagues might say of an employee belonging to a racial minority, "He works so hard because he has to compensate for his lack of intelligence." Or they might claim that this person's success was the result of favoritism from a boss sensitive to pressures to incorporate minority individuals into high positions.

The second element is the token role. If supervisors or fellow workers feel that a member of a racial minority received a position because of affirmative action, they are likely to assume the individual is incompetent, able to obtain the job only when given unfair advantage because of race. This reality can create ambivalent feelings for the individual in question. In a study of Northern Plains Native Americans, a respondent explained that she had received a position through affirmative action, indicating that she was a hard worker and thus had earned it. Then she added, "But I've got a mixed bag of feelings, because I think that at times some people's outlook is that 'they've got to give it to them and the standards don't have to be as high' " (Juntunen et al. 2001, 280).

The third element in the triple jeopardy is the solo role. As the only or almost only member of their group in the work unit, African Americans or members of other racial minorities are likely to experience unrealistic evaluation from whites, who have often had little or no previous contact with racial minorities. Ernest Jones, the first black manager in his company, said, "I was out of the 'place' normally filled by black people in the company, and since no black person had preceded me successfully, it was easy for my antagonists to believe I was inadequate" (Jones 1973, 114). Sometimes minority solo employees find the opposite—that expectations are unusually high. In either case, they are considered different from whites and are not evaluated realistically, deprived of constructive feedback that provides a helpful evaluation of their progress on the job.

Because they often find themselves in a solo role, minorities in management can be isolated from social networks, creating disadvantage when seeking promotion, which is most likely to succeed in a context of effective relations with co-workers and superiors. A black middle manager described a situation in which a black supervisor working for her demanded an overdue merit raise. Convinced that he deserved it, the middle manager gathered relevant documentation and went to the appraisal meeting. That meeting was with several white male colleagues who spoke without documentation of their respective candidates, voted down her nominee, and awarded merit raises to several of their own people. According to the black middle manager, a "buddy system" existed. She explained, "It turned out to be a matter of 'Joe, you did a favor me last week, so I'll support you in getting your person in this week. You owe me one, old buddy' " (Jones 1986, 89). Within this system African Americans, who are often new arrivals, are likely to be victims of clear discrimination.

In business, high-level executives often become sponsors of younger subordinates, but a prominent white consultant told Edward Jones that white managers are usually uncomfortable sponsoring African Americans, fearing negative reactions from other whites (Jones 1986, 89). Furthermore, many black executives claim that their superiors withhold more strategic information from them than from their white colleagues, thereby making blacks less effective on the job (Campbell 1982). The practices just described are subtle, seldom disclosed realities demonstrating the racialized social system's impact in management, where many Americans believe blacks' opportunities equal whites'.

The impact of the triple jeopardy and limited access to social networks for black managers is that they find themselves in the unique situation described by the subtitle of an article written by Sharon M. Collins: "up the corporate ladder but out on a limb" (Collins 1997).

Collins did in-depth interviews with seventy-six top African American executives in major Chicago-based white corporations. Her respondents had such titles as comptroller, trust officer, manager, director, vice president, and chief officer, indicating that their positions were prestigious and high-ranking.

Nonetheless, about two-thirds of these executives had had one or more racialized jobs focused on affirmative action or urban affairs. Among a comparison group of twenty white executives, only one had received a racialized position.

Collins divided the sixty-four respondents who had had fourteen or more years in corporate management into three categories—those with a history of only mainstream jobs; those with at least one but not a majority of racialized positions; and those with a majority of racialized jobs. The three categories each represented about a third of the respondents.

The dominant finding was that the management personnel in the mainstream positions had advanced farther than their counterparts in racialized positions, which the respondents characterized as "dead-end jobs [that had] no power," "nigger jobs," and "money-using" versus "money-producing" jobs.

These racialized positions were necessary for companies, resulting from pressures created by federal legislation and by protests in urban black communities. As the jobs developed, however, they represented very limited, unchallenging work. An executive for a clothing manufacturer and retailer endorsed that point in summarizing his experience.

> {The company} sent me to Chicago for a week long workshop on affirmative action. In that one week I learned all I needed to know about affirmative action, and I haven't learned much since. It's the kind of field that nothing, well, a few laws might change, but the concept doesn't. You don't branch out. There's nothing, oh, now how can I explain it? There's not a lot of specialties . . . in affirmative action. You deal with 6 or 7 basic laws, or regulations, and . . . once you know those there's not an awful lot more to learn. (Collins 1997, 62)

Other observers have backed Collins's conclusion about the peculiar location of blacks in management. Ellis Cose, a well-known journalist, concluded that

> black executives have landed out of all proportion to the numbers, in community relations and public affairs, or in slots where their only relevant expertise concerns blacks and other minorities. The selfsame racial assumptions that make minorities seem perfect for certain initially desirable jobs can ultimately be responsible for trapping them there as others move on. (Cose 1999, 22)

Blacks, Cose also noted, have begun to obtain some specialized management positions because they have the expertise and group contacts to most effectively handle them. For instance, because of African Americans' increasingly extensive involvement in Washington, D.C.'s political and economic activities, it has become almost inevitable that the *Washington Post*'s city editor would be African American.

The context in which managerial positions exist, in short, can help determine the ethnic- or racial-group members that receive those jobs. Data from the Multi-City Survey of Urban Inequality supported this conclusion, indicating that work groups' race and ethnicity were important social characteristics influencing employers' choice of supervisors. Latinos, for instance, were likely to obtain supervisory control over Latino groups, Asians over Asian groups, and blacks over black groups. In the study the numbers were impressive, with minority supervisors seven times more likely to maintain control over work groups composed largely of their own members than over a mixed workforce. However, the survey indicated that this ethnic or racial matching of supervisors to work groups declined at higher levels of the wage hierarchy, most likely because, as Sharon Collins's findings suggested, white leadership sets limits on minorities' upper managerial participation (Elliott and Smith 2001).

Looking at the overall minority employment picture, one might ask what is the key factor to overcoming racialized practice? To begin, one must acknowledge that practically all medium-to-large American organizations have written nondiscrimination policies and have made public assertions that they both value diversity in their workers and do not discriminate against them.

I. Job-candidate stage	II. Job-screening stage	III. Job-promotion stage
Employer: use of their own social networks; also selective recruitment	Employer: use of advertising, screening interviews, testing	Supervisor: possible reliance on the triple jeopardy; use of social networks
Candidate: access to social networking varied for groups	Candidate: need to demonstrate a variety of job-related skills	Employee: possible relevance of the triple jeopardy; access to varied social networks

FIGURE 5.1   Stages and Issues in the Racialized Pipeline

The problem is that many organizations, including some of the nation's largest, most prominent companies, continue to systematically exclude most minority-group members from their ranks because senior executives view their greater inclusion as a threat to what they perceive as a currently effective work setting. The challenge is to convince such leaders that their companies can establish more inclusive personnel policies and not cripple organizational functioning, neither curtailing relaxed, flexible relations among employees, nor making the delegation of authority more difficult, nor restricting the exercise of judgment by lower-level managers and workers (Bielby 2000).

It is, to be sure, not a simple task. As we have already noted, racism and ethnic prejudice often reside in the top corporate ranks, and some corporate leaders might claim that their reason for opposing new personnel policies is the disruption they will cause, when in reality the root of their resistance is simply racism.

Figure 5.1 represents the stages and principal issues that appear in the racialized pipeline. Moving on, we keep analyzing minorities' job process, but only for one severely challenged segment of the population.

Women of Color as Family Heads in the Welfare-to-Work Program

At times the media have been fairly positive about welfare reform. An analysis of 250 stories on welfare to work and caseload declines found in the nation's leading newspapers between January 1998 and September 2000 indicated that over half (51.6 percent) were either wholly or generally positive, and about a quarter (24.4 percent) were wholly or generally negative. While offering some modest reservations, the typical story suggested that to date welfare reform has had "remarkably positive results" (Schram and Soss 2001, 51). For these journalists, the authors of the study cautioned, "positive" had a very specific meaning: It referred to cutbacks in the welfare roles.

Many specialists on the topic have opposed such single-mindedness, emphasizing the need for attunement to the well-being of families in transition. As the upcoming discussion of the development of the welfare system indicates, controversy is hardly new to this topic.

Brief History of American Welfare

To begin, human societies have always offered help to needy people, but invariably such assistance is provided in the context of reigning cultural beliefs and values.

In the United States, it appears that most citizens not only subscribe to the value that a man should be the chief breadwinner but assume that this standard is the one that families maintain. That has never been the case for all families. Through death, desertion, and out-of-wedlock births, some women have always been left alone with dependent children, and since a woman's wages have traditionally been half a man's or less, female-headed families have been both poor and stigmatized for not attaining the national standard.

Between 1910 and 1920, a movement developed in support of public assistance for female-headed families. To gain widespread support, advocates focused on programs for widows, who at the time represented the majority of single mothers. Describing widows as models of morality, hard work, and good housekeeping, proponents of public assistance successfully established programs for widows and their children in forty out of forty-eight states. Although this financial aid helped widows and their families, deserted and unmarried women and their children were excluded. Even widows could not escape the stigma that touched all lone-mother families. Supporters of public assistance insisted that to qualify, widows had to submit to interviews and site visits evaluating their housekeeping quality, children's cleanliness, and personal habits, with major prohibitions including the consumption of alcohol and intimate relations with men.

By the 1920s advocates of public assistance sought to include unwed mothers in the program. Even the most sympathetic analyses described them as deficient, emphasizing that such women were "feebleminded"—slightly less harsh than the earlier claim of "hereditary depravity."

During the 1940s social workers modernized their explanation, designating unwed mothers as the product of backward cultures and moral standards imported by eastern and southern European immigrants.

Then in the 1950s and 1960s as African Americans pressed for inclusion in welfare programs, social workers observed their high out-of-wedlock birth rates and interpreted that outcome as evidence of cultural inferiority. Meanwhile, when unmarried middle-class white girls became pregnant and gave birth, parents often hired psychiatrists who were likely to diagnose their clients as emotionally disturbed. Historian Linda Gordon noted that in contrast, black girls, who could not afford psychiatric consultation,

> were not suspected of having individual personality attributed to them; they were merely expressing the standard "low" culture and upbringing of their people. As white unwed mothers became increasingly individualized, medicalized, and interesting, black mothers remained a mass, objects not of medical but of sociological and anthropological investigation. (Gordon 2001, 19)

Blacks were eventually accepted in welfare programs, and from the 1960s to the present, they have made up 35 to 40 percent of the total number of recipients. In recent years Asian and Latino participation has increased as their proportions of the overall population has risen. About two-thirds of recipients today are African American, Asian American, Hispanic, and Native American (Burnham 2001, 42–46; Mink 2001, 81). In recent years this distinctly racialized group has encountered a drastically different experience.

The Dynamics of Welfare to Work

In 1996 Congress passed the Personal Responsibility and Work Opportunity Reconciliation Act, and President Clinton signed it into law. The new program reflected the influence of the Republican-controlled Congress elected in 1994. It emphasized the pivotal importance of marriage and responsible fatherhood and motherhood, and a chief means of establishing these conditions was the reduction of teen pregnancy, which, according to the legislation, the current welfare system encouraged. The new law indicated that welfare recipients should become independent wage earners as quickly as possible, and to this end the program provided Temporary Aid to Needy Families (TANF) to support new wage earners while they established themselves.

The multiethnic participants in this welfare-to-work program in Riverside, California, are likely to vary considerably in their abilities to meet the challenges they must face in obtaining and retaining jobs.

Welfare-to-work programs are based on values consistent with the long-established cultural image of the family as a two-parent entity with a husband/father as the dominant breadwinner. Lone women heading families do not achieve the desired model and to many Americans represent a questionable level of deservedness, especially if they have had children out of wedlock. Advocates of welfare reform suggest that their redemption lies in hard work, contending that it is both morally correct and practical to require that welfare recipients become independent wage earners.

Most critics of the new legislation are willing to admit that the old welfare program was in disarray and needed reform. However, they refuse to accept the traditional conclusion that just because women-headed families do not follow the two-parent model those families are less worthy and that the children within them are less worthy of effective nurturing. These observers are deeply concerned about the damage welfare to work inflicts on many, disproportionately minority families (Gordon 2001, 22; Zuckerman 2000, 588–94).

While the opponents of current welfare reform consider the new legislation inhumane, its creators appear to believe that they have established an effective system. These legislators are often upper-middle-class white males who are unaware of the specific challenges facing welfare recipients—individuals who are primarily poor women of color heading families rapidly propelled into the work world. Soon after an early welfare-reform bill was passed, a pair of critics wondered "how many of the men who sit in the halls of Congress have ever played a parenting role in which they had the opportunity to engage in such tasks for even, let us say, one week" (Wilkerson and Gresham 1989, 128).

In analyzing the process of moving from welfare to work, I focus on some of the specific challenges recipients face, challenges often exacerbated by the impact of the racialized social system:

1. One distinct issue involves the chronic low pay. While it is true that welfare rolls have declined dramatically since 1996 and adults leaving welfare have often obtained new jobs and increased income, a number of dire results are also evident. Most women leaving the welfare rolls do not achieve financial independence, lacking the education and work experience for anything but low-paid insecure jobs that, when the full economic picture is taken into account, leave them worse off than when on welfare. Data from 1999 indicate that three years after leaving welfare for work, the median income among former welfare recipients was $10,924—well below the poverty line of $14,150 for a family of three. These women received wages and an earned income-tax credit but lost at least as much income with the cutbacks in welfare and food stamps. Not surprisingly, the number of children in extreme poverty, receiving less than half a poverty-level income, has increased (Albelda 2001, 67; Mink 2001, 87–89; Zuckerman 2000, 597). In the course of welfare reform, access to the Food Stamp Program has become more bureaucratized and confusing. As one national study concluded, that complication, along with widespread lowered income, has meant that "[t]he bottom line is that . . . for millions of households, work force participation has been accompanied by hunger" (Burnham 2001, 42).

2. Evidence from a large random sample of welfare recipients suggested that half of the participants had one or more of the following difficulties: mental-health disorder, substance dependence, and a physical health problem or disability. When one or more of these barriers existed along with limited education or training, the likelihood of obtaining employment significantly decreased. Few state welfare programs provide consistent quality assessments of and services for these kinds of problems, and yet until such formidable issues are competently addressed, the women in question will be incapable of functioning well in the work world (Danziger, Kalil, and Anderson 2000; Jayakody and Stauffer 2000).

3. Research demonstrates that many welfare mothers have low educational attainment and lack recent job experience, impeding their entry into the job market and once there almost guaranteeing low wages. In addition, as noted earlier, job readiness is also important, involving the ability to present oneself effectively to a prospective employer. A black manager in a Chicago insurance company observed that the perception exists that young black people

> don't have the proper skills . . . they don't know how to write. They don't know how to speak. They don't act in a business fashion or dress in a business manner . . . in a way that the business community would like. And they just don't feel that they're getting a quality employee . . .
> *Interviewer:*   Do you think—is that all a false perception or is something there or—?
> *Respondent:*   I think there's some truth to it. (Wilson 1997, 131)

4. Another important problem is child care. Women in two-parent households have frequently found it an almost impossible problem to solve, both because of the cost and because of the unrelenting need to coordinate an often complex job schedule with the child or children's schedules. The "arithmetic" simply doesn't work out. So law professor Lucie E. White raised a compelling question when she asked, "How, then, could the lowest-income single-parent families be expected to solve this care problem?" (White 2001, 136). To be sure, not effectively. Research has indicated that low-income mothers, like all parents, want care that is affordable, convenient, and safe. The vast majority of these women use informal arrangements with family members, friends, or neighbors, and such child care is seldom monitored or regulated. In addition, unlike formal programs, where parents can be certain that child care is the focus, informal arrangements are less predictable. After switching to formal care, one greatly relieved woman said, "I know that when I get up in the morning they'll be open" (Henly and Lyons 2000, 700).

5. A final challenge is transportation. Poor minorities, especially African Americans, have historically been forced to live in isolated areas that prove convenient for the dominant group but do not allow residents easy access to jobs. Increasingly, many businesses are moving out of declining downtown sections of a city and into the urban periphery or suburbs. Poor people, such as welfare mothers, can usually reach these sites only by public transportation. The job commute might take an hour or more and often requires a transfer to a second bus or train. Transportation, of course, involves not only getting to and from work but also the compounded challenge, sometimes under intense time pressure, of reaching a variety of other, often widely dispersed sites like day-care facilities, schools, stores, medical offices, and hospitals. It is hardly surprising that in an interview when asked about her short-term future, one welfare recipient immediately replied, "Hopefully, I'll be working on my driver's license and a car" (Scott, London, and Edin 2000, 740).

S O C I O L O G I C A L   I L L U S T R A T I O N

When Pranks Become Harassment:
The Case of African American Women Firefighters

Psychologists Janice D. Yoder and Patricia Aniakudo (1996) conducted a study of the harassment of African American female firefighters using both a lengthy mailed questionnaire and an hour-long telephone interview. Starting with a set of fifteen names of African American women firefighters obtained from the International Association of Black Professional Firefighters, the researchers generated a list of forty-eight possible respondents. Twenty-two of these women (46 percent) located around the country responded positively to the request to participate in the study.

These women were pioneers in an occupation that white men dominate. Over 95 percent of firefighters are men and 83 percent are white, and majority-group members hardly applauded black women's presence on the job, often responding aggressively and hostilely.

As far as the incidence of sexual harassment was concerned, twenty members (91 percent) of the sample indicated that as firefighters they had experienced unwanted sexual teasing, jokes, or questions. Seventeen (79 percent) said that as firefighters they had been sexually harassed, and fourteen (64 percent) reported that on the job they had experienced unwanted deliberate touching, leaning over, cornering, or pinching.

Most of the respondents had found critical designations scrawled across their pictures or featured in notes—such terms as "bitch," "bitch whore," "dyke," "rebel," "militant," and "outspoken"—and many described fraternity-like pranks: eggs and syrup in boots, short-sheeting of beds, pails of water dangerously balanced on doors and lockers, intrusions into bathrooms, and flashing. A few pranks produced serious results. One woman slipped in water that doused her and her locker, tore cartilage in her knee, required surgery, and afterward goodnaturedly claimed to be able to use the injured knee to predict the weather. Although new male recruits also experienced pranks, it was usually a preliminary step to male bonding—hardly the outcome experienced for the study's respondents.

Consistently, the women in the study described an inhospitable climate in which some or even many men ignored their presence. One respondent said, "I'll go into a room and they act like I'm not here; like I'm invisible" (Yoder and Aniakudo 1996, 260). Part of the general treatment involved disregarding competence and magnifying mistakes. Seldom, the interviewees explained, did a female firefighter even receive credit for doing a job well, generally just being ignored, but if she made a mistake, she became the center of critical attention. Furthermore, a double standard clearly seemed to exist. While the women heard frequent complaints about their deficient upper-body strength, many, in truth, were in peak form, having trained as runners, bodybuilders, and athletes who became firefighters because of its physical demands. In contrast, one respondent noted that "you have men on the equipment who were so grossly overweight, they couldn't even tie their shoe-strings. They had to get boots and pull them up!" (Yoder and Aniakudo 1996, 261).

Finally, as African Americans these women had to face questions and insinuations about affirmative action, suggesting that the only reason they obtained the job was to fulfill that requirement. As a firefighter of nine years who was the first African American in her house explained, "They felt that I have been given special preference to get onto the job. And those were the types of rumors that I heard as time went on: that I was hired because I was a Black woman, that I could not perform" (Yoder and Aniakudo 1996, 262).

Although most hostility toward the respondents occurred in low-key, indirect ways, the black female firefighters experienced various situations that clearly spelled out the men's opposition to their presence. Three women reported that male peers asked for transfers to avoid being partnered with them. Another described a captain who "fought tooth and nail to make sure I was not gonna get on his shift" (Yoder and Aniakudo 1996, 264). A sixteen-year veteran provided the starkest case of rejection when she indicated that

(continued)

the first day I came on, the first day I was in the field, [my captain] told me he didn't like me. And then he said: "I'm gonna tell you why I don't like you. Number one, I don't like you cuz you're Black. And number two, cuz you're a woman." And that was all he said. He walked away. (Yoder and Aniakudo 1996, 263)

Although most incidents the respondents described appeared linked with their being female rather than being black, the women consistently considered the two factors intertwined. As one of them summarized, "it [is] double edged[d]: being black and being female" (Yoder and Aniakudo 1996, 266).

In spite of frequent rejection, the respondents almost unanimously embraced their jobs, describing them as challenging, satisfying, fascinating, enjoyable, worthwhile, and pleasant. One firefighter, who

was the first African American and the first woman in her department, explained,

> It's been wild. It's just been 14 of the most exciting years of my life, I'll tell you. I can't imagine what would I have done, if, you know, what my life would be, if it hadn't been for the fire department. The knowledge that I've acquired, the opportunity to travel . . . And I've learned a lot. That's how I've learned, you know. [I]t's just been amazing. I've made some wonderful friends. It's just amazing. (Yoder and Aniakudo 1996, 266)

In conclusion, the black female firefighters found themselves in a setting that was both racialized and genderized. As they themselves noted, the two conditions were intertwined, often promoting a relentlessly hostile work setting.

Mounting evidence suggests that the easily placed welfare recipients have already moved into the work world. Those who remain are deficient in critical capital—for instance, the cultural capital of job-readiness skills, the human capital of job training and education, and the financial capital of a car for reaching far-flung jobs sites—but unfortunately welfare-reform programs have provided little support for overcoming such disadvantages (Albelda 2001, 71).

Although the challenges many women of color confront in the work world appear to be somewhat less formidable than those just described, the previous Sociological Illustration indicates that the blend of race and gender can be important factors adversely affecting adjustment on the job.

As this chapter draws to a close, it seems useful to pull together some of its central ideas in Table 5.1, which demonstrate that certain race- and ethnicity-related issues prove to be definite assets for job placement while others are just as decisively debits.

Conclusion

Looking at Table 5.1, we can see that both historically and currently advantage in access to the job world varies considerably with ethnic and racial groups.

Yet whether or not they are the beneficiaries of those conditions, Americans often appear to share a general outlook on their jobs. After interviewing Americans in over one hundred occupations, journalist Studs Terkel wrote, "No matter how bewildering the times,

TABLE 5.1   Outstanding Race- and Ethnicity-Related Assets and Debits for the Urban Job World

Groups Assets	Group Debits
Early entrance into the process of ethnic succession	Late entrance into ethnic succession or during earlier eras such severe restrictions as slavery or reservation location impeding occupational progress
Access to occupational advancement offered by such structures as political organizations, unions, and ethnic enclaves	Limited or no access to these opportunities
Beneficiaries of structural mobility	Location in society offering limited or no access to structural mobility

Characteristics to do well in the racialized job pipeline:
    Membership in racial or ethnic group recruiters regard well
    Access to relevant job networks
    Good job-readiness skills
	Characteristics to encounter problems in the racialized job pipeline:
	    Membership in racial or ethnic group recruiters view in stereotyped way
	    Limited or no access to relevant job networks
	    Poor job-readiness skills

Most privileged group: corporate community, with membership 90–95% male, 95% white; often born into the upper class	Distinctly disadvantaged category: female family heads in welfare-to-work transition; two-thirds minorities, with limited education and training and a complex set of challenges

no matter how dissembling the official language, those we call ordinary are aware of a sense of personal worth—or more often a lack of it—in the work they do" (Terkel 1974, xxiv).

How is the future likely to affect Americans' sense of personal worth on the job? In the summer of 2002, a panel of the Appellate Division of the New York Supreme Court ruled that the state must only provide what Justice Alfred D. Lerner writing for the majority called a "minimally adequate educational opportunity," meaning an eighth-grade education. Lerner went on to indicate that "society needs workers at all levels of jobs, the majority of which may be very low-level" (Gehring 2002, 2).

Racial minorities—blacks, Hispanics, Native Americans, recently arrived immigrants from a number of countries and their children—are a substantial portion of the pool of workers Lerner accepted as trapped in low-level service jobs. What would be the societal impact of such a bleak, exclusionary vision?

DISCUSSION QUESTIONS

1. Analyze the significance of ethnic succession, comparing two ethnic or racial groups that are very differently positioned in relation to it.

2. Are you aware of any individuals or families that have benefited from belonging to ethnic enclaves? If so, discuss. Then examine bonded solidarity and enforceable trust, illustrating these activities with any examples you have observed or otherwise encountered.

3. Discuss Hi Duk Lee's vision for Koreatown. Does it appeal to you, or does it seem old fashioned or in some other way misguided?

4. Examine the process of job discrimination, describing any incidents of which you are aware and highlighting situations in which its occurrence is subtle but effective.

5. Discuss possible approaches to combating job discrimination, indicating why they are or are not likely to be effective.

6. Evaluate the welfare-to-work program, describing its strengths and weaknesses and suggesting possible ways of reforming welfare reform.

BIBLIOGRAPHY

Alba, Richard. 1985. *Italian Americans: Into the Twilight of Ethnicity.* Englewood Cliffs, NJ: Prentice-Hall.

Albelda, Randy. 2001. "Fallacies of Welfare-to-Work Policies." *Annals of the American Academy of Political and Social Science.* 577 (September): 66–78.

Bailyn, Bernard et al. 1977. *The Great Republic.* Lexington, MA: Heath.

Bendick, Marc, Jr., Charles W. Jackson, Victor A. Reinoso, and Laura E. Hodges. 1993. "Discrimination Against Latino Job Applicants: A Controlled Experiment," pp. 86–93 in John A. Kromkowski (ed.), *Race and Ethnic Relations 97/98,* 7th ed. Guilford, CT: Dushkin.

Bielby, William T. 2000. "Minimizing Workplace Gender and Racial Bias." *Contemporary Sociology.* 29 (January): 120–29.

Braddock, Jomills Henry, II, and James N. McPartland. 1987. "How Minorities Continue to Be Excluded from Equal Employment Opportunities: Research on Labor Market and Institutional Barriers." *Journal of Social Issues.* 43: 5–39.

Burnham, Linda. 2001. "Welfare Reform, Family Hardship, and Women of Color." *Annals of the American Academy of Political and Social Science.* 577 (September): 38–48.

Burris, Val. 2000. "The Myth of Old Money Liberalism: The Politics of the *Forbes* 400 Richest Americans." *Social Problems.* 47 (August): 360–78.

Burum, Linda. 2001. "Authentic Ethnic." *Los Angeles Times.* (January 25). www.bridgecreek.com/articles/Little Saigon Has its Fill of Delights.htm

Campbell, Bebe Moore. 1982. "Black Executives and Corporate Stress." *New York Times Magazine.* (December 12): 36–39+.

Chun, Ki-Taek. 1993. "The Myth of Asian American Success and Its Educational Ramifications," pp. 175–85 in Young I. Song and Eugene C. Kim (eds.), *American Mosaic.* Englewood Cliffs, NJ: Prentice-Hall.

Collins, Sharon M. 1997. "Black Mobility in White Corporations: Up the Corporate Ladder but Out on a Limb." *Social Problems.* 44 (February): 55–67.

Cose, Ellis. 1999. "A Dozen Demons," pp. 18–24 in Christopher G. Ellison and W. Allen Martin (eds.), *Race and Ethnic Relations in the United States: Readings for the 21st Century.* Los Angeles: Roxbury.

Danziger, Sandra K., Ariel Kalil, and Nathaniel J. Anderson. 2000. "Human Capital, Physical Health, and Mental Health of Welfare Recipients: Co-occurrence and Correlates." *Journal of Social Issues.* 56: 635–54.

Darity, William A., Jr., and Patrick L. Mason. 1998. "Evidence on Discrimination in Employment: Codes of Color, Codes of Gender." *Journal of Economic Perspectives.* 12 (Spring): 63–90.

Domhoff, G. William. 1998. *Who Rules America? Power and Politics in the Year 2000,* 3rd ed. Mountain View, CA: Mayfield.

Doob, Christopher Bates. 1967. *The Development of Peer Group Relationships Among Puerto Rican Boys in East Harlem.* Unpublished Ph.D. dissertation.

Eichenwald, Kurt. 1996. "The Two Faces of Texaco." *New York Times.* (November 10): sec. 3, p. 1+.

Elliott, James R., and Ryan A. Smith. 2001. "Ethnic Matching of Supervisors to Subordinate Work Groups: Findings on "Bottom-up" Ascription and Social Closure." *Social Problems.* 48 (May): 258–76.

Gehring, John. 2002. "New York Appeals Court Rebuffs Lower Court's School Aid Ruling." *Education*

Week. (July 10): 1–3. www.edweek.org/ew/newstory. cfm?slug=42nyc.h21.

Gitter, Robert J., and Patricia B. Reagan. 2002. "Reservation Wages: An Analysis of the Effects of Reservations on Employment of American Indian Men." *The American Economic Review.* 92 (September): 1160–68.

Gordon, Linda. 2001. "Who Deserves Help? Who Must Provide?" *Annals of the American Academy of Political and Social Science.* 577 (September): 12–25.

Hacker, Andrew. 1992. *Two Nations: Black and White, Separate, Hostile, Unequal.* New York: Scribner.

Hamill, Pete. 1994. *A Drinking Life: A Memoir.* Boston: Little, Brown.

Healey, Joseph F. 2003. *Race, Ethnicity, Gender, and Class: The Sociology of Group Conflict and Change,* 3rd ed. Thousand Oaks, CA: Pine Forge Press.

Henly, Julia R., and Sandra Lyons. 2000. "The Negotiation of Child Care and Employment Demands Among Low-Income Parents." *Journal of Social Issuees.* 56: 683–706.

Hirschman, Charles, and Morrison Wong. 1986. "The Extraordinary Educational Attainment of Asian-Americans: A Search for Historical Evidence and Explanations." *Social Forces.* 65 (January): 1–27.

Hondagneu-Sotelo, Pierrette. 2001. *Doméstica: Immigrant Workers Cleaning and Caring in the Shadows of Affluence.* Berkeley and Los Angeles: University of California Press.

Ingham, John N. 1978. *The Iron Barons.* Westport, CT: Greenwood Press.

Jayakody, Rukmalie, and Dawn Stauffer. 2000. "Mental Health Problems Among Single Mothers: Implications for Work and Welfare Reform." *Journal of Social Issues.* 56: 617–34.

Jaynes, Gerald David, and Robin M. Williams Jr. (eds.). 1989. *A Common Destiny: Blacks and American Society.* Washington, DC: National Academy Press.

Johnson, Kirk. 1997. "Black Workers Bear Big Burden as Jobs in Government Dwindle." *New York Times.* (February 2): 1+.

Jones, Edward W., Jr. 1973. "What It's Like to Be a Black Manager." *Harvard Business Review.* 51 (July/August): 108–16.

Jones, Edward W., Jr. 1986. "Black Managers: The Dream Deferred." *Harvard Business Review.* 64 (July/August): 84–93.

Juntunen, Cindy L., et al. 2001. "American Indian Perspectives on the Career Journey." *Journal of Counseling Psychology.* 48 (July): 274–85.

Kantowicz, Edward R. 1994. "The Changing Face of Ethnic Politics: From Political Machine to Community Organization," pp. 179–95 in Timothy Walch (ed.), *Immigrant America: European Ethnicity in the United States.* New York: Garland.

Kenny, Kevin. 2000. *The American Irish: A History.* Harlow, England: Longman.

Lai, Tracy. 1998. "Asian American Women: Not for Sale," pp. 209–16 in Margaret L. Andersen and Patricia Hill Collins (eds.), *Race, Class, and Gender: An Anthology,* 3rd ed. Belmont, CA: Wadsworth.

Li, Wen Lang. 1982. "Chinese Americans: Exclusion from the Melting Pot," pp. 303–28 in Anthony Gary Dworkin and Rosalind J. Dworkin (eds.), *The Minority Report: An Introduction to Racial, Ethnic, and Gender Relations,* 2nd ed. New York: Holt, Rinehart and Winston.

Light, Ivan H. 1972. *Ethnic Enterprise in America.* Berkeley and Los Angeles University of California Press.

Light, Ivan, and Steven J. Gold. 2000. *Ethnic Economies.* San Diego: Academic Press.

Logan, John R., and Harvey L. Molotch. 1987. *Urban Fortunes: The Political Economy of Place.* Berkeley: University of California Press.

Lopez, Felix. 1976. "The Bell's System's Non-Management Personnel Selection Strategy," pp. 226–27 in Phyllis A. Wallace (ed.), *Equal Opportunity and the AT&T Case.* Cambridge, MA: MIT Press.

Lyman, Stanford M. 1974. *Chinese Americans.* New York: Random House.

Massey, Douglas. 1996. "The Age of Extremes: Concentrated Affluence and Poverty in the Twenty-first Century." *Demography.* 33 (Winter): 395–412.

McCall, Nathan. 1994. *Makes Me Wanna Holler: A Young Black Man in America.* New York: Random House.

Miller, William. 1949. "American Historians and the Business Elite." *Journal of Economic History.* 9 (November): 184–208.

Mink, Gwendolyn. 2001. "Violating Women: Rights Abuses in the Welfare Police State." *Annals of the American Academy of Political and Social Science.* 577 (September): 79–93.

Moberg, David. 2001. "Organization Man." *Nation.* 273 (July 16): 23–24+.

Neckerman, Kathryn M., and Joleen Kirschenman. 1999. "'*We'd* Love to Hire Them But . . . ': The Meaning of Race for Employers," pp. 276–87 in Charles A. Gallagher (ed.), *Rethinking the Color Line: Readings in Race and Ethnicity.* Mountain View, CA: Mayfield.

Ostrander, Susan. 1984. *Women of the Upper Class.* Philadelphia: Temple University Press.

Pager, Devah. 2003. "The Mark of a Criminal Record." *American Journal of Sociology.* 108 (March): 937–75.

Parrillo, Vincent N. 2003. *Strangers to These Shores: Race and Ethnic Relations in the United States,* 7th ed. Boston: Allyn and Bacon.

Pettigrew, Thomas F., and Joanne Martin. 1987. "Shaping the Organizational Context for Black American Inclusion." *Journal of Social Issues.* 43: 41–78.

Portes, Alejandro, and Robert D. Manning. 1986. "The Immigrant Enclave: Theory and Empirical Examples," pp. 47–68 in Susan Olzak and Joane Nagel (eds.), *Competitive Ethnic Relations.* Orlando: Academic Press.

Portes, Alejandro, and Min Zhou. 1992. "Gaining the Upper Hand: Economic Mobility Among Immigrant and Domestic Minorities." *Ethnic and Racial Studies.* 15: 513–18.

Portes, Alejandro, and Min Zhou. 1999. "The New Second Generation: Segmented Assimilation and Its Variants," pp. 494–503 in Christopher G. Ellison and W. Allen Martin (eds.), *Race and Ethnic Relations in the United States: Readings for the 21st Century.* Los Angles: Roxbury.

Powell, Thomas. 1969. *Race, Religion, and the Promotion of the American Executive.* Columbus: Ohio State University Press.

Quinones, Sam. 2001. "The Koreatown That Never Was." *Los Angeles Times.* (June 3). www.calendarlive.com/top/1,419.L-LATimes-Search-X!ArticleDetail-34897,00.html.

Rader, Benjamin G. 1983. *American Sports: From the Age of Folk Games to the Age of Spectators.* Englewood Cliffs, NJ: Prentice-Hall.

Schram, Sanford F., and Joe Soss. 2001. "Success Stories: Welfare Reform, Policy Discourse, and the Politics of Research." *Annals of the American Academy of Political and Social Science.* 577 (September): 49–65.

Scott, Ellen K., Andrew S. London, and Kathryn Edin. 2000. "Looking to the Future: Welfare-Reliant Women Talk About Their Job Aspirations in the Context of Welfare Reform." *Journal of Social Issues.* 56: 727–46.

Segura, Denise A. 1999. "Chicanas in White-Collar Jobs: 'You Have to Prove Yourself More,' " pp. 79–88 in Christopher G. Ellison and W. Allen Martin (eds.), *Race and Ethnic Relations in the United States: Readings for the 21st Century.* Los Angeles: Roxbury.

Shannon, William V. 1989. *The American Irish: A Political and Social Portrait,* 2nd ed. Amherst: University of Massachusetts Press.

Sklar, Holly. 1995. "Imagine a Country," pp. 121–30 in Paula S. Rothenberg (ed.), *Race, Class, and Gender in the United States: An Integrated Study,* 2nd ed. New York: St. Martin's Press.

Stolzenberg, Ross M., and Marta Tienda. 1997. "English Proficiency, Education, and the Conditional Economic Assimilation of Hispanic and Asian Origin Men." *Social Science Research.* 26 (March): 25–51.

Terkel, Studs. 1974. *Working.* New York: Pantheon Books.

Torres, Joseph. 1999. "Invisible Ink?" *Hispanic.* 12 (October): 22+.

Waldinger, Roger D. 1996. *Still the Promised City.* Cambridge: Harvard University Press.

Ward, Carol. 1998. "The Importance of Context in Explaining Human Capital Formation and Labor Force Participation of American Indians in Rosebud County, Montana." *Rural Sociology.* 63 (September): 451–80.

Wahl, Jenny B. 2003. "From Riches to Riches: Intergenerational Transfers and the Evidence from Estate Tax Returns." *Social Science Quarterly.* 84 (June): 278–96.

Wellner, Alison Stein, and John Fetto. 2003. "Worth a Closer Look." *American Demographics.* 25 (June): 29–37.

Western, Bruce. 2002. "The Impact of Incarceration on Wage Mobility and Inequality." *American Sociological Review.* 67 (August): 526–46.

White, Lucie E. 2001. "Closing the Care Gap That Welfare Reform Left Behind." *Annals of the American Academy of Political and Social Science.* 577 (September): 131–43.

Wilkerson, Margaret, and Jewell Handy Gresham. 1989. "Sexual Politics of Welfare: The Racialization of Poverty." *Nation.* 249 (July 24/31): 126–30+.

Wilson, William Julius. 1997. *When Work Disappears: The World of the New Urban Poor.* New York: Vintage Books.

Woo, Deborah. 1998. "The Gap between Striving and Achieving: The Case of Asian American Women," pp. 247–55 in Margaret L. Andersen and Patricia Hill Collins (eds.), *Race, Class, and Gender: An Anthology,* 3rd ed. Belmont, CA: Wadsworth.

Yoder, Janice D., and Patricia Aniakudo. 1996. "When Pranks Become Harassment: The Case of African American Women Firefighters." *Sex Roles.* 35 (September): 253–70.

Yoon, In-Jin. 1999. "The Growth of Korean Immigrant Entrepreneurship in Chicago," pp. 123–31 in Christopher G. Ellison and W. Allen Martin (eds.), *Race and Ethnic Relations in the United States: Readings for the 21st Century.* Los Angeles: Roxbury.

Zhou, Min. 2001. "Contemporary Immigration and the Dynamics of Race and Ethnicity," pp. 200–42 in Neil J. Smelser, William Julius Wilson, and Faith Mitchell (eds.), *America Becoming: Racial Trends and Their Consequences,* vol. I. Washington, DC: National Academy Press.

Zuckerman, Diana M. 2000. "Welfare Reform in America: A Clash of Politics and Research." *Journal of Social Issues.* 56: 587–600.

6 Exclusion or Inclusion? Access to the Halls of Urban Power

In a mid-nineteenth-century eastern city, a practical joker's stunt made it clear that this rough-and-tumble era no longer nurtured an aristocratic type of urban politician. A newsboy the trickster had hired ran into the aldermanic chamber and shouted, "Hey, mister, your saloon's on fire." In an instant the room had cleared.

Though no longer in the saloon business, modern political leaders still maintain the same basic motivation: to win and hold political power. One of the first African American politicians elected mayor of a large American city stressed a valuable tactic. In campaigning throughout the city's diverse neighborhoods, he emphasized a single set of ideas and actions, altering only the designation of which group would be the potential beneficiary. Later, a well-known Hispanic mayor, who became a cabinet member in the Clinton administration, indicated that a successful, urban-based minority-led campaign requires carefully planned speeches in which candidates both nail down votes from their own ethnic group by clear if discrete references to support for members' interests and also obtain substantial majority-group backing by promoting prominent citywide concerns (Hero and Beatty 1989).

Modern urban politicians, it appears, are salespeople in a complicated, demanding setting. They must be attuned to diverse needs and interests—such players as local corporate groups, various public and private occupation-linked organizations, and constituents from different races and ethnicities. All political action occurs in a setting where other layers of political activity, most notably the economy and the federal government, play a frequently changing, often increasingly intricate role. Observations suggest that urban politicians tend to be impossibly busy, usually energetic people, who almost always run late for appointments and meetings and try, often quite convincingly, to convey that they are committed to satisfying the needs their petitioners express.

In this chapter we consider four historical periods of American city government and then examine current urban political activity for large categories of racial and ethnic groups.

Urban Political Realities across Time

Through the centuries American cities have formed, grown, and constantly altered in appearance and function. One consistent element, however, has been an intimate if not always smooth relationship between the respective members of the local political and economic leadership. Invariably, politicians keep this relationship in mind, and it influences many important decisions. Often the outcome is that elected officials talk more about providing support for less affluent groups' needs and interests than actually addressing those realities.

The first of the four eras started over three hundred years ago.

The Emergence of a Nearly Aristocratic Elite

By the 1680s, the children and grandchildren of the original colonies' first English inhabitants were the political leaders of the towns, exploiting the growing economic stakes. Not only did these men and their families possess the increasingly valuable land their ancestors had started cultivating, but their political leadership gave them control of the vast amounts of still undivided territory, which they could sell to new arrivals, greatly enriching themselves in the process. A grandson of John Winthrop, the founder of the Massachusetts Bay colony, explained that it was little enough reward "for the waste of that plentiful estate which my predecessors joyfully laid down to begin the growth and prosperity of this country" (Bailyn et al. 1977, 135). Wealth from the sale of lands then helped the members of this elite group consolidate power in their local regions.

In the port cities of Boston and New York, later in Newport, Philadelphia, and Charlestown, a select group of merchants, who engaged in trade in the colonies and with Caribbean ports, also joined the local political leadership group. Both the large landowners and successful merchants were set apart from other settlers, and their manor houses and town houses were visible testimony to those leaders' superior wealth. However, though they were better off than others, they did not form a distinctly separate class, clearly lacking the great wealth and aristocratic tradition of Europe's well-established nobility.

In the colonies, newly obtained wealth, was the basis for obtaining superior rank and power, but it could disappear in a flash in an era when liquid funds (assets easily converted to cash) scarcely existed. As a result, even a modest challenge to an individual's economic fortune could produce bankruptcy. In 1707 Samuel Lillie, who held shares in 108 vessels,

42 of which he owned outright, was not only Boston's leading shipowner but one of its most powerful political leaders. Yet when faced with the need to pay a debt for a few hundred pounds, he was unable to do so, fleeing to England, never to be heard from again. Many others also tumbled out of wealth and power into poverty and obscurity.

Another problem for early town political leaders was that they often faced direct challenge from those who felt left out in the pursuit of wealth. When second- and third-generation colonists began forming exclusive landholding companies to control the yet undivided land, later arrivals who wanted a piece of the fertile pie challenged them. The leaders' most frequent response was to meet separately outside the normal town meetings, carrying on with their plans to sell the yet undivided land and sometimes offering bribes to the most vocal opponents or those with special claims. Occasionally, the excluded individuals brought their case to the General Court, where most decisions favored heirs of the original settlers (Bailyn et al. 1977, 135–48).

In the early nineteenth century, as American cities grew larger and more complex, political leadership also began to change.

Entrepreneurial Leadership in an Era of Growing Governmental Demands

The British American urban elite had the greatest staying power in the older eastern ports, where wealthy, leisured men like Mayor Philip Hone of New York City felt it was the natural, proper thing that they provide an elevated municipal guidance, always, of course, discreetly protecting their own substantial economic interests along the way. By the 1830s, however, vigorous, ambitious new arrivals began elbowing themselves into leadership positions. Meanwhile in the faster-growing interior cities like Pittsburgh, Cincinnati, Louisville, St. Louis, and New Orleans, new entrepreneurs committed to shepherding their expanding economic interests took control, often to leave political office once their cities had established firm growth patterns.

By the middle nineteenth century, in fact, the growing complexity of urban problems made political officials' role increasingly demanding. These rapidly expanding cities required leaders who would address pressing issues such as the following ones:

■ *Health and housing:* By the 1850s city leaders showed growing appreciation of the relationship between filthy neighborhoods and disease, particularly the likelihood that epidemics started or flourished in slum neighborhoods. In the wake of New York City's Tenement Law of 1901, over forty American cities developed fairly well-enforced building codes.

■ *Police and fire control:* In 1845 New York City was the first American city to establish a uniformed police force, and other prominent cities quickly followed. In 1900 cities with 30,000 or more inhabitants maintained a national total of over 28,000 uniformed policemen. By that date the fire departments in Boston and New York City were widely considered the best in the world, and Chicago's force had as many men as London's and more horses and steam engines, even though the American city was only a third as large as the English metropolis.

■ *Public parks:* From the 1870s city leaders considered parks important for community health, particularly as wholesome areas for poor residents and children to pursue recreation. Under the supervision of Frederick Olmsted, a distinguished landscape architect, New York City in 1858 began the construction of Central Park. Within thirty years, most American cities began looking for land that could be converted into parks (Glaab and Brown 1967, 172–78).

As Chapter 3 indicated, Boss Tweed played a prominent role in the development of Central Park, steadfastly pursuing the project and readily violating laws to keep moving ahead.

The bosses stood in bold contrast to most incumbent city leaders, who were often incompetent at confronting the new administrative problems just described and lacked the experience to communicate with the increasingly more diversified ethnic mix entering American cities.

New arrivals, in fact, were ideal clients for bosses, whose organizations provided "government with a human face." A greenhorn just off the boat, alone and understandably terrified in a new, strange land and in immediate, often desperate need of food, shelter, and a job for himself and often for other family members "must have breathed a sigh of relief when the machine's ward-heeler [a low-level member of the organization] greeted him with a smile and an outstretched hand" (Kantowicz 1994, 179–80).

A **political machine** is an organization designed to use both legal and illegal means to run a city, county, or state government. Representatives of these mid-nineteenth-century political machines not only found food, housing, and jobs for Irish or other newly arrived immigrants but also accompanied them to naturalization hearings and attended their weddings, wakes, and religious celebrations.

Besides the specific assistance they provided, the bosses' political machines gave the groups they served both recognition and leverage. For instance, if a machine boss gave a German, Irish, Polish, or Italian immigrant a job or designated one of his bright, ambitious sons to run for elective office, then that opportunity would reflect not only on the immediate recipient but also on the entire ethnic community, whose members could readily appreciate that others might follow a similarly successful occupational path. Furthermore, the machines provided new immigrants a certain political leverage, locating them on the power ladder's lower rung, where the more adept could start tinkering with such challenges as playing one political machine against another or mobilizing the local ethnic community to convince the leadership to address some mutually shared goal (Kantowicz 1994, 180).

In their cities, the bosses ran the main economic game, controlling the distribution of all contracts for both private and public building as well as the allotment of municipal services, the establishment of various utility rates, and authority over the city's police force (involving such lucrative activities as tavern and liquor regulations, prostitution, and gambling). For the political machines, it was an enormously profitable operation. From 1868 to 1871, Boss Tweed of the machine known as Tammany Hall diverted between $30 million and $100 million of public funding to himself and his henchmen, astronomically accelerating the traditional 10 percent machine "take." A courthouse project, for instance, which originally was supposed to cost $250,000, eventually soaked the public for $14 million,

This cartoon shows Tammany Hall, Boss Tweed's political machine, reduced to rubble following the election of November 1871. Boss Tweed is the large man in the middle, and Mayor Hall clings to a remnant of the building.

with more than 90 percent of the overruns going toward payoffs, bribes, and fake contracts (Judd and Swanstrom 2002, 60–61).

Once bosses' theft of public funds was well publicized, they became the topic of frequent negative exposure in newspapers and magazines. Around the country cartoonists represented the boss in a stereotyped manner, showing him either jovial or smiling, often wearing a derby hat, smoking a cigar, and "usually portrayed with his hand in the public till, surrounded by ill-washed, grinning, and rough-looking cronies" (Glaab and Brown 1967, 202).

In spite of stereotyped representations, machine politics varied from city to city. Although Irish politicians favoring Irish immigrants dominated most of the large, nineteenth-century political machines, there were substantial exceptions. Chicago, for instance, perhaps because of its extremely rapid growth and sprawling geography, never fell under a single boss's control; instead, various bosses catered to different groups, with one boss appealing to Irish Catholics, another to blacks, and a third and a fourth dividing the support from middle-class whites of northern European ancestry (Glaab and Brown 1967, 208–09; Judd and Swanstrom 2002, 63).

The pattern of political machines' success bore a close relationship to the immigration trends, and when in the 1880s and beyond those trends began to change, the machines were adversely affected.

From the Demise of Bossism
to the Dawn of the Modern Era

Two factors contributed to political machines' decline. The bosses depended on support primarily from Irish and secondarily from German immigrants, to whom they supplied various types of assistance in exchange for political support. They were less comfortable with the southern and eastern Europeans who in the 1880s replaced the earlier arrivals as the primary immigrant groups. Like other established whites, the members of the political machines tended to see these newcomers as possessing inferior racial stock and cultural traditions, and the new residents, in turn, recognized the prejudice directed against them and were reluctant to solicit the bosses' help.

Besides the difficulty gaining new recruits, the bosses also had to face the gradual loss of their core constituency, the earlier immigrants whose support they could rely on in exchange for petty favors and patronage. Descendants of these groups became the beneficiaries of upward mobility, improving their jobs and residential locations and no longer finding the bosses' assistance either necessary or desirable (Judd and Swanstrom 2002, 103–04).

At the beginning of the twentieth century, just as the bosses' machines were suffering serious decline, the progressive movement developed. It was an era of expanding mass media—newspapers and magazines in which "muckraking" journalists like Lincoln Steffens described in great detail the "inside stories" of vice and corruption their investigative reporting produced. In 1904 Steffens published a best-selling book entitled *The Shame of the Cities,* which along with other writers' articles and books, including popular novels by Theodore Dreiser and Upton Sinclair, portrayed urban reform as a dramatic, critical necessity (Judd and Swanstrom 2002, 80–81).

These reformers, some of whom were women, generally came from northern European Protestant upper-class backgrounds. They included wealthy industrialists, lawyers, newspaper editors and publishers, medical doctors, real-estate brokers, and bankers. Most reformers were college graduates at a time when that accomplishment, particularly for women, was unusual.

They believed that well-educated experts with extensive training and experience should control city services. They contended that just as scientists and inventors were revolutionizing life with a host of increasingly efficient machines, competent specialists could apply scientific principles to government, much as they had previously done to business organizations.

The urban reformers supported middle-class, business-oriented candidates and interests. In contrast, immigrants from central and southern Europe represented a disproportionate share of the poor and working-class residents and generally opposed the reform movement, particularly in larger cities, where coalitions of immigrants and other working-class groups engaged in political actions against key elements in the reform programs (Glaab and Brown 1967, 219–20; Judd and Swanstrom 2002, 91–92, 99–100).

Emphasizing efficient, business-style government, the reformers found such opposition both irritating and destructive. In an 1890 issue of *Forum,* Andrew D. White, the first president of Cornell University, lashed out:

> The questions in a city are not political questions. . . . The work of a city being the creation and control of the city property, it should logically be managed as a piece of property by

those who have created it, who have a title to it, or a real substantial part in it . . . [and not by] a crowd of illiterate peasants, freshly raked in from the Irish bogs, or Bohemian [Czech] mines, or Italian robber nests. (Judd and Swanstrom 2002, 83)

Although some reformers would have liked to disenfranchise immigrants, such a proposal was unfeasible a century ago in an era where widespread support for popular democracy existed.

In Chapter 4, discussion indicated that popular democracy did little to support blacks moving to northern and midwestern cities. Isolated in ghetto areas, they fell victim to the urban renewal program, which during the 1950s and 1960s supported a variety of affluent, prominent political and economic interests but only exacerbated the crowded, dilapidated conditions residents faced. In the modern era, it becomes apparent that this legacy has had an effect on urban political activity.

In addition, as American cities advanced toward modern times, immigrants continued to arrive, and like their predecessors, they often found barriers to participation in the political realm. Table 6.1 summarizes features of the four political eras described in the chapter.

The Contemporary Ethnic and Racial Array of Political Participants

Nowadays over three hundred American cities have minority mayors. Most are African American, and almost every large city, including the three biggest—New York, Los Angeles,

TABLE 6.1   Features of Four Political Eras in American Cities

Era	Years Covered	Politicians' Racial and Ethnic Character	Prevailing Political Approach
Emergence of a nearly aristocratic elite	Mid-17th century until first third of the 19th century	British American	Maintenance of political and economic control in the hands of a select few
Entrepreneurial leadership in a time of growing governmental demand	Early 19th century until last third of the 19th century	Primarily northern Europeans, with a growing Irish American presence	Recognition of the need to address expanding cities' needs, with corrupt practices prevalent
From the demise of bossism to the dawn of the modern era	Last third of 19th century until about the middle 1960s	Upper-class northern European reformers opposed by more recent immigrants from southern and central Europe	Reform of urban corruption to promote scientifically maintained government coordinated with smoothly running business activities
Contemporary ethnic and racial array of political participants	Middle 1980s to present	A gradually increasing proportion of blacks and other racial minorities	A dominant role for the pro-growth framework and the self-help ideology

and Chicago—has had a black man as its top elected official. A number of mayors have been Hispanic, including four in three major Texas cities. In the next fifty years, a projected sharp increase of both Hispanic and Asian Americans is likely to mean more candidates from both groups attaining top political positions in American cities (Gottdiener and Hutchison 2000, 248–56; McWhirter 2000).

Besides the politicians themselves, the modern players in urban politics have included the business elite, middle-class reformers, professional city planners, private developers, various racial and ethnic interests, and administrative leaders focused on planning, engineering, and the distribution of basic services.

Although each of these factions has its own goals and can become entangled in squabbles or disputes to promote them, the overriding reality has been a commitment to what some observers call a "pro-growth" framework focusing on American cities' transition from an industrial to a prostindustrial or corporate phase. Dominant elements in this framework include the following:

- Dispersion of manufacturing from the inner city toward the outskirts of the city, its suburbs, and often beyond the region.
- Movement of retail commerce from downtown to the suburbs and replacement by corporate structures.
- Flight of working-, middle-, and upper-class residents toward the urban periphery with a steady influx into the inner city of poor, disproportionately minority residents, many of whom are employed in low-paying service jobs (Reed 1999, 84–86).

As the new urban paradigm emphasizes, this is a framework in which corporate interests tend to dominate.

It is important to recognize that whether conservative, liberal, or middle-of-the-road, the major participants in the pro-growth coalition appear to have accepted these elements, seldom opposing them. In particular, members of the pro-growth coalition do not challenge the conventional distribution of income, which leaves a large core of poor, primarily minority workers and most of their descendants locked into a timeless pattern of servicing the corporate economy.

According to political scientist Adolph Reed Jr., the pro-growth coalition has endorsed a "self-help" ideology—a set of guidelines that Reagan administration members developed for dealing with poor, inner-city minorities. In the middle 1980s, federal government officials concluded that the social pathologies of inner-city, largely black ghettos are beyond the scope of publicly financed and controlled programs. Seeking to establish a policy consistent with Daniel Patrick Moynihan's ethnic pluralism perspective discussed in Chapter 2, they argued that the most viable option is to put control of rehabilitative efforts in the hands of knowledgeable, middle-class blacks. This conclusion has generally received support from racially and politically diverse urban leaders.

The federal government has sponsored the pro-growth framework and the self-help ideology, producing such programs as the recent Empowerment Fund, which has hired black leaders to oversee the distribution of large sums of money to designated cities, where the goal has been to develop programs that help local poor people remove themselves from poverty. As the upcoming Sociological Illustration about Detroit illustrates, the economic and personnel commitment has tended to be insufficient to produce meaningful inroads into cities' current level of poverty.

Reed indicated that although he has strongly supported grassroots activism, the self-help scheme puts the groups that engage in it in an isolated, highly disadvantaged position for accomplishing their goals. He wrote:

> Each attempt by a neighborhood or church group to scrounge around the philanthropic world and the interstices of the federal system for funds to build low-income housing or day care or neighborhood centers, to organize programs that compensate for inadequate school funding, public safety, or trash pickup, simultaneously concedes that black citizens cannot legitimately pursue those benefits through government. (Reed 1999, 126)

Minority politicians, who have little alternative to joining pro-growth coalitions, find themselves in cities where these difficult, self-help–related issues arise. As Figure 6.1 emphasizes, they must function within a racialized social system that is likely to keep many of their minority constituents in a position of sustained disadvantage. The next section examines such modern political realities.

FIGURE 6.1   The Pro-Growth Framework and the Racialized Social System

---

Chief characteristic of pro-growth framework: Transition of cities from their industrial to corporate phase:

- Loss of manufacturing and retail commerce with replacement by corporate structures
- Flight of working-class and middle-class residents, with inner-city areas disproportionately composed of poor minorities involved in low-paying service work

Means by which the pro-growth framework supports a racialized social system:

- White groups decisively advantaged in positions of power and affluence while poor minorities entrenched in residential and economic disadvantage
- Once in place, the system self-perpetuates: mayors, including minority mayors like Dennis Archer in Detroit, surviving politically by catering to affluent whites' interests and downplaying or ignoring poor minorities' economically related deprivations
- Politicians and other leaders in support of the "self-help" ideology, providing the appearance of effectively addressing poverty-related issues but generally producing little or no progress

Possible counter strategies mentioned in the second portion of the chapter:

- Linkage or other arrangements requiring corporations established in cities to subsidize well-planned efforts to improve local poor residents' housing, schools, and other basic resources
- Interest groups, often involving multiracial coalitions, that lobby and protest for their low-income membership seeking to receive a bigger piece of the economic pie

Power to the People?

Political scientist Robert A. Dahl (1961) hypothesized that an ethnic group's members move through three stages in the passage to political assimilation:

■ In stage one recent immigrants are employed in unskilled, low-paying jobs and possess little status or political influence. Over time, however, a few more active participants in the group begin to serve as intermediaries between their own members and established political leaders in more assimilated groups, and eventually some of these ethnic subleaders run for minor offices such as alderman, where the voters primarily come from that person's ethnic group. Politically, members of the group think and act quite homogeneously, not only sharing their ethnicity but also finding it useful to support candidates who have been at least somewhat attuned to the needs and interests of low-wage earners victimized by periodic unemployment and nativist groups' discrimination.

■ In the second stage, the group in question has diversified, with a substantial number of members obtaining higher-paying, more prestigious white-collar jobs and moving out of their poor, ethnically homeogenous neighborhoods. Higher status, increased income, and greater self-confidence allow a few members of the group to start challenging established political leaders for more important political offices, leading to charges of ingratitude or betrayal. If members of the group run for such citywide offices as sheriff, treasurer, or mayor, they need to obtain votes from diverse ethnic groups. Although at this stage members' political outlooks become more varied, all of them still retain a strong sense of their ethnic roots.

■ In the third stage, an increasing number of group members move into the middle class. They live, attend school, work, and socialize in very diverse ethnic settings and find their ethnicity increasingly less significant and sometimes even embarrassing. Candidates for political office may occasionally cite their ethnicity as a source of pride, gaining votes from their own members by doing so. To win citywide office, however, they must represent positions that will appeal to the general middle-class constituency, and by so doing they are likely to split open their ethnic group's support, losing less affluent members' backing (Dahl 1961, 34–36).

Dahl's scheme represents a useful description of various European groups' assimilation into the urban political process. Like the structural-functional framework presented in Chapter 2, however, it currently seems unduly optimistic in two regards. It does not concern itself with blacks' history, where systemic discrimination has thwarted large numbers from moving into the middle class and where the pro-growth strategy appears likely to sustain that condition, and in a related vein, it does not consider that in a postindustrial context, many recently arrived members of racial minorities also face a bleak economic and political future.

A growing number of white Americans, in fact, have felt that they too are trapped in either dead-end jobs or unemployment when postindustrial technological advances increasingly displace workers. About 25,000 whites belong to about three hundred white-supremacist organizations that might be considered political, seeking to build support for what members consider exclusively whites' interests (Dobratz and Shanks-Meile 2000, 25).

Milton Kleim, a former member of the white-power movement, commented on its participants:

> Most of the people who join the movement are not evil, though they may be violent. They are lost kids, like myself once was, bitter at a society they perceive as betraying them, very similarly to how many black youth perceive their betrayal by a racist society that has little or no place for them. (Dobratz and Shanks-Meile 2000, 279)

Moving into the heart of this section, we might keep in mind the issue of how effectively minority politicians promote their members' movement into the economic and political mainstream. The discussion begins with a look at black urban politics.

African Americans' Political Participation

Conflicting perceptions can arise on this topic. On the one hand, greater inclusion over time is apparent. Between 1970 and 2000, the number of blacks elected to political office, most of them in cities that were losing whites to the suburbs, rose sixfold, with women steadily increasing in number so that they now represent over a third of the total. In the 1950s and 1960s, blacks began creating coalitions combining blacks and white liberals, and as a result they started winning some urban elections. The first African American mayor of a large city was Carl Stokes in Cleveland in 1967, followed by Coleman Young in Detroit in 1973. By 2000 there were forty-seven African American mayors of cities with populations over 50,000, and more than half resided in cities where the majority of the population was white. At that time twenty-six African American mayors headed cities with populations of 100,000 or more (*AntiRacism Net* 2002; McWhirter 2000).

Although black urban political leadership has become more prominent, many of the cities where African Americans have been elected have had serious financial problems, and so these leaders find themselves in difficult negotiations with such central players as business leaders, middle-class professionals, public officials, union leaders, and poor minorities. The complicated, sensitive issues black mayors face are hardly unique to their experience, but the cities they inherit are likely to face particularly dire conditions, thus complicating these mayors' relations with the array of groups with which they must deal. In particular:

■ When attempting to convince corporate groups to locate or to remain in their downtown areas, black leaders recognize that these major businesses can be significant sources for subsidizing various public programs that provide services for the city's poorest citizens. However, to assure that corporations remain in their cities, politicians are usually willing to limit themselves to distinctly modest taxation, curtailing the funds that would aid their low-income members.

■ In seeking fiscal stability, African American mayors can be motivated to provide their municipal service workers low wages and meager benefits, but these decisions alienate unions, which are a traditional support group for the primarily Democratic black mayors.

■ While promoting revitalization of their downtown areas, African American leaders have faced the danger of alienating local residents, many of whom are poor minorities. In the second half of the twentieth century, the impact of urban redevelopment on the largely minority residents of affected areas has been widely criticized, often ignoring their rights by ruthlessly removing them from their communities and relocating them in increasingly ghettoized, cramped, and cheaply constructed public housing.

■ When encouraging affluent, middle-class people to move into the city, mayors are inclined to provide them tax breaks or choice residential locations, thus either curtailing important funding sources that will help pay for poor residents' basic needs or forcing those low-income individuals out of their communities (McWhirter 2000; Reed 1999, 105–06).

In spite of these complexities, African American city administrations have assisted their black constituents in distinct ways. In various cities, including Gary, Oakland, Newark, Atlanta, and Detroit, black administrations have significantly curbed police brutality, which often was among black residents' most pressing concerns. One means of promoting this goal has been substantial gains in employing black police officers.

Black administrations have also obtained various city contracts and municipal employment in professional and administrative jobs that have primarily aided middle- and upper-middle-class African Americans. The main reason this result has been skewed upward is that while the higher positions are exempt from civil-service classification, lower-level city positions are often covered by these regulations, restricting the use of affirmative action (Reed 1999, 97–98).

Like most administrations located in economically depressed American cities, black administrations generally accept the pro-growth framework. Some observers oppose this strategy, arguing that even in the most depressed industrial cities, the resident corporations have historically enjoyed substantial growth and, if required to do so, could readily afford and would probably accept the inevitability of a payment that would help defray the costs for such urban necessities as decent low-cost housing, adequately funded schools, and effective health-care systems.

Nearly all the big-city black administrations govern in cities that are either national or regional economic and administrative centers, which normally contain many large, successful businesses. If economic recovery occurs in the new century's opening years, many of these corporations should be able to afford **linkage,** a municipal procedure requiring developers or other corporate players doing business in a city to provide a substantial fee for low-cost housing or some other commodity or service aiding a city's less affluent residents. In the late 1980s in Boston, Mayor Ray Flynn became a major proponent of linkage, and six years after he initiated its use, developers had committed over $76 million in linkage funds for low-cost housing (Doob 1995, 110; Wayne 1992).

In the upcoming Sociological Illustration, I refer to linkage as well as other issues raised in these pages.

Besides having the longest urban political tradition of any racial minority, African Americans have created a host of organizations that have championed members' political, economic, and social rights. The first of these organizations was the National Association of Colored People (NAACP), which was formed by both blacks and whites in 1909 and

SOCIOLOGICAL ILLUSTRATION

Detroit during the Dennis Archer Watch

On April 17, 2001, even Dennis W. Archer's staff was caught unaware by his decision not to seek a third term as mayor of Detroit. Apparently, Archer had spent weeks deliberating over the decision, weighing the pros and cons and like many of his constituents finding that the results of his regime had been mixed.

Archer's campaign for a first term generated great interest and support as he offered the vision of a "world class city" in which crime would be minimal, education high-quality, and the job climate excellent. Toward the end of the campaign, he declared, "Upon election as mayor, I will immediately move to restore the quality of basic public services, i.e. police and fire services and public transportation, with an emphasis on residential and neighborhood areas" (Bray 2001).

Certainly, Mayor Archer was successful in attracting new business and redeveloping downtown areas. He was the driving force in the construction of new baseball and football stadiums for the Detroit Tigers and the Detroit Lions and also the creation of three new casinos generating about $1 million a day in business. In addition, because of Archer's close links with the Clinton administration, Detroit was awarded $100 million over ten years from the federal Empowerment Fund to promote economic development in the city. Finally, Archer also convinced both General Motors and Compuware to build their headquarters downtown.

Because of the economic development Archer spearheaded, the new regime was able to rid the city of an $88.5 million deficit and produce a string of balanced budgets that have given Detroit an "A" credit rating (Jones 2001; McWhirter, McConnell and Nichols 2001; Nichols and McWhirter 2001).

In Archer's reelection bid, voters responded positively, giving him over 83 percent of the vote (Jones 2001). While most observers acknowledged Archer had been a skilled campaigner, critics said that he lacked a quality highly valued in politicians—the ability to engage in the standard give-and-take of cajoling, arguing with, perhaps even bullying politicians and other civic players to push

through the part of his program dedicated to poor minorities' needs.

This was one reason why the mayor failed to deliver on his campaign pledge to restore basic services and revitalize neighborhoods. Despite some service-related gains involving such issues as the replacement of street lights and the removal of thousands of junked cars, systemic problems in city government involving understaffing, underfunding, and lack of coordination among departments persisted. Driving through poor areas, observers would see ample evidence of extensive dumping, nonenforcement of laws on property upkeep, and the deterioration of public parks, recreation facilities, and vacant buildings and lots. All in all, poor neighborhoods continued to lose vitality throughout the Archer watch (McWhirter, McConnell, and Nichols 2001).

Linkage might have provided badly needed funding for poor neighborhoods, but Archer's regime never established it as a priority. In fact, the essence of what made Archer a successful politician actually steered him away from linkage and other strategies that would have benefited the poor. A community activist declared, "You don't win [reelections] by having a good training program; you win again by having cranes in the sky" (Lawless 2001).

Like the mayor's emphasis on such large projects as the construction of stadiums and casinos, his use of substantial tax abatements to coax white-owned businesses into the city was politically popular and widely defended even though it was not constructive for minorities. The head of a city economic development agency described the approach as encouraging "feasible economic projects." She added:

> If this means more "white pioneers" moving . . . downtown that's fine. It would be a mistake for me to suggest that because you are not African American you do not have the right to build or provide jobs for people in Detroit. (Lawless 2001)

A number of African American critics concluded that Archer gave minimal attention to blacks' needs and interests. As one key player in the

(continued)

planning department explained, "[H]e thinks like a whitey; his friends are white; all he has done is to bring the suburbs to the city" (Lawless 2001). Such observers argued that as a result African Americans invariably lost out.

Like other black mayors, Archer has faced a major dilemma. "If they don't accommodate the white community, they run the risk of being shut out by it and by the white-dominated suburbs," said political scientist Wilbur C. Rich. "If they do accommodate, they run the risk of being labeled Oreos (blacks who accede to whites' interests) by a portion of their poor black constituency" (McWhirter 2000). The outcome is that like Archer most African American mayors end up implementing a pro-growth approach, which keeps a racialized social system alive and well in their cities.

It's a tough road that undoubtedly comes with the territory for black mayors elected in American cities. One can speculate whether or not a mayor with a clearer, more sustained commitment to fulfilling a social contract more inclusive of poor minorities' needs could have succeeded in a city as diverse and problem-laden as Detroit. Perhaps it would have been possible. My sense, however, is that Dennis Archer's overall success on the job was better than most mayors of any race or ethnicity will currently achieve in large American cities with such an ample supply of poverty-related challenges.

---

throughout its proud history has engaged in a variety of legal and civil actions to promote the political, educational, social, and economic equality of all minority people. During the civil rights era, other organizations, most notably the Southern Christian Leadership Conference headed by Dr. Martin Luther King Jr. until his death in 1968 and the Core of Racial Equality, were in the forefront of the southern protests to desegregate public facilities and secure blacks' voting rights.

Nowadays, however, the most powerful African American force on behalf of its members' interests is distinctly political—namely, the Congressional Black Caucus, which in 2003 had thirty-nine members, many representing urban districts. Elijah E. Cummings, the chair, indicated that the group's priorities include

> building wealth by creating new jobs and businesses; universal health care for every American; ensuring equity in the education of our children; strengthening and enforcing our civil rights laws; and providing both homeland and hometown security. (Cummings 2003)

Like blacks, Hispanics face formidable issues when moving into urban politics. However, they often have the advantage that the cities with substantial Hispanic populations, where they are likely to seek political office, are more prosperous, perhaps making their tenure in office somewhat less taxing.

The Growing Hispanic Political Presence

It is an expectant era for Latinos in American politics. In 2001 first-time Hispanic mayors were elected in Hartford, Austin, and Houston, a second Mexican American mayor won in San Antonio, and in Miami a Cuban American challenger defeated a Puerto Rican incumbent. Hispanic voters also played an important role in the mayoralty elections of the nation's two largest cities. In New York City following a divisive primary, Hispanic voters, who generally vote Democratic, evenly split their votes, thereby helping elect the Republican. Although in 2001 a black candidate defeated his Hispanic adversary in Los Angeles, the fact that the steadily increasing Hispanic proportion of the population was 47 percent strongly supports the likelihood of a Latino mayor in the near future. Numbers, in fact, are important to consider when analyzing Hispanic political participation. The 2000 census revealed that the Latino population was 12.5 percent of the nation's total and over the next few decades most likely will continue to grow rapidly (DiPasquale 2001; Segal 2001).

At present, however, Hispanic voting power does not correspond with the group's proportion of the population. Many Latinos are too young to vote, and those who are older can be undocumented immigrants, lacking the citizenship required of voters. While in 2001, 47 percent of Los Angeles was Latino, that contingent contained only 22 percent of the voters.

In that election, however, blacks represented an even smaller percentage of voters—17 percent. Belonging to a less populous group than his opponent, the African American candidate nonetheless defeated his Hispanic adversary because he won support from white voters, and, in particular, from the powerful white business community.

That particular support is often critical. In San Antonio, Ed Garza was elected mayor, with almost no Latino-targeted advertisement. However, he sought and obtained strong backing from the white business establishment. According to sociologist Victor Rodríguez,

In an increasing number of American cities, Hispanic politicians like Mayor Henry Cisneros in San Antonio are able to obtain strong support from the growing number of Hispanic voters.

the "rules are fashioned by the Anglo business elite, and as the saying goes, whoever designs the rules also wins. Garza won because he played by their rules" (Rodríguez 2001).

This conclusion is consistent with the pro-growth approach, which all modern urban politicians, including minority mayors, have needed to support. Yet as their proportion of some cities' electorate increases, Latino candidates might decide that they can downplay even powerful white business interests as long as they are highly responsive to their own ethnic constituency. As one writer phrased it, "Now, with the Hispanic population exploding and both major political parties competing for those voters, a new and less accommodating model may be emerging" (Navarette 2001).

All in all, certain general conditions now accelerate more Hispanic involvement in urban politics. Latinas' growing interest in political activity has made them an increasing proportion of Latino/a elected officials, receiving support from Latino/a organizations that help prepare them primarily to serve on local school boards and in municipal government. They hold about a third of all Hispanic-occupied offices, about twice the proportion of female-held elected positions in the nation overall.

A second major factor supporting a surge of Hispanics into politics has been a set of conditions mobilizing immigrants to seek naturalization. These conditions included efforts by the Clinton administration to speed up the process; the willingness of six Latin American countries to permit dual citizenship, thus allowing those individuals to become naturalized U.S. citizens without losing full rights in their country of origin; and new anti-immigration policies and laws such as California's Proposition 187, which has denied undocumented immigrants access to public education and state social services and has helped them realize that their most fruitful course is to naturalize, thus becoming eligible for those rights (Montoya, Hardy-Fanta, and Garcia 2000; Sierra, Carrillo, DeSipio, and Jones-Correa 2000).

Besides their increasing involvement in mainstream politics, urban Hispanics continue a tradition of seeking political engagement by other means. Both Mexican Americans and Puerto Ricans have had a history of creating organizations within their communities that help protect them from racial discrimination and procure benefits they otherwise would not obtain. For Mexican Americans the first support organizations were *mutualistas,* mutual-aid societies that starting in the 1840s in the Southwest supplied members funeral insurance, created credit unions and libraries, and published newspapers. Following World War II, groups like the League of United Latin American Citizens (LULAC) and the Mexican American Movement formed in order to protect their people from the repetition of such injustices as the forced deportation of 500,000 Mexican immigrants during the Great Depression. Then in the 1960s, Cesar Chavez and other organizers founded the United Farm Workers Union, which not only led strikes against farm employers but instigated a national boycott of grapes, lettuce, and table wine that eventually won California farmworkers a stable union, their first multiyear contracts, and unprecedented gains in wages, benefits, and working conditions.

Puerto Ricans' engagement outside the conventional political process began with the Young Lords, a group that started as a Chicago street gang and within several years established chapters in twenty cities, where they presented a thirteen-point program detailing the oppressive conditions requiring change, including the end to U.S. control of Puerto Rico. During their few years of existence, the members suffered persistent police repression and yet in various cities promoted demonstrations, discussions, and temporary programs for food and clothing distribution (Feagin and Feagin 1996, 352–53; Marquez and Jennings 2000).

Presently, various types of Latino organizations engage in politically related tasks outside the formal political process:

- *Large national organizations addressing Hispanics' basic needs.* Founded in 1929, LULAC has a middle-class membership, which had formed over 150 chapters by 1960. LULAC has promoted reforms in voter registration, equal employment, and other areas where Hispanics have traditionally suffered discrimination. The Mexican American Legal Defense Fund (MALDEF) is another large organization serving Hispanics' needs. Since 1968 MALDEF has sought to promote programs that will protect Mexican Americans and other Latino residents. Its activities have included civil rights litigation; development of new procedures for elections, hiring, and promotion; advocacy of census adjustment, seeking to have all Hispanic residents included; and training Latinos to serve on policy-making boards and commissions at various governmental levels (MALDEF 2002).

- *A wide variety of grassroots organizations helping Hispanics obtain workplace safety, access to health care, economic stability, and educational skills.* Some of the individuals leading these initiatives have realized that they can use such accomplishments to gain access to the political arena. John Herrera, a Costa Rica native, has been vice president of Latino-Hispanic affairs at the Self-Help Credit Union in Durham, North Carolina, spearheading efforts to integrate Latinos into the local economy. Using the support he had built up, Herrera ran for the board of alderman. He explained, "Hopefully it will open a lot of doors, and raise the hope that if a Latino can be elected to a municipal office in North Carolina, if we do that, that means a Latino can be elected to be president of the United States one day" (Elliston 2001).

- *Partnering between various Hispanic political organizations and prominent mainstream organizations.* In March 2002, at Estes Park, Colorado, the National Education Association (NEA) joined with some 300 Hispanic community activists representing a variety of groups to galvanize support in local communities for candidates and legislation that promote Latino interests. Bob Chase, the president of NEA, explained that the members of his organization visualized a vibrant interplay between public education and the quality of American life. Chase said, "Empowering Hispanic voices will enrich American democracy and help provide a quality education for every child" (National Education Association 2002). While the weekend gathering was supposed to mobilize participants' involvement, its most practical contribution was the provision of specialized information on such topics as campaign planning and strategy, coalition building, communication with the media and the public, and the encouragement of voter participation.

In the course of Latinos' political empowerment, adjustments need to occur. Recent immigrants are likely to resent being labeled as simply Latinos or Hispanics, with no acknowledgment of their country of birth. "Suddenly we were grouped and we didn't like it, we felt like we lost identity," said Nolo Martinez, a prominent activist for Hispanic rights in North Carolina. "But then we realized that this identity gives you some political influence in a democracy. It's kind of like an awakening of how the political process works" (Elliston 2001).

When Asian Americans, whose membership has originated from many countries, seek political involvement, they can probably experience a similar awakening.

Asian American Political Participation

Early Asian American immigrants had direct exposure to harsh political realities. Congress passed the Chinese Exclusion Act of 1882, which simply eliminated the influx of Chinese migrants. At the state and local level, officials followed the national lead, establishing discriminatory taxes for Chinese Americans or restrictions on such rights as intermarriage and land ownership. Some early Asian American citizens rejected such restrictions. Between the 1880s and the 1920s, they filed over a thousand lawsuits demanding equal rights in federal and state courts; organized boycotts, petitions, and letter-writing campaigns; and founded newspapers and magazines to promote their causes (Aoki and Nakanishi 2001; *Asian-Nation* 2001).

In modern times Asian Americans have become active politically. Although their total population is barely 12 million, they represent an increasingly visible political force in the nation and, in particular, in cities. Between 1978 and 2000, the overall number of Asian American elected officials accelerated nearly threefold, from 120 to 328. At the local level, mainly in cities, the number expanded nearly fivefold, from 52 to 248, with most of those elected serving on city councils and school boards.

Unlike both blacks and Hispanics who enter politics, Asian American candidates usually reside in districts where their racial compatriots comprise less than half the population. As a result, election often depends on a "crossover effect," meaning the ability to gain support from a diverse constituency by focusing the campaign on interests resonating for various racial and ethnic groups (Lai, Cho, Kim, and Takeda 2001).

Nonetheless, Asian Americans' political activities have been greatest in districts where their numbers are substantial. Their voter turnout, for instance, has been higher where the Asian American population is dense—thus Hawaii leads California, with all other states trailing. Furthermore, since the early 1980s a number of cities including New York, Houston, San Diego, and San Francisco have developed high-density Asian American residential areas, and so in the years ahead, an increasing number of Asian American elected officials are likely to emerge from those locales (Leadership Education for Asian Pacifics 2000; Lien, Collet, Wong, and Ramakrishnan 2001).

Sometimes political mobilization has hinged on a single event. In Lowell, Massachusetts, there are over 30,000 Cambodian Americans, who have tended to be politically dormant since starting to settle there in the early 1980s. In 1999 Chanrithy Uong ran for the city council and won with the support of a multiracial coalition. Uong, though an upbeat, friendly person, has not been reluctant to emphasize the injustices and mistreatments Cambodian Americans and other Asian Americans have suffered both in Lowell and elsewhere in the country. Uong's election has led to a doubling of Asian American voter registration in Lowell as well as a willingness to express long harbored complaints. Ratha Paul Yem, executive director of the Cambodian American League of Lowell, said that in emphasizing the injustices occurring to Asian Americans in the larger society, politicians like Uong have been performing a valuable service. "Many people have probably heard about those scandals a little bit," Yem said. "But the thing is that . . . [such leaders as Uong] are making the connections for people between those things, and their local struggles. We do that to build self-sufficiency, and that includes political empowerment" (Fletcher 2000).

That process can require the Asian American political leadership to address difficult relations with other groups. The widespread destruction of Korean Americans' businesses in Los Angeles in 1992, for instance, graphically demonstrated that in some cities tensions between Asian Americans and blacks have been strong. It is less well known that in some communities hostility between Hispanics and Asian Americans has developed, and evidence indicates some conflict between different Asian groups, such as claims that in Hawaii Asian Americans have oppressed Native Hawaiians (Aoki and Nakanishi 2001, 606).

The process of developing political awareness, in fact, requires participants to be attuned not only to diversity among Asian American groups but also to differences in experiences, outlooks, and opportunities that exist within a single ethnic category. Touring Koreatown in Los Angeles with fellow members of UCLA's Asian American studies program, Jessica Kim, a Korean American, became aware that her experience growing up in a suburban setting an hour's drive from this community was very different from that of the residents facing such problems as poor housing, inadequate schools, and unsafe and unpleasant working conditions. Kim suggested that leading such politically oriented tours could help make students more aware of residents' problems and also mobilize them politically. Such trips, Kim concluded, should be "more than cultural experiences or entertaining day-trips. Instead, we will listen to the needs of people who live and work in these communities and follow their lead as they struggle for economic and social justice" (Kim 2002). This suburban versus urban distinction in life experience corresponds with different social-class locations—contrasting situations in which suburban residents are generally more affluent and have better mainstream opportunities than their urban Korean American counterparts.

While becoming more active in mainstream urban politics, Asian Americans have also been involved in various interest-group activities. In the 1970s and 1980s, for example, Japanese Americans engaged in grassroots protest and lobbying Congress to obtain redress for members' relocation during World War II. The eventual result was that President Reagan signed legislation that provided both an official apology and monetary compensation to survivors. Then in the 1980s, the nationwide Justice for Vincent Chin Campaign spearheaded by Chinese Americans galvanized an array of Asian American groups against racial violence.

In recent decades various urban-based Chinese American groups have organized to promote members' interests. In 1971 residents of Boston's Chinatown formed the Free Chinatown Committee to preserve their territory from the New England Medical Center's expansion effort. Since then, businesses from both the retail and financial districts have also tried to move into their area. Chinese American residents have used public demonstrations, mass publicity, and outside alliances in this continuing struggle to survive. Similar confrontations have occurred in such cities as San Francisco, Los Angeles, and Philadelphia, where development projects ejected residents and small businesses from well-established urban villages. Although the protest groups have often lacked the political clout to win the struggle, they have either demonstrated the ability to sustain an impressive opposition or, as in the case of Japanese Americans in Los Angeles's Little Tokyo, have rebuilt the portion of the ethnic community that survived redevelopment. In a few instances, such as in Philadelphia, the local ethnic protest effort was successful. Led by the Philadelphia Chinatown Coalition to Oppose the Stadium, a number of Asian American groups rallied to defeat the construction of a new baseball stadium near Philadelphia's Chinatown (Aoki and Nakanishi 2001; Liu 2001).

Besides focusing on their residential communities, Asian American groups have organized around a variety of topics including health care, immigrants' rights, and job-related issues. In September 2000 in San Jose, over three hundred Indian and Pakistani cab drivers nearly shut down South San Jose, protesting the lack of police protection following an Indian driver's death.

New York City, however, has been where the most memorable Asian American–led protest occurred. In 1998 the New York Taxi Workers Alliance (known as the Alliance), whose members have been primarily from India, Pakistan, and Bangladesh, led a strike in which about 98 percent of the city's 24,000 yellow cabs withheld their labor for 24 hours, protesting a sharp increase in municipal fines for minor violations (Geron, Cruz, Saito, and Singh 2001).

At that time the Alliance had 3,000 members, and by the middle of 2002, 300 more cab drivers had joined. One of the reasons for the Alliance's growing strength has been that its membership has assisted other Asian American groups in obtaining such important benefits as health-insurance coverage and unemployment compensation (Malhotra 2002; Marx 2002).

Bhaivavi Desai, an Indian woman, has been the Alliance's chief organizer. Arriving in the United States in 1979 when she was six, the family moved to New Jersey, where her father ran a grocery store and her mother worked in a factory. Desai explained, "I grew up in a working class household. I have always had a job and going to college was not a given" (Sharma 2002).

Yet Desai went to college, majored in history and women's studies, and decided to become an organizer working with and for Asian Americans. Her first step was to join Manavi, an organization assisting South Asian women who were victims of domestic violence. Within three years Desai and several others formed the Alliance, which began with seven hundred cab drivers and steadily expanded.

Following the destruction of the World Trade Center, Desai found that the Alliance's largely Muslim, Asian American members faced increased discriminatory treatment from customers as well as many instances of detention, particularly for Pakistani Americans held by the Immigration and Naturalization Services. But while the Alliance staff has confronted new, difficult challenges, Desai has remained optimistic, immersed in her working-class Asian American community. She declared, "My family were my first set of comrades. They represent the best in working-class people. I don't want to stray from that" (Sharma 2002).

Like the New York Taxi Workers Alliance, many politically oriented organizations containing minorities have been most successful when incorporating different groups. That issue arises in the final commentary.

Conclusion

The early northern European settlers and their descendants have often managed to keep a firm, often controlling involvement in many American cities. Over time, however, local political leadership has steadily diversified from northern European supremacy, first featuring access to political office for an increasing array of European groups and then gradually including racial minorities—blacks, Hispanics, and Asian Americans.

Since racial minorities are a fairly small proportion of the population, their clout in such areas as winning elections or building a political organization's membership increases if they produce multiracial coalitions. Research evidence indicates that such multiracial alliances are most likely to succeed under the following conditions:

- Participating groups have access to personnel and resources that can provide their members such requisites as leadership training and knowledge about the process of community mobilization.
- The groups in these coalitions build communication and understanding that promote collaborative efforts.
- The various groups emphasize fundamental issues of urban change, recognizing the role of race but refusing to pursue narrow, race-based goals (Kim and Lee 2001, 632).

The last point strikes me as particularly reminiscent of a theme running through much of this chapter, namely, the relevance of the pro-growth framework. If the participants in multiracial coalitions are capable of clearly spelling out to their constituencies (a) how the pro-growth framework helps perpetuate a racialized social system and (b) that they as minority-group members can join a coalition with the power to force the corporate leadership to provide funding to alleviate poor minorities' critical deficiencies in jobs, schooling, housing, and health care, then the coalition membership will be able to observe and enjoy positive results from their collaborative effort. That would certainly represent the onset of a bright new political day.

DISCUSSION QUESTIONS

1. Analyze the conditions promoting both the rise and fall of political machines in American cities, indicating the role that ethnicity played in these activities.

2. Provide an overview of racial minorities' participation in the urban politics of the postindustrial era. Include references to both the pro-growth framework and the self-help ideology, describing the impact of race.

3. Assess how race and social class impact on blacks' political activity in cities.

4. Summarize the principal current realities of Hispanic urban politics.

5. What are some challenges Asian Americans face in engaging in political activity in U.S. cities?

6. Drawing from material in the text as well as available personal sources, discuss the feasibility of groups forming effective multiracial political coalitions.

BIBLIOGRAPHY

AntiRacismNet. 2002. "Count of Black Elected Officials Shows Dramatic Increase over Three Decades." (April 15). www.antiracismnet.org/arn041502-head5.html.

Aoki, Andres, and Don T. Nakanishi. 2001. "Asian Pacific Americans and the New Minority Politics." *PS.* 34 (September): 605–10.

Asian-Nation. 2001. "Participating in Politics." www.asian-nation.org/issues5.html.

Bailyn, Bernard et al. 1977. *The Great Republic.* Lexington, MA: Heath.

Bray, Thomas J. 2001. "Dennis Archer: The Transitional Mayor." *Detroit News.* (April 29). www.detnews.com/2001/editional/0104/29/a15–217863.htm.

Cummings, Elijah E. 2003. "The Online Home for the Congressional Black Caucus." www.house.gov/cummings/cbc/cbchome.htm.

Dahl, Robert A. 1961. *Who Governs? Democracy and Power in an American City.* New Haven: Yale University Press.

DiPasquale, Domenick. 2001. "2001 Elections Demonstrate Voting Power of U.S. Hispanics." *U.S. Deparment of State International Information Programs.* (November 8). www.usinfo.state.gov/usa/race/diversity/a110801.htm.

Dobratz, Betty A., and Stephanie L. Shanks-Meile. 2000. *The White Separatist Movement in the United States.* Baltimore: Johns Hopkins University Press.

Doob, Christopher Bates. 1995. *Social Problems.* Fort Worth, TX: Harcourt Brace.

Elliston, Jon. 2001. "The Next Step." *The Independent Weekly.* www.indyweek.com/durham/2001–09–12/triangles.html.

Feagin, Joe R., and Clairece Booher Feagin. 1996. *Racial and Ethnic Relations,* 5th ed. Upper Saddle River, NJ: Prentice Hall.

Fletcher, Michael A. 2000. "Asian Americans Using Politics as a Megaphone." *Washington Post. (*October 2). www.washingtonpost.com/ac2/wp-dyn?pagename=article&node=world/asia&contentId=A57358–2000)oct1.

Geron, Kim, Enrique de la Cruz, Leland T. Saito, and Jaideep Singh. 2001. "Asian Pacific Americans: Social Movements and Interest Groups." *PS.* 34 (September): 619–24.

Glaab, Charles N., and A. Theodore Brown. 1967. *A History of Urban America.* New York: Macmillan.

Gottdiener, Mark, and Ray Hutchison. 2000. *The New Urban Sociology,* 2nd ed. New York: McGraw-Hill.

Hero, Rodney E., and Kathleen M Beatty. 1989. "The Election of Federico Peña as Mayor of Denver: Analysis and Implications." *Social Science Quarterly.* 70 (June): 300–10.

Jones, Larry. 2001. "Detroit Mayor Dennis W. Archer Decides Not to Seek Reelection." *U.S. Mayor Newspaper.* (April 30). www.usmayors.org/uscm/us_mayor_newspaper/documents/04_30_01/archer.asp

Judd, Dennis R., and Todd Swanstrom. 2002. *City Politics: Private Power and Public Policy,* 3rd ed. New York: Longman.

Kantowicz, Edward R. 1994. "The Changing Face of Ethnic Politics: From Political Machine to Community Organization," pp. 179–95 in Timothy Walch (ed.), *Immigrant America: European Ethnicity in the United States.* New York: Garland.

Kim, Claire Jean, and Taeku Lee. 2001. "Interracial Politics: Asian Americans and Other Communities of Color." *PS.* 34 (September): 631–37.

Kim, Jessica. 2002. *Asian American Studies Classweb.* (Winter Quarter). www.sscnet.ucla.edu/aasc/classweb/winter02/aas197a/jkim_pt.html.

Lai, James S., Wendy K. Tam Cho, Thomas P. Kim, and Okiyoshi Takeda. 2001. "Asian Pacific-American Campaigns, Elections, and Elected Officials." *PS.* 34 (September): 611–17.

Lawless, Paul. 2001. "Urban Policy and Politics in Two American Cities: Jersey City and Detroit." Centre for Regional Economic and Social Research. www.by-og-byg.dk/eura/workshops/papers/workshop2/lawless.htm.

Leadership Education for Asian Pacifics. 2000. "A Guide to Asian American Empowerment." *Model Minority.* www.modelminority.com/society/leap4.htm.

Lien, Pei-te, Christian Collet, Janelle Wong, and S. Karthick Ramakrishnan. 2001. "Asian Pacific-American Public Opinion and Political Participation." *PS.* 34 (September): 625–30.

Liu, Michael. 2001. "The Asian American Movement Today." *Asian American Revolutionary Movement. www.aamovement.net/history/as am my today.html.*

MALDEF. 2002. "About Us." www.maldef.org/about/index.htm.

Malhotra, Priya. 2002. "64% of South Asians in Queens Don't Have Health Insurance." *Desi Talk in New York.* (May 10). http://desitalk.newsindia-times.com/2002/05/10/queens-8-top.html.

Marquez, Benjamin, and James Jennings. 2000. "Representation by Other Means: Mexican American and Puerto Rican Social Movement Organizations." *PS.* 34 (September): 541–46.

Marx, Eric. 2002. "Workers Claim Inequality in Unemployment Insurance Benefits Program." Columbia University Graduate School of Journalism. www.jrn.columbia.edu/studentwork/deadline/marx-unemployment.asp.

McWhirter, Cameron. 2000. "Black Mayors, Big Cities." *Detroit News.* (February 13). www.detnews.com/special/reports/2000/blackmayors/lead/lead.htm.

McWhirter, Cameron, Darci McConnell, and Darren A. Nichols. 2001. "The Archer Legacy: Progress Made and Delayed." *Detroit News.* (December 30). www.detnews.com/specialreports/2001/archer/lead/lead.htm.

Montoya, Lisa J., Carol Hardy-Fanta, and Sonia Garcia. 2000. "Latina Politics: Gender, Participation, and Leadership." *PS.* 34 (September): 555–61.

Navarrette, Ruben, Jr. 2001. "Political Rebels Shake Up Latino Image." *The Washington Post Writers Group.* www.postwritersgroup.com/archives/nava1206.htm.

NEA. 2002. "NEA Joins the Nation's Leading Hispanic Organizations to Promote Hispanic Empowerment." (March 8). www.nea.org/nr/nr020308.html.

Nichols, Darren A., and Cameron McWhirter. 2001. "The Archer Legacy: Downtown Was Archer's Star." *Detroit News.* (December 30). www.detnews.com/specialreports/2001/archer/downtown/downtown.htm.

Reed, Adolph, Jr. 1999. *Stirrings in the Jug: Black Politics in the Post-Segregation Era.* Minneapolis: University of Minnesota Press.

Rodríguez, Victor M. 2001. "L.A. Election: Prologue or Epilogue?" *Hispanic.* 14 (July/August): 112.

Segal, Adam. 2001. "Hispanic Voters Leave Imprint on 2001 Elections." *Johns Hopkins Journal of American Politics.* www.wcjournal.org/hispanic_voters.htm.

Sharma, Kalpana. 2002. *The Hindu.* (May 19). www.hinduonnet.com/thehindu/mag/2002/05/19/stories/2002051900260300.htm.

Sierra, Christine Marie, Teresa Carrillo, Louis DeSipio, and Michael Jones-Correa. 2000. "Latino Immigration and Citizenship." *PS.* 34 (September): 535–40.

Wayne, Leslie. 1992. "New Hope in Inner Cities: Banks Offering Mortgages." *New York Times.* (March 14), pp. 1+.

CHAPTER

7

Smorgasbord I: Race, Ethnicity, and Socialization to Community Life

Growing Up in American Communities
Era Up to 1840
Era Extending from 1840 to 1924
Era Covering 1924 to the Present

Contemporary Struggles
Homelessness
Deficient Health Care
Conclusion

Americans generalize from what they see and hear. Furthermore, many believe that modern minorities get special treatment and that racial and ethnic distinctions are fast losing significance.

At one point I saw Mackie with whom I have discussed racial and ethnic issues many times. He started the conversation with his latest illustration of how a minority professional got a break for an infraction while a white counterpart didn't. As on previous occasions, I conceded that unfairness but then emphasized that the bigger issue appeared to be that the vast number of poor minority individuals never get such favored treatment—quite the opposite.

As the conversation progressed, however, it took another turn. "Things are different with my boys," Mackie said. "They like the black kid or the white kid for what they say or do, not who they are."

"Do you think they're going to grow up in a world where a person's race has less impact?"

"Who knows."

It's hard to know. It's difficult, for instance, to make a prediction about Mackie's own children. He's a very involved parent, who spends a lot of time with his sons, and undoubtedly they are exposed to, perhaps influenced by the kinds of claims about minorities I've heard him express. On the other hand, he has made a point of hiring minorities to work for his home-improvement business, and the relationships have been mutually productive—a situation to which his sons have also been exposed.

In this chapter and the next, the focus is on **socialization,** which is the process by which a person becomes a social being, learning the necessary cultural content or behavior to become a member of a group or society. As with Mackie and his children, people's communities influence their socialization in the areas of race and ethnicity.

The opening section extends from the seventeenth century to the present, contrasting basic conditions in urban communities over time. Then we center on important problems and challenges modern urban residents face in their locale.

Growing Up in American Communities

Looking across American urban history, I am using a three-part division of time: up to 1840; 1840 to 1924; and 1924 to the present. Although the eras are broad and could readily be subdivided, interesting and important distinctions emerge with the current classification.

Era Up to 1840

When speaking of communities, some sociologists prefer the term *enclave* (Abrahamson 1996, 1–2) or *lifestyle enclave* (Bellah et al. 1985, 71–75), feeling they make sharper reference to shared elements in the residential area. It appears that people seek out others who are like themselves as neighbors and intend to obtain mutual advantage by so doing. Within these residential communities, commercial organizations develop—grocery stores, restaurants, bars, theaters, social and recreational clubs, and churches. Sometimes, as in the case of San Francisco's Chinatown, which has elaborately decorated portals, the boundaries are well marked; often they are not. Once an ethnic community forms, major events, such as political or economic turmoil in the homeland, will affect influx into the area. In many instances, those new inhabitants have entered voluntarily, but as we have already observed in the cases of various European and Asian groups and, most emphatically blacks, often they had little or no option on where to live (Abrahamson 1996, 1–11).

The early American cities were small and homogenous. By the start of the Revolution, the five largest—Philadelphia, New York, Boston, Charleston, and Newport—had a combined population of 90,000 residents representing about 3.6 percent of the colonies' total.

Until the beginning of the eighteenth century, the immigrant flow came primarily from England. In the early 1700s, it included about five or six thousand French Huguenots and several thousand Scots. However, the two largest sources from outside England were Irish Protestants—the so-called Scotch-Irish, who had originally come to Ireland from Scotland—and Germans. Together they represented about 20 percent of the inhabitants when the first national census occurred in 1790. While these two new groups added substantially to the population, their early arrivals often felt that both the government and the nativist citizenry viewed them as inferior and often sought to exploit them. So instead of moving into cities, they tended to settle in the backcountry and become farmers (Bailyn et al. 1977, 164–68).

Within cities social-class ranking could affect residential location. Around 1800, first in Boston's Beacon Hill and soon afterward in Philadelphia's Chestnut Hill, there developed elite communities composed of upper-class English families who had maintained both economic and social prominence for several generations. Some of the names are well known—

Adams, Cabot, and Lodge in Boston; Ingersoll and Biddle in Philadelphia; and later Roosevelt and Jay in New York City (Abrahamson 1996, 19–27).

English was the dominant language, and British American customs were the order of the day. The naturalization act of 1790 limited citizenship to "free white persons," most of whom came from somewhere in Great Britain. These British American pioneers set themselves apart from and above other European groups when these groups immigrated into cities. Philadelphia had some Germans, who, according to Benjamin Franklin, were not really white, sharing with Spanish, Italians, French, Russians, and Swedes "what we call a swarthy complexion" (Jacobson 1998, 40), and, as a quotation from Franklin in Chapter 3 indicated, maintaining what he considered disturbing, alien customs.

In the middle nineteenth century, such race-related dissatisfactions erupted into major outbursts.

Era Extending from 1840 to 1924

This time period begins with Irish immigration during the 1840s, encompasses the influx of central and southern Europeans, and concludes with the passage of the National Origins Act of 1924. A massive increase in immigrants was a major factor during the era. Although they were welcomed as a source of cheap labor, many nativists sensed an invasion.

Race-related fears were at the core of that sense of invasion. What we now perceive as ethnic groups—the Irish, Italians, Poles, Russian Jews, Greeks, Hungarians, Czechs, Spaniards, and others—they considered racial groups with stereotyped traits that were believed to transmit from generation to generation. The Dillingham Commission, whose conclusions strongly influenced restrictive legislation, described "South Italians" as "individual[s] having little adaptability to highly organized society," Poles as "high strung," and gypsies as tribal people who "resent the restraint of a higher social organization . . . [finding] laws and statutes are persecutions to be evaded" (Jacobson 1998, 79). And on and on about other central and southern European "racial" groups.

During this era a popular book was Madison Grant's *The Passing of the Great Race* in which the author asserted that Europe had produced several races, ranging from the superior Nordics of northwestern Europe to the inferior southern and eastern races of the Alpine and Mediterranean regions. Most untrustworthy and despicable were Jews, who seemed to be everywhere in Grant's native New York City. For Grant and his prominent associates, the unrelenting nightmare was race mixing.

These were influential men, who, as we saw in Chapter 3, developed the eugenics movement, whose proponents claimed that science could improve the quality of the human species, particularly by promoting the "purification" of the "Anglo-Saxon race." In 1918 Grant and Charles B. Davenport organized the Galton Society to support research, promote eugenics, and lobby for restrictive legislation. In fact, eugenics researchers, who included Lewis Terman, Henry Goddard, and Robert Yerkes, the developers of the "intelligence tests," had already obtained results showing that 80 percent of the arriving immigrants they measured were "feebleminded." What the researchers conveniently and shockingly overlooked was that the tests were delivered in English, a condition that considerably disadvantaged the vast majority of takers (Brodkin 1998, 28–29).

Eugenics proponents focused on recent immigrants' allegedly distinctive physical characteristics as well as their supposedly inborn personality traits and behavioral tendencies. The inevitable conclusion was that the new arrivals were distinctly different from and inferior to white Anglo-Saxon Protestants and ideally should have been barred from the country, and this goal was eventually achieved with the restrictive legislation the National Origins Act of 1924 imposed.

Although the eugenics movement remained strong early in the twentieth century, its impact in the modern era declined.

Era Covering 1924 to the Present

With the passage of the National Origins Act, the eugenics movement triumphed. As a result its supporters no longer felt the previous panic about hordes of unkempt, racially inferior groups inundating them. Now established whites focused their fears on blacks newly arrived from the South, imposing restrictions on them. Both of these broad conditions supported a gradual reduction of earlier racial distinctions among the European groups. By the mid-twentieth century, these groups were not only widely accepted as "white" but also classified as "Caucasian," bringing "the full authority of modern science to bear on white identity" (Jacobson 1998, 94)

No longer the objects of racial discrimination, modern urban white ethnics now live in what sociologist Mary C. Waters designated "a costless community," where they can pick and choose when to acknowledge their ethnicity. If it is convenient to do so, then that is fine: mention their ethnic heritage and when appropriate talk about the family experience, attend the group's ethnic festivals, and retain the traditional way of celebrating the holidays. Or do not: According to Waters, modern whites' ethnicity is a sufficiently flexible label that they can embrace as part of their community, or if they find the affiliation distasteful or inconvenient, they can exercise their individuality to reject it. The situation permits a sense of ethnic community but allows one's individuality and sense of freedom to assert itself—a situation, in short, with which most modern Americans are likely to be comfortable (Waters 1990, 147–50).

Waters's respondents addressed their sense of ethnic affiliation, often indicating that they valued it. Joe Bajko, for instance, concluded that being Lithuanian made him special:

> It's nice to feel that you are one of a thousand. You are not exactly in a big crowd. In fact, rarely do you find any Lithuanians around. It's nice to feel that you are in an elite group. Like in grade school, when everyone would brag, like saying, "I'm Italian." I would say, "I'm Lithuanian." (Waters 1990, 154)

After acknowledging ethnicity's potential importance, respondents like Liz Field were careful to make it clear that commitment to ethnicity should be limited.

> While I don't feel that my ethnic heritage needs to be dominant in my awareness, I do have an awareness of it and I am encouraged to learn a bit more about the type of people I may have come from. The type of traditions that I might have way back there somehow gotten exposed to. By knowing OK, I am X and X, or XY and Z. Then I don't have to pay any more attention to it. (Waters 1990, 155)

Such ethnic affiliations seem superficial, lacking quality and depth and no longer involving the material circumstances of people's everyday lives. In some instances that

While white ethnics like these Polish Americans in Yber City, Florida, might sometimes celebrate their ethnic affiliation, such behavior is not likely to be a frequent occurrence.

superficial approach to ethnicity produces criticism when those belonging to a given ethnicity encounter members from the home country, who are more firmly grounded in the traditional culture. Sociologist Stephen Steinberg described a group of affluent Americans of Scottish descent who returned to Scotland for the International Gathering of the Clans. Replete with kilts and bagpipes, they spent two rapacious weeks scouring the countryside in search of their roots. Not only did they offend many locals by making spectacles of themselves, but, in particular, they were condemned for fraternizing with the wealthy clan chiefs whose ancestors had driven their own ancestors out of Scotland (Steinberg 2001, 62).

In this instance shared economic status seemed to prove more compelling than kinship ties. Economically successful Scottish Americans probably felt more affinity with the clan chiefs, whose social-class placement more closely resembled their own, than with their relatives, who tended to be less affluent. Steinberg appeared dubious about the strength of such continuing ethnic affiliations, suggesting the "[t]he ultimate ethnic myth, perhaps, is the belief that the cultural symbols of the past can provide more than a comfortable illusion to shield us from present-day discontents" (Steinberg 2001, 262).

This conclusion does not appear applicable to all whites. In *Habits of the Heart,* Robert Bellah and associates suggested that some white Americans belong to what they call "communities of memory" derived from their families' ethnic traditions that can resonate powerfully in later life. Ruth Levy, a therapist, explained that fifteen years after leaving parental households she and her husband decided to make a renewed commitment to the local synagogue, seeking the nurturing of a community beyond their family. Part of locating themselves in that community was a ritual practice that provided stability. Levy explained:

> I keep kosher because of structure, because at some point I remember thinking, twelve years ago or so, the universe is chaotic, there is so much going on, so much turbulence, and the only thing that imparts meaning isn't some external source. . . . (Bellah et al. 1985, 136)

The authors concluded that for individuals like Levy and her husband, their ethnic affiliation and the rituals accompanying it could provide a major source of stability in their lives.

Whether or not whites value their ethnic affiliation, they generally have the option of discarding it. Furthermore, the respondents in Waters's study tended to generalize from their own situation, concluding that because they could move effortlessly in and out of their ethnic roles that others, including people of color, have equally flexible options. Tim McDonald explained:

> I think black people and Hispanic people face discrimination. Definitely. I think a lot of it they bring on themselves. They talk too much about it. If they would let it go it would be better. (Waters 1990, 160)

This perspective seems to illustrate color-blind racism, in which white people assume that like them minority-group individuals have encountered no significant disadvantage, living in a costless community much like the one they experience. As the concept of color-blind racism suggests, this outlook overlooks or downplays historical and current evidence documenting disadvantaging conditions that continue to impact on racial minorities' lives. Indeed, Waters indicated, it would be a progressive reality if participants in all groups had an equal opportunity to embrace or discard their ethnicity. For many people of color, she contended, that flexibility simply does not exist (Waters 1990, 167–68).

Most majority-group members are unaware of the range of challenges minorities can face in their daily lives. For instance, they fail to appreciate the quiet efficiency with which housing discrimination can occur in urban neighborhoods. As we noted in Chapter 4, realtors and bankers sometimes engage in it, but community members can also collaborate. Greenpoint, a working-class neighborhood in Brooklyn, is an example. It divides into two sections—a northern portion, which is heavily Hispanic, primarily Puerto Rican, and part Polish, and a southern portion, which contains Polish, Irish, Italian, and a few Hispanic residents. The widely recognized boundary between the two sections is Greenpoint Avenue. As one southern inhabitant explained, "I always remember, once you cross Greenpoint Avenue, except for a few white blocks, that wasn't the good section of Greenpoint" (DeSena 1999, 278).

Many Polish, Irish, and Italian residents of the southern area have been committed to controlling who lives there. Few apartments or houses are listed for sale or rent. Instead, the informal social network of gatekeepers, primarily local women, handles the task. As one inhabitant explained, "There are some ads in the local paper, but I think most of the time it's by word of mouth. . . . They're very hush or word of mouth. Even if they're not Hispanic, they still watch who they rent to" (DeSena 1999, 279).

The gatekeeping process can involve intimidation—for example, neighbors some-times exert pressure on one another about potential tenants or homeowners. One resident of the southern section indicated:

> This house was almost bought by a Cuban gentleman, and the lady on this side of us told our landlord that they are not welcome here, in very choice words she used; and they almost threatened him, "don't sell," and the sale did not go through.
>
> When the guy across the street was selling his house, somebody came out and said, "I hope you're not selling to blacks." (DeSena 1999, 280)

Outsiders are often unaware of such tactics. Isolated from ethnic groups' community activities, they can rush toward hasty generalizations. Many majority-group members, for example, are likely to lump all recent Hispanic or Asian immigrants together: Hispanics or Asians are simply members of their respective groups, and so why bother looking further? The reason to do so is that the ethnic group can contain members whose life chances are highly varied—an outcome that can reveal itself within communities. Consider, for instance, the distinction between traditional immigrants and exiles.

Traditional immigrants are likely to be men seeking their fortunes; women and chil-dren generally follow later. These men usually take low-income service jobs with little mobility. They establish no lasting bond to any community because it is unlikely to assure them either lucrative employment or helpful political ties. So they readily shift from one residential location to another.

In contrast, exiles, who are escaping persecution, usually bring the entire family because all members have become vulnerable in the home country. As a rule, the very fact that they are objects of governmental persecution suggests that they are above average in prominence, income, and education. Arriving in the United States, their economic resources and family support can make it feasible to establish successful businesses and, if they choose, become politically active. Exiles, in short, have a higher social-class ranking and possess more valuable resources than traditional immigrants.

Cubans in Miami demonstrate these two types. Between 1965 and 1973, about 340,000 Cuban refugees landed in Miami, and most remained in its Cuban community, known as "Little Havana." Many of these exiles were well-educated professionals or experi-enced businessmen, and some had amassed large fortunes, which they could invest in new ventures in Florida. In addition, after the immigrants' arrival, a number of small Latin Amer-ican banks employing local Cuban Americans with banking backgrounds in Cuba provided start-up capital for some of their new business ventures, which often stressed the link to the homeland—for instance, the sign in front of the Caballero Funeral Home stating "since 1857," a date that preceded the Miami opening by a full century. Both to support ethnic sol-idarity and to obtain cheap, reliable workers, these businesses have generally hired newly arrived Cuban refugees.

The so-called *Marielitos,* who left Cuba in 1980 from the port of Mariel, contrasted with these earlier Cuban arrivals. Although differences of opinion exist about their members' characteristics, there is little doubt that they were less well educated and affluent than the majority of their predecessors. The *Marielitos,* in fact, fitted a more traditional pattern of immigrants than earlier Cuban arrivals, finding it necessary to take low-paying, unskilled jobs, often moving from place to place and encountering suspicion and hostility from various estranged groups, including Little Havana's residents (Abrahamson 1996, 88–94, 99–100).

Exiles and other recently arrived immigrant groups well-positioned to obtain economic success can inadvertently contribute to a locale's interracial tensions. While this has been the case with Cubans in Miami, the most publicized modern instance has involved Korean merchants and black residents in south central Los Angeles (known simply as "South Central"). When prolonged rioting occurred in South Central following the jury decision in the celebrated Rodney King case exonerating four Los Angeles police officers charged with the beating of a black man, Korean merchants in South Central suffered a disproportionate share of the losses, totaling over $158 million.

Racial polarization within the community provided a fertile context for rioting. A substantial number of black residents considered the Korean merchants, who owned many gas stations, liquor stores, and other retail outlets in the community, the most recent representatives of a government-sponsored plan that left the South Central area impoverished following deindustrialization. A black cosmetologist, for example, explained: "Now that Jews have left and Asians come in—which the whites have consciously allowed . . . the whites, or the system, won't allow blacks to get into these business positions" (Ong, Park, and Tong 1999, 412).

The Korean merchants unwittingly contributed to the polarized situation. Except for commercial dealings, the merchants were isolated from the customer base. Most lived outside of South Central and both to be economical and to help establish kinship members, theirs were usually Korean-staffed organizations. Furthermore, because of limited resources and significant start-up costs, the businesses were often marginal operations, maintaining high prices, no-return policies, and other practices that appeared exploitative. Not surprisingly in this context of mutual isolation, some Korean American merchants bore very negative stereotyped views of their black customers. South Central, in short, provided a highly polarized community setting, where rioting readily spread once it broke out.

Although the Los Angeles case is dramatic, many other cities share the same turbulent interracial potential, including New Haven, which is featured in the Sociological Illustration describing my involvement in its inner-city communities. Figure 7.1 sums up the three historical stages just described.

FIGURE 7.1   The Racialized Nature of Community Life in American Cities

  I. Up to 1840: British immigrants in fairly homogenous communities, with the majority of early Irish and German arrivals settling in rural areas

 II. 1840 to 1924:

   (a) Irish immigrants and later newcomers from central and southern Europe designated members of inferior races and subjected to extensive discrimination, including the eugenics movement and ultimately the restrictions of the National Origins Act

   (b) Early discrimination against blacks migrating to cities described in previous chapters

III. 1924 to the present:

   (a) All white ethnic groups receive the Caucasian designation and share "a costless community"

   (b) Racial minorities subjected to different degrees of racial discrimination while whites often fail to recognize the racialized nature of the prevailing social system

SOCIOLOGICAL ILLUSTRATION

The First Four Years

Several years ago a local political leader remarked that for the kind of community work in which I am involved a background in sociology seems surprising. I agreed that the connection wasn't obvious but that there is one.

Involving myself in the activity described here, in fact, began while I was working on the third edition of my book *Racism: An American Cauldron.* As the revision progressed, I felt a growing sense of restless inadequacy: Although producing an effective text on racism was a significant effort, it now felt necessary not only to analyze the problems but to make at least some effort toward alleviating them.

I had an idea about how to proceed and wrote up a proposal and gave it to the university's vice president for academic affairs. He liked it, but in the next few months was so busy we had almost no chance to talk. The last time I saw him we ran into each other in an office adjoining his, where he gave me a hug and said, "Chris, I really appreciate your project. Set up an appointment with my secretary, and we'll get started."

He died suddenly soon afterward. His successor had a different approach, more readily delegating authority and immediately giving control of my project to Richard Gerber, his chief assistant. Dr. Gerber was pleased with my basic plan: to have Southern Connecticut State University (SCSU) host a series of meetings in which local political, business, educational, and neighborhood leaders would meet to develop more effective means of addressing the city's array of race- and poverty-related issues.

We convened an advisory group of faculty and administrators who discussed the project and eventually decided that instead of taking on the entire city and its problems I should focus on a locale near the university, specifically the West Rock community, a largely black residential area and the poorest, most resource-deprived section of the city. My activity would support a portion of the university's mission statement, which emphasizes providing productive services to the local community—"be a good neighbor" is how Dick Gerber summarized it.

Just how to go about being a good neighbor wasn't entirely clear at first. I didn't know a single person in the West Rock area, and so I consulted a knowledgeable university administrator who mentioned two local agencies with which I should start. I also contacted the mayor's office, residential officers of six public-housing projects, and the West Rock representatives of New Haven's federally funded Empowerment program.

The first arrival for the opening meeting was the head of a large public-service organization. As soon as we introduced ourselves, he asked to see my agenda for the meeting. After glancing at it, he said, "You know, Chris, if this is all you have to offer, they'll eat you alive in there." While hardly comforted by his words, I replied that my initial task was to listen and learn about the participants' priorities for the West Rock area.

After several meetings of widely ranging discussion, the chief executive officer of Empower New Haven joined the group, which soon accepted her suggestion to pursue an employment initiative. The plan was that residents from the West Rock area would recruit local individuals interested in undergoing a job-training course at a nearby agency preparing them for entry-level jobs in such places as fast-food outlets and retail stores. The initial contacts were promising as over a dozen residents showed up for three meetings, where two specialists on job training discussed the challenges the recruits would face both in the upcoming training and in the job world itself.

Through most of these sessions, there was little for me to do but observe. My most tangible contribution was to order and deliver an assortment of sandwiches and sodas from a nearby Subway outlet. Overall I was pleased with the initiative's general progress, particularly when thirteen individuals signed up for the set of job-readiness classes.

The morning of the first session, however, only one person appeared. I was caught off guard, stunned, and even the veteran staff members of the agency prepared to provide the training seemed somewhat surprised. The head of its employment group, however, indicated that such an outcome could quite readily develop; the residents we had lined up all had histories featuring repeated difficulties holding a job along with such personal baggage as drug and alcohol problems and, as a result, undoubtedly were feeling ill equipped to take on the job world again.

The next year and a half in West Rock followed a generally unproductive trend. For about nine months, I ran a discussion group composed of several elected officers from the area's public-housing projects, staff members from the mayor's office and the housing authority, and also the director of the adjacent city-sponsored neighborhood corporation that was supposed to help local residents address various poverty-related issues. Although we amply discussed such local problems as unemployment, deficient housing and schooling, drugs, and violence, no concerted action emerged from that group.

Over that eighteen months, Dick Gerber and Pat Whalen, another university administrator, and I had lunch with each of three successive directors of the neighborhood corporation. We listened as each, in turn, laid out plans for improvements to the local community, featuring ways that SCSU could collaborate. Two of the three directors were eloquent, enthusiastically detailing how the university's assistance with computer training, basic literacy, and recreational programs could prove invaluable in the center's effort to help local children. During each meeting Gerber told the respective director that we were eager to press ahead but before doing so we needed to have a brief written statement describing just what the university's contribution to the impending partnership would entail.

None of the directors ever provided a written statement. I followed up each meeting with phone calls and visits to the center and even indicated that I would happily assist in putting the statement together. Each director, in turn, indicated such assistance wasn't necessary—that the statement was forthcoming. I never found out why they didn't follow through. All I knew was that in each case we had reached the moment when deeds needed to support words, and none of the directors made that transition.

After the third director didn't respond, I gave up trying to work in West Rock. In this most resource-deprived section of the city, I had focused on starting partnered activities with the sole agency that people who knew the area agreed offered some promise of effective collaboration. It was a locale so severely deprived by its racialized setting that my associates and I saw little opportunity for someone with my limited resources to make a positive contribution.

It was time to look elsewhere. I contacted Ian Skoggard, an anthropologist who had taught at SCSU and also conducted recreation programs in the West Rock area as a prominent member of the advocacy group, Elm City Congregations Organized (ECCO). Dr. Skoggard indicated that working through churches can be particularly potent in poor neighborhoods, where sometimes few other effective community organizations exist.

Skoggard felt that a collaboration between SCSU and ECCO was promising. He suggested that we contact the pastor of the Varick Memorial A.M.E. Zion Church, which belonged to ECCO, and that if he was interested it could be productive to set up a small computer-training program in the adjoining Varick Family Life Center. That project, which took about a year to establish, has succeeded.

At a press conference announcing the computer-training center's opening, several local political and educational leaders participated, applauding the contribution to the immediate community. Toward the end I briefly addressed the steering committee's role in setting up the enterprise.

Through our shared experience, I had learned that such committees are the powerful little engines that can drive effective community partnerships. Although disagreements and disputes are inevitable, progress occurs when the participants stay "zoned in" on the common task—in our case, to help poor children obtain the basic chance to develop computer-related skills that give them a better shot at mainstream success. In such groups it is apparent that individuals range in their capacity to stay focused on the collective goal and to subordinate personal insecurities and ego needs. When individuals' personal drives distract participants from the collective goal, then trouble, sometimes race-linked, can break out. All in all, such situations can provide participants a new, frequently provocative experience in which the setting, fellow workers, and other

(continued)

issues are often different from what they've previously experienced—not necessarily a comfortable, easy context in which to function but one where moral growth and understanding can flourish and clients can obtain meaningful benefits.

The computer-training program now includes math tutoring, with SCSU's math department playing a pivotal role, and the university is also involved in an exploratory effort to resurrect the neighborhood corporation in the West Rock area. Throughout all this activity, I have learned not to become too optimistic about any specific initiative, recognizing that these activities have unfolded in the context of the pro-growth framework described in Chapter 6: Any significant urban enterprise, in short, requires support from the reigning economic and political groups. As in so many cities, political alliances in New Haven are highly factionalized, meaning that while our ventures receive some powerful support, they can encounter opposition from others. Furthermore, as small projects largely dependent on volunteers, they at best can obtain short-term commitments of personnel and resources. For instance, each time our math tutoring program has started a new semester, we have needed to locate new funding; new teachers and other key personnel such as teaching assistants, a van driver, and a cook (to prepare the Southern-style breakfast included in the program); new students; and some new equipment—a process that at times can be interesting and challenging but also wearisome. Unlike schools, underfinanced and inefficient though they often are, programs like this one have no sustained support from public funding.

These are difficult programs to implement. On the other hand, it has become apparent that once these collaborative projects are under way, effective individuals and groups with whom one can partner are likely to emerge. The process is provocative, sometimes exhilarating, encouraging us to extend our contacts and relationships for the program's advantage. All in all, my community work now positions me to make some interesting firsthand observations of how individuals of diverse backgrounds labor together, sometimes effectively and sometimes not, to promote change in their urban communities. One potential is that this collaborative activity might be laying the foundation so that the university will be able to host the sort of discussions of urban issues originally conceived.

Moving ahead into a discussion of current issues, we examine two major, intractable issues facing the poor, largely minority residents of urban communities—homelessness and deficient health care.

Contemporary Struggles

All of us are aware that modern formal organizations are often large and impersonal, staffed by individuals who can seem alien, even hostile. In Ken Kesey's *One Flew Over the Cuckoo's Nest,* the narrator, an inmate of a mental hospital, described the system in which he and his fellow patients were immersed as a "fog machine," which spewed out a thick, skim-milk-like substance making it almost impossible to see and creating a timeless void in which longtime patients became permanently lodged. It was a lost world of forgotten people who remained technically alive but suffered a numbed, diminished existence.

Individuals and families served by the organizations processing homelessness and health care find themselves in similarly alienating systems, and a major contributing factor appears to be their racialized nature. These are large, difficult issues that the American government and most urban communities have not effectively addressed.

Homelessness

David Bright, a ten-year-old, homeless black boy from New York City, testified before the House Select Committee on Hunger in Washington, D.C. When he grows up, David explained, he wants to become president so that he can make certain that "no little boy like me will have to put his head down on his desk at school because it hurts to be hungry" (Hayes 1987, 58).

David's statement left few dry eyes in the hearing room. From Mayor Edward Koch, however, it aroused an angry reply. Koch indicated that David's testimony "simply doesn't reflect reality. New York does more for the homeless than any other city in America" (Rimer 1986, 42). David Bright took the developing feud in stride, saying that the root of the problem might be jealousy produced by the fact that "I've got hair, and he doesn't." David's school principal declared that while Koch had an effective public presence, "he's no match for this kid" (Rimer 1986, 42).

Although David Bright had his moment in the sun, much of his life has been dreary and painful. At the time of the hearing, he was living with his mother and three siblings in two small rooms in New York City's crowded Hotel Martinique, along with 1500 homeless children and their families. Sometimes his mother would become so depressed that she would tell the children to leave her alone in one room so that she could cry.

But while adults suffer because of homelessness, children appear to suffer more. There is no physical place, even were it to fall far short of the ideal, that provides a basic sense of stability, a home, during their developmentally influential early years. As one writer indicated, homelessness destroys "the inner beauty of a child" (Hayes 1987, 66).

During a typical day, between 900,000 and 1.4 million American children are homeless. Individuals and families often move quickly in or out of homelessness, with four to five as many experiencing it at some point in a year as suffer it on a given day. In the late 1990s, between 2.3 and 3.5 million Americans experienced homelessness in the course of a year.

Statistics about homelessness have been gathered from homeless assistance programs around the country. Participants in these programs have been 61 percent lone men, 15 percent lone women, 15 percent adults with children, and 9 percent two or more adults without children. Homeless individuals' racial and ethnic composition has involved about equal proportions of blacks and whites, each about 40 to 41 percent of the total, 11 to 12 percent Hispanics, 6 to 8 percent Native Americans, and 1 percent some other group, primarily Asian Americans. Racial minorities, in short, are distinctly overrepresented.

Geographically, homelessness has been mainly an urban phenomenon, with 71 percent located in central cities, 21 percent in suburban or urban-fringe areas, and 9 percent in rural districts. Among homeless people a variety of disabilities have been prevalent. Nearly half (46 percent) reported chronic physical conditions. About a third (31 percent) indicated a combination of problems with mental illness and drugs and/or alcohol, and 17 percent described a substance-abuse dependency and no mental illness. Only one in four homeless adults claimed to be free of both mental illness and substance-abuse problems (Burt

TABLE 7.1   Characteristics of Individuals in Homeless Assistance Programs

The Participants

Lone men	61%
Lone women	15
Adults with children	15
Adults without children	9

Racial and Ethnic Composition

Black	40 to 41%
White	40 to 41
Hispanic	11 to 12
Native American	6 to 8
Another race	1

Location

Central cities	71%
Suburban or urban fringe	21
Rural areas	9

Disabilities[1]

Chronic physical conditions	46%
Mental illness and substance abuse	31
Substance abuse	17
Alcohol abuse	12
Mental illness	15

[1]Total exceeds 100 percent because chronic physical conditions can accompany any of the other disabilities.

Sources: Data from Martha R. Burt. "What Will It Take to End Homelessness?" Urban Institute, 2001. *www.urban.org/housing/homeless/endhomelessness. html;* Martha R. Burt, Laudan Y. Aron, and Edgar Lee. *Helping America's Homeless: Emergency Shelter or Affordable Housing?* Washington DC: Urban Institute Press, 2001.

2001; Burt, Aron and Lee 2001). Table 7.1 summarizes these data on homeless people's characteristics.

To understand the causes of homelessness, we should appreciate that the issue illustrates C. Wright Mills's perspective on history and biography—a situation in which broad economic and political forces converge with certain individuals' and families' vulnerabilities. In particular:

- Declining housing markets for very poor single adults and families have been relentlessly pricing them out of what once were financially manageable rents.
- Dwindling jobs for people with a high-school education or less schooling are contributing to a widening gap between those who are at least fairly well off economically and those who are not.
- Cutbacks in traditional publicly financed care for individuals with severe mental illness have basically left this category of adults out on the streets.
- Widespread racial and ethnic discrimination in housing along with zoning restrictions that prohibit public housing in many urban and suburban areas have increasingly curtailed locations for low-cost dwellings.

Many observers' greatest concern regarding homelessness has been homeless children, who are much more likely than housed children to experience such major difficulties as physical, cognitive, emotional, and mental problems—problems that leave a lasting impact and make it much more likely that homelessness will persist in adulthood (Burt 2001; Burt, Aron, and Lee 2001).

Shelters themselves can add to homeless people's burdens, particularly for residents who do not speak English. Two common ways program managers deal with this difficulty is to hire bilingual or bicultural staff and to arrange for staff members to receive training involving cross-cultural issues. Some managers like the following one, whose clients were Hispanic, black, and white, took a comprehensive approach. She explained, "We hire bilingual/bicultural staff at every opportunity we can. We have books, audiotapes, and videotapes in both languages. We provide translators (staff or volunteers) at all groups and educational programs" (Friedman 2000, 202).

Although many program organizers are attuned to racial and ethnic groups' customs and needs, misunderstandings and conflict are distinctly possible. Obviously emotional about it, one manager indicated that some whites who had recently become poor and homeless often claimed superiority over the other inhabitants of the shelter. He explained:

> A woman feels as though there should be air-conditioning in the shelter. She pulls up in a Buick Park Avenue. Her attitude is that she shouldn't be here. "I'm not like the rest of these people. I wasn't brought up like this." Now she's with black people, Vietnamese, Hispanic. (Friedman 2000, 203)

In another shelter after several robberies, white occupants simply assumed that a certain individual who was ethnically different from them must be responsible. The program manager indicated:

> People pointed their fingers at an Hispanic male . . . in the house meeting and in individual meetings. It could have been anybody. We had to reiterate that people are innocent until proven [guilty]. The young man got teed off from others [including a staff member] staring at him and accusing him. He had a bad experience as a child with being accused. So this incident brought up a lot of issues for him. We do express to families that living in the shelter is not easy. Everyone has different problems and stuff going on. . . . It's not easy at all. (Friedman 2000, 203)

People living in shelters can face a difficult, debilitating experience. Specialists on the topic of homelessness have asserted that a number of specific safeguards could keep most individuals and families from facing the predicament. They include competent public or private officials who negotiate with landlords and assist clients with bad credit histories; various rental-assistance funds alleviating such short-term costs as unpaid back rent or security deposits; and programs that encourage developers to build or renovate attractive low-cost apartment buildings and houses (Burt 2001, 3).

Kitty Cole, an administrator for a Chicago agency that has battled homelessness, indicated that an aggressive posture could produce a solution, that

> [w]e just need the political will and the resources to do it. If we dealt with the small number of people who are chronically homeless and provided good preventative services for families that are on the edge, we could solve the problem. I know we could. (Marks 2001, 2)

Like homelessness, health care has also been a growing crisis that has disproportionately affected racial minorities.

Deficient Health Care

When Elvia Marin, a Mexican immigrant, went with her husband to an emergency room in Oakland, California, neither of them in their halting English had the vocabulary to help identify her ailment—urinary tract stones that produced an intense pain that Marin described as worse than giving birth. She left the hospital untreated but was forced to return shortly afterward when the pain returned. "I felt really desperate and also frustrated at my inability to communicate in English and explain my problem," Marin said in Spanish. "I feel like we're not being listened to, not being paid attention to. We're not considered important" (Kong 2002, 2A).

This kind of situation has sparked ongoing debate. While some observers argue that the only reasonable solution is for immigrants to learn effective English, many others contend that translators could readily resolve most situations. However, such additional staff can prove prohibitively expensive. Meanwhile, with at least 21 million American residents unable to speak English well, the problems and controversy will continue.

Health care, in fact, is a resource area where inequalities abound. Racial minorities are about twice as likely as whites to have no medical coverage. Trying to encapsule the significance of this deficiency in the world's most affluent nation, Eric Krakauer of Massachusetts General Hospital's Palliative Care Service said, "I think our kids and grandkids will look back and wonder, 'how could we allow forty million Americans, disproportionately minorities, to be without health insurance?' " (Crenner and Fox 2002).

Because the nation's teaching hospitals have remained willing to provide free care to individuals who cannot afford to pay, their patient load has significantly grown as the number of uninsured Americans rose in the 1990s. Between 1991 and 1996, teaching hospitals' number of unpaid cases increased by over 40 percent, creating an oppressive volume of patients, diminishing the effectiveness of care, and undermining these hospitals' financial stability (Commonwealth Fund 2001).

Besides being disproportionately represented among uninsured patients, racial minorities appear disadvantaged even when their medical coverage is comparable to whites'. In *Unequal Treatment: Confronting Racial and Ethnic Disparities in Health Care,* members of the National Academies' Institute of Medicine indicated that racial and ethnic minorities tend to receive lower quality health care even when medical-insurance coverage, income, and severity of condition is at whites' level. As a rule, African Americans and sometimes Hispanics have been less likely than whites to obtain appropriate cardiac medication, cardiac bypass surgery, hemodialysis and kidney transplantation, effective cancer diagnostic tests, diabetes care, and high-quality clinical services such as intensive care (Smedley, Stith, and Nelson 2002).

Data showing racial minorities' disadvantage exist, but much of the time the data come from hospital records, creating a situation in which, as medical researcher Sally Satel indicated, "key questions cannot be asked directly of the very people being studied: for example, did subjects in the study want or refuse a specific treatment? Did physicians offer it, and if not, why?" (Satel 2001, 131).

There are two broad categories of issues to consider here—minority responses to medical care and experts' recommendations for system improvements.

Minority Responses to Medical Care   Blacks, particularly in the South, have been exposed to many stories about discriminatory health-care treatment, resulting in death or serious disability. Some, like the claim that blues singer Bessie Smith bled to death because of being turned away from a whites-only hospital following a 1937 automobile accident, have turned out to be untrue. Many, however, including the numerous accounts of the infamous Tuskegee experiment have proved accurate (Smith-King 2002).

The Tuskegee study, which began in 1932, was a research project in which the Public Health Service (and later the Centers for Disease Control) decided to record the natural course of syphilis by observing four hundred infected black men *without treating them.* Recruited from churches and clinics throughout the South, the men were simply told that they had "bad blood" and were not provided the standard 1930s treatment involving mercury and arsenic compounds, nor penicillin when in 1947 it was found effective for treating syphilis.

This study continued for forty years, ending abruptly in 1972 when a lawyer informed about the research went public with his knowledge. That would appear to have been the tragic end of the damage done, but not so. For many southern blacks, the Tuskegee experiment created a legacy of distrust. For instance, one woman being treated for AIDS told her doctor that as a child she was warned to get home before dark because otherwise the Tuskegee researchers "would snatch her off the street and experiment on her in the basement at night" (Stryker 1997, 4). Such stories were common, symptomatic of a massive, persistent mistrust. Many blacks, particularly those living in the rural South, have believed that HIV, the virus causing AIDS, was produced in laboratories to kill African Americans; that AZT, a prominent drug for combatting AIDS, was meant to poison blacks; and that both condom-use and needle-exchange programs have been part of the conspiracy to wipe out African Americans. A 1990 poll among nearly 2,000 black churchgoers provided consistent information, indicating that 35 percent of the respondents believed that AIDS was meant to produce black genocide (Stryker 1997).

In contemporary times some evidence exists that racial minorities are more inclined than whites to either refuse treatment, delay seeking it, or fail after consultation to follow treatment regimes effectively. Such medically nonproductive outcomes can occur because of poor communication and understanding between medical staff and patients belonging to distinctly different cultural traditions, users' mistrust based on either poor relations with current medical personnel or previous bad experiences with health-care systems, or simply from the inability to make effective use of such systems (Smedley, Stith, and Nelson 2002, 6–7).

Additional differences between racial minorities and whites are apparent. Research has demonstrated that with similar insurance coverage, African Americans and Latinos are about twice as likely to rely on either a teaching hospital or a public hospital as a regular source of care. Why this difference occurs is not entirely clear. It well might be that patients' minority status is the key component leading to the choice of hospitals as primary providers. Racial minorities are disproportionately poor, and as a result find themselves susceptible to the following conditions that seem to encourage the choice of hospitals for medical care:

- A preference for hospitals' flexible hours, especially for low-income patients in jobs unlikely to provide payment for time away from work
- Financial barriers like copayment requirements generally associated with private practices (Lillie-Blanton, Martinez, and Salganicoff 2001)

Because of the realities of modern medical treatment, however, patients opting for hospitals as their chief source of regular medical care can lose out. Let me explain.

Nowadays the major form of cost containment that most health-insurance plans follow is what is called "managed care," where private and public organizations subscribe to specific health plans that permit their employees to receive subsidized medical coverage. For patients managed care is complex, with many rules to follow, officials to consult, and forms to fill out in seeking both optimal medical treatment and limited financial cost. The most fundamental step a patient can take to obtain positive outcomes is to develop a sustained relationship with a physician, whose detailed knowledge of and concern for that individual is likely to promote effective treatment. However, the disproportionately minority patients under managed care who go to a hospital as a regular source of care are much less likely to develop such a relationship, simply receiving care from whoever is on duty at the time they appear (Smedley, Stith, and Nelson 2002, 120–21).

Besides analyzing minorities' care in the current health-care structure, medical researchers have suggestions for bettering it.

Experts' Recommendations for System Improvements   Ours is a stereotype-laden society in which recent survey data have demonstrated that between half and three-quarters of white Americans believe that compared to themselves African Americans are less intelligent, more violent, and more inclined to prefer living off welfare. In this intolerant context, it is distinctly possible that such perceptions influence health-care providers in interacting with minority patients. Although the limitations of research have made it impossible to provide actual documentation showing that medical personnel's biases have affected the quality of care for minority patients, a body of experimental studies have suggested that when faced with matched medical diagnoses involving black and white subjects, white physicians have been inclined to prescribe more extensive treatment and medication for whites. Research findings on this significant topic are fragmentary, suggesting the importance of continuing investigation on the topic (Smedley, Stith, and Nelson 2002).

Evidence from studies is also limited regarding the improvement of health care delivery to minorities, but medical researchers have emphasized two steps that patients can find productive:

- Establish a comfortable, sustained relationship with a medical provider, preferably a physician, that serves as the central link to effective health care.
- Communicate fully and openly with various staff people in the system, realizing that one's welfare or one's family members' welfare is at stake and thus overcoming any traditional sense that it is disrespectful to ask a lot of questions (AfricanAmerican-Therapists.com 2000; Johns Hopkins School of Public Health 1999).

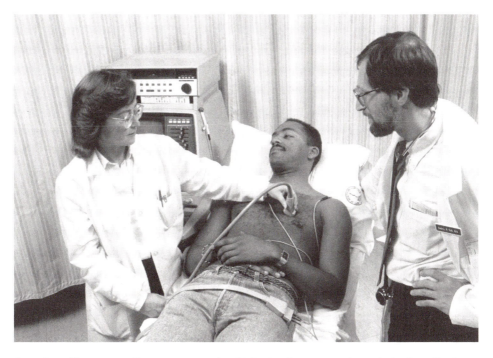

A number of factors contribute to a pattern in which minority-group patients receive less effective medical care than majority-group members.

While such individual steps are useful, experts also emphasize the utility of overhauling the medical-delivery system:

■ To reform and revitalize American health care so that those who are poor and disproportionately minority obtain overall high-quality treatment comparable to what more affluent citizens currently receive. At present the system is distinctly racialized, with minorities heavily represented in health-care contexts where they have inferior coverage or none at all, limiting the range of expensive tests, procedures, and drugs available, and, perhaps equally important but often overlooked, influencing the prevailing atmosphere in the health-care setting—in short, affecting whether or not providers are pleasant, relaxed, and respectful.

■ To support a growth in minority medical staff, especially physicians. Minority patients are more likely to establish the trustful relationships with minority physicians and other health-care personnel that can lead to their following the various steps that will maximize good health. In addition, people of color are more likely to serve in inner-city hospitals, which have tended to be chronically understaffed. The challenge that currently faces those seeking to increase the numbers of African American, Hispanic, and Native American medical personnel involves developing and promoting procedures that will locate and nurture minority students to become effective doctors and nurses (Community Catalyst 2002; Smedley, Stith, and Nelson 2002 11–12).

Sporadically, the topic of minorities' inferior health care receives some political attention. In the fall of 2002, members of the Congressional Black Caucus, which contains most of the black members of the House of Representatives, convened a forum in which House members, medical researchers, and health-care activists discussed the urgency of the situation, advocating the mobilization of a health-care movement. According to David Williams of the University of Michigan, there has been "absolutely no progress in reducing the racial health gap." Gary King, a participant from Penn State University, suggested that what is needed to promote effective minority health care is a mobilization modeled on the civil rights movement. King said, "This campaign will require sustained advocacy and pressure before health care can be conceived as a right and not a privilege" (W. K. Kellogg Foundation, 2002).

Health care, at least health care for poor, minority Americans, is clearly in disarray, and that is one contributing factor to the larger community reality we now consider.

Conclusion

Several years ago in a small community meeting, Father Tim Dempsey sat in a folding chair, his massive body almost enveloping its frame. Discussion had fallen off, and Father Dempsey, who was usually brisk and businesslike, was toned down, even pensive. He explained how in the early 1950s as a young priest he'd come to New Haven from a town in the northern part of the state—at a time when the city still had thriving ethnic communities. "The Irish, the Italians, the Jews—they hadn't yet fled to the suburbs. It was exciting, it was diverse." Gesturing enthusiastically, he recalled the pleasant task of walking through the various neighborhoods, talking to parishioners and others. "Crime was low, scarcely visible. Many groups didn't have much, but there was hope. Winchester's [a major firearms manufacturer] was always willing to hire, and people could visualize their way up in the world."

Father Dempsey rose slowly to his feet, shaking his head sadly. "That was a long time ago."

I'm not trying to suggest that Father Dempsey was mired in the past. He was always actively involved in a variety of housing and employment initiatives intended to help the city's poor minorities, and although he admitted that various groups and interests, including the incumbent mayor who campaigned for the restoration of vibrant communities, contributed to the rehabilitative efforts to which he devoted most of his energy, it was a difficult setting in which to gain ground.

"In the summer," Father Dempsey continued, "I sit out on the front porch of my beach house every night, listening to the gentle waves breaking on the shore. I love it—the quiet, regular peacefulness of it all. And then I think of the city—how in the past I felt almost that very same way and how it is now—and wonder whether in this postindustrial age people will ever be able to get a renewed sense of that wonderful old feeling."

DISCUSSION QUESTIONS

1. Indicate how the nineteenth- and early twentieth-century conception of race affected relations in urban communities.

2. Examine Mary C. Waters's claim that modern white ethnics live in a costless community. Do you have information that has been personally obtained or comes from family members or friends that either supports or disputes this conclusion?

3. Review the reasons why homelessness occurs, evaluating whether it is likely to continue in the future. Indicate how race and ethnicity play into the process.

4. Analyze how the issues of race and income link to the choice of a primary health-care provider.

5. Discuss important improvements to be made in health-care delivery, with special attention directed toward means of eliminating racism.

6. Have you been involved or would you like to become involved in some activity assisting poor urban residents? Discuss, indicating, in particular, how the issues of race and ethnicity are likely to prove relevant.

BIBLIOGRAPHY

Abrahamson, Mark. 1996. *Urban Enclaves: Identity and Place in America.* New York: St. Martin's Press.

AfricanAmericanTherapists.com. 2000. "Medical Treatment & Black Consumers of Care." Africanamericantherapists.com/Medical%20Treatment%20and%20Blacks.htm.

Bailyn, Bernard, et al. 1977. *The Great Republic: A History of the American People.* Lexington, MA: Heath.

Bellah, Robert N., et al. 1985. *Habits of the Heart: Individualism and Commitment in American Life.* Berkeley: University of California Press.

Brodkin, Karen. 1998. *How Jews Became White Folks & What That Says About Race in America.* New Brunswick: Rutgers University Press.

Burt, Martha R. 2001. "What Will It Take to End Homelessness?" Urban Institute. www.urban.org/housing/homeless/endhomelessness.html.

Burt, Martha R., Laudan Y. Aron, and Edgar Lee. 2001. *Helping America's Homeless: Emergency Shelter or Affordable Housing?* Washington, DC: Urban Institute Press.

Commonwealth Fund. 2001. "Teaching Hospitals Provide Significantly More Free Care to the Poor and Uninsured Than Any Other Hospitals." www.cmwf.org/media/releases/ahc_indigent_release04182001.asp.

Community Catalyst. 2002. "Barriers Block Minority Progress in the Medical Profession." www.communitycatalyst.org.

Crenner, Christopher, and Ken Fox. 2002. "Minority Patients Face Barriers to Optimum End-of-Life Care." *Massachusetts General Hospital News & Information.* www.mgh.harvard.edu/news/releases/011002barriers.htm.

DeSena, Judith N. 1999. "Local Gatekeeping Practices and Residential Segregation," pp. 276–84 in Christopher G. Ellison and W. Allen Martin (eds.), *Race and Ethnic Relations in the United States.* Los Angeles: Roxbury.

Friedman, Donna Haig. 2000. *Parenting in Public: Family Shelter and Public Assistance.* New York: Columbia University Press.

Hayes, Cheryl D. 1987. *Risking the Future: Adolescent Sexuality, Pregnancy, and Childbearing.* Washington, DC: National Academy Press.

Jacobson, Matthew Frye. 1998. *Whiteness of a Different Color: European Immigrants and the Alchemy of Race.* Cambridge: Harvard University Press.

Johns Hopkins School of Public Health. 1999. "Following ER." www.er.jhsph.edu/Erwork/072999.htm.

Kong, Deborah. 2002. "Diagnosis: Acute Misunderstanding." *Maine Sunday Telegram* (June 23): 2A.

Lillie-Blanton, Marsha, Rose Marie Martinez, and Alina Salganicoff. 2001. "Site of Medical Care: Do Racial and Ethnic Differences Persist?" www.academic.udayton.edu/health/03access/access01.htm.

Marks, Alexandra. 2001. "US Shelters Swell—with Families." *Christian Science Monitor* (November 29). www.csmonitor.com/2001/1129/p1s1-ussc.html.

Ong, Paul, Kye Young Park, and Yasmin Tong. 1999. "The Korean-Black Conflict and the State," pp. 409–18 in Christopher G. Ellison and W. Allen Martin (eds.), *Race and Ethnic Relations in the United States.* Los Angeles: Roxbury.

Rimer, Susan. 1986. " 'Hotel Kid' Becomes Symbol for the Homeless." *New York Times.* (March 6): 42.

Satel, Sally. 2001. "Health and Medical Care." Hoover Press. www-hoover.stanford.edu/homepage/books/fulltext/colorline/127.pdf.

Smedley, Brian D., Adrienne Y. Stith, and Alan R. Nelson. 2002. *Unequal Treatment: Confronting Racial and Ethnic Disparities in Health Care.* Washington, DC: National Academy Press. http://.books.nap.edu/books/030908265X/htm1.

Smith-King, Tonya. 2002. "The Color of Death 10 Years Later." *The Jackson Sun.* (November 6). www.jacksonsun.com/fe/cod/distrust.shtml.

Steinberg, Stephen. 2001. *The Ethnic Myth: Race, Ethnicity, and Class in America,* 3rd ed. Boston: Beacon Press.

Stryker, Jeff. 1997. "Tuskeegee's Long Arm Touches a Nerve." *New York Times.* (April 13): sec. 4, p. 4.

Waters, Mary C. 1990. *Ethnic Options: Choosing Identities in America.* Berkeley: University of California Press.

W.K. Kellogg Foundation. 2002. "Capitol Hill Forum Examines Racial Disparities in Health Care." *Community Voices: HealthCare for the Underserved.* www.communityvoices.org/Article.aspx?ID=246.

8

Smorgasbord II: Race, Ethnicity, and Socialization to American Urban Families and Education

When public officials, urban experts, and committed citizens seek to figure out ways to address difficult family- and education-related issues, sharp differences of opinion can arise in the struggle toward understanding and consensus. Consider the following illustration.

In the city and surrounding towns, Susan Jeannette was renowned as the driving force for most major humanitarian and artistic public programs. She and her husband, the former dean of the university's law school, not only served on an array of major boards that put them in direct touch with most influential groups and individuals in the state, but with their wealth they could make an opening contribution to a new project that would immediately establish its prominence.

When, as this afternoon, Jeannette arrived late to a community meeting, rapidly reciting the day's crowded schedule to explain her tardiness, all eyes turned toward her and discussion ceased—a reaction normally reserved for a major political official.

This day's topic was a newly established after-school program at a local middle school. Jeannette was pleased the program was up and off the ground and well funded by the city's board of education, but she questioned its direction. "Ladies and gentlemen," she said, "what these children need badly is nurturing, cultural nurturing, what so often is called "enrichment." She paused to scan her audience. "After all, they have regular classes at school—reading, writing, arithmetic, and computers too. What they desperately need is cultural growth—the art, music, literature that unlike middle-class students they aren't exposed to in their culturally deprived homes."

At this time Milton Jackson, the school's principal, who always attended the meetings and normally spoke little except to answer questions about school procedures, appeared agitated. "Madame," he began with exaggerated gentleness:

> I am at a loss how to respond to you. I don't know whether to begin by following up on the personal insult I feel as an African American heading up a school whose families are largely minorities or whether I should start by addressing the folly of simply ignoring the necessity of making this program's priority seeking to overcome our children's disadvantage in basic educational skills. I know your intentions are good, but . . .

Do you agree with Ms. Jeannette or with the principal, or is another conclusion preferable?

That issue aside, an important reality is that with distinctly limited resources available, community groups seeking to improve inner-city schools have difficult choices to face. In the last portion of the chapter, we consider some of those, but first we continue the previous chapter's analysis of socialization by examining the related topics of family and education. The family is usually the first setting in which individuals' socialization occurs, and once children reach school age, the education system assumes some of these functions.

The brief historical section divides into two time periods, examining both family and education. The first segment focuses on the years when Europeans dominated immigration, and the second involves a racially and ethnically more diversified time span.

Era Up to 1924

Arriving in the American wilderness, the earliest immigrants struggled to survive. Life was centered on work—long hours with family members and little time or opportunity for formal schooling. In addition, the first pioneers also emphasized religious practice.

The Family

According to the Calvinist doctrine that guided the Puritans, people who God had destined for salvation were living in accord with biblical teachings. Even though the Puritans believed that it was impossible to influence God's decisions, parents hammered away at the primacy of biblical instruction and pious behavior. The children, however, often lacked their parents' religious zeal. Undeterred, the elders "intensified the campaign to win the children; they wrote, they preached, they prayed, they threatened—but to no avail" (Morgan 1966, 185).

Yet the Puritans remained unrelenting, enacting increasingly strict laws to hold children in line. In Connecticut, Massachusetts, and New Hampshire, children who struck their parents faced severe punishment, including the possibility of death. As family discipline appeared to slacken, towns passed statutes requiring parents to enforce discipline on their children, and when those measures appeared insufficient, officials took the educational function out of parents' hands and assumed control of it themselves.

By the second and third generation, however, economics exercised more influence in family life than religion. Land was plentiful, labor in short supply, and children needed to be nurtured so that they became effective workers—whether on farms or in cities. Focusing on living a sin-free, pious life was not going to promote such productivity (Mintz and Kellogg 1988, 17).

This "silent revolution," which by the onset of the eighteenth century influenced nearly all white families in the early cities, featured a new set of family functions. Now the urban white family had become a "buffer, filter, and sorting mechanism"—providing a protected setting in this new, often harsh world where challenging, often confusing options about residential location, marital choice, work, education, and various other issues could be discussed and debated in relation to traditional standards (Habenstein 1998, 19–20).

An Italian mother, her two daughters, and her son arrive at the Ellis Island processing center in 1905 during the peak time of immigration from southern and eastern Europe.

Early immigrants often faced conditions that affected family structure and effectiveness. The Irish arriving in the 1840s lived in poorly constructed, crowded housing in deplorably rundown slums—conditions that made family life unsettled and turbulent. Infant-mortality rates, longevity rates, and the number of illegitimate births all rose sharply and stayed high for about thirty years until the Irish started to become more established occupationally. In addition, during that same time period, Irish American women, in part because they lost their husbands to dangerous occupations, headed a relatively high 14 to 18 percent of households, which, because of women's chronically low pay, tended to be particularly poor (Horgan 1998, 47–48).

For early blacks migrating north, conditions varied greatly—from the harsh and impoverished to the well settled. In Philadelphia, W. E. B. DuBois observed that the poorest, who he considered the products of "the looseness of plantation life," where "home life was protected only by the caprice of the master," displayed "much sexual promiscuity and the absence of a real home life" (DuBois 1973, 192). DuBois indicated that, in contrast, the majority of the city's black citizens, who were working-class, maintained "a family life of distinctly Quaker characteristics. One can go into such homes . . . and find all the quiet comfort and simple good-hearted fare that one would expect among well-bred people" (DuBois 1973, 195).

While facing many hardships, blacks were at least able to create families and gain the comfort, protection, and assistance such structures can provide. In contrast, the vast majority of early Chinese laborers entered as unaccompanied men to earn as much money as quickly as possible as laborers and then planned to return to China, often to wives and children in the home village (Wong 1998, 287–88).

Like other newly arrived immigrant groups, Italians faced difficult conditions, but their cultural traditions played a distinctive role in their adaptation. The majority of Italian immigrants to the United States came from the Mezzogiorno region of southern Italy, where families, including extended family members such as parents, grandparents, aunts, uncles, and godparents, were the most valued social unit. An individual's personal identity derived from the family, and family membership was critical in defining one's place in society.

The significance of the last point was that if some of the New World standards or expectations clashed with the traditional family code, then, at least among early generations, the new ways would lose out. Traditionally, Italians had supported the idea of children being *ben educato* (well educated), but their particular use of the term focused on developing values, attitudes, habits, and skills that promoted the welfare of the family. To the first generation of Italians, schools failed in this regard, criticizing *la via vecchia* (the old ways) and keeping young people from what were considered the more important lessons to be learned on the job (Squiers and Quadagno 1998, 102–05).

Like the family, education played an important function—one that over time became more salient and controversial.

Education

Children, the Puritans believed, were born ignorant and evil, and education—learning to read so that they could obtain firsthand knowledge of the Bible—was the clear path to salvation. Learning to read often occurred at home, where pious parents approached the task as a sacred trust (Morgan 1966, 92–97).

Although the Puritans and other early groups developed schools, they served a small percentage of urban children. In Massachusetts in 1650 there was about one school for every 212 households, declining to one school for every 352 households forty years later. At that time New York had one school for every 200 households and Virginia one for every 900.

Far from feeling chagrined at what modern Americans would consider his state's dire deficiency, Lord Berkeley of Virginia stated, "I thank God that there are no free schools nor printing, and I hope that we shall not have these [for a] hundred years." Berkeley, who was governor at the time, agreed with many other wealthy, powerful individuals of his era that "learning has brought disobedience, and heresy and sects into the world" (Rury 2002, 36).

A century later, basic schooling was still very limited. A Massachusetts law required towns to provide elementary schools six months of the year, and no legal restriction excluded Boston's 766 free black children. However, few attended, primarily because of the hostile reception they received, and so in 1798 a group of black parents petitioned for separate schools. The request was denied, authorities declaring that if they gave blacks their own schools they would need to do the same for other groups. At this time the black parents turned to wealthy whites for philanthropic help and produced a school that lasted only a few months. Two years later the parents made another effort to open a private school, and then in 1806 the Boston School Committee accepted the idea of separate schools, which were maintained with a combination of public and private funding.

By the 1820s, however, many blacks questioned the wisdom of separate schools, particularly noting the low quality of teachers. A subcommittee of the Boston School Committee issued a report, which indicated the blacks' schools were inferior in both teaching and physical facilities. The report declared, "After all, Black parents paid taxes which helped to support white schools. They deserved a more equal return on their share of the city's income" (Spring 1994, 166). The dispute continued for over two decades, finally reaching a resolution when in 1855 the governor signed into law a bill prohibiting exclusion from schools based on race or religion (Spring 1994, 166–67).

This was the era of the so-called "common school," where the general argument went that if children from a variety of ethnic, religious, and social backgrounds were educated in common, there would be a decline in hostility and conflict. In addition, educational leaders advocated their use as an instrument of governmental policy, promoting a unified nation where students would learn to obey the law and live peacefully and harmoniously (Spring 1994, 63–64).

Educators knew that the political leadership was very concerned that the mass of arriving immigrants would be rebellious and noncooperative. Needing politicians' support to establish public education, they were willing to contribute to a strenuous effort to Americanize all children: to focus on speaking and writing English while discouraging, sometimes even denigrating other languages and cultural traditions; to emphasize Protestantism; and, above all, to exult the worthiness of the capitalist system (Binzen 1970, 41–42).

Believing that drunkenness was one of the traits needing to be discouraged, teachers sermonized endlessly about its evils, even working the idea into arithmetic problems. An example from one text read: "There were 7 farmers, 3 of whom drunk rum and whisky and became miserable. The rest drank water and were happy. How many drank water?" (Binzen 1970, 43).

Besides facing relentless propagandizing, urban students suffered abysmally low-quality education. In 1893 Joseph Rice, a freelance writer, visited schools in thirty-six states. In New York City, for instance, he found that young children attended

> a hard, unsympathetic, mechanized drudgery school, a school into which the light of science has not yet entered. Its characteristic feature lies in the severity of its discipline, a discipline of enforced silence, immobility and mental passivity. The primary reading, is, as a rule, so poor that the children are scarcely able to recognize new words at sight at the end of the second year. Even the third year reading is miserable. (Binzen 1970, 45)

Various conditions encouraged some ethnic groups to develop antagonistic relations with the schools. Italians' focus on the traditional sense of family values militated against standard public education. Italian Americans tended to believe that schools might undermine family unity and that they would impede children's economic contribution to the family, which in Italy began at the age of twelve. Because of this reaction to schools, Italian children in the early twentieth century were more likely than children from other ethnic groups to be late, truant, and involved in disciplinary infractions. For several decades this disadvantage adversely affected some Italian Americans' employment potential (Squiers and Quadagno 1998, 111–12).

Although blacks never opposed receiving mainstream public education, differences of opinion existed about the schooling available to them. Early in the twentieth century, Booker T. Washington spoke in favor of segregated industrial education that would prepare blacks to be low-paid laborers in the industrial world. W. E. B. DuBois condemned such a program, declaring it would signify "the legal creation of a distinct status of civil inferiority for the Negro" (Spring 1994, 173). Instead, he wanted African Americans to receive the kind of education that would develop a leadership dedicated to protecting their people's social and political rights and keeping them aware of the need for relentless struggle.

Like blacks, early Chinese immigrants found access to mainstream public education difficult to obtain. When in 1884 a Chinese couple tried to enroll their child in the school system, the San Francisco board of supervisors issued a stern warning, declaring that at all cost the Chinese should be kept out of the schools

> in enforcement of the law of self-preservation, the inculcation of the doctrine of true humanity and an integral part of the iron rule of right by which we hope presently to prove that we can justify and practically defend members from this invasion of Mongolian barbarism. (Spring 1994, 163)

Undeterred, the Chinese couple went to court where the ruling was that the child should be admitted to the school. Officials in the San Francisco school district responded by asking the California assembly to establish separate facilities for Chinese students, and within a decade Sacramento followed San Francisco's example. In 1905, however, the segregationist policy was undermined when the board of education allowed Chinese students to attend the regular high school.

Younger Asian American children, however, still faced segregated schooling, and in 1906 the San Francisco Board of Education established a new school expressly for Chinese, Japanese, and Korean children, claiming that not only did it relieve congestion in the system but it also served "the higher end that our children should not be placed in any position where their impression may be affected by association with pupils of the 'Mongolian race'" (Spring 1994, 164).

Japanese parents were furious, boycotting the school and seeking to win public opinion in Japan to their side as a means of forcing compliance from the U.S. government. It worked. Editorials in Tokyo newspapers claimed the segregation was an insult to their nation, and the U.S. ambassador warned President Theodore Roosevelt of the developing international furor. Roosevelt, in turn, threatened the San Francisco school board with federal action, and the Asian American students were permitted back in regular primary school.

Moving up to the current period, we encounter new issues and challenges for various racial and ethnic groups with families and education.

Era from 1924 to the Present

Are American families and schools better off now than a century ago? In brief, although the blatant racist pronouncements and acts of the past no longer occur now, it is apparent that elements in the racialist social system have solidified.

The Family

In the 1958 edition of Broom and Selznick's prominent text *Sociology,* there was a lengthy chapter about the family. Perusing this material, I found an almost complete absence of information describing diversity. While there was a short subsection entitled "family types," the authors concentrated on such cross-cultural distinctions as whether marriages are monogamous or polygamous and did not mention the ethnic and racial diversity already established in American society (Broom and Selznick 1958, 367–68). In describing women's role in the family, they did list several options, including "the partner role," which, they contended, entails equality on various issues, including financial matters, but curiously there was no reference to women actually working outside the home. Furthermore, the study from which these options were drawn was done in 1934—hardly making it cutting-edge, even in 1958 (Broom and Selznick 1958, 384–85). My sense is that the authors were not trying to avoid analyzing racial, ethnic, and gender diversity in families; it simply did not occur to them that this broad issue should be included.

Once the civil rights era had begun, however, racial characteristics of families began to receive extensive public attention, particularly in a 1965 report entitled *The Negro Family: The Case for National Action.* This document became known as "The Moynihan Report" after its chief writer, then Harvard professor and later New York Senator Daniel Patrick Moynihan. It emphasized that while the white family had achieved a great deal of stability, the black family, especially the lower-class black family, was highly unstable, with an increasing percentage of female-headed families. The report stated that slavery, which prevented blacks from establishing stable families, and the postslavery tradition of restricting blacks' rights, particularly the black man's right to work, had necessitated women becoming family heads. The combination of poverty, the absence of fathers, and exposure to crime and delinquency, which the Moynihan Report designated "the tangle of pathology," made it virtually impossible for most blacks to perform effectively in school and in the workplace. The document concluded that "the case for national action" was clear. The United States needed an effective strategy, and because of the extent of current pathology in the black family, it could only focus on one place. The report declared:

> In a word, a national effort toward the problems of Negro Americans must be directed toward the question of family structure. The object should be to strengthen the Negro family so as to enable it to raise and support its members as do other families. (Office of Policy Planning and Research, United States Department of Labor 1965, 47)

The report created a furor. Critics considered it a simplistic indictment of the African American family and thus African Americans. Psychologist William Ryan asserted that the situation represented a clear instance of blaming the victim. He concluded:

> Moynihan was able to take a subject that had previously been confined to the Sociology Department seminar room . . . and bring it into a central position in popular American thought, creating a whole new set of group stereotypes which support the notion that Negro culture produces a weak and disorganized form of family life, which in turn is a major factor in maintaining Negro inequality. (Ryan 1976, 64)

Sociologists readily agree that discrimination and poverty have produced dire effects. The emphasis, however, needed to shift from Moynihan's stereotyping conclusions about "the black family" to the structural process having an impact on "black families."

Social-Class Division in Minority Families   Within any racial or ethnic group, families fall into various social-class categories.

In *A New Look at Black Families,* for example, Charles Willie (1991) concluded that his study of black families indicated that they should roughly be divided into three more-or-less equal-sized categories—poor blacks, working-class blacks, and affluent or middle-class blacks. As already noted, poor black families possess various problems rooted in poverty. For instance, the stress poor parents experience can make it more difficult to be supportive and involved like their wealthier counterparts. In recent years black men's rising unemployment has undermined their ability to marry or maintain families, thus contributing to a high rate of female-headed poor families (Hill 2001, 500–01). Willie indicated that sometimes these families are rebellious, rejecting the society that has rejected them, trusting few if any outsiders, and appearing uncommitted to anyone or anything. However, mothers remain loyal to their children, and brothers and sisters generally accept the obligation to help one another.

Among working-class black families, life is a struggle requiring cooperative activity for family members. Both spouses tend to be employed, with husbands sometimes maintaining two jobs. The sense of unity in this type of family is often less the result of understanding and tenderness than of the joint effort to avoid major economic hardship. Because their salaries tend to be low, working-class black families find that any reduction in their overall income is likely to push them below the poverty level.

Affluent black family members are generally well educated, with one or both spouses college graduates. The adults generally work hard, obtaining positions in the public sector, industry, education, and private business. Work is often a consuming experience; little time remains for recreation and other activities, with the possible exception of regular church attendance. Because of the income limitations of jobs available to blacks, wife and husband usually both work and as a result produce a total income at or above the national average. A study of forty-one black professional couples concluded that while the respondents considered work a significant part of their lives, they heavily depended on their marriages for happiness and psychological well-being (Thomas 1990).

Middle-class African Americans want the home to be a pleasant, often elegant place to live—"their home is their castle," Willie indicated—and so they emphasize modern furnishings and appliances.

Affluent blacks tend to have two or fewer children and to encourage them to go to college directly after high school. The parents hope that their children will have more opportunities than they did, and they consider a college degree critical for success in the work world. Middle-class African Americans try to develop in their children the same positive emphases on work and thrift that dominate their own lives (Willie 1991). While expecting their children to be obedient, they tend to be somewhat more lenient than parents in lower income categories (Hill 2001, 500).

Like blacks in general, these middle-class parents are aware of persistent racism and recognize that their children, who often live in predominantly white neighborhoods, have been spared exposure to the harsh realities of the outer world. The parents are aware of the unfolding of these realities in their children's teen and adult years, and so they often seek to discuss the issues with them (Toliver 1998).

A highly select portion of the affluent group is upper class, containing members who are highly publicized athletes, actors, or entertainers; or the recipients of inherited wealth. The latter category is likely to involve descendants of blacks achieving freedom before the Civil War—individuals who are usually lighter skinned than most blacks. Like the members of the corporate community described in Chapter 5, upper-class blacks generally attend elite private schools, belong to their own exclusive country clubs, and seek marital partners within their own ranks. Although many upper-class people continue to enter elite black colleges, they are increasingly inclined to attend prominent integrated schools (Starbuck 2002, 178–79).

In other racial and ethnic groups, members' background and opportunities also vary, resulting, as for blacks, in families dividing into distinct social-class groups. Vietnamese Americans, for instance, have been most economically successful when they have arrived in the United States as intact family units in which the male head of either an extended family or simply a nuclear family has been able to establish himself in some occupational niche and both assist and encourage various family members in seeking education and good jobs. In many instances, however, there has been no such guiding presence, and facing this new, sometimes forbidding social world, young Vietnamese have found it difficult or impossible to move beyond low-paying, service employment (Tran 1988, 270–71).

In Puerto Ricans' case, there is also considerable variation in family types. Since the early 1980s, a substantial number of young Puerto Rican professionals have migrated to the mainland United States. Like all Puerto Ricans, they face the distinct possibility of discrimination, but their advantages over lower-income members of their ethnic group include higher occupational and educational status, better command of English, and both the income and professional credentials to move into middle-class Anglo-American residential areas (Sánchez-Ayéndez 1998, 211; Toro-Morn 2002).

Looking beyond these individual groups, Table 8.1 presents the range of family income as well as other characteristics showing diversity within the nation's four major racial groups. Besides the social-class variations just mentioned, families within a given category differ in other significant ways.

Composition and Gender within Minority Families   In contrast to the prominent nuclear family, some minority groups feature extended family arrangements. African Americans, for instance, often contain extended kinship members at the core—the mother and another adult relative; grandparents; a grandmother alone or with another adult relative. One sociologist asserted that this tradition, which appears to be a carryover from West Africa, signifies that "[m]arriages may end but blood lasts forever" (McAdoo 1998, 368). These arrangements have been important for helping to cope with the fragmentation widely occurring for families in economic crisis. A study of black grandmothers indicated that over two-thirds took on the task because they wanted to protect the children from living in foster care (Rodgers-Farmer and Jones 2002, 380).

Other minority groups have also depended on the extended family. When Cubans first moved to the United States, they often sought refuge in these structures, particularly during the first three years of adjustment. A pair of circumstances, however, could break the pattern—the economic necessity to depart from the Miami area or the assessment that the likelihood of mainstream occupational success increases if they sever close ties with highly traditional, economically marginal extended kin (Suárez 1998, 179–80).

Living in extended family arrangements can also provide unique benefits. Growing up spending many intimate hours listening to her grandmother's stories, which had been passed down through countless generations, one Native American woman indicated that "I learned what it means to be a Dakota woman, and the responsibility, pain, and pride associated with such a role" (Wilson 2002, 49).

Another important issue involving family composition is interracial marriage. Considering American culture's inordinate emphasis on racial "purity," it seems reasonable to accept sociologists Joe R. Feagin and Melvin P. Sikes's statement that "[e]ven in relatively liberal white areas, interracial dating and marriage are probably anathema to most white parents" (Feagin and Sikes 1994, 266). One of Feagin and Sykes's informants in a study of middle-class blacks indicated that living in white suburbs was often "very uncomfortable particularly if they have young black sons, you know, and [are facing] the dating situation" (Feagin and Sikes 1994, 266).

TABLE 8.1   Social and Economic Characteristics of American Citizens in 2000

	White	**Black**	**Asian**	**Hispanic**
Population				
Under 5 years	6.1%	8.1%	6.5%	10.5
5–14 years	13.4	18.3	13.3	19.2
15–44 years	42.5	46.9	51.3	51.6
45–64 years	23.9	18.6	21.0	13.7
65 and older	14.4	8.1	7.8	4.9
Family Income				
Under $10,000	4.7%	14.6%	6.6%	10.0%
$10,000-$24,999	15.8	25.1	13.8	28.6
$25,000-$49,999	28.5	28.9	23.9	32.6
$50,000-$74,999	22.1	15.8	18.5	15.9
$75,000 or more	29.7	15.6	37.1	12.8
Unemployed	2.3%	5.0%	2.6%	3.9%
Families Below Poverty Level	9.8%	23.6%	10.7%	22.8%
Educational Attainment				
High-school grad or more	84.9%	78.5%	85.7%	57.0%
Bachelor's degree or more	26.1	16.5	43.9	10.6
Advanced degree	8.8	5.1	15.3	3.3

In this table, several patterns emerge. First, all four racial categories demonstrate economic and educational diversity, suggesting a distinct range in life chances within each of them. Second, configurational differences among the groups emerge. Thus Asians and whites, who tend to be more affluent and better educated than the other two categories, also exhibit a somewhat older age profile.

Source: U.S. Census Bureau. *Statistical Abstract of the United States: 2001,* No. 37.

In such an unsettled cultural context, it is notable that both interracial marriages and intimate relationships have been increasing. Table 8.2 demonstrates a distinct increase over time in interracial marriage, but these data do not reveal an additional important reality: According to a study based on census data for people aged 18 to 30, young American women and men in all four racial groups were more likely to live with a member of another race than to marry such a person. The most dramatic cases involved white women and black men, where the respective parties were 3.5 times more likely to live with each other than to marry while Asian women and white men were nearly twice as likely to cohabit as to marry. "Our findings suggest that there is much greater intimate contact between the races than

TABLE 8.2   Interracial Marriages

	1980	1990	2000
Whites			
Total number of couples with white partner	45.5 million	48.1 million	50.3 million
White/white	98.6%	98.1%	97.2%
White/black	.4	.4	.7
White/other (excluding blacks)	1.0	1.5	2.1
Blacks			
Total number of couples with black partner	3.5 million	3.9 million	4.4 million
Black/black	94.3%	93.8%	90.6%
Black/white	4.7	5.4	8.2
Black/other (excluding whites)	1.0	.8	1.1
Hispanics			
Total number of couples with Hispanic partner	2.8 million	4.3 million	6.5 million
Hispanic/Hispanic	68.1%	72.1%	73.1%
Hispanic/other	31.9	27.9	26.9

Over two decades, whites and blacks have shown a modestly increasing tendency to marry outside their own racial group, whereas Hispanics have become less inclined in this regard. In general, however, Hispanics have been much more likely to intermarry than the other two categories.

Source: U.S. Bureau of the Census. *Statistical Abstract of the United States: 2001,* No. 50.

marriage data imply," commented sociologist David R. Harris. "Consequently, the social distance between racial groups is not as great as other studies indicate it is" (University of Michigan News and Information Services 2000).

Although the statistics are instructive, it is important to appreciate the factors influencing people's reluctance or willingness to intermarry. Looking across American history, one can readily conclude that a sense of racial purity has played a major role. In some instances, however, cultural compatibility has appeared more significant. In a study of second-generation Chinese and Korean Americans, the researcher discovered that the respondents' desire to marry other Asian Americans came from a pervasive sense of a generally shared culture—that, as one woman assessed her situation, "it's important that Chinese have the same work ethic and the same sense of family as Koreans" (Kibria 2002, 117).

Besides their view on family composition, modern minority families vary in their conception of gender roles. A study of Korean immigrants, for instance, indicated that husbands were often stunned when once located in the United States their wives demanded a role in family decision making (Jo 1999, 101–03), and among Dominican families the traditional pattern has involved men's control over the family budget (Pessar 2002, 67).

However, in the United States, where both women and men tend to be employed, minority women generally not only have gained a greater voice in budgeting decisions but also have increasingly found their husbands involved in household tasks. In a study of Dominican immigrants, many women indicated that "the changes just happened." As one respondent, who worked nine hours a day, explained, "I am bringing in a lot of money to help my husband . . . He actually does things around the house now without my even asking" (Pessar 2002, 69).

Although the traditional, male-dominated pattern has become less prominent, couples within a given group establish varied arrangements about the distribution of outside work and domestic activity. A study of twenty middle-class Mexican American couples, for instance, found that slightly less than half had a traditional arrangement in which husbands were the main provider and wives were considered innately more attuned to dealing with domestic tasks and child care. If wives worked in such arrangements, it was strictly out of economic necessity. One main-provider husband explained, "I would prefer that my wife did not have to work, and could stay at home with my daughter, but finances just don't permit that" (Coltrane 2000, 471). Such men sought to perform as few household and child-care duties as possible.

In contrast, slightly more than half the respondents were co-providers, with the wife working similar jobs but because of gender bias often receiving lower pay. Husbands in this group divided quite evenly between those who accepted a fairly equitable division of the domestic tasks and those who did not. However, even those who accepted a significant share were often unsatisfied with the arrangement. One typical informant said:

> I think I do more housework. It's probably not fair, because I do more of the dirtier tasks. . . . Also, at this point, our solution tends to favor her free time more than my free time. I think that has more to do with our personal backgrounds. She has more personal friends to do things with, so she has more outside things to do whereas I say I'm not doing anything. (Coltrane 2000, 477)

Although it appeared that many or most of the respondents in this study faced continuing dialogue and struggle in resolving these issues, one point seemed clear: For Mexican Americans as well as some other racial and ethnic families, earlier descriptions of men as macho controllers and women as tradition-bound, subservient helpmates have become vast oversimplifications.

In other gender-related areas, modern families are also varied. Across racial and ethnic types, there has been an increasing tendency for lesbians and gays to raise children. Audre Lorde, a black lesbian, discussed the challenges she has faced bringing up two children, particularly her son Jonathan. Lorde indicated that the task before her was to raise a black man who would both develop the ability to analyze and, when he deemed necessary, resist an oppressive system and also the capacity to understand and be comfortable with his own relationships, including intimate, loving contacts with others.

Lorde concluded that the most important lesson she could help Jonathan to learn was how to be the person he wanted to be. That person would develop in a family in which his mother was a lesbian with a live-in lover. Lorde asked her fourteen-year-old son what were the strongest negative and positive elements in growing up with lesbian parents. She explained:

> He said the strongest benefit he felt he had gained was that he knew a lot more about people than most other kids his age that he knew, and that he did not have a lot of the hang-ups that some other boys did about men and women.
> And the most negative aspect he felt, Jonathan said, was the ridicule he got from some kids with straight parents.
> "You mean from your peers?" I said.
> "Oh no," he answered promptly. "My peers know better. I mean other kids."
> (Lorde 1997, 287)

Audre Lorde's relationship with her son went smoothly because she talked freely with him about her own lesbianism and gender- and sex-related issues in general. In many families, however, such openness has not been the standard. A study of Asian American parents with gay and lesbian children revealed that in a tradition where sexuality has rarely been discussed, discovering one's child is either gay or lesbian can be disorienting, often leaving the parent with the uncomfortable sense of not knowing the child in some fundamental way.

In this setting where friends, family members, and neighbors often respond adversely to gays and lesbians, parents sometimes felt ashamed, in part or wholly responsible for their children's gender preference. Some of them, however, disclosed the news to siblings or close friends, and several were more outgoing, participating in panels involving Asian American parents with gay and lesbian children (Hom, 2002).

In schools as in their families, urban racial and ethnic minorities now face both controversy and change.

Education

Recognizing the disadvantages minorities can face in schooling and jobs, a government-supported directive called affirmative action has required schools and employers to develop timetables and goals for increasing educational and employment opportunities for women and minorities. The roots of affirmative action appeared in the Civil Rights Act of 1964, an executive order issued by President Lyndon Johnson in 1965, and a Labor Department statement produced in 1970. Although no federal legislation supports the policy, the U.S. Supreme Court affirmed the practice in its 1978 decision in the case of *Regents of the University of California v. Bakke.*

Supporters of affirmative action in education have argued that the racialized social system within American society has put African Americans, Hispanics, and Native Americans at a distinct disadvantage and that continuing, often subtle racist practices still restrict many members of these groups. Opponents, on the other hand, discard the necessity of such compensation, saying that in an increasingly tolerant world, government-mandated slots for minority students gives them an unfair competitive advantage.

Beginning in the late 1990s, affirmative action has come under steady attack, with California's Proposition 209 calling for an end to racial and gender preferences in public education, state hiring, and state contracts. In both California and Texas, the percentage of enrolled black and Hispanic undergraduate and law students in public universities sharply dropped (Doob 1999, 150–52).

In 2003 the Supreme Court heard two cases involving affirmative action at the University of Michigan—one about a white undergraduate applicant and the other a white law school applicant, who claimed they had been unfairly barred from admittance because of their race. Speaking in opposition to affirmative action, President Bush said that while he supports diversity, "the Michigan policies amount to a quota system that unfairly rewards or penalizes prospective students, based solely on their race" (White House 2003).

Mary Sue Coleman, president of the University of Michigan, countered that while she was pleased to learn that the president supported diversity, especially racial diversity, she was convinced that he misunderstood the university's admissions policy—that neither the undergraduate nor the graduate programs had quotas and that while race was taken into account, the point system used in admissions was complex, with academic qualifications accounting for nearly three-quarters of each student's total. Coleman concluded:

> There is no substitute for the careful consideration of race as one of many factors in a competitive admissions process. No alternatives can achieve the goal of a diverse student body while maintaining the high academic standards for which we strive. (News Service: University of Michigan 2003)

In July 2003 the Supreme Court reached split decisions. The judges provided a 6–3 vote against the undergraduate admissions scheme because in the majority's eyes the automatic awarding to underrepresented minorities of 20 points on a 150-point scale represented a quota that lacked the individualized assessments mandated in the landmark Bakke case. On the other hand, the Court ruled 5 to 4 in favor of Michigan's graduate admissions approach, which according to Justice Sandra Day O'Connor, who wrote the majority decision, used an individualized, nonquantitative decision-making process that met the Bakke requirement of incorporating race in "a flexible, nonmechanical way." While proponents of affirmative action criticized the undergraduate decision, saying its 20-point boost for minority candidates represented just the sort of "plus" factor the Bakke case mandated, most were pleased that the graduate ruling permitted the continuing use of affirmative-action procedures.

By the fall of 2003, university officials had brought the undergraduate admissions procedures in line with the Supreme Court decision, eliminating the point system while establishing academics as the priority factor and race as just one of a set of equally weighed additional considerations. Critics of the university's admissions policies indicated that they would stay vigilant, evaluating the process to determine that race was not put ahead of the other factors (Foner 2003; Liptak 2003; Winter 2003).

It should be kept in mind that the University of Michigan is an elite school with the opportunity to develop a racially diverse student body. Meanwhile in most cities, African Americans and other racial minorities face extensive segregation. In 1994, forty years after the landmark case *Brown v. the Topeka* [Kansas] *Board of Education,* which outlawed racially separate schools and designated that city as the cradle of the desegregation movement, the schools were just as segregated as they were in 1954. The key to the situation has been that since residential districts largely determine school districts, segregated living areas have promoted segregated schools (Celis 1995).

Recent research involving 329 metropolitan areas found a sharp correlation between housing segregation and school segregation. As in Chapter 4, the measurement used has been the **index of dissimilarity,** which indicates the percentage of a particular racial group that would need to change residential location in order to achieve racial evenness—a condition in which that racial group's representation throughout a city's census tracts would be dispersed proportionate to its overall representation in relation to non-Hispanic whites in the city. The reality is that the higher a group's index of dissimilarity, the greater its segregation.

Figure 8.1 indicates the close relationship between the extent of children's residential segregation and the level of segregation in their primary schools. On both measures African Americans fall in the mid-60s, Asian/Pacific Islanders in the mid-40s, and Hispanics in the 50s (Rickles and Ong 2001). Thus, all three racial groups are significantly segregated, with blacks facing the greatest amount of it but even Asians, the least segregated of the three, confronting a situation in which the typical young Asian American child lives in an area and attends a primary school where the minority population distinctly exceeds racial evenness. These research findings signal the impact of the racialized social system, demonstrating how the racially segregated nature of one structural element, namely housing, has influenced another—schooling.

Segregated education poses at least two major problems. First, it separates minorities from the majority group. Although the opportunities to be together can have a modest impact on minorities' short-term academic performance, studies have shown that black stu-

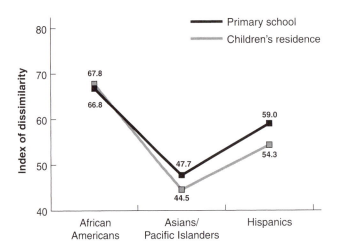

FIGURE 8.1   Racial Groups' Residential and School Segregation Levels
This graph demonstrates that the level of children's residential segregation and the extent of segregation in their primary schools are very closely correlated.

Source: Data from Jordan Rickles and Paul M. Ong. "Relationship Between School and Residential Segregation at the Turn of the Century." Center for Regional Policy Studies, 2001, p. 3. www.sppsr.ucla.edu/lewis.

dents who attended integrated elementary or secondary schools were more likely to enroll in integrated colleges, to complete these programs, to have white social contacts and friends, to work in desegregated businesses, and to live in integrated housing areas. The investigators indicated that "[d]esegregation put majorities and minorities together so that they can learn to coexist with one another, not so they can learn to read" (Braddock, Crain, and McPartland 1984, 260).

In addition, segregated schools suffer a decisive funding disadvantage in the American education system, in which a substantial portion of the yearly budget comes from local property taxes. As a result in poor, inner-city areas, students are often forced to endure old, rundown buildings; outdated, overused books, computers, and other supplies; and large, crowded classes.

Several years ago I did a brief study at New Haven's oldest middle school, which was located in a rundown, outdated building and primarily served students belonging to racial minorities. When entering its vestibule I found it hard to see clearly. The venerable chandelier-like light system, which contained outlets for fifteen bulbs, had just three still shining. In one of the room's murky corners, there was a plaque for "Student Citizen of the Year," beginning in the middle 1940s with about a decade of northern European awardees and then by the late 1950s featuring various central and southern ethnicities, particularly Italians. The list stopped abruptly at 1972—no more winners. Based on my observations at the school, the unintended message seemed painfully clear—students coming from that locale have usually been denied the chance to develop effective educational skills.

Although integrated schools are likely to provide a more effective education, they can still leave minority students at disadvantage. Quite often black students encounter tracking procedures administered by guidance counselors and teachers that can funnel them into vocational slots. In a study of middle-class blacks, one parent explained:

> I get a sense that often my children, as well as other black children, have been steered into vocational type subjects and given to believe that that's "best for them," quote, unquote, "best for them." And I have certainly encouraged my children that I would like [them] to take the academic courses and to do well in them. . . . And it takes a lot to stay in there with them, and try to make sure that nobody's undermining my goal for them. (Feagin and Sikes 1994, 84)

Another problem that racial minorities face in integrated high schools and colleges is that campus activities are generally geared to the white clientele and that in all or most activities minority students must make the adjustment and never or very seldom the other way around. A black college student explained:

> To integrate means simply to be white. It doesn't mean fusing the two cultures; it simply means to be white, that's all. And we spend so much effort in passing into the mainstream of American society. They have no reason to know our culture. But we must, in order to survive, know everything about their culture. Racism is simply preferring straight hair to an Afro; that's certainly more acceptable in our society today. Black vernacular, it's not seen as a cultural expression, it's seen as a speech problem. When you look at something as simple as just a group of people talking, black people are given . . . a much higher regard if they are seen in an all-white group laughing and talking, . . . and probably taking care of something important. (Feagin and Sikes 1994, 96)

Regardless of where they go to school, black students are often somewhat isolated from mainstream society, and one negative impact appears with standardized testing. A recent study of results from Standard Aptitude Tests (SATs) released by the College Board found that members of the high-school class of 2003 obtained an average composite score of 1026 on the verbal and math tests. The scores for various groups were:

- Asian or Pacific Islanders, 1,083
- Whites, 1,063
- American Indians or Alaskan Natives, 962
- Hispanics (except for Puerto Ricans and Mexican Americans), 921
- Puerto Ricans, 909
- Mexican Americans, 905
- Blacks, 857 (Toppo 2003)

African Americans' comparatively low scores appear to be an impact of American society's racialized social system, restricting most blacks to more time spent in racially segregated settings than even such newly arrived immigrant groups as southeast Asians. Political scientist Andrew Hacker wrote:

> Blacks with middle-class jobs and incomes may have greater opportunities to meet and mingle in this world, but those contacts are seldom allowed to develop to the fullest extent. The fact that black modes of perception and expression, which are largely products of segregation, become impediments to performing well on tests like the SAT reveals that racial bias remains latent not only in the multiple-choice method, but in the broader expectations set by the modern world. (Hacker 1992, 146)

As the next section indicates, such widely implemented racialized practices pose the danger of putting minority children out of mainstream schooling where their self-image and development suffer.

Ghosts in the Classroom

In sociology a prominent concept related to socialization is Charles Horton Cooley's **looking-glass self**—the idea that individuals' understanding of what kind of person they are is based on how they think they appear to others. Members of racial minorities in inner-city schools have often received limited positive response from teachers, and thus their sense of self as students is diminished. In Nat Hentoff's haunting phrase, they become "ghosts in the classroom."

Once Hentoff read and discussed poetry with the primarily minority children in an inner-city high school, acting against the advice of the regular teacher, who had explained that the children were not interested in reading. At the end he was approached by an extremely shy young woman who asked if he could tell her something more about that Emily Dickinson. Later she told Hentoff that while it was weird, she felt some of the same things that Emily Dickinson had felt so long ago. Then, very hesitantly, she handed Hentoff some of her poems, indicating that she had never shown them to anyone because she had suspected that nobody would believe she could write poetry. It was the first time that anyone in the classroom had communicated with this young woman in a way that suggested the possibility of interest in her work and, as a result, began to draw her out of the ghost world.

John Simon has been a teacher who has regularly accomplished such tasks. He has taken tough, often delinquent, inner-city, primarily minority-group children and turned them into effective readers, writers, and eventually college students. Simon indicated that there is nothing special about his approach. It is neither revolutionary nor does it require a charismatic personality, but it does take time. Simon told Hentoff:

> First of all . . . you have to listen. When I start working with a child I don't know too well, I spend a lot of time listening to him before I try to suggest a course of study. I have never fallen in with that dumb notion that you have to start "teaching" from the very first day of class—as if teaching is something that happens in a vacuum without having to take account of where each student is, in his head, on that first day. (Hentoff 1989, 145)

Structural impediments, however, often block such straightforward progress. Our nation has come a long way from the one-room schoolhouse, where a single teacher and a group of local, largely or wholly white students met each day for a few hours of rudimentary instruction. The United States is a diverse, problem-laden society, where demands on the educational system have grown and become complicated (Rury 2002, 224). The 1995 Luxembourg Study of child poverty in seventeen developed nations placed American society at the top with 22 percent of children in poverty, with those under eighteen displaying the highest rate of any American age group. Racial minorities have been disproportionately represented, and over a third of both black and Hispanic children fall into the poverty category (Hodgkinson 2002).

In this section we examine three important system issues that impact decisively on poor minorities—quality of day care; the current state of school funding; and evaluation of leaks in the educational pipeline. Once again, it becomes apparent that the racialized setting of American society plays a role with these issues.

Quality of Day Care

"I'm very happy with the care my children get here," said Yanira Mejia through an interpreter. "The teachers are helpful and really involved. They always let me know what my children did during the day, if they misbehaved and things like that. And I also like the fact that the Center is very secure and safe. I'm really satisfied." Mejia could not afford to send her two children to the Rainbow Children's Center without a state subsidy provided by the Mexican-American Opportunity Foundation, one of the two organizations involved in its creation.

"Our whole emphasis is on helping children get ready for school," said Rosa Maria Sanchez, the manager of this Los Angeles–based center. "Our program exposes children who come from a predominately Spanish-speaking background to English so that they can function in both languages," Sanchez explained. "We talk with them in whichever language they are most comfortable with, but we expose the children to English in the daily learning activities of language, numbers, shapes, and so forth. That way, they go into the school environment better armed with the skills they need to succeed" (Rainbow Children's Center 2001).

The creators of this program seemed to consider two fundamental issues of successful day care—first, the importance of making certain that during the time away from home children are safe and secure, not exposed to some form of child abuse or any other physical danger, and second, the significance of providing a positive learning environment. As educator Harold Hodgkinson wrote to school principals, "The evidence is very clear that the first five years of life are the most important learning years for all children. By supporting good child care and preschool programs in your service area, you make your job a lot easier when those children reach kindergarten" (Hodgkinson 2002).

While day care is an issue involving all racial, ethnic, and social-class groups, over a third of clients, about 37 percent, belong to racial minorities (National Center for Education Statistics 2002). However, because racial minorities tend to be particularly poor, representing about two-thirds of those on welfare at the end of the twentieth century (Burnham 2001; Mink 2001), their members often face a great struggle, most notably perhaps those just moving into the work world (Pungello and Kurtz-Costes 2000).

A study found that for a sample of poor women obtaining jobs, the distinct majority opted for informal day care—family members, friends, or neighbors. While often more affordable and convenient than more formal programs, such arrangements can be unreliable in either their quality, safety, or availability (Henly and Lyons 2000). With informal arrangements the last problem is common. "[W]hat happens when your kid gets sick?" Faye Ensey, a black office worker wondered.

> Or when the baby sitter's kids get sick? I lost two jobs in a row because my kids kept getting sick and I couldn't go to work. Or else I couldn't take my little one to the baby sitter because her kids were sick. They finally fired me for absenteeism. I didn't really blame them, but I felt terrible anyway. It's such a hassle, I sometimes think I'd be glad to just stay home. But we can't afford for me not to work, so we had to figure out something else. (Rubin 1997, 269)

In Europe (excluding Great Britain), the cost of day care is less burdensome because in most countries parents contribute only 25 percent of the cost compared to the United States, where they often bear the full responsibility (Joshi et al. 2002). European countries' financial support is particularly pronounced in the first year: Sweden provides 51 weeks of day care at 90 percent of cost, France 16 to 30 weeks at 84 percent of cost, and Germany 14 weeks at 100 percent of cost (Caminiti 1994, 140).

Whether in Europe or the United States, parents value high-quality day care. The evaluation process is still in its infancy, currently providing few firmly established measures of quality assessment (Jaeger, Shlay, and Weinraub 2000; NICHD Early Child Care Research Network 1999).

One of the best-known systems has been the family day care rating scale, which requires that an outside observer assess thirty-three items, with each item ranging from a "1," meaning "inadequate," to a "7," representing "excellent." From the sum of the ratings, the evaluator obtains an overall score (Deiner 1992).

Some of the principal variables in quality assessment are the stability of care, the numbers issues, and staff training. The chief means of measuring stability of care is to determine the rate of staff turnover. In one of the few studies to use stability of caretakers as a quality indicator, effective centers were those in which children had no more than one or two primary caregivers over a year-long period and low-quality centers were those with three or more primary caretakers during the year (Deiner 1992). At the well-known Calvin Hill Day-Care Center in New Haven, the director has set salary and benefits high enough so that staff members would want to stay; in addition, she has treated them "like professionals, not baby sitters" (Polk 1997, 2).

In analyzing the numbers issues, Carollee Howes, a prominent evaluator of day-care programming, noted that research has shown that when the ratio of children to caregivers exceeds more than about three to one or when there are more than about eight to ten infants or toddlers in a group, the staff members "tend to become more managers rather than loving and playful providers" (Howes 1990, 28).

The third major factor is staff training, with better trained personnel providing such benefits as greater social stimulation, better cognitive and language skills, less negative emotion, and fewer restrictions (Howes 1990, 29). Research has found that if shortly after birth disadvantaged children are taken five days a week to special centers where well-trained staff provide a rich educational curriculum in a loving atmosphere, they score 15 IQ points higher than matched peers not receiving that treatment. A practical challenge to achieving this result is that it will prove very expensive; intervention in this study began earlier than most experts had anticipated it needed to occur (Blakeslee 1995).

Assessing the quality of current day-care programming, experts have concluded that only 30 percent of children in day-care centers and 12 percent in regulated family care (provided in private homes) receive quality care producing optimal child development (Zigler 1995, 6). "There is so much bad child care that when I see a [good] place I rejoice," said psychologist Edward Zigler, the founder of the renowned Head Start program (Polk 1997, 2). Using the knowledge already available, the current challenge is to produce more such centers. Funding, of course, is at the core of such a challenge, just as it is with the next issue.

Current Status of School Funding

The primary source of public-school funding has been local property tax, where throughout a state, homes and businesses are assessed at a standard rate. Invariably, significant disparity in district funding results because the values of buildings in different areas vary considerably. In the early 1920s, national educational policy developed a "foundation program," which sought to reconcile the rights of local districts to support and govern their own schools with state obligations to compensate for greatly reduced financial assets in certain areas.

Although the general policy of the foundation program emphasized that the state should compensate for poor communities' low funding, the standard reality has been that state officials tend to be most closely attuned to affluent groups' interests. The frequent consequence has been the development of a policy that has been described as "a reasonable minimum," which usually produces very modest funding for poor sections. As a result, the schools in various districts have often been vastly different in quality, with those in poor, minority-dominated areas providing only the rudimentary education preparing people for low-level service jobs—the stance represented in the judge's statement described at the end of Chapter 5.

In other western nations, public schools normally receive equal funding based on the number of enrolled students (Slavin 1999, 520). That difference means that residing in a poor American school district puts young residents at a distinct disadvantage in relation to educational funding compared to their low-income peers in many other countries.

In the late 1990s in forty-one states, poor districts received less total funding than affluent districts, and in fourteen states minimum funding was less than half the state's average funding. In fact, in a survey of over 7,000 school districts, 20 percent received less than $5,000 per pupil per year and 6 percent over $10,000. African Americans and Hispanics are consistently overrepresented in the underfunded areas (Biddle and Berliner 20002a; Whitington 2000).

An important issue to examine is whether or not funding has a significant impact on academic performance. A number of studies have concluded that the level of funding has been unrelated to student achievement. These investigations have usually been based on small samples, not representing the full range of schools, and most of them have used questionable measurements and statistical techniques (Biddle and Berlinger 2002a, 5–6).

Another body of studies has concluded that the level of school funding produces a significant impact on academic performance. This research has used sizable samples that have included both well-funded and poorly financed schools, and they have tended to establish statistical controls for level of income, socioeconomic status, or other factors that could influence students' performance level. In addition, this second group of surveys has had validated measuring and scaling techniques for analyzing data (Elliott 1998; Harter 1999; Payne and Biddle 1999).

How does greater school funding improve students' level of performance? The most important factor appears to be the increased capacity of more affluent school districts to attract better educated, more experienced, more competent teachers who then generate a higher level of student achievement. The second, most significant advantage of greater school funding involves class size; the wealthier districts are better able to afford smaller classes, which seem to promote more effective learning, at least in the early grades and particularly for poor and minority students (Biddle and Berliner 2002b; Darling-Hammond and Post 2000; Elliott 1998; Ferguson and Ladd 1996).

As far as quality of teaching is concerned, the poorer, minority-dominated districts, which tend to be at the bottom of job candidates' preferences, can even face the prospect of sometimes having no permanent teachers in place. Pamela Barker-Jones, the dedicated math supervisor for New Haven middle and high schools, informed me that often in the course of an academic year her most pressing task has been to find a qualified math teacher for an inner-city school. It can be hard to accomplish. For instance, once in February Barker-Jones indicated that she had finally filled a slot where until that time the students had experienced a succession of substitute teachers. Exposure to such fragmented teaching is probably sufficient in itself to put students at a distinct disadvantage. For the most part, however, the American public receives little information about such persistent inequalities.

School funding issues create a strong public reaction, where those well situated often resist efforts to increase expenditure while those with limited funding and their supporters demand a greater share (Augenblick, Myers, and Anderson 1997). At election time candidates

These photos sharply contrast the public-school settings different districts provide: conditions so crowded in this inner-city area that these minority-group elementary students must use the floor of a corridor as a makeshift classroom, and a spacious classroom with individual laptops for these majority-group suburban high schoolers.

are likely to represent the opposing interests. For instance, during the 2002 campaign to become lieutenant governor of Texas, David Dewhurst, the Republican candidate, claimed that the legislature would be too busy addressing several important financial issues to implement the so-called Robin Hood law requiring a city's wealthier districts paying large amounts of property taxes to fund local public education to share revenues with the poorer districts. On the other hand, John Sharp, the Democratic candidate, felt the issue was important enough to address quickly. He explained, "With the condition some schools are in, I'm not sure you can wait" (Graves 2002).

Texas has had over a thirty-year history of struggle with the school-funding issue, beginning in 1968 with a prominent civil suit that led to a series of referendums and eventually to the law just mentioned. At least three-quarters of the states have had suits involving challenges about the inequality of school funding in different districts. These suits have tended to stimulate both public interest and sometimes, as in Texas, reform legislation. The redistribution of funds following such actions have tended to reduce but not eliminate districts' funding inequities (Biddle and Berliner 2002a). However, a major drawback in the reform measures has been the conclusion that the only way to obtain sufficient popular support to pass reform legislation has been to offer financial "sweeteners" to all districts. So while the legislation might pass, the monetary benefit to poor districts is likely to be modest (Biddle and Berliner 2002a; Kozol 1991, 209).

In concluding their article "A Research Synthesis: Unequal School Funding in the United States," Bruce J. Biddle and David C. Berliner summarized the perception shared by those seeking an equalization of school funding:

> This vision has stressed the need for a public school system that generates the informed citizenry needed for democratic government, embraces the welfare of all children in the nation, upholds the ideal of equal opportunity, and stresses the belief that public education can and should provide a level playing field. [Philosopher John] Dewey's maxim, now a century old, applies here: "What the best and wisest parent wants for his child, that must be what the community wants for all its children." (Biddle and Berliner 2002a, 11)

The following Sociological Illustration appears consistent with Dewey's maxim, providing various opportunities that benefit poor, largely minority children with limited access to various important resources.

Elsewhere, minority groups' advocates often find themselves seriously challenged to keep the existing pipelines functioning for college-bound students.

Evaluation of Leaks in the Educational Pipeline

Though diminutive, Elvira in actuality is a giant—a volcano of motivated energy, and when she came in to see me that great energy was focused on the result of her first test. A "51" was completely out of kilter with her effort. Not that she was blaming me. She simply wanted to know what to do to improve her grade. We went over the test, and I made some suggestions about how to learn the material and prepare for the next test, especially its lengthy essay portion. "I'll do much better the next time," she declared.

SOCIOLOGICAL ILLUSTRATION

New Beginnings: A Successful Experiment

Launched in 1988 in San Diego, New Beginnings has been an interagency program in which top officials of city and county organizations, the school district, an area college, and the state university have been exploring new ways of meeting the needs of the children and the families they serve. The program has been located at Hamilton Elementary School and focused on its school district, where residents are poor, primarily Hispanic and African American families (Coalition for Community Schools 2002).

To make the program work, various organizations have needed to contribute key personnel. Hamilton Elementary provided a nurse and a guidance counselor; the local hospital supplied a doctor; a variety of other agencies donated personnel to work as family advocates, communicating with one or more other agencies to make sure that a child's or a family's specific needs have been effectively met.

For over a decade, New Beginnings has been just that—a "new beginning" for many poor families. Pam Nowling, an African American client with twin ten-year-old sons, indicated that "some of the things they helped me deal with, I don't think I could have dealt with by myself. I would have gone into a little shell," she explained, putting her hands over her eyes and said, "What do I do next?" Nowling worked with Ken Byrd, a family-service advocate provided by Hamilton Elementary. Contacting various local agencies, he was able to get one of the boys extra help after school; obtain government subsidies for food, gas, and electric bills; and also get Nowling into an adult-education program where she could complete her high-school degree.

New Beginnings not only has obtained help for its clients but has done so in a way that is often more dignified and pleasant than poor minorities experience in what are often racialized settings. As Nowling indicated, "I had to curse out my welfare worker a number of times. Even though I'd set up appointments, I'd go there, and it's like, 'Who are you? Give me your papers.' I'm a person too" (MacNeil/Lehrer Report 1993).

The organizers of New Beginnings were fully aware of such problems. Before the program got under way, they did a feasibility study and found out that although the various agencies servicing the school district were putting a great deal of money into the area, their efforts were ineffective. Tom Payzant, the superintendent of schools, who was a driving force early in the program, indicated that the study provided "the best information to make the argument that we couldn't do any worse than we were doing, and there had to be some efficiencies and improvement of services" (MacNeil/Lehrer Report 1993). Apparently, there was a shared willingness to do the difficult and inconvenient—to forsake the traditional punitive patterned responses to poor, often minority clients.

Payzant indicated that the array of agencies affiliated with the program were not used to cooperating with each other. Traditionally, each of these organizations has had its own turf; now they have been in frequent contact with each other—not making decisions about clients on their own but consulting with each other and finding the need to discuss, sometimes to give way to another opinion, or at least compromise. As Connie Busse, the director of New Beginnings, said, "You have to think of using resources differently, of using workers differently. I don't think you really need a lot of money. You need to open your mind. You need to think of how you're going to do something differently" (MacNeil/Lehrer Report 1993).

Doing things differently has the potential of creating opportunities that normally are not available to poor minorities. Sandra Daley, the doctor who has been with New Beginnings since it started, indicated that the program provides an excellent context for effective medical participation. She explained:

> Physicians are usually chosen for their ability to work alone. We are good at making emergency decisions. We're not trained to work by committee, but there are times when we're taking care of

(continued)

patients when we need to cooperate with others. You need to know who you should be setting up relationships with over time in order to maintain a high level of education and economic sustainability in that community. (UCSD School of Medicine 2002)

The development of these relationships requires effective communication, starting with the simple willingness to listen. At community meetings, Daley indicated, she always has had residents speak first, even if she had distinct ideas about what is needed. "Then you say, 'This is what I have. Do you think it will be useful? Does it shed more light on this issue?'" She added, "I offer this as a strategy. We're all very good-hearted people, but we frequently alienate our colleagues who are part of the solution" (UCSD School of Medicine 2002).

Besides providing health-care assistance, Daley has decided that New Beginnings's medical outreach can also involve local schools, where she and other medical personnel can encourage poor, often minority children to pursue health and science careers. She explained, "We're setting up a pipeline of students and a network of participating schools, as well as interested healthcare providers and scientists to nurture these students" (UCSD School of Medicine 2002).

For Daley this part of the program is particularly dear to her heart. She knows what it is like to grow up in deprived circumstances, having been raised by her grandmother in Panama, where they lived in a one-room dwelling with no plumbing or electricity, requiring her to study her lessons by the light of a kerosene lantern. Moving to Los Angeles at age twelve, Daley indicated that "[w]hen I look at the kids on the playground at Hamilton, I really think of myself when I first came to this country" (UCSD School of Medicine 2002).

All in all, New Beginnings appears well established, with over a decade of accomplishment. As Dr. Sandra Daley and her colleagues have shown, they can establish new channels or pipelines that in various ways help local residents improve their lives.

Although these achievements might appear quite commonplace, the ability of the organizers to effectively unify the efforts of so many agencies and organizations for many years is a most impressive accomplishment that has opposed traditional ineffective patterns. Many individuals involved in similar activities could find exposure to such an interagency model both instructive and inspiring.

"It looks like you will," I replied. "You certainly are getting a sense of how to prepare more effectively."

She came back a week later and showed me how she was following the suggestion to write out a summary of the key material so that it would imprint more effectively in her memory. We went over several points in the reading that were not clear, and she left, looking calmly confident. The second test, actually a slight disappointment to Elvira, was a 30-point improvement. Once again, she vowed to do better next time.

Now I do not encounter many quick success stories like this one. Elvira, a black freshman from inner-city Hartford, was highly motivated, clearly had a positive self-image, and as a result, in spite of her initial difficulty could visualize improvement as inevitable. Minorities' disadvantaged situation often means that they have not had the chance to develop the psychological and intellectual tools to rapidly raise their performance.

All of us, students and teachers alike, encounter evidence of students' efforts. What escapes many people's detection are the following factors, which not only affect everyone's chances of getting into college and completing a degree but also often put minorities at a disadvantage:

- *Immediate passage to college:* Although during the last three decades of the twentieth century whites, blacks, and Hispanics have all been increasingly inclined to go directly from high school to college, minorities were less likely to do so. In 1998 the respective percentages for those three groups were 68.5, 61.9, and 47.4 (O'Brien and Shedd 2001, 1). Mainstreamed students, who tend to be disproportionately white, have the advantage of being more likely to grow up with the expectation that they will attend college, and from infancy onward are more likely to receive supports at home and in school for achieving that outcome.

- *Significance of high-school grades:* A strong predictor of students' persistence in college is their high-school grades. That success, in turn, links to the quality of schooling, with low-income minority students more likely to come from substandard schools where classes tend to be large and impersonal, with minimal learning-enhancing teacher–student interaction.

- *Importance of college grades:* Once enrolled, students' college grades appear to be the single most potent predictor of the chances of receiving a degree. Because low-income minorities are less likely to attend affluent high schools with demanding curricula and college-preparatory programs, including advanced-placement courses, they tend to be less effectively prepared for college, increasing the likelihood that their grades once there will be lower (Blair 2002; O'Brien and Shedd 2001).

- Tricia, a thirty-year-old Hispanic respondent in a large study on poor minorities' adjustment to college, indicated that Upward Bound, a precollege program, "helped me with the language barrier. . . . I was scared of college but it helped me overcome the fear, it made me feel that I could do it" (O'Brien and Shedd 2001, 35). In particular, the program prepared her for college-level science and math.

- *Role of social integration.* Whether belonging to a minority or majority group, students' most common time to drop out of college is shortly after arrival, which is the moment when they are least involved in college life. Research has demonstrated that blacks and Hispanics actually have an advantage on integration—compared to white students they are more involved in clubs and social organizations and also more active in tutoring, mentoring, and other campus-based support programs.

- *Financial aid.* A variety of studies has established that with increased financial aid students are more likely to complete their degrees. While this conclusion is hardly breathtaking, it is significant when one considers that minority students tend to be poorer than whites and thus increased economic assistance could make their likelihood of completing college more equitable (Nora 2001).

It is notable, however, that not all types of aid have the same relationship with persistence in schooling. One national study found that while providing black and Hispanic students with an extra $1,000 in grant money significantly increased their likelihood of staying in school, an additional $1,000 in loan money actually diminished blacks' likelihood of remaining there. The latter conclusion is consistent with the finding that over time African

Americans have been less likely than whites of comparable family income to seek government loans for education, probably because the discriminations they have historically faced have made them feel more vulnerable (Jaynes and Williams 1989, 343; O'Brien and Shedd 2001, 7).

Certainly, all low-income students can find taking on loans burdensome. In the survey of poor minorities' adjustment to college, Dan, a first-generation Asian American student, addressed frustration about his loan. He explained, "I prayed and hoped the aid would be enough . . . but the school's grant started big and then decreased so I had to borrow more" (O'Brien and Shedd 2001, 35).

Advocates of financial aid to poor minorities have been particularly critical of recently redesigned state programs, which have sharply curtailed scholarship aid to poor minority students. This type of program, which had become active in thirteen states in 2002, took much of the scholarship money meant to compensate promising minority students for their initial educational disadvantage and reallocated it to the state's academically top high-school graduates, seeking to convince those students to remain in the state and attend a leading public university. Georgia's HOPE program, which started in 1993, is the longest-running effort of this type. It "has widened the gap in college attendance between blacks and whites," said Susan Dynarski, a Harvard researcher, who studied the HOPE program. "It has also widened the gap between those from low- and high-income families" (Fletcher 2002).

Since public systems of higher education are supposed to extend equal educational opportunities to all individuals within a state, reliance on standards that favor highly advantaged students is distinctly questionable and arguably racist in implication (Astin 1999, 338).

■ *Diversity in minority faculty.* Although this issue has received extensive attention, its impact on minority students' retention appears to be more indirect than direct, occurring because strong relations with faculty can help achieve good grades and satisfaction with the institution—factors that in turn link directly to students' persistence (O'Brien and Shedd 2002, 6).

There appear to be two principal reasons why a small proportion of minority faculty creates an arid climate for minority attendance. First, since minority faculty members are among the major recruiters of minority students, their absence deprives a school of this important recruiting resource. In addition, minority students are less inclined to apply to a college with few minority faculty, because students conclude that such a school is just modestly committed to equal opportunity for minority groups (Epps 1989, 24). With such thoughts in mind, the following statistics are instructive: In American society over one-third of the workers are people of color, and so are more than one-fourth of college students. However, the percentage of racial/ethnic minorities who are faculty members in higher education are about 5 percent African American (heavily represented in black institutions), 4 percent Asian American, and 2 percent Hispanic. To be a faculty member in a college or university, an individual often needs a doctorate, and minority representation here is disproportionately low (Abraham and Jacobs 1999).

All in all, this set of factors indicates that minority students often face various potent issues that threaten their retention in school. The entire section, in fact, has documented that conclusion. The racialized social system operates here. Low-quality day care, a common reality for poor minorities, can help establish early disadvantage. In addition, poor minorities' segregated housing location can lead to poorly funded early schooling, which impedes their later educational development.

Throughout this section we have seen that in major ways the education system is often unresponsive to minority students' needs. The chapter ends with a final commentary on that theme.

Conclusion

Perusing the questionnaires from students completing our math-tutoring program, the school principal suddenly held one up. "This has to be Carlos's," she said, shaking her head. "I can almost feel the frustration bursting off the page."

It was different from the others. While most of the students, who were the school's top seventh and eighth graders in math, seemed pleased with the experience, this sheet conveyed a different response.

"What was the program's best feature?"
"The breakfast."
"Would you participate in a follow-up?"
"Maybe."
"What did you learn?"
"Nothing at all."
The principal indicated that on standardized tests Carlos had scored unusually high in both math and English. "Research shows that with inner-city schools gifted students are often the most dissatisfied clients. We just can't stimulate them." She sighed and explained that she hoped to extend Carlos's immediate opportunities with special tutoring. Perhaps I could help with the contacts.

A few minutes later I asked Carlos about his specific interests. "Both math and science," he replied.
"Does one interest stand out?"
"Nuclear physics." He started telling me about an article he read describing how a high-school student had built his own reactor.
"You'd like to be involved in that kind of work?"
"I would," he said, enthusiastic for the first time.

I recalled John Dewey's quotation about the optimal outcome for public education, realizing how far the system needed to go in a community like this one to approach that ideal.

DISCUSSION QUESTIONS

1. Examine how Calvinist doctrine impacted on colonial families and schooling.

2. Evaluate the strengths and weaknesses of late nineteenth-century public education.

3. Discuss social scientists' representation of family diversity in the second half of the twentieth century.

4. Examine the extent of segregated schooling for specific racial and ethnic groups, evaluating the possible disadvantages and also considering whether or not groups can find it advantageous in certain settings.

5. Why is effective day care important, and what are the most significant criteria in evaluating it? Indicate the challenges that particular racial and ethnic groups encounter.

6. Examine equity in school funding, indicating why it is a particularly salient issue for American minorities and whether or not it actually makes a difference in students' performance.

7. Discuss plugging leaks in the educational pipeline, pointing out what you consider the most troublesome leaks for racial minorities and making observations based on personal experience or that of others you know.

BIBLIOGRAPHY

Abraham, Ansley, and Walter R. Jacobs Jr. 1999. "Diversity in College Faculty: SREB States Address a Need." Southern Regional Education Board. www.sreb.org.

Astin, Alexander. 1999. "Educational Equity and the Problems of Assessment," pp. 330–38 in Christopher G. Ellison and W. Allen Martin (eds.), *Race and Ethnic Relation in the United States*. Los Angles: Roxbury.

Augenblick, John G., John L. Myers, and Amy Berk Anderson. 1997. "Equity and Adequacy in School Funding." *The Future of Children*. (Winter). www.futureofchildren.org/information2826/information_show.htm?doc id=73377.

Biddle, Bruce J., and David C. Berliner. 2002a. "A Research Synthesis: Unequal School Funding in the United States." *Educational Leadership*. 59 (March): 1–15. www.ascd.org/readingroom/edlead/0205/biddle.html.

Biddle, Bruce J., and David C. Berliner. 2002b. "Small Class Size and Its Effects." *Educational Leadership*. 59 (March): 12–23.

Binzen, Peter. 1970. *Whitetown, U.S.A.* New York: Random House.

Blakeslee, Sandra. 1995. "In Brain's Growth, Timetable May Be Crucial." *New York Times*. (August 29): C1+.

Blair, Julie. 2002. "Study: Inequalities Persist in Access to Higher Education." *Education Week*. www.edweek.org/ew/vol/18/01deseg.h18.

Braddock, Jomills Henry II, Robert L. Crain, and James S. McPartland. 1984. "A Long-Term View of School Desegregation: Some Recent Studies of Graduates as Adults." *Phi Delta Kappan*. 66 (December): 259–64.

Broom, Leonard, and Philip Selznick. 1958. *Sociology: A Text with Adapted Readings,* 2nd ed. Evanston, IL: Row, Peterson.

Burnham, Linda. 2001. "Welfare Reform, Family Hardship, and Women of Color." *Annals of the American Academy of Political and Social Science*. 577 (September): 38–48.

Caminiti, Susan. 1994. "Who's Minding America's Kids?" pp. 140–42 in Ollie Pocs (ed.), *Marriage and Family 94/95,* 20th ed. Guilford, CT: Dushkin.

Celis, William, III. 1995. "40 Years after Brown, Segregation Persists," pp. 30–33 in John A. Kromkowski (ed.), *Race and Ethnic Relations 95/96,* 5th ed. Guilford, CT: Dushkin.

Coalition for Community Schools. 2002. "New Beginnings, San Diego, California." www.communityschools.org/newbegin.html.

Coltrane, Scott. 2000. "Stability and Change in Chicano Men's Family Lives," pp. 470–82 in Anne Minas (ed.), *Gender Basics: Feminist Perspectives on Women and Men,* 2nd ed. Belmont, CA: Wadsworth.

Darling-Hammond, L., and L. Post. 2000. "Inequality in Teaching and Schooling: Supporting High-Quality Teaching and Leadership in Low-Income Schools," pp. 127–67 in Robert D. Kahlenberg (ed.), *A Nation at Risk: Preserving Public Education as an Engine for Social Mobility*. New York: Century Foundation Press.

Deiner, Penny L. 1992. "Family Day Care and Children with Disabilities, pp. 129–45 in Donald L. Peters and Alan R. Pence (eds.), *Family Day Care: Current Research for Informed Public Policy.* New York: Teachers College Press.

Doob, Christopher Bates. 1999. *Racism: An American Cauldron,* 3rd ed. Reading, MA: Longman.

DuBois, W. E. B. 1973. *The Philadelphia Negro.* Milkwood, NY: Kraus-Thomson Organization. Originally published in 1899.

Elliott, M. 1998. "School Finance and Opportunity to Learn: Does Money Well Spent Enhance Students' Achievement?" *Sociology of Education.* 71: 223–45.

Epps, Edgar R. 1989. "Academic Culture and the Minority Professor." *Academe.* 75 (September/October): 23–26.

Feagin, Joe R., and Melvin P. Sikes. 1994. *Living with Racism: The Black Middle-Class Experience.* Boston: Beacon Press.

Ferguson, R. F., and H. F. Ladd. 1996. "How and Why Money Matters: An Analysis of Alabama Schools," pp. 265–98 in H. F. Ladd (ed.), *Holding Schools Accountable: Performance-Based Reform in Education.* Washington, DC: Brookings Institution.

Fletcher, Michael A. 2002. "Mixed Grades: States Draw Criticism on Scholarship Programs." (June 4). www.washingtonpost.com/ac2/wp-dyn/A54871-2002Jun3?language=printer.

Foner, Eric. 2003. "Diversity Over Justice." *Nation. 277* (July 14): 4–5.

Gordon, Jane. 2002. "Back on the Bus." *New York Times.* (October 6): sec. 14, p. 1+.

Graves, Rachel. 2002. "Candidates Differ When to Mend School Funding." *Houston Chronicle.* (October 3). www.chron.com/cs/CDA/story.hts/metropolitan/1599640.

Habenstein, Robert W. 1998. "A 'Then and Now' Overview of the Immigrant Family in America," pp. 13–38 in Charles H. Mindel, Robert W. Habenstein, and Roosevelt Wright Jr. (eds.), *Ethnic Families in America: Patterns and Variations,* 4th ed. Upper Saddle River, NJ: Prentice-Hall.

Hacker, Andrew. 1992. *Two Nations: Black and White, Separate, Hostile, Unequal.* New York: Scribner.

Harter, E. A. 1999. "School Resource and Student Performance." *Journal of Education Finance.* 24 (September): 281–302.

Henly, Julia R., and Sandra Lyons. 2000. "The Negotiation of Child Care and Employment Demands Among Low-Income Parents." *Journal of Social Issues.* 56: 683–706.

Hentoff, Nat. 1989. "Anonymous Children/Diminished Adults." *Proceedings of the Academy of Political Science.* 37: 137–48.

Hill, 2001. "Class, Race, and Gender Dimensions of Child Rearing in African American Families." *Journal of Black Studies.* 31 (March): 494–508.

Hodgkinson, Harold L. 2002. "The Demographics of Diversity." *Principal Online.* November/December. www.naesp.org/comm/p1102b.htm.

Hom, Alice Y. 2002. "Perspectives of Asian American Parents with Gay and Lesbian Children," pp. 156–61 in Nijole V. Benokraitis (ed.), *Contemporary Ethnic Families in the United States.* Upper Saddle River, NJ: Prentice-Hall.

Horgan, Ellen Somers. 1998. "The Irish-American Family," pp. 39–67 in Charles H. Mindel, Robert W. Habenstein, and Roosevelt Wright Jr. (eds.), *Ethnic Families in America: Patterns and Variations,* 4th ed. Upper Saddle River, NJ: Prentice-Hall.

Howes, Carollee. 1990. "Current Research on Early Day Care," pp. 21–35 in Shahla S. Chehrazi (ed.), *Psychological Issues in Day Care.* Washington, DC: American Psychiatric Press.

Jaeger, Elizabeth A., Anne B. Shlay, and Marsha Weinraub. 2000. "Child Care Improvement: Evaluating a Low-Cost Approach to Improving the Availability of Quality Child Care." *Evaluation Review.* 24 (October): 484–515.

Jayakody, Rukmalie, and Ariel Kalb. 2002. "Social Fathering in Low-Income, African American Families with Preschool Children." *Journal of Marriage and Family.* 64 (May): 504–16.

Jaynes, Gerald David, and Robin M. Williams Jr. (eds.). 1989. *A Common Destiny: Blacks and American Society.* Washington, DC: National Academy Press.

Jo, Moon H. 1999. *Korean Immigrants and the Challenge of Adjustment.* Westport, CT: Greenwood Press.

Joshi, Sunil, et al. 2002. "A Case of Social Responsibility or Competitive Advantage?" Human Resources Department of Georgia Institute of Technology. www.Worklifebalance.com.

Kibria, Nazli. 2002. "Intermarriage and Ethnic Identity among Second-Generation Chinese and Korean Americans," pp. 110–19 in Nijole V. Benokraitis (ed.), *Contemporary Ethnic Families in the United States.* Upper Saddle River, NJ: Prentice-Hall.

Kozol, Johnathan. 1991. *Savage Inequalities: Children in America's Schools.* New York: Crown.

Liptak, Adam. 2003. "Scholars Say Justices Sent Murky Message." *International Herald Tribune.* (June 25): 2.

Lorde, Audre. 1997. "Man Child: A Black Lesbian Feminist's Response," pp. 282–87 in Estelle Disch (ed.), *Reconstructing Gender: A Multicultural Anthology.* Mountain View, CA: Mayfield.

MacNeil/Lehrer Report. 1993. "New Beginnings."

McAdoo, Harriet Pipes. 1998. "African-American Families," pp. 361–81 in Charles H. Mindel, Robert W. Habenstein, and Roosevelt Wright Jr. (eds), *Ethnic Families in America: Patterns and Variations,* 4th ed. Upper Saddle River, NJ: Prentice-Hall.

Mink, Gwendolyn. 2001. "Violating Women: Rights Abuses in the Welfare Police State." *Annals of the American Academy of Political and Social Science.* 577 (September): 79–93.

Mintz, Steven, and Susan Kellogg. 1988. *Domestic Revolutions: A Social History of American Family Life.* New York: Free Press.

Morgan, Edmund S. 1966. *The Puritan Family: Religion & Domestic Relations in Seventeenth-Century New England.* New York: Harper & Row.

National Center for Education Statistics. 2002. "Digest of Education Statistics, 2001." www.nces.ed.gov/digestprograms/.

News Service: University of Michigan. 2003. "President Mary Sue Coleman Responds to Bush Administration Announcement on Affirmative Action. www.umich.edu/~newsinfo/Releases/2003/Jan03/r011503c.html.

NICHD Early Child Care Research Network. 1999. "Child Outcomes When Child Care Center Classes Meet Recommended Standards for Quality." *American Journal of Public Health.* 89 (July): 1072–77.

Nora, Amaury. 2001. "How Minority Students Finance Their Higher Education." Eric Clearinghouse on Urban Education. www.eric-web.tc.columbia.edu/digest/dig171.asp.

O'Brien, Colleen, and Jessica Shedd. 2001. "Getting Through College: Voices of Low-Income and Minority Students in New England." Nellie Mae Foundation. www.NellieMae.org.

Office of Policy Planning and Research, United States Department of Labor. 1965. *The Negro Family: The Case for National Action.* Washington, DC: United States Department of Labor.

Payne, Kenneth J., and Bruce J. Biddle. 1999. "Poor School Funding, Child Poverty, and Mathematics Achievement." *Educational Researcher.* 28 (June): 4–13.

Pessar, Patricia R. 2002. "Grappling with Changing Gender Roles in Dominican American Families," pp. 66–70 in Nijole V. Benokraitis (ed.), *Contemporary Ethnic Families in the United States.* Upper Saddle River, NJ: Prentice-Hall.

Polk, Nancy. 1997. "Day Care: What Works, What's Needed." *New York Times.* (May 25): sec. 13, p. 2.

Pungello, Elizabeth Puhn, and Beth Kurtz-Costes. 2000. "Working Women's Selection of Care for Their Infants: A Prospective Study." *Family Relations.* 49 (July): 245–55.

Rainbow Children's Center. 2001. "Providing Affordable Community Day Care." www.whitememorial.com/pages/YourHealth/RainbowCenter.html.

Rickles, Jordan, and Paul M. Ong. 2001. "Relationship Between School and Residential Segregation at the Turn of the Century." UCLA School of Public Policy and Social Research. www.sppsr.ucla.edu/lewis.

Rodgers-Farmer, Antoinette Y., and Rosa L. Jones. 2002. "Black Grandmothers Raising Their Grandchildren," pp. 378–84 in Nijole V. Benekraitis (ed.), *Contemporary Ethnic Families in the United States.* Upper Saddle River, NJ: Prentice-Hall.

Rubin, Lillian B. 1997. "The Transformation of Family Life," pp. 263–72 in Estelle Disch (ed.), *Reconstructing Gender: A Multicultural Anthology.* Mountain View, CA: Mayfield.

Rury, John L. 2002. *Education and Social Change: Themes in the History of American Schooling.* Mahwah, NJ: Erlbaum.

Ryan, William. 1976. *Blaming the Victim,* rev. ed. New York: Vintage Books.

Sánchez-Ayéndez, Melba. 1998. "The Puerto Rican Family," pp. 199–222 in Charles H. Mindel, Robert W. Habenstein, and Roosevelt Wright Jr. (eds.), *Ethnic Families in America,* 4th ed. Upper Saddle River, NJ: Prentice-Hall.

Slavin, Robert E. 1999. "How Can Funding Equity Ensure Enhanced Achievement? *Journal of Education Financee.* 24: 519–28.

Spring, Joel. 1994. *The American School 1642–1993,* 3rd ed. New York: McGraw-Hill.

Squiers, D. Ann, and Jill S. Quadagno. 1998. "The Italian-American Family," pp. 102–27 in Charles H. Mindel, Robert W. Habenstein, and Roosevelt Wright Jr. (eds.), *Ethnic Families in America: Patterns and Variations,* 4th ed. Upper Saddle River, NJ: Prentice-Hall.

Starbuck, Gene H. 2002. *Families in Context.* Belmont, CA: Wadsworth.

Suárez, Zulema. 1998. "The Cuban-American Family," pp. 199–222 in Charles H. Mindel, Robert W. Habenstein, and Roosevelt Wright Jr. (eds.), *Ethnic Families in America: Patterns and Variations,* 4th ed. Upper Saddle River, NJ: Prentice-Hall.

Thomas, Veronica G. 1990. "Determinants of Global Life Happiness and Marital Happiness in Dual-Career Black Couples." *Family Relations.* 39 (April): 174–78.

Toliver, Susan D. 1998. *Black Families in Corporate America.* Thousand Oaks, CA: Sage.

Toppo, Greg. 2003. "SAT Takers Are Sharpening Up." *USA Today.* (August 27): 5D.

Toro-Morn, Maura I. 2002. "Puerto Rican Migrants: Juggling Family and Work Roles," pp. 232–39 in

Nijole V. Benokraitis (ed.), *Contemporary Ethnic Families in the United States.* Upper Saddle River, NJ: Prentice-Hall.

Tran, Thanh Van. 1988. "The Vietnamese-American Family," pp. 254–83 in Charles H. Mindel, Robert W. Habenstein, and Roosevelt Wright Jr. (eds.), *Ethnic Families in America: Patterns and Variations,* 4th ed. Upper Saddle River, NJ: Prentice-Hall.

UCSD School of Medicine. 2002. "Medicine in the Context of Community Medicine." www.meded.ucsd.edu/Catalog/36.html

University of Michigan News and Information Services. 2000. "Intimate Relationships between Races More Common Than Thought." www.umich.edu/~newsinfo/Releases/2000/Mar00/r032300a.html.

White House. 2003. "President Bush Discusses Michigan Affirmative Action Case." www.whitehouse.gov/news/releases/2003/01/20030115-7.html.

Whitington, Daphne. 2000. "Equity in School Funding." Equity in Education Project. www.geocities.com/-schoolfunding/equity in education projec.html.

Willie, Charles V. 1991. *A New Look at Black Families,* 4th ed. Dix Hills, NJ: General Hall.

Wilson, Angela Cavender. 2002. "Grandmother to Granddaughter: Learning to Be a Dakota Woman," pp. 49–53 in Nijole V. Benokraitis (ed.), *Contemporary Ethnic Families in the United States.* Upper Saddle River, NJ: Prentice-Hall.

Winter, Greg. 2003. "U. of Michigan Alters Admissions Use of Race." *New York Times.* (August 29): A12.

Wong, Morrison G. 1998. "The Chinese-American Family," pp. 284–310 in Charles H. Mindel, Robert W. Habenstein, and Roosevelt Wright Jr. (eds.), *Ethnic Families in America: Patterns and Variations,* 4th ed. Upper Saddle River, NJ: Prentice-Hall.

Wu, Frank H. 2002. *Yellow: Race in America Beyond Black and White.* New York: Basic Books.

Zigler, Edward F. 1995. "Meeting the Needs of Children in Poverty." *American Journal of Orthopsychiatry.* 65 (January): 6–9.

9 The Canadian Multicultural Mosaic: How Different from the United States?

The Development of Canadian Ethnic Pluralism

    History of Canadian Immigration

    The Development of Multiculturalism

Race and Ethnicity in Canadian Daily Life

    Important Current Realities

    Employment Equity

Conclusion

How are Canada and Canadians different from the United States and Americans? For one thing the country is larger, colder, and less populated than the United States; slaves escaped there and over a century later so did young American men resisting the military draft. Their quarters and dimes filter into our cash transactions and are likely to be rejected by salespeople and vending machines. Their accent has distinctive vowel sounds, and while spelling like the British person, they, unlike Americans, officially use the meter system. But these are superficialities. Is there a fundamental difference?

While a three-element phrase from the Declaration of Independence—"life, liberty, and the pursuit of happiness"—summarizes American citizens' inalienable rights, the closest to a Canadian counterpart, which opens section 91 of the *Constitution Act, 1867,* is quite different—"peace, order, and good government." The American statement is distinctly individualistic, whereas the Canadian focus is more collective.

This Canadian emphasis carries into racial and ethnic relations, where diversity is widely embraced. Canadians, many native observers say, are relativists, recognizing that the standards and goals of all people of color* as well as those of women, gays and lesbians,

---

*In Canada most people of color are referred to as "visible minorities." Because of their unique history, Canadian Indians, who are called "Aboriginal people," are often listed separately.

and disabled people must be respected and incorporated. Sociologist Reginald W. Bibby wrote, "Canada, we have concluded, will be a multinational society, a multicultural mosaic of people from varied backgrounds who will have the freedom to live as they see fit" (Bibby 1990, 7). Canada, in short, is supposedly like a mosaic work of art, where instead of patterns of stone or glass, the focus is on discrete clusters of people who remain largely free to express their varied values, beliefs, and norms and maintain their own customs. The Canadian cultural emphasis on ethnic pluralism is quite different from the American focus on assimilation, where the approach is "to discard one's cultural past and conform to the dominant culture" (Bibby 1990, 7). Whereas the Canadian citizen remains somewhat group-oriented, the American individual is relatively unrestricted by group ties in pursuing his or her personal ambitions. Culturally speaking, Americans display less of a social conscience regarding the welfare of the general citizenry. Furthermore, unlike Canada, in the United States "there is no official recognition of cultural or ethnic pluralism at the federal level" (Goldberg and Mercer 1986, 40).

Why the difference? In the upcoming section, we see the important role that history has played in shaping Canada's pluralistic emphasis. Then discussion shifts to biographical topics, examining situations in which Canadian minorities have experienced discriminatory treatment and finally analyzing current efforts to establish reforms in employment. First, however, a look back in time.

The Development of Canadian Ethnic Pluralism

An interesting, important quality of Canada has been that unlike other Western nations it had two founding groups—the British and the French. In 1759 following the French and Indian War, France lost control of Quebec, and all of Canada came under British control. However, English-speaking authorities made no effort to occupy Quebec. Each cultural group remained separate—alone in its own vast territory. Reginald Bibby wrote:

> Historians tell us that the reality of the two solitudes has represented Canada's central nation-building problem. For almost 350 years—from just after 1600 until the 1960s—we wrestled with the question of how the two dominant groups could comprise one country. (Bibby 1990, 25)

Although Canada differs from the United States in having two founding national groups, its overall immigration pattern has often resembled the American one. We consider that pattern and then the multiculturalism it precipitated.

History of Canadian Immigration

Established urban Canadians responded to mid-nineteenth-century Irish immigrants in an ambivalent manner—much like their contemporaries in American cities. In Toronto, Hamilton, and London (all in the province of Ontario), the new arrivals were appreciated as a source of cheap labor for taxing jobs, but their poverty, Irish brogue spiced with Gaelic words and phrases, their Catholicism, and other alien ways encouraged fierce stereotypes and discriminatory action. In 1858 George Brown, editor of *The Globe* in Toronto, declared:

> Irish beggars are to be met everywhere, and they are as ignorant and vicious as they are poor. They are lazy, improvident and unthankful; they fill our poorhouses and our prisons, and are as brutish in their superstitions as Hindoos [sic]. (Nicholson 1991, 334)

Canadians also responded to both Chinese and Japanese immigrants in a hostile manner that closely paralleled their southern neighbors' reaction. In the 1880s Canada received an influx of Chinese workers to lay track for the transcontinental railroad. Although these men did their job admirably, pressure from labor unions and other groups developed to curtail Chinese entry, and a decade later restriction on Japanese immigration was also imposed. Again, as in the United States, citizens of Japanese descent were forced to relocate during World War II, suffering confiscation of their property and imprisonment in concentration camps in the interior of British Columbia until the end of the war (Weinfeld and Wilkinson 1999, 58).

At that time government officials gave Japanese Canadians the choice of moving to Japan or into Canada's interior east of the Rocky Mountains but not the option of returning to their coastal homes, where many had lived for two or three generations. In both cases, the internees would supposedly be allowed to bring along their personal possessions. The plan was to conduct interviews in which the choices were carefully laid out, but in actuality an understaffed contingent of immigration officers gave hurried interviews and pressured or tricked many families into moving to Japan. When the war ended, nearly 5,000 Japanese Canadians petitioned to be removed from the repatriation list, but in spite of support from church leaders and several large eastern newspapers, William Lyon MacKenzie King, the deputy labor minister and future prime minister, issued an order allowing the cabinet to send away anyone it pleased. On January 16, 1946, the first of five ships deporting former Japanese Canadian citizens left for Japan. A reporter for the *Vancouver Daily Province* wrote:

> Six hundred and seventy solemn-faced Japanese . . . sailed from Vancouver Friday night bound for the land of the rising sun. . . . There were few smiling faces among the boatload. Solemnness was written on their faces; only indifference they showed. (Boyko 1995, 145)

Up to 1967 when legislative reform occurred, both Japanese and Chinese immigration to Canada remained highly restricted. The situation was more complicated with Indians. Because India and Canada both belonged to the British Commonwealth, the expectation prevailed that individuals and families could pass freely from one member country to another. Considering that this situation would produce an unwanted influx of alien people, Canadian legislators performed a neat trick. In 1908 they passed the Continuous Journey Stipulation, not outrightly denying Indians' entry but permitting them to immigrate only if they journeyed from their homeland to Canada nonstop. The convenient catch for the Canadian lawmakers was that no throughfare tickets to Canada were available in India, and thus immigration from that country was thoroughly yet discretely shut off (Weinfeld and Wilkinson 1999, 58–59).

In their general outlook on immigrants, urban Canadian leaders of northern European descent responded much like their American counterparts, appreciating a source of cheap labor but fearing an alien inundation. Like the Americans, the leaders of Canadian cities felt uninhibited about giving bold, frank expression to their views. In 1900, for instance, writing in a local newspaper, a prominent citizen of Winnipeg expressed his anxiety about the growing Ukrainian presence.

> Increased population, if of the right sort, will be of great benefit. . . . But we should be careful that we do not bring in an imported population of such a character as will be an injury, not a benefit to our people. . . . Anglo-Saxons, Germans, and Scandinavians in general we can take in any number, but we cannot assimilate more than a limited number of immigrants of radically different race. The Galician [Ukrainian] is as yet an experiment; we do not know how he will turn out; and we cannot afford to make the experiment on too grand a scale. (Artibise 1991, 372)

Historically, Canadian immigration policy was responsive to concerns about the numbers of immigrants coming from outside of northern European countries. The Immigration Act of 1952 removed prohibitions against the Indians, Japanese, and Chinese but continued to give preference to arrivals from Great Britain, Ireland, other European countries, Australia, New Zealand, and the United States. Ten years later the immigration act was updated, making employment skills a major criterion for immigrant selection and removing the reference to preferred status for citizens of the countries just mentioned. However, unlike whites, visible minorities already living in Canada still found it difficult to bring sponsored relatives into the country.

With the passage of the Immigration Act of 1967, that situation changed. Now legislators established a point system based on applicants' education, technical and professional training, employment experience, and knowledge of one or both official languages, and admission required a minimum of 50 points out of a total of 100.

Why did immigration policy change in the 1960s? One reason was that because Canada's system of higher education was still largely undeveloped, the country faced a clear shortage of professional and skilled workers, and to meet the needs of an expanding economy, some of these individuals had to come from outside the country. In addition, Canada was trying to create a positive image on the world stage as a helpful, resourceful middle power. John Humphrey, a Canadian, had drafted the UN Declaration of Human Rights in 1948, and Prime Minister Lester Pearson received the Nobel Peace Prize for his major role in resolving the 1956 Suez War and developing the concept of United Nations' peacekeeping. Receptiveness to immigration from diverse nations only enhanced the image of contributing to a more positive world order (Weinfeld and Wilkinson 1999, 59).

At this time the ethnic and racial composition of Canada was significantly changing. In 1881 people of British and French origin represented 90 percent of the population; other Europeans, mainly Germans, were 7 percent, and Asians were less than 1 percent. Through the next century, British immigration steadily declined, comprising only 7.5 percent of the total arriving between 1981 and 1991, and the pattern was comparable for other European groups.

Meanwhile, dramatic increases in visible minorities have occurred. While between 1996 and 2001, 19 percent of immigrants came from Europe and 3.1 percent from the United States, 8.3 percent arrived from South and Central America (including the Caribbean), 8.3 percent from Africa, and a massive 59.4 percent from Asia and the Pacific.

Foreign-born Canadians represent about 17 percent of the nation's population and are most heavily settled in three cities. Primarily composed of visible minorities, this group of citizens comprises 42 percent of the population in Toronto, 38 percent in Vancouver, and 18 percent in Montreal (*Statistics Canada* 2001; Weinfeld and Wilkinson 1999, 62–63). Table 9.1 provides recent figures for most Canadians' ethnic origins.

In the course of diversification, Canada's urban life has stayed vibrant. Unlike in the United States, there has not been a large, ghettoized inner-city population. Canada never had a large slave population whose descendants were subjected to the relentless housing segregation described in earlier chapters. Black Canadians have often been the objects of racist mistreatment, but their numbers are smaller and the discriminatory patterns of political, economic, and residential restriction are less historically entrenched than in the United States.

TABLE 9.1 Canadian Ethnic Origins: 2001

Total population	29.64[1]
British Isles	14.46
French	4.67
Western European	3.79
Total visible minorities	3.98
Chinese	1.03
South Asian	.92
Black	.66
Latin American	.22
Arab	.19
West Asian	.11
Korean	.10
Japanese	.07
Other ethnicities	.17
Eastern European	2.52
Southern European	2.33
Aboriginal	1.32
Northern European	.96

[1]All figures in millions.

Sources: Data from tables entitled "Population by Selected Ethnic Origins, Provinces, and Territories" and "Visible Minority Population by Age." *Statistics Canada 2001.* www.statcan.ca/english/Pgdb/demo26a.htm and www.statcan.ca/english/Pgdb/demo50a.htm.

A second difference between the two countries related to diversity has been that since French- and English-speaking citizens have been bound into a single political entity, Canada's historical pattern has emphasized language and culture instead of race. In 1971 Canada adopted a multicultural policy with the stated purpose of preserving the language and traditions of all ethnic groups and removing barriers to their equality. In 1988 this policy was legalized with the passage of the Canadian Multiculturalism Act (Boyd 2000, 143), and its impact on the nation has been significant.

The Development of Multiculturalism

In addressing the smoldering conflict between French- and English-speaking Canadians, historian Arthur Lower concluded, "[W]here you have a country of two primary cultures, two primary religions, and two pulls on fundamental allegiance . . . only one attitude becomes possible, short of endemic civil war, the attitude of compromise" (Lower 1958, 382).

In 1965 the Royal Commission on Bilingualism and Biculturalism released the first of seven volumes, indicating that Canada was in the throes of a major crisis that would pass only when the citizens of Quebec believed that the linguistic, economic, and occupational inequalities they were experiencing could be resolved. One of the commission's recommendations was that since Canada had two founding people each speaking its own language, hereafter the nation would have two official languages—French and English—and with the passage of the Official Languages Act in 1969, that idea became enshrined in law.

Throughout Canada road signs are in both official languages, serving as frequent reminders of the bilingual emphasis throughout the country.

At this juncture, Reginald Bibby indicated, "the first of Canada's two major intergroup building blocks—bilingualism—was dropped into place" (Bibby 1990, 49).

The second major intergroup topic needing resolution involved the place in society for the remaining cultural groups. We have already seen that the Immigration Act of 1967 established a point system, opening entrance into the country for a growing number of racial and ethnic groups. The mere right to enter the country, however, did not resolve the issue of how these groups would be received. Finally, after focusing four volumes of its report on the French-English conflict, the Royal Commission shifted attention to this topic. The general recommendation was that citizens of various cultural backgrounds should have the chance to retain the positive elements of their heritage and that in the process the nation would be enriched. Addressing a Ukrainian group in 1972, Prime Minister Pierre Trudeau indicated that Canada's array of multicultural groups was one of the country's finest attributes. He declared:

> Each of the many fibers contributes its own qualities and Canada gains from the combination. We become less like others; we become less susceptible to cultural, social, or political envelopment by others. We become less inclined—certainly less obliged—to think in terms of national grandeur; inclined not at all to assume a posture of aggressiveness, or ostentation, or might. Our image is of a land of people with many differences—but many contributions, many variations in view—but a single desire to live in harmony. (Christiano 1990, 19–20)

Clearly, Trudeau was implying, Canada's multiculturalism policy contributed to a national image that contrasted positively with what its more contentious southern neighbor projected.

Sociologist Morton Weinfeld, who had been highly critical of how the federal government had traditionally treated minorities, could enthusiastically declare in 1988, "The Canadian state has moved from active oppression and past indifference to championing the rights of minority groups. The state and its institutions are formally committed to ensuring for Canadian minority groups both equal opportunity and continued cultural survival" (Reitz and Breton 1998, 59).

In 1988 the passage of the Canadian Multicultural Act produced two significant impacts: It emphasized the symbolic importance of diversity in Canadian society and also encouraged the development of various ethnic associations that have lobbied local, provincial, and federal government departments on behalf of their constituents (Boyd 2000, 143).

One notable consequence of the 1988 law has been extensive government support for second-language teaching in the schools. While French is by far the most commonly taught second language in English-dominant provinces and English the one most often included in French-dominant areas, at least forty so-called "heritage" languages associated with newly arrived immigrant groups are part of the formal curricula of schools in the country's major cities. Furthermore, in Ontario instruction in seven Aboriginal people's languages occurs in various communities. Besides teaching the language itself, the more established programs provide content-based instruction, creating a classroom setting in which over time students can become very comfortable with and capable in the second language (Cumming 2001). One important implication is that the established presence of these instructional programs, particularly with subsidy by provincial governments, represents a legitimacy of ethnic groups' significance in Canadian society—a legitimacy without American parallel.

In spite of its success with second languages in the schools, many current observers of multiculturalism consider the policy vague, referring to inequalities but not specifying just what those inequalities are nor how to remove them. Anthropologists Frances Henry and Carol Tator, in fact, concluded that the language of the Canadian Multiculturalism Act is unduly optimistic and simply assumes that in spite of some cases of discriminatory treatment, justice and equity will prevail (Henry and Tator 1999, 96).

According to Henry and Tator, Canadian society displays a more complicated picture, one in which three general outlooks on multiculturalism prevail:

■ The first view, which was analyzed for American society in Chapter 2, involves an assimilationist model, where immigrants downplay their own cultural traditions and blend into Canadian culture and society. While perhaps continuing to maintain various traditional ways, the new arrivals acknowledge the dominant significance of the common culture in which everyone shares the same history, traditions, values, and norms.

■ The second approach involves verbal advocacy of multiculturalism but little actual implementation. In reality, this position holds minorities' cultural traditions at the margins, not encouraging full inclusion, equity, and empowerment. It is a policy of containment, where visible minorities and Aboriginal people are seldom induced to seek powerful positions from which they can shape policy, and if their members call for access and inclusion they are likely to be labeled "unreasonable" or "radical."

■ The final outlook, "critical multiculturalism," emerged in the 1990s when it became clear that the Multiculturalism Act was not making it possible for many people of color to obtain full participation in Canadian society. This perspective, which fits with conflict theory examined in Chapter 2, considers minorities full partners in the political and economic process, not merely interest groups petitioning to have specific needs addressed. It emphasizes that multiculturalism focuses on the centrality of restructuring and transforming communities, serving as a challenge to white mainstream control of knowledge and cultural and institutional practices (Henry and Tator 1999, 94–99). This approach emphasizes the fact that visible minorities are disproportionately lower class, facing similar disadvantages in schooling, housing, and jobs to those their American counterparts encounter.

In the 1990s the multiculturalism policy encountered stiff opposition. Critics asserted that it represents ethnic separation, encouraging arriving groups to produce self-contained ghettoes alienated from the mainstream. Although such an outcome represents a logical possibility, evidence has not been supportive. Since the inception of the multiculturalism policy in 1971, visible minorities arriving in Canada have demonstrated the opposite of such a trend. In particular, they have shown high naturalization rates; extensive involvement in mainstream politics, including election to Parliament; high rates of mastery for at least one of the official languages; and a steadily increasing tendency to intermarry. Compared to their counterparts in the United States, newly arrived immigrants are much more inclined to become integrated on these four dimensions (Kymlicka 1997; Kymlicka 1998).

TABLE 9.2   **Historical Events Influencing Canada's Multicultural Mosaic**

Date	Event
Early 1600s	Foundation by two nations: Great Britain and France
1967	Report of the Royal Commission on Bilingualism and Biculturalism
1971	Adoption of the multiculturalism policy
1986	Employment Equity Act
1988	Canadian Multiculturalism Act
1995	The Ontario government's Act to Repeal Quotas and to Restore Merit-Based Employment Practices

Nonetheless, opposition to multiculturalism is likely to persist. As in the United States, the political and economic leadership is disinclined to share power and decision making, and the citizens themselves do not appear enthusiastic about such a development.

A comparison of Canadian and American outlooks on race and ethnicity indicates a general similarity. Examining the two sets of available survey research, sociologists Jeffrey G. Reitz and Raymond Breton (1998) concluded that in both countries blatant racist views and expression are marginal, with 85 to 90 percent of citizens in the two nations committing to the belief that all races are created equal. Although social separation between the majority and minorities has been steadily declining in both countries, it has been consistently less pronounced in Canada, particularly in relation to intermarriage. Two factors that appear to contribute to this difference are (1) that economic disparities, which normally encourage a sense of group separation, are less distinct in Canada and (2) that, overall, its proportion of minorities is smaller, perhaps inclining majority-group members to be less motivated to isolate themselves for the protection of group interests.

As we have seen, however, the proportion of visible minorities is high in such cities as Toronto, Vancouver, and Montreal, and extensive evidence suggests that many whites are inclined toward racial stereotyping; racial discrimination in housing, employment, and other important areas; and opposition to government intervention to reduce discrimination and inequality.

Moving into the second principle section of this chapter, we continue to see both similarities and differences between the two countries. Table 9.2 lists the distinctive features of Canadian history linked to multiculturalism.

Race and Ethnicity in Canadian Daily Life

Canada is a country in which the majority of the citizenry appears to support some multiculturalist policies. However, a large body of research offers an important, decisive conclusion: Most Canadians believe that the more different a given group's culture is perceived to be from those of the nation's two founding groups and the stronger that group's identity and involvement in its own ethnic community, the longer it will take the members to obtain full and equal access to the society's mainstream resources—quality housing, schooling, health care, jobs, and so forth (Kalbach 2000, 70–71).

That conclusion serves as a theme for the following discussion of Canada's contemporary racial and ethnic complexity.

Important Current Realities

We examine housing, health care, gender-related challenges, and at greater length, employment.

Housing   While the most residentially concentrated racial or ethnic group in the United States is blacks, in Canada it is Jews. In 1996 half the Jewish population of Montreal lived in 1.8 percent of the census tracts and 90 percent in 7 percent of the tracts—concentrations that actually increased from five years earlier. In Toronto, the other Canadian city with a substantial Jewish population, the residential concentration of Jews has been just slightly less pronounced. Italians and Poles are more residentially concentrated than the northern European groups but less so than visible minorities, which are also heavily represented in these two cities.

In Montreal, where the concentrations of visible minorities are highest, half the South Asians in 1996 lived in 4.8 percent of census tracts, and for the Chinese and blacks the respective figures were 8.4 and 12.4 percent. At that time in Toronto, the city with the largest number of visible minorities, half the Chinese, South Asians, and blacks resided in 8.8, 12, and 14.4 percent of the census tracts, respectively. In 1996 in the western cities of Winnipeg, Calgary, Edmonton, and Vancouver, half of South Asians lived in about 8 percent of the census tracts (Balakrishnan 2000, 126–29).

Although their cities are less ghettoized and therefore perhaps less threatening to whites than American cities, many modern Canadian urban dwellers still express fearful, hostile stereotypes toward racial minorities and engage in housing discrimination against them. In Toronto this practice is widespread, somewhat undercutting the official motto "Diversity, Our Strength."

Amina Ahmed, who helps poor people of color locate housing, indicated that the manager of an attractive building with modest rents would put up a no-vacancy sign in his window when he saw her coming. "It's a nice building, but you would never be able to get any of my clients in there," Ahmed explained. "I've been there with many people and, miraculously, the vacancies disappear every time."

David Hulchanski, a professor of housing policy at the University of Toronto, supported this conclusion after intensive interviews with 180 poor people seeking housing. "If you're poor and you have an accent and don't speak English too well, you're going to be excluded by some landlords," Hulchanski said. "But as soon as your skin is black, there's no comparison between the level and extent of discrimination" (Philip 2000).

Established immigrants can be among the most hostile urban inhabitants, tending in one study to emphasize a sharp distinction between "new" and "old" immigrants. In explaining his decision to move out of a multiethnic neighborhood in Montreal in which he had lived for over thirty years, a Greek factory worked said:

> Waiting in line at the bank, in front of me, was this Indian guy dressed in his native clothes, barefoot, and smelling as they all do. Now, thirty years ago, one never saw a Greek man walking in the streets in traditional costumes. These people have no respect for others, no sense of decency. They've destroyed the neighborhood. White families, the working people like us, they're moving to decent areas. These new immigrants are filthy, and what can we do? They're like that, it's their cultures, they'll never change, they just don't want to live like us. (Noivo 1998, 235)

With health care, visible minorities also can face a discriminatory response.

Health Care   Social researchers Joan Anderson and Sheryl Reimer Kirkham concluded that in spite of the national emphasis on the centrality of multiculturalism "[w]hat is striking today is the invisibility of so-called 'visible minority groups' within the public arena in Canada" (Anderson and Kirkham 1998, 251).

In the area of health care, this is a growing problem. Although Canada prides itself on an internationally recognized system of health care for all residents, severe spending cuts during the 1990s had a disproportionate impact on poor people of color (Randall 2002).

Drawing on a variety of studies, including their own research with both health-care users and practitioners, Anderson and Kirkham cited several ways that the combination of race, gender, and social class had a negative impact on visible minorities to produce unsatisfactory health-care outcomes:

■ Patients who speak neither English nor French will often find that communication with medical providers is difficult or impossible, seriously impeding the passage of information and therefore treatment of a disease or injury.

■ Many health-care programs schedule clinic hours that make it difficult for members of some groups to attend. Those encountering problems are primarily people who do not have the privilege of taking time off from work (with pay)—a situation most frequently found among immigrants, particularly women, who are paid only for the hours they work and sorely need the money. Getting to a clinic during set hours can also be difficult because of the need to coordinate one's arrival with taking care of children and/or bringing along an interpreter, who is often a family member or friend likely to lose pay for taking time off during work. Clearly, the more complicated the details of an individual's life, the greater the challenge a rigid clinical schedule represents.

■ Even when patients from other societies overcome such practical issues, they can encounter cultural barriers. Instructional styles and material may not be geared to them, and their frameworks for meaning and interpretation may differ significantly from those of the health professionals supplying care. As one provider explained, "I feel there are a lot of professional people, they have their own cultural superiority sense, and this has done a lot of harm to the relationship between the care people and people being cared for . . . I dare not tell you some bad habits I have." Another health-care server added, "I think that a fair number of people of colour communities perceive that they can't get decent health care from the dominant community because there's just so many things they perceive that the current medical model doesn't understand and accept" (Anderson and Kirkham 1998, 253).

■ It is difficult or impossible for frontline health professionals, who tend to be women in such roles as nurses, occupational therapists, and physiotherapists, to address the kinds of problems just described because they are powerless to establish basic policies. As one physician explained, "It's not a health care system, it's a medical industry, and that's all it is. It's got some applications of some business principles, but there is no sense of greater social responsibility or accountability" (Anderson and Kirkham 1998, 254)

Such a criticism has been directed against the American health-care system, but it might carry more weight in Canada, where a multiculturalist outlook is more prevalent.

Because gender is often a factor in dealing with health care and housing, it is the focus for the next topic. As this topic unfolds, one might keep in mind the possibility that the Canadian emphasis on multiculturalism offers ethnic groups more leverage, particularly male family members in relation to female family members, for enforcing traditional ways than occurs within American ethnic groups.

Gender-Related Challenges   It is unquestionable that in Canadian society female members of racial minorities as well as males face complicated, often difficult adjustment. For instance, women belonging to visible minorities entering the highly competitive Toronto job market can find that to succeed they might need to forsake their group's cultural standards and practices. In a study of South Asian (Indian) community workers associated with immigrant centers, one respondent explained that

> South Asian women are forced to give up their own tradition. They have to cut their hair . . . [and] change their dress, especially the women who wear saris. [When such a woman] comes to me . . . I have to tell her as a counselor, you don't put the red dot on, you can't wear a sari and go to work. (Agnew 1996)

Such women, this respondent suggested, have been located in two different worlds, and while they might want to preserve their traditional sense of self, the demands of mainstream society have been opposing that practice. She added, "We don't know which direction to take and what's the best solution" (Agnew 1996).

As South Asian women in Toronto have encountered such upheaval, Jamaican women have often found the prospects of life in that city more comfortable than back on the island. In Jamaica women were often considered subservient to men, expected to be full-time homemakers while men were breadwinners and otherwise free to live a highly independent life outside the home. Although many Jamaican women arrived as domestic workers, some have become white-collar employees. Often their jobs are better paid and more satisfying than those for men, whose fit with the current job market is often less effective. Men's level of depression is often greater as they find themselves subservient not only within the general society but also within their own households, where wives' and girl friends' income is often substantially greater.

Meanwhile, living in Canada and developing economic independence, Jamaican women have changed their standards of what they seek in a man. Most would like to have a husband or boyfriend who is communicative, supportive, effective as a father, and helpful around the house. Locating such an individual is difficult enough for young women, but those in their forties or older often find few such Jamaican men available for long-term relationships. As one woman explained:

> We would love to find that. It's a hope, it's like a dream. When you come across two or three who have those characteristics, it's wonderful, because they're very far and few between. However, in the Caribbean I grew up in, that characteristic was there. It was lost somewhere along the way between leaving the Caribbean and coming here. (Billson 1995, 154)

In Vancouver, Chinese Canadian women also struggle with conflicting cultural standards affecting work and domestic issues. Many come from well-established families and have the opportunity to pursue high-level careers, but as women of Chinese ancestry they often expect subtle discriminations from various sources. A university student majoring in social work had wanted to become a lawyer but had been warned that it would be "really hard" to get business as a Chinese woman lawyer. She explained:

> First of all, Caucasians might not trust you. It doesn't matter whether you're a man or a woman, but because you're Chinese maybe you don't get the business. If you're a Chinese woman lawyer, it's even harder, because the Chinese don't trust you—they don't trust women as much as men! (Billson 1995, 285–86)

Another hurdle Chinese Canadian women face is the frequent family expectation that they will marry young and have children. Most younger women will either delay marriage or work only part-time once children arrive. Many seek partners who will help them balance the demands of career and family. One woman explained that her husband would not prevent her from pursuing a career "because he's trying to be the modern supportive person," but added that both he and her father would question her choices. "He'd say, 'Hmm, she didn't put me top on the list of priorities.' Being a good wife or girlfriend should come first" (Billson 1995, 291).

Women in other Canadian ethnic communities confront a similar struggle. A respondent from a Greek neighborhood in Calgary discussed the situation women encounter growing up in a tradition where men have been socialized to believe they are superior—so-called Greek princes.

> I have felt it all of my life, although I may say that on the surface they seem to have changed, especially the Canadian Greek. But I don't believe it for a minute. I have engaged in intellectual battles with the most educated of them, and no matter what you talk about, it is always in the back of their minds, you know it is. It's the thought that no matter how educated you might be, how many degrees you may hold, or how intelligent and successful you are, you are still "only" a Greek woman. (Panagakos 2000)

Nonrecognition for mainstream accomplishments is one barrier women from various ethnic groups can face. They also must confront the reality that in Canada they often lack the supports they received in their traditional settings. Consider South Asian women's current vulnerability to violence. In their traditional communities, a woman whose husband beat her could turn to one of his female relatives, asking her to intervene and stop the mistreatment or face a serious loss of reputation. One research subject indicated that such a protection no longer exists in Canada, "where everyone is on his own, where even husbands and wives are at war with each other. Practically, a woman who doesn't work is totally at the mercy of her husband and society" (Agnew 1996).

This situation emphasizes the role of social networks, which are important for survival and mobility as well as for emotional support. Women who are people of color and/or recently arrived immigrants appear to be best off when they proceed to assess their location in society, figuring out what combination of contacts they need to pursue in order to establish themselves psychologically, economically, and socially in an increasingly complex and competitive Canadian society.

In the modern Canadian context, gender-related challenges have received modest public attention, but the issue of employment equity has been both publicized and controversial.

Employment Equity

In 1986 the Employment Equity Act became a federal law in Canada, stating that its purpose was "to achieve equality in the workplace, and to correct the conditions of disadvantage in employment experienced by designated groups" (Henry and Tator 1996, 96). Those groups include women, Aboriginal people, and visible minorities. The law applied to private companies and governmental organizations and agencies with one hundred employees or more and starting in June 1988 required employers to file an annual report with the Canada Employment and Immigration Commission.

A distinct difference between Canada's employment equity and the United States' affirmative action has been that Canada legislated the policy whereas the American federal government only implemented it informally, never passing laws to legitimize the practice. The Canadian approach seems to have been quite effective.

After the employment equity law's first decade of existence, the proportion of visible minorities in the labor force doubled, from about 6 percent in 1986 to 12 percent in 1996. Indications were that the private sector raised its representation more than did the public-service organizations (John Samuels & Associates 1997).

In spite of the improvement, visible minorities have expressed the view that racial discrimination has remained prevalent in the workplace. A study of public-service employees and managers listed such criticisms as the following:

- The widespread failure to include visible-minority representation in hiring boards.
- Difficulty in obtaining information on jobs and their requirements both for people coming into public service and for those seeking promotion within it.
- A reluctance to bring visible minorities into senior management, meaning that members of these groups do not see themselves represented in the top echelons and so as a result are likely to be discouraged from seeking such positions.
- An overall sense that from the top down management has not been committed to increasing visible minorities' representation and the accompanying realization that

there has been little or no training to elevate management's understanding of how to help make diversity a comfortable, effective condition in the modern economy (John Samuels & Associates 1997).

Not surprisingly, research has shown that in the work world visible minorities lag behind the general populace. A study released by the Canadian Race Relations Foundation concluded that although visible minorities have attained higher levels of education than white Canadians, they still suffer lower levels of employment and income; that Aboriginal peoples and visible minorities still have a harder time than others in finding employment in all regions of Canada; and that foreign-born visible minorities have the greatest difficulty finding what they consider suitable jobs, with only half of those with a college degree having high-skill jobs and overall earning 78 cents for every dollar earned by foreign-born white Canadians.

Several informants observed that the higher up the organizational ladder one looked, the lighter the skin color. As a member of one visible minority explained, "I look around and think—there's no chance of getting ahead. Of all the people in senior positions, no one is from an ethnic group" (Canadian Race Relations Foundation 2001).

Furthermore, opposition to employment equity has solidified. In 1995, driven by leadership from the New Democratic Party (DNP), the Ontario legislature launched its "commonsense revolution," passing a bill entitled "An Act to Repeal Job Quotas and to Restore Merit-Based Employment Practices." As anthropologists Frances Henry and Carol Tator indicated, "The government's rhetoric regarding employment equity was framed in racialized discourse. It used a vocabulary disassociated from both a historical context and contemporary social conditions" (Henry and Tator 1999, 104). This situation appears to demonstrate color-blind racism, where in the name of equal opportunity the majority declares that disadvantaged conditions linked to minority status play little or no role in affecting racial minorities' life chances.

Seeking to enlist public support, the NDP created a discourse based on code phrases that asserted claims manifesting color-blind racism:

- Employment equity is reverse discrimination.
- Fairness is best achieved by treating everyone the same.
- Employment equity ignores the merit principle.

Equality-seeking groups have challenged the Ontario government's authority to eliminate the Employment Equity Act, but the courts have ruled that it is a political action the provincial government has the right to implement. Encouraged by a public response that appears to support their "commonsense revolution," the DNP-led leadership has eliminated a number of other policies and programs, including the Anti-Racism Secretariat of the Ontario government, an agency responsible for overseeing antiracist policies and strategies for almost two decades (Henry and Tator 1999, 104–06).

While advocates of employment equity recognize that they face opposition not only in Ontario but throughout the country, widespread support exists for policies that could further its progress. Such policies could involve the following:

■ Maintenance of full employment and a tight job market, thereby encouraging or even compelling employers to acknowledge and recognize skills and invest in training. Evidence from the United States in the late 1990s suggested that with a high level of employment, benefits began to trickle down to poor urban minorities, starting to reduce the income gap between the poor and middle-class groups.

■ The development and implementation of workplace plans, representing cooperative efforts between employers and workers. Although the idea of employment equity has caught many Canadians' imagination, there has been legislative resistance in a number of provinces, with Ontario's counterlegislation the most salient case in point. In such an atmosphere, the initiation of workplace plans seems the most feasible place to begin the process (Jackson 2001).

For two reasons employment equity seems to be a promising policy. First, it focuses on an important, practical issue—namely, work and the income derived from it—for establishing people's place in the mainstream world. Second, as just indicated, the road to increased employment equity seems quite concretely marked, encouraging its advocates to focus in their workplace and then, if inclined like some of the participants in the upcoming Sociological Illustration, to extend themselves into a broader regional or national participation.

Beyond the issue of employment equity, Canada's multicultural mosaic has provided some interesting comparisons with the American pattern of racial and ethnic relations.

Conclusion

It seems helpful to review the principal points covered in this chapter. An important historical difference between the two countries is that whereas the United States originated with a single primary culture—namely, the English—Canada developed from two—the English and the French, providing a foundation for the nation's stronger interest in multiculturalism. Furthermore, Canada is a much smaller country, with its people of color heavily concentrated in a few major cities. There are no large urban ghettos, whose residents appear locked into a multigenerational pattern of poverty. Compared to the United States, therefore, Canada has a racial heritage in which a small proportion of racial minorities are disadvantaged in social-class position.

In addition, Canada maintains the standard of a multicultural mosaic. It seems to be a society with a more collective, group-oriented tradition where racial and ethnic groups will find their rights more clearly outlined than in the United States. The fruits of that advantage have been most apparent in the legislation involving both multiculturalism and employment equity but might also reveal themselves with issues like gender-role relations and housing.

The comparison between Canada and the United States can serve as a gateway to the complexity of the racial and ethnic confrontations in other countries, where dramatically different schemes often prevail. Brazil, for instance, offers a convincing veneer of racial harmony, which obscures long-entrenched disciminatory practices against blacks. South Africa has undergone a rapid transformation from a white-supremacist political structure to a full-fledged democracy, where sharp economic differences among the major racial groups

S O C I O L O G I C A L   I L L U S T R A T I O N

The Canadian Labor Movement and Employment Equity

The leaders of the Canadian labor movement embrace the idea that the overall elevation of society should begin with employment equity—decently paid, satisfying, sustainable jobs for all workers. To promote this goal, the labor movement has produced sources of information on the topic—the development of course curricula, the production of audiovisual resources, and the creation of workshops, all for both workers and management. In the Canadian Auto Workers (CAW), for instance, the provision of courses and workshops reached over 4,000 workers, giving them the chance to learn about, discuss, and evaluate employment equity.

Organizers find that many white workers are ambivalent about the subject, often wanting to be fair but accepting the color-blind-racist slogans developed by the Ontario government and other powerful, influential organizations. Susan Spratt, a CAW official, said, "Reaction is negative because of insecurity and right wing backlash. Instead of being against banks and corporations, we're mad at people of colour" (Das Gupta 1998, 326–27).

Because many white union members have feared that visible minorities would encroach on their jobs, the progress of employment equity within unions has been modest, particularly in leadership positions. For instance, Harminder Magon, a member of the Canadian Union of Public Employees (CUPE), indicated that his organization's most important challenge is to build representation of visible minorities and Aboriginal people on its national executive board. Progress is slow. Magon explained,

In Toronto, members of the Hotel Employees and Restaurant Employees International Union, who are strong supporters of employment equity, leave the Sheraton Centre following a four-hour "study session," where participants considered the possibility of a strike.

"Right now, there is one black sister out of fourteen" (Das Gupta 1998, 327)

Nonetheless, indications of change have been occurring. In November 2000 at the Aboriginal/ Workers of Colour Conference, most of the 122 delegates present were in leadership positions in their own local unions. Jenny Ahn, the president of CAW Local 40, applauded this outcome and stated, "I think that . . . we will take on the struggle of making sure that there is representation [of people of color] within our union, whether it is elected positions or appointed positions" (CAW/TCA Canada 2000).

Once in authoritative positions, minority leaders face challenges promoting employment equity, sometimes finding opponents seek to subtly undermine their efforts. In 1990 Bev Johnson, a union official at the Ontario Public Service Employees Union (OPSEU), spearheaded the creation of the twelve-person Race Relations and Minority Rights Committee, which was formed to curtail or eliminate discrimination in the workplace. While not outrightly condemning the efforts of this committee, opponents declared that its activities should be controlled by elected groups at the individual worksites. With people of color's modest representation in OPSEU's locals, this policy certainly would have restricted their efforts to fight discrimination and promote employment equity.

One subtle, normally undeclared strategy that seems to be unfolding in some unions is a form of tokenism, in which all positions dealing with equity-related issues are held for visible minorities and Aboriginal people. Such an approach can keep people of color from sharing in general policy setting for union activities, which could significantly impact both their influence and the growth of employment equity. Bev Johnson of OPSEU said: [People of color] are not in the meat and potatoes of the union . . . same thing with grievances . . . not too many staff reps of colour in all unions" (Das Gupta 1998, 329).

Visible minorities promoting employment equity often find subtle resistance apparent in the treatment they receive, particularly when moving into leadership positions. The top union leadership is likely to restrict their access to travel funds or office supplies and communicate with them minimally, isolating them from important networking opportunities. Meanwhile, white colleagues engaged in less controversial projects don't face such constraints. Over time such treatment can be discouraging, even alienating. Bev Johnson explained, "On paper, we're progressing. In actual fact, you get removed, you can't go to the Convention or are taken off a committee" (Das Gupta 1998, 329).

All in all, union activists seeking employment equity have characterized their efforts as filled with contradiction. They mentioned that union leadership issued strong statements on behalf of employment equity and antiracist activity and that it was profoundly empowering to reach thousands of their fellow workers through the channels their unions provided. On the other hand, they also cited the constant constraints on bringing visible minorities into leadership positions as well as personal harassment, lack of colleague and leadership support, and the danger of burnout. The election of a Conservative government in Ontario has been a major setback in their work, directly opposing efforts to promote the interests of people of color (Das Gupta 1998, 333–34).

Yet a look at the websites for CAW, OPSEU, the Coalition of Black Trade Unionists, and other selected unions demonstrates that they remain active in seeking employment equity, possibly less for themselves than for their children.

still prevail. In recent years Rwanda, the Sudan, and Bosnia have experienced brutal ethnic confrontations killing thousands, and at this writing Middle Eastern countries, most notably Iraq and Israel, are in the throes of violent ethnic struggle.

Nonetheless, Canada offers a moderate, provocative contrast with the United States, and looking toward the future one might wonder whether the standard of the multicultural mosaic will unfold in new and unexpected ways. Will employment equity make significant advances? Will some currently unanticipated initiative championing visible minorities' rights move to the forefront? And how, if at all, will American racial and ethnic relations be influenced by Canadian actions?

DISCUSSION QUESTIONS

1. Examine the history of Canadian immigration, indicating detailed features that were similar to and different from the American pattern.

2. Evaluate the assertion that for racial and ethnic relations Canada has pursued an ethnic pluralism model and the United States an assimilationist pattern.

3. Summarize central features of housing for various Canadian ethnic groups.

4. List and describe major challenges visible minorities face in the Canadian health-care system.

5. Address the most provocative point you found in the subsection about gender-related challenges.

6. If you belonged to a union or some other work-related organization and a major part of your job involved promoting employment equity, how would you go about it? What do you think would be the major challenges? In the course of the discussion, indicate whether you feel such activity is a productive course of action.

BIBLIOGRAPHY

Agnew, Vijay. 1996. "Women's Work with Women: The South Asian Context." *Polyphony.* www. collections.ic.gc.ca/magic/mt30.html.

Anderson, Joan, and Sheryl Reimer Kirkham. 1998. "Constructing Nation: The Gendering and Racializing of the Canadian Health Care System," pp. 242–61 in Veronica Strong-Boang, Sherrill Grace, Avigail Eisenberg, and Joan Anderson (eds.), *Painting the Maple: Essays on Race, Gender, and the Construction of Canada.* Vancouver: UBC Press.

Artibise, Alan F. J. 1991. "Divided City: The Immigrant in Winnipeg Society, 1874–1921," pp. 360–91 in Gilbert A. Stelter and Alan F. J. Artibise (eds.), *The Canadian City: Essays in Urban and Social History,* rev. ed. Ottawa: Carleton University Press.

Balakrishnan, T. R. 2000. "Residential Segregation and Canada's Ethnic Groups," pp. 121–36 in Madeline A. Kalbach and Warren E. Kalbach (eds.), *Perspectives on Ethnicity in Canada: A Reader.* Toronto: Harcourt Canada.

Bibby, Reginald W. 1990. *Mosaic Madness: The Poverty and Potential of Life in Canada.* Toronto: Stoddart.

Billson, Janet Mancini. 1995. *Keepers of the Culture: The Power of Tradition in Women's Lives.* New York: Lexington Books.

Boyd, Monica. 2000. "Ethnicity and Immigrant Offspring," pp. 137–54 in Madeline A. Kalbach and Warren E. Kalbach (eds.), *Perspectives on Ethnicity in Canada: A Reader.* Toronto: Harcourt Canada.

Boyko, John. 1995. *Last Steps to Freedom: The Evolution of Canadian Racism.* Winnipeg: Watson and Dwyer.

Canadian Race Relations Foundation. 2001. "Unequal Access: A Canadian Profile of Racial Differences in Education, Employment and Income." www.crr.ca.

Christiano, Kevin J. 1990. "Federalism as a Canadian Ideal: The Civic Rationalism of Pierre Elliott Trudeau." Quoted in Reginald W. Bibby, *Mosaic Madness: The Poverty and Potential of Life in Canada.* Toronto: Stoddart. 1990.

CAW/TCA Canada. 2000. "Aboriginal/Workers of Colour Conference." www.caw.ca/news/videonews/recent/ Aboriginal-Workers_of_Colour_Conference.asp.

Cumming, Alister. 2001. "Second Language Education in Schools in Canada." www.cal.org/ericcll/countries. html.

Das Gupta, Tania. 1998. "Anti-Racism and the Organized Labour Movement," pp. 315–34 in Vic Satzewich (ed.), *Racism and Social Inequality in Canada: Concepts, Controversies & Strategies of Resistance.* Toronto: Thompson Educational Publishing.

Goldberg, Michael A., and John Mercer. 1986. *The Myth of the North American City: Continentalism Challenged.* Vancouver: University of British Columbia Press.

Henry, Frances, and Carol Tator. 1999. "State Policy and Practices as Racialized Discourse: Multiculturalism, the Charter, and Employment Equity," pp. 88–115 in Peter S. Li (ed.), *Race and Ethnic Relations in Canada,* 2nd ed. Don Mills, Ontario: Oxford University Press.

Jackson, Andrew. 2001. "Poverty and Racism." *Perception.* Spring. www.ccsd.ca/perception/244/racism.htm.

John Samuels and Associates. 1997. "Visible Minorities and the Public Service of Canada." www.chrc-ccdp.ca/ee/vismin/contents.asp?1=e.

Kalbach, Warren E. 2000. "Ethnic Diversity: Canada's Changing Cultural Mosaic," pp. 59–72 in Madeline A. Kalbach and Warren E. Kalbach (eds.), *Perspectives on Ethnicity in Canada: A Reader.* Toronto: Harcourt Canada.

Kymlicka, Will. 1997. "Immigrants, Multiculturalism and Canadian Citizenship." www.pearson-shoyama.ca/Hot Button/immigran.htm.

Kymlicka, Will. 1998. *Finding Our Way: Rethinking Ethnocultural Relations in Canada.* New York: Oxford University Press.

Lower, Arthur R. 1958. *Canadians in the Making.* Toronto: Longmans, Green.

Nicholson, Murray. 1991. "The Other Toronto: Irish Catholics in a Victorian City 1850–1900," pp. 328–59 in Gilbert A. Stelter and Alan F. J. Artibise (eds.), *The Canadian City: Essays in Urban and Social History,* rev. ed. Ottawa: Carleton University Press.

Noivo, Edite. 1998. "Neither 'Ethnic Heroes' nor 'Racial Villains': Inter-Minority Group Racism," pp. 223–41 in Vic Satzewich (ed.), *Racism and Social Inequality in Canada: Concepts, Controversies and Strategies of Resistance.* Toronto: Thompson Educational Publishing.

Panagakos, Anastasia N. 2000. "Revisiting the Immigrant Family: The Impact of Transnational Migration on Family and Marriage in the Greek Diaspora." Annual American Antropological Association Meeting. www.uweb.ucsb.edu/~panagako/notesdecember1.html.

Philip, Margaret. 2000. "Poor? Coloured? Then It's No Vacancy." *Toronto Globe and Mail.* July 18. www.geocities.com/CapitolHill/6174/povyrace.html.

Randall, Vernellia R. 2002. "Health and Racism in Canada." http://academic/udayton.edu/health/06world/canada01.htm.

Reitz, Jeffrey G., and Raymond Breton. 1998. "Prejudice and Discrimination in Canada and the United States: A Comparison," pp. 47–68 in Vic Satzewich (ed.), *Racism & Social Inequality in Canada: Concepts, Controversies & Strategies of Resistance.* Toronto: Thompson Educational Publishing.

Statistics Canada, 2001. 2003. www.statcan.ca/english/Pgdb/demo26a.htm. www.statcan.ca/english/Pgdb/demo50a.htm.

Weinfeld, Morton, and Lori A. Wilkinson. 1999. "Immigration, Diversity, and Minority Communities," pp. 55–87 in Peter S. Li (ed.), *Race and Ethnic Relations in Canada,* 2nd ed. Don Mills, Ontario: Oxford University Press.

10 Urban Racial and Ethnic Relations: The Road Ahead?

History and Biography Briefly Revisited
Some Potentially Productive Initiatives
   Two Major Reforms

Two More Modest Proposals
   Everyday Interactive Investment
Final Commentary

About a century ago, the often contentious leading figures in sociology agreed that both the social bonds and the conflicts associated with ethnicity and race were preindustrial qualities and would rapidly recede in the industrial world (Bell-Fialkoff 1994; Blauner 1972, 3–4). One evening while my race and ethnicity class was divided into discussion groups, I pondered that conclusion as bits of dialogue drifted my way: a middle-aged woman angrily condemning the Bush administration's attack on Iraq as the latest illustration of the nation's harsh, often violent international policy toward people of color; a young man analyzing Malcolm X's impact on a white public never previously exposed to such fiery, race-laden rhetoric. For most participants it was late in a long day, and yet they were animatedly involved in the exchanges.

Clearly, the issues and problems associated with race and ethnicity have not disappeared, and as in the class just described, many people remain interested and concerned. In fact, my sense is that nurturing people's interest in these topics can widen the gateway leading toward the examination of various other national and international issues involving equal opportunity. After reviewing the book's principal conclusions, I offer several suggestions about productive steps that can supply improvements.

History and Biography Briefly Revisited

A priority for American society has been the work ethic and economic success—an outlook that initially linked to a sense of heavenly salvation but ultimately centered on occupational activity.

The importance of economic success was a distinct impetus for accepting newcomers to cities—first, immigrants from various European countries, at the turn of the twentieth century blacks from the South, and in recent decades increasing numbers from Latin America, Asia, and Africa. Many new arrivals have been limited to menial jobs for low pay and have often encountered discriminatory treatment in various areas. Historically, within a generation or two, a significant proportion of most groups were able to advance occupationally and residentially, finding better-paying jobs and as a consequence moving into more desirable mainstream housing and receiving in the process various educational, economic, and social benefits. Over time African Americans, who have been subjected to sustained discrimination in housing and suffered myriad consequences from their isolation, have been the most distinct exception.

In current urban America, many citizens, most notably whites, reside in what Mary Waters has called a "costless community," where they can choose when to acknowledge or to discard their ethnicity and can practice color-blind racism by ignoring or minimizing the adverse conditions that continue to put large numbers of people of color at a disadvantage.

The outcomes that color-blind racism denies are apparent in the racialized social system that we examined through the chapters:

- In housing, some racial minorities, especially blacks, continue to suffer the impact of discriminatory conditions, in which such historical factors as racially restrictive covenants as well as current racist practices have limited their residential locations and as a result have had a negative effect on schooling, jobs, and the pursuit of mainstream opportunities. At present it appears that many whites are fearful of inner-city blacks, strongly desiring to reside far away from them.

- In examining work we saw that this country has maintained an ethnic succession that has benefited members of those groups who arrived early or have had such advantages as membership in an ethnic enclave. Blacks, who as a rule have not been beneficiaries of these assets, have often continued to be pronounced victims of discrimination in the three stages of the current job process reviewed in the text.

- In politics the ethnic and racial range of elected urban officials has steadily broadened over time, but regardless of who fills elected offices, many American cities remain in the grip of the pro-growth framework and self-help ideology, making big-business interests the priority and doing little to improve the conditions of disadvantaged, largely minority citizens.

- In health care, homelessness, education, and family issues, racial minorities continue to be disproportionately disadvantaged—realities that are well documented in the text's analysis of the racialized nature of such issues as the following: minorities' relations with their health-care providers, the composition of homeless people, and public expenditure on primary and secondary education.

- In Canada, while ethnic and racial relations provide many historical and current parallels with those in the United States, that nation's cultural approach has been more ethnically pluralistic than assimilationist, making it likely that their citizens more readily than Americans support a minority-attuned issue like employment equity.

TABLE 10.1   Illustrations of Minorities' Widely Unperceived Disadvantages

Macrosociological: Development of American Cities	Examples
Fundamental influence of historical conditions	Systematic restriction of blacks' residential location in northern and midwestern cities, establishing the modern ghettos
Underlying contribution of social class, encouraging a victim-blaming approach	Invidious comparison between rates of mainstream success for African Americans and selected Asian Americans, ignoring various social-class advantages accruing to some Asian Americans
Self-fulfilling realities having an impact on minority groups	Widespread use of standardized testing, which heavily favors children with mainstream contacts and thus "confirms" isolated minorities' intellectual deficiencies
Deceptive system "improvements," which fail to address the conditions promoting basic inequalities	Federally developed policy for the delivery of the welfare-to-work program

Microsociological: Location in a Racialized Social System	Examples
An array of race- and poverty-linked disadvantages	Poor minorities' largely hidden vulnerability to homelessness, deficient health care, ineffective school performance, or unemployment
Limited access to the process of accumulating various types of capital	Deficient social capital such as exclusion from gatekeepers' social networks; for housing; limited financial capital such as welfare-to-work clients' often impeded access to jobs.
Psychological impact	Large classes, chronically underpaid teachers, and other debilitating conditions leading to a classroom setting that can encourage students to give up the pursuit of formal education

Throughout the book, readers have encountered a steady flow of situations that illustrate the types of issues summarized in this table.

Often, as Table 10.1 indicates, majority groups fail to see adverse circumstances impinging on minorities' lives. In the upcoming section, discussion focuses on some means of addressing minorities' disadvantages.

Some Potentially Productive Initiatives

Moving from the macrosociological to the microsociological level, we examine a number of initiatives that potentially address the kinds of conditions discussed throughout this book.

Two Major Reforms

Both of these topics center on financial capital, involving material sources individuals can use to produce other valued capital. The first topic is the development of living-wage initiatives, and the second considers the possibility of dismantling ghettoes.

A number of living-wage proposals have been established, with mixed results as these three cases indicate:

■ In Chicago the City Council voted unanimously to increase the city's living wage, originally set in 1998, from $7.60 to $9.05 per hour, with the new standard starting in January 2003.

■ In 2001 the Santa Monica City Council passed an ordinance mandating hourly wages of $10.50 with health care or $12.25 without it for city contractors and also for selected city businesses. Opponents of the measure gathered enough signatures to force a referendum, and outspending the living-wage supporters three to one, prevailed in a close election.

■ In November 2002 Oregon voters passed a ballot initiative raising the state's living wage from $6.50 to $6.90 an hour. As with Chicago's living wage, Oregon's is adjustable for inflation based on the Consumer Price Index (Mitchell 2002).

Along with living-wage initiatives, some advocates for racial minorities have called for the general upgrading of lower-level jobs. Sociologist Pierrette Hondagneu-Sotelo, for instance, has proposed various measures that would improve domestic employment, which has become a major job source for many Latino/a and Caribbean immigrants. The measures include bringing domestic work into conformity with state regulations by providing basic protections involving wages and hours, particularly overtime demands on live-in employees; and establishing a reasonable working context, including a fairly comfortable working schedule, decent food and living conditions, and dignified, pleasant relations with the employing family (Hondagneu-Sotelo 2001, 211–18).

Whereas living-wage initiatives and related strategies develop at the local or state levels, another proposal would require federal subsidy—a major effort to dismantle the nation's urban ghettos. In *A Way Out: America's Ghettos and the Legacy of Racism,* legal scholar Owen Fiss proposed that because black ghettos have become self-perpetuating sites of poverty, crime, family fragmentation, violence, and hopelessness, the federal government should allot $50 billion a year to relocate their inhabitants to more affluent, primarily white communities, where preliminary projects have produced such benefits as better health, more advancement in education, and improved job prospects (Fiss 2003).

Agreeing about the seriousness of the ghetto issue, commentators nonetheless raised various criticisms: notably, that on the very unlikely prospect that the government allotted this level of funding, the communities receiving the influx of newcomers have their own psychological and moral pathologies (Coles 2003) and are unlikely to be receptive to an influx of poor African American families (Orfield 2003; Thompson 2003); that such a proposal can produce negative impacts for both those who move (Hochschild 2003) and those in the receiving community (Sleeper 2003); and finally, that in spite of the difficult conditions of inner-city life, a variety of established churches, community organizations, clubs, and social networks remain viable and should serve as the basis for a revitalized, democratically driven empowering process for those residents who choose to or must stay put (Meares 2003; Thompson 2003).

Because of such widespread opposition as well as the prohibitive cost, ghetto dismantling does not appear to be in the imminent American future. What does seem both possible and productive is more modest ventures such as the Gautreaux Demonstration Project or the Move to Opportunity Program, where Housing and Urban Development (HUD) supplied subsidies allowing scattered numbers of black public-housing residents to move to predominantly white suburbs. The results demonstrated that the participants who moved had greater success in education and employment than a comparable group who remained in the ghetto (Fiss 2003, 39–43; Massey 2001, 427; Rosenbaum and Popkin 1991).

In line with the HUD initiative, the following suggestions are fairly modest in conception and scope.

Two More Modest Proposals

In earlier discussions it has been apparent that various minority groups are disadvantaged in both job preparation and educational attainment. These topics focus on human capital, which involves the acquisition of skills and abilities to obtain material success. Although difficulties in both of these areas can be the result of accumulated disadvantages in the racialized system and thus are difficult to resolve, once again it is possible to propose some practical steps that can help to alleviate the problems.

Reviews of the most productive experiments to move people from welfare to work have reached some distinct, revealing conclusions:

■ The move into the work world often does not follow a simple progression. Agencies and organizations assisting in the transition must recognize that if they are going to help individuals be successful in the process, they need to assist in addressing clients' various difficulties, including extensive treatment for substance abuse and illness and the location of fairly low-cost, reliable child care.

■ Effective job-training and placement programs are attuned to both the demands of the labor market and employers' specific requirements. As we noted in Chapter 5, employers not only seek workers with the requisite abilities but also want employees who are punctual, efficient, cooperative, and receptive to improving their current skills.

■ Programs that focus on prompt job placement may have effective short-term outcomes, but in the long run they can prove counterproductive, failing to provide the educational or training foundation to sustain self-sufficiency (Albelda 2001; Schorr 1997, 176–77; Zuckerman 2000).

Clearly, effective schooling is an essential form of human capital for individuals' advancement in the postindustrial urban world. At the end of a lengthy article reviewing testing gaps comparing white versus black and Hispanic children, Ronald J. Ferguson (2001, 384–85) concluded that over the past thirty years testing gaps have narrowed, but that the differences remain significant. What is needed, he suggested, is a more responsive culture committed to closing the gap, featuring teachers and parents increasingly committed to that goal.

Like the previous suggestions provided in this chapter, the following one could benefit from public subsidy, particularly for poor students in educationally underresourced areas—students who could most decisively benefit from a practice that has already been widely used.

Many Asian American children, whose academic performance is often well above average, have been attending "cram schools," which have had a long tradition in the Far East. Around New York City, starting in the third grade and continuing through high school, hundreds of Korean and Chinese American students along with increasing numbers from other groups attend these private tutoring programs, whose signs dot storefronts announcing themselves with such names as "Harvard Academy," "Ivy Prep," and "Elite Academy." Although the programs typically prepare students for college-admission tests and for entrance into the city's specialized science high schools, they are more focused on developing effective study habits than enhancing test-taking abilities.

Cram schools tend to be less expensive than the more prevalent after-school study centers, thus making them more accessible to a wider range of income groups. Yet the quality of instruction tends to be good; they use trained teachers who usually are employed in local area schools. Their growing popularity is apparent at a program like Elite Academy, where about a quarter of the children were neither Korean nor Chinese but Indian, Greek, Hispanic, and African American.

Some parents welcome the dominant presence of Asian American students. Dimitra Pangopoulos, a Greek American, explained, "You go to the library, those are the kids that are there." He added, "They're the ones interested in learning" (Luo 2003, B7). Norma Murray, who is African American, spent three summers bringing her three children to the school. "Some kids don't need it," she said. "My kids need a little push, a little shove" (Luo 2003, B1).

Elite's most potent claim to success is that every year it sends about 110 students to leading city high schools and its placement of students in prestigious colleges is well above the city average. While not liking the concept of cramming, I can concede that if such programs help students overcome their current skill disadvantages and prepare them for the educational challenges ahead, then they can prove useful. In addition, their modest cost is a distinct asset.

My own experience with an inner-city math-tutoring program suggests how helpful additional academic assistance can be. Whether it is cram courses or some other arrangement, the compelling goal might be that in our nation's diversified educational settings, competent authorities should assess the major local learning deficiencies and then either inside or outside the regular program provide tutoring help to improve students' basic skills so that they can continue to advance effectively through the educational system. Such programming should occur at public expense so that those too poor to pay will not be denied the critical opportunity.

To this point the proposals offered, whether grandiose or modest, have been planned initiatives. One of the interesting realities about racial and ethnic relations is that many important, unanticipated encounters can also occur.

Head Start, which has emphasized intense contacts between staff members and children, has been a successful, federally funded program, helping thousands of poor children like this Asian American boy working on a coloring project confront their poverty-associated educational disadvantage.

Everyday Interactive Investment

In the course of daily events, many individuals have the chance to assist others, including members of racial and ethnic minorities. The focus here is on social capital, which is the ability to secure advantage through the organizations and social networks to which individuals belong, as well as cultural capital, which involves the development of a sense of how the social world works, particularly a competence at engaging in the practices necessary to move toward mainstream success.

For poor minorities a dominant reality can be isolation, a situation in which the inhabitants of racialized inner-city areas tend to lack access to useful social and cultural capital. A single individual can make an enormous difference in overcoming this isolation. Consider the case of Brent Staples, who eventually obtained a Ph.D. in psychology and became a well-known, talented editorial writer for the *New York Times*. As a high-school senior, however, he was drifting, unclear of his future and with no plans for attending college. Then he met Eugene Sparrow, a sociologist teaching at a local college, who was impressed by this young black man's intelligence. Sparrow, who was also black, inquired about Staples's future and eventually suggested he attend his college, which was seeking to increase its black enrollment. Staples resisted, saying he was a secretarial student, that he had not taken the SATs, and that besides his family had no money.

> Sparrow frowned and gestured at me with his cigarette.
>   "Come on, baby. Hear me out. Listen to me, man." The next words he underscored heavily. *"Never mind about the money."*
>   By then I was clinging to every syllable.
>   "And never mind about the College Boards," he said. "You can take them in the fall."
>   He took out a notebook and scribbled the name and number of Vincent Lindsley, the director of admissions.
>   "Call him. Tell him I told you to call."
> I did, from home, the next day.
>   I wanted this badly. The future that Sparrow had suggested was the only one that would do." (Staples 1994, 160–61)

Although such individual success stories are significant and uplifting, the impact is more far-reaching when organizations develop policies that promote such individualized assistance. As we noted earlier, productive job-placement programs contain staff who recognize that they must be flexible in enhancing their clients' needs for social and cultural capital. As Sister Mary Paul said of her successful neighborhood program for poor minorities in Brooklyn's Sunset Park, "No one ever says, this may be what you need, but it's not part of my job to help you get it" (Schorr 1997, 5). That same diffuse orientation to addressing children's diverse needs and problems was apparent in the successful New Beginnings program discussed in Chapter 8.

As the following situation illustrates, the problem is that often the majority-group individuals who could provide such capital are not attuned to that reality. Paul Kivel (2002) offered two hypothetical dialogues between a white teacher and a Latino student. In each case the student was furious and frustrated, telling the teacher that even though he was fully qualified for a computer-programming job, he was rejected, clearly in his mind the object of blatant discrimination. In the first instance, the teacher, though seeking to help, downplayed the recruiter's response by suggesting that the student either misunderstood or was too sensitive. When the student rejected the explanation, indicating that with whites in spite of "talk about equal opportunity, . . . it's the same old shit" (Kivel 2002, 129), the teacher ended up defending the job recruiter and himself, making his defensiveness readily apparent and further alienating the student. In contrast, in the second situation, the teacher was not only sympathetic but also receptive to the student's evaluation, and after asking him what action he wanted to take agreed to assist him in assessing the prospect of challenging his rejection for the job.

My guess is that many white people have found themselves in crossroads situations like this one, in which they feel reluctant to get involved in a potentially volatile situation requiring them to side with a minority-group individual against a fellow white person. However, if the individual in question is willing to push carefully ahead, he or she can provide invaluable assistance in showing the wronged person how to combat racism and perhaps also be rewarded with a revitalized insight into how such situations can move toward a positive outcome. I call this a crossroads situation because the majority-group member's reluctance or willingness to supply cultural capital—in this case, knowledge about the process of pro-ducing a job-discrimination complaint—can also significantly affect the other's future trust or mistrust about whites' likelihood of taking discriminatory incidents seriously.

By refining their own cultural capital, teachers and other hands-on professionals can interact with their students or clients in ways that can elevate those individuals and help them advance themselves. An earlier discussion of education indicated that effective teach-ers realize that in order to reach children who have been educationally disadvantaged, they need to focus on communicating well with them, leading off by listening carefully. In work-ing with clients of varied backgrounds, particularly those with whom linguistic contact is difficult, sensitive social workers have learned that they are more effective if they improve certain communications skills, such as using the most simple terms possible, speaking loudly, avoiding slang, or using art therapy. One social worker who was inter-viewed indicated that the focus should be on developing effective communication, not dealing with a client deficient in English. She discussed a client who like her had learned English as an adult:

> I could see her going through the same struggle where she wasn't sure if she was clear with me or if I understood. I just kept trying, checking out with her that she understood, being honest with her if I didn't understand. We just struggled through it together. (Russell and White 2001, 82)

Perhaps "we" is the key word in that quotation. Instead of the social worker perceiv-ing herself as providing instruction, she embraced the reality that the two of them, the client and she, were working together toward a shared solution.

We have seen evidence of some small productive advances, but what's ahead for American race and ethnic relations?

Final Commentary

Occasionally in class I suggest to my students that we discuss the establishment of policies that could set the country on a more equitable path for the diverse population.

One issue that invariably receives attention is the nation's spending priorities. Partic-ipants note that as long as the flow of billions of dollars goes to war and occupation in Iraq, Afghanistan, and other countries, there will be only the most modest funding to address the many growing problems discussed in this and other chapters. It seems clear that in spite of political leaders' lip service to improving minorities' disadvantages, the overall commit-ment to champion any significant improvements is distinctly modest.

We classroom planners would divert a significant portion of that military funding into domestic projects, providing jobs for students and others who wanted to devote their lives, or at least a portion of their lives, to helping eliminate the kinds of disproportionately minority problems discussed in this book. It is hardly a new idea: In the 1930s a potent model was the Works Project Administration, which helped galvanize a national sense of people pulling together to address the nation's serious domestic problems. The ultimate goal would be distinctly inclusive: a better, safer, more pleasant, equitable, and healthier world for all citizens.

With dollars to disperse, our advisory group would earmark the bulk of funding for the programs that had already proved successful and that could detail specific deficiencies that impeded them from achieving greater success. Those might seem obvious requirements, but throughout this book I have indicated that funding often goes to groups that are well connected politically and whose leaders do a good public-relations job but have proved neither their commitment to nor their capacity for effectively addressing the challenges at hand.

Citizen interest exists for such a mobilization. Many colleagues with whom I talk report that students are animated in courses with subject matter involving race and ethnicity. They want to understand what is going on, and their involvement with the topics in their internships, jobs, and volunteer work is often highly motivated. Furthermore, as many of us can find when we get into community projects, there are extensive, often diverse individuals and groups whom one can encounter in productive projects, and in the course of events we can receive new insights and understandings about this constantly changing, interesting, and admittedly difficult world of unequal opportunity in which we now reside.

DISCUSSION QUESTIONS

1. After reading the first section of this chapter and thinking about the contents of this book, discuss its most memorable conclusion. Explain why you make the choice. It is possible that you have found nothing memorable, and if that's the case, then indicate why you feel that way.

2. If you could introduce two measures to improve the lives of poor minorities, what would they be?

3. Are you aware of situations in which interaction between members of different racial or ethnic groups has led to individuals improving their social or cultural capital?

4. Looking toward the future of American racial and ethnic relations, indicate two things: a major development you expect to occur and a major development you hope occurs.

BIBLIOGRAPHY

Albelda, Randy. 2001. "Fallacies of Welfare-to-Work Policies." *Annals of the American Academy of Political and Social Science.* 577 (September): 66–78.

Bell-Fialkoff, Andrew. 1994. "Ethnic Conflict," pp. 198–204 in John A. Kromkowski (ed.), *Race and Ethnic Relations 94/95,* 4th ed. Guilford, CT: Dushkin.

Blauner, Robert. 1972. *Racial Oppression in America.* New York: Harper & Row.

Coles, Robert. 2003. "Better Neighborhoods?" pp. 57–59 in Joshua Cohen, Jefferson Decker, and Joel Rogers (eds.), *A Way Out: America's Ghettos and the Legacy of Racism.* Princeton: Princeton University Press.

Ferguson, Ronald F. 2001. "Test-Score Trends Along Racial Lines, 1971 to 1996: Popular Culture and Community Academic Standards," pp. 348–90 in Neil J. Smelser, William Julius Wilson, and Faith Mitchell (eds.), *America Becoming: Racial Trends and Their Consequences,* vol. I. Wshington, DC: National Academy Press.

Fiss, Owen. 2003. "What Should Be Done for Those Left Behind?" pp. 3–43 in Joshua Cohen, Jefferson Decker, and Joel Rogers (eds.), *A Way Out: America's Ghettos and the Legacy of Racism.* Princeton: Princeton University Press.

Hochschild, Jennifer. 2003. "Creating Options," pp. 68–73 in Joshua Cohen, Jefferson Decker, and Joel Rogers (eds.), *A Way Out: America's Ghettos and the Legacy of Racism.* Princeton: Princeton University Press.

Hondagneu-Sotelo, Pierrette. 2001. *Doméstica: Immigrant Workers Cleaning and Caring in the Shadows of Affluence.* Berkeley and Los Angeles: University of California Press.

Kivel, Paul. 2002. "How White People Can Serve as Allies to People of Color in the Struggle to End Racism," pp. 127–35 in Paula S. Rothenberg (ed.), *White Privilege: Essential Readings on the Other Side of Racism.* New York: Worth.

Luo, Michael. 2003. "Taking Lessons from Another Culture." *New York Times.* (October 20): B1+.

Massey, Douglas. 2001. "Residential Segregation and Neighborhood Conditions in U.S.. Metropolitan Areas," pp. 391–434 in Neil J. Smelser, William Julius Wilson, and Faith Mitchell (eds.), *America Becoming: Racial Trends and Their Consequences,* vol. I. Washington, D.C.: National Academy Press.

Meares, Tracey L. 2003. "Communities, Capital, and Conflict," pp. 51–56 in Joshua Cohen, Jefferson Decker, and Joe Rogers (ed.), *A Way Out: America's Ghettos and the Legacy of Racism.* Princeton: Princeton University Press.

Mitchell, Mike. 2002. "Elections a Mixed Bag for 'Living Wage' Proposals." *Labor Letter.* www.laborlawyers. com.

Orfield, Gary. 2003. "Exit and Redevelopment," pp. 74–78 in Joshua Cohen, Jefferson Decker, and Joshua Rogers (eds.), *A Way Out: America's Ghettos and the Legacy of Racism.* Princeton: Princeton University Press.

Rosenbaum, James E., and Susan J. Popkin. 1991. "Employment and Earnings of Middle-Class Blacks Who Move to Middle Class Suburbs," pp. 342–56 in Christopher C. Jencks and Peter Phillip Peterson (eds.), *The Urban Underclass.* Washington, DC: Brookings Institution.

Russell, Mary N., and Bonnie White. 2001. "Practice with Immigrants and Refugees: Social Worker and Client Perspectives." *Journal of Ethnic and Cultural Diversity in Social Work.* 9: 73–92.

Schorr, Lisbeth B. 1997. *Common Purpose: Strengthening Families and Neighborhoods to Rebuild America.* New York: Anchor Books.

Sleeper, Jim. 2003. "Against Social Engineering," pp. 92–101 in Joshua Cohen, Jefferson Decker, and Joshua Rogers (eds.), *A Way Out: America's Ghettos and the Legacy of Racism.* Princeton: Princeton University Press.

Staples, Brent. 1994. *Parallel Time: Growing Up in Black and White.* New York: Pantheon Books.

Thompson, J. Phillip. 2003. "Beyond Moralizing," pp. 60–67 in Joshua Cohen, Jefferson Decker, and Joshua Rogers (eds.), *A Way Out: America's Ghettos and the Legacy of Racism.* Princeton: Princeton University Press.

Zuckerman, Diana M. 2000. "The Evolution of Welfare Reform: Policy Changes and Current Knowledge." *Journal of Social Issues.* 56: 811–20.

GLOSSARY TERMS

assimilation a group's access to all culturally valued rights, opportunities, and experiences within a society

blockbusting a realtor's attempt to convince individuals to vacate an area where they own or rent property, telling them that an influx of a nearby racial or ethnic group is imminent

camouflaged racism distinctly racist behavior that bursts into public view from individuals whose racist outlooks and behavior generally remain hidden behind public statements and actions favoring racial equality

capital the material or nonmaterial means that provide resources or access to resources promoting mainstream success

city a large, densely settled concentration of people permanently located within a fairly confined geographical area where nonagricultural occupations are pursued

color-blind racism an ideological position asserting whites' frequently proclaimed desire to live in a society in which race no longer matters

concentric-zone hypothesis a proposition asserting that the groups occupying a given space push outward from the city center in a fairly symmetrical pattern along local transportation lines

culture all human-made products associated with a society

discrimination behavior by which an individual prevents or restricts a minority-group member's access to scarce resources

ethnic agglomeration effect the causal impact produced when increasing numbers of a given ethnic group settle in a city and create more jobs for the group's members

ethnic enclaves interconnected sets of small businesses belonging to a single ethnic group, located in its own neighborhood, and usually serving both the immediate ethnic community and the society at large

ethnic pluralism a perspective describing ethnic groups' respective contributions to American society, stressing both their current distinctive qualities and their important functions

ethnic succession the process by which the presence of established ethnic groups affects the economic opportunities of the groups arriving afterward

ethnicity a classification of people into a particular category with distinct cultural or national qualities

eugenics movement an initiative founded by late nineteenth-century intellectuals who claimed science could improve the quality of the human race, primarily by promoting "purification of the Anglo-Saxon race"

formal organization a group characterized by formally stated rules, clearly defined members' roles, and distinct goals

gender the general behavioral standards that distinguish females and males in a given culture

ghetto an area of a city, often within its inner portion, where one ethnic or racial group predominates, usually because of restrictions the majority group imposes

group structure in which two or more interacting people share certain expectations and goals

ideology a practical set of ideas and concepts that provides a working theory of everyday life

index of dissimilarity the percentage of a particular racial group that would need to change residential location in order to achieve racial evenness—a condition in which that racial group's representation throughout a city's census districts would be dispersed proportionate to its overall representation in relation to non-Hispanic whites

index of isolation, the citywide average of a particular racial or ethnic group's membership within the selected neighborhoods where that group resides

jury nullification the acquittal of a defendant, basing the decision on the alleged injustice the criminal-justice system has historically delivered to the defendant's racial or ethnic group and not on the evidence at hand

linkage a municipal procedure requiring developers or other corporate players doing business in a city to provide a substantial fee for low-cost housing or some other commodity or service aiding a city's less affluent residents

looking-glass self the idea that individuals' understanding of what kind of person they are is based on how they think they appear to others

macrosociological involving the large-scale structures and activities that exist within societies and even between one society and another

majority group a category of people within a society who possess distinct physical or cultural characteristics and maintain superior power and resources

microsociological involving the structure and activity of small groups

minority group any category of people with recognizable physical or cultural traits that place it in a position of restricted power and inferior status so that its members suffer limited opportunities and rewards

new urban paradigm a theory that focuses on the factors determining why cities develop their respective forms and functions

political machine an organization designed to use both legal and illegal means to run a city, county, or state government

prejudice a highly negative judgment toward a minority group, focusing on one or more characteristics that are supposedly uniformly shared by all group members

race a classification of people into categories falsely claimed to be derived from a distinct set of biological traits

racialized social system a social system in which people's racial classification partially determines their access to valued economic, political, and social resources

racially restrictive covenant a contract among property owners in an area prohibiting selected minorities from buying, leasing, or occupying property in that locale

redlining the discriminatory practice toward minorities of refusing to provide mortgage loans or property insurance or only providing them at accelerated rates for reasons not clearly associated with any conventional assessment of risk

role a set of expected behaviors associated with a certain position in a group or society

selective recruitment a policy of pursuing racially restrictive population segments in an effort to produce a workforce with certain targeted characteristics

sexism a set of beliefs emphasizing that actual or alleged differences between women and men establish the superiority of men

social class a large category of people who are similar in income level, educational attainment, and occupational prestige ranking

social Darwinism an ideology loosely borrowing from Darwinian thought and emphasizing that the most capable groups will rise to the top of economic, political, and social hierarchies and establish the most productive arrangement for the distribution of wealth and power for society at large

socialization the process by which a person becomes a social being, learning the necessary cultural content or behavior to become a member of a group or society.

social network a set of contacts involving friends, acquaintances, or business associates that individuals use to obtain information about or advantage in seeking jobs or other valued opportunities

social system a society's fairly enduring set of interrelated institutions, which the society's elite seeks to control both to maximize its own interests and to ensure its citizens' survival and reproduction

steering a real-estate agent's effort to direct customers toward residential areas where their racial or ethnic group is concentrated

stereotype an exaggerated, oversimplified image, maintained by prejudiced people, of the characteristics of the group members against whom they are prejudiced

structural mobility changes in the economy and the labor market affecting workers' advancement

suburb a politically independent municipality that develops next to or in the vicinity of a central city

urban village a city-based community where the members of one or more ethnic groups seek to adapt their own cultural standards and activities to the new, sometimes disorienting setting

INDEX

Concepts written in **boldface** type are defined in the text, often on the first page listed in the index, and also in the glossary at the end of the book.